WAKEFIELD PRESS

Germans
Travellers, Settlers and Their Descendants in South Australia

Germans
Travellers, Settlers and Their Descendants
in South Australia

edited by Peter Monteath

Wakefield Press

Wakefield Press
16 Rose Street
Mile End
South Australia 5031
www.wakefieldpress.com.au

First published 2011

Copyright © Peter Monteath and individual authors, 2011

All rights reserved. This book is copyright. Apart from any fair dealing for the purposes of private study, research, criticism or review, as permitted under the Copyright Act, no part may be reproduced without written permission. Enquiries should be addressed to the publisher.

Cover design by Liz Nicholson, designBITE
Typeset by Wakefield Press

National Library of Australia Cataloguing-in-Publication entry

Title:	Germans in South Australia/edited by Peter Monteath.
ISBN:	978 1 86254 911 1 (pbk.).
Subjects:	Germans – South Australia – History.
	South Australia – History.
Other Authors/ Contributors:	Monteath, Peter, 1961– .
Dewey Number:	994.2300431

Government of South Australia

Contents

Acknowledgements	vii
Introduction Peter Monteath	ix
Hermann Koeler's observations on South Australia in 1837 and 1838 Peter Mühlhäusler	1
A vision frustrated: Lutheran missionaries to the Aborigines of South Australia 1838–1853 Christine Lockwood	17
The Moravian Church in South Australia Bill Edwards	41
Nothing pleasing to impart? H.A.E. Meyer at Encounter Bay, 1840–1848 Mary-Anne Gale	63
The Grand Duke, the Town Council and the Bützow Butchers' Guild: The tradesman's plight and Mecklenburg migration to South Australia Lois Zweck	81
The hospital that never was Michael Bollen	95
Richard Schomburgk: Explorer, natural scientist and Botanic Garden director Pauline Payne	126
'Essentially South Australian': The artist Alexander Schramm Janice Lally and Peter Monteath	144
The man of the law: Ulrich Hübbe Horst K. Lücke	166
Erhard Eylmann: Ethnographer and explorer Wilfried Schröder	188
Colonial *Wissenschaft*: German naturalists and museums in nineteenth-century South Australia Philip Jones	204

Wine, women and so on: Female labour in the Barossa Julie Tolley	237
A region, its recipes and their meaning: The birth of *The Barossa Cookery Book* Angela Heuzenroeder	251
National Socialism in South Australia Barbara Poniewierski	269
South Australia's Lutheran churches and refugees from Hitler's Germany Peter Monteath	304
Penguins that flew: Paul Pfeiffer and Modernism in war and peace John Miles	326
No man's land: A tale of love and longing during wartime Christine Winter	345
The educator: Karl Mützelfeldt Volker Stolle	364
Hermann Sasse's way: Scholar, churchman, immigrant Maurice Schild	384
Nora Heysen: Art and war for a German-Australian family Catherine Speck	402
Joining the club: German immigrants to South Australia after 1945 Ingrid Münstermann	418
Notes on contributors	437
Index	445

Acknowledgements

For some years there have been signs of a renewed interest in South Australia's Germans. One of the driving forces behind that revival has been Lee Kersten, who in 2005, and then again in 2010, organised conferences at the University of Adelaide devoted to the multiple contributions of Germans to the history of this state and of Australia more broadly. For many of the authors gathered here, those conferences both triggered an engagement with the topic and also provided an invaluable opportunity to air their knowledge and their ideas. Similarly, a workshop devoted to German pioneer women in South Australia, organised by a group around Pauline Payne and Lois Zweck and held in History Week 2010, was a catalyst for a good deal of thinking and writing on things German. On that occasion too, the generous provision of space and facilities by Ray Choate and his team at the Barr Smith Library was invaluable. Without these promptings, and without the communal exchange of ideas that such forums provide, this collection would not have come to fruition.

Without funding, too, this book might not have moved beyond the phase of a mere germ of an idea. Essential injections of publication support have been most gratefully received from History SA, from the Faculty of Social and Behavioural Sciences at Flinders University, and from the University of Adelaide.

The efforts made by Penelope Curtin and Michael Deves at Wakefield Press in converting a variety of documents and images into a handsome volume fell nowhere short of the heroic. As for my fellow contributors, both in Australia and in Germany, let me thank them for their dedication to the project, for their generosity in sharing their profound and wide-ranging knowledge, and above all for their patience.

Peter Monteath
Adelaide, January 2011

Introduction

Peter Monteath

One thing really troubled me in Australia, and more so here in Adelaide than in Sydney – because there was more cause for concern here – and that was the disunity of my countrymen. It is true it should have been no surprise, it was unfortunately by no means an unusual phenomenon, and I would have been taken aback if it had been any different, but nonetheless it does hurt me to recognize that a great and a most malevolent curse appears to weigh upon our poor nation. A scattiness is cultivated not just at home in our own nest but has been transported with anxious care into distant parts of the world, where it grows like weeds in fertile foreign soil. In North America the very devil is among them, in Chile they hoe into each other, just as they do in California. All of that was simply confirmed here, and the only place thus far where I have found my German countrymen really unified was in Tahiti – where there lived just one of them, and the arrival of another will make a fool of me.[1]

These are the words of the irrepressible Friedrich Gerstäcker, who knew a thing or two about Germans. He was one, he grew up among them in Hamburg, and then, as he toured the globe, he observed them in many of its corners. The young colony of South Australia, too, was on his expansive itinerary. He managed to fit it in after visits to California, various Pacific islands and Sydney, followed by a paddle down the Murray and a trek of over 1000 kilometres to Adelaide, which he was to describe as the wildest and most dangerous of his life.[2]

His recollections of Adelaide remind us of a feature of South Australia's Germans which we all too readily forget, and that is their sheer variety. True, there were the pious Lutherans who settled in the Barossa Valley and other parts of the colony, religious refugees from their native Prussia. But in truth Germans made their way to South Australia from other German lands as well, at different times, and for many different reasons. They were farming folk from villages scattered across many parts of Europe, but they came from towns and cities too. Many stayed, but others were simply passing through. Their contributions were overwhelmingly positive, and they encompass both a breadth and a depth not easily fathomed.

South Australia can boast German connections which reached to the very pinnacle of politics and society on the other side of the world. Britain's reigning monarch at the time of the colony's foundation, King William IV, had a consort who went by the name of Queen Adelaide. By birth she was German royalty, hailing from the duchy of Saxe–Meiningen and christened with the regally prolix name Adelheid Amalie Luise Therese Carolin. In its corrupted form she was to give the first of those names to a place far removed from her German home, but which nonetheless was to bear the stamp of German influence long after Adelheid and the duchy of Saxe-Meiningen were no more.

The ascent of Queen Victoria to the British throne did nothing to weaken these lofty links with German Europe. For more than two decades through the middle of the nineteenth century, and during a crucial phase in the development of South Australia, the monarch was married to another German consort, this time in the person of her handsome cousin Prince Albert. The Prince had been born in the same year as Victoria, and, as coincidence would have it, with the help of the same midwife. Although the Queen's choice of consort provoked initial misgivings in some quarters, Albert came to be a valued and admired member of the British royal family. Victoria's grief at his premature death in 1861 was shared widely through the realm. When her son Alfred visited South Australia in 1869, both rural and urban Germans vied with one another to outdo the British in demonstrating their loyalty to the British prince.

Powerful German links were formed among more modest folk as well. Religious refugees of German peasant stock played an invaluable role in populating the infant colony of South Australia with a rural workforce. Through their trademark toil on the land they helped provide the colony with the food it so desperately

Introduction

needed. In time they more than repaid the gift of religious freedom with their industry and tractability during the colony's tenuous formative years, and far beyond. In many regards they were the model human building blocks for the new colony.

These South Australian connections with Germany, high and low, are deeply inscribed in South Australians' historical consciousness; indeed they remain visible to this day in a multitude of forms, from the streetscapes of Hahndorf and the Barossa townships, the architecture of Adelaide, the foods and wines we consume, to the names of streets, towns and people. In Adelaide and beyond, a German heritage is omnipresent. What purpose, then, should be served with a new collection of essays on the contributions of Germans to this part of the world?

There are at least a couple of answers to this. The dogged persistence of the story of the devout and stolid German farmers doing more than their share to establish the colony of course has a foundation in reality, but there is quite a dose of myth as well. As Gerstäcker well knew, there is much more to be said about so many other Germans who made their way to the Antipodes, settlers and travellers from quite different backgrounds and driven by a multitude of reasons. Secondly, since the age of Adelaide and Victoria there has been more than another century of German migration, settlement and activity. For Germans, and indeed for others, there are parts of the often vexed history of Germans in South Australia's twentieth century they might prefer to forget. With the onset of a new century, however, the time has arrived to look at it closely and honestly, without ignoring obvious sensitivities, but with a commitment nonetheless to telling that age's stories truthfully.

*　*　*

From the perspective of almost any point of time in the past 100 years, the nineteenth century British admiration and respect for many things German is difficult to comprehend. Yet in the 1800s it was palpable. Even during the decades before 1871, when there was still no such thing as a unified German state, there was much to approve and no shortage of Britons prepared to say so. Having played their role in ridding Europe of the tyrant Napoleon

Bonaparte, Germans had excelled in music, philosophy, literature, and indeed in virtually every branch of the sciences. In the largest and most powerful of the German states, Prussia, a series of reforms had created an apparatus of state and a military organisation which was the envy of the rest of the world. Moreover, the Prussians, still mindful of the ignominious years of French subjugation, introduced systems of education and training widely held to be the best anywhere, with many passing through Prussia's exemplary institutions taking their skills and knowledge to the rest of the world. As for those who stayed behind, unification presented them with the opportunity to contribute to the emergence of Germany as a major global power, its rise observed with liberal quantities of esteem, respect and, as the *fin de siècle* drew near, some trepidation as well.

The first sizeable group of Germans to settle in South Australia had no inkling of how a future Prussian chancellor's *Realpolitik* would shape their homelands. In their day Germany was at best a cultural nation, a community with a shared sense of historical and linguistic identity, but no more than that. To the state of Prussia they felt little loyalty, since the king had imposed an unwanted liturgy upon them, and they had been deprived of their citizenship on receiving their hard-won emigration permits. For these rural folk from the eastern provinces of Brandenburg, Pomerania, Posen and Silesia, the primary allegiance was to a higher realm, to the worship of their Lord. When secular authorities interfered with that allegiance, they were prepared to cut their ties with the state and depart in search of the religious freedom that the South Australian colony offered.

Yet these first immigrants, united in their reasons for leaving their homelands, were by no means a homogeneous mass whose collective genes somehow shaped their identity and that of all who followed. Even on matters of religion the first fault lines soon appeared – as early as 1846 the Old Lutherans, not so many years earlier united in their opposition to an imposed liturgy they could not accept split into two separate groups, one led by Pastor August Kavel and the other by Pastor Gotthard Daniel Fritzsche. It was a division among the Lutherans which, in numerous permutations and varying degrees of rancour, persisted into the 1960s. In time

Introduction

came Catholics and, albeit in much smaller numbers, Jews.

Not all were farmers. As Lois Zweck points out in a fascinating case study of the dynamics of early migration, there were numerous craftsmen and tradesmen, including butchers. Miners, too, came in significant numbers in the late 1840s and early 1850s, many of them from the Harz Mountains. Despite the persistence of the myth, not all Germans came to escape religious persecution, especially when persecution gradually gave way to tolerance after the death of Frederick William III in 1840. Increasingly, the Germans came as what we might call in today's parlance – with its troubling pejorative undertone – 'economic refugees'. And while it is true that for the first decade or so about half of the Germans came in closed congregational groups, that changed from around the middle of the century, even as family or group migrations continued. For the remainder of the 1800s there were German immigrants who continued to make their way out to the rural communities, but more and more chose life in Adelaide, where eventually they gathered in sufficiently large numbers to support, for a time at least, the existence of not just one but two German clubs. One of those clubs, patronised by Germans of the upper middle class, was housed in opulent circumstances in Pirie Street, and promoted German language and culture, while the other, the so-called South Australian General German Club (*Süd-Australischer Allgemeiner Deutscher Verein*) catered for a membership drawn largely from the working classes and garnered something of a reputation for itself as a hotbed of socialist radicalism.

The variety among the Germans in South Australia of course becomes especially evident when one looks beyond the main groups of immigrants to individuals. A fascinating early example is that of a traveller rather than an immigrant, namely Dr Hermann Koeler. As Koeler's title alone suggests, he was a man of education, whose medical training had served to secure him the role of ship's doctor, but whose intellectual curiosity embraced a world of knowledge far beyond his chosen vocation. Both the scope of his inquisitiveness and the range of knowledge exhibited by the doctor anticipate those qualities in so many Germans who followed in his wake and elected to stay much longer.

Foremost among Koeler's interests, as Peter Mühlhäusler

shows in his chapter, were the indigenous people Koeler encountered, on whom he cast the untrained yet observant eye of the lay anthropologist. Koeler's interest was replicated among many Germans, with the result that it is a recurrent theme in this collection. Though their impulse was quite different from that of Koeler, the German missionaries, too, displayed a keen interest in understanding the new colony's original inhabitants. Whether of Lutheran training and persuasion, like those discussed by Christine Lockwood and Mary-Anne Gale, or the Moravians investigated by Bill Edwards, the unrelenting efforts to comprehend the indigenous people and their culture are a remarkable constant in German missionary work in South Australia. The missionaries' efforts were not always rewarded – at least not in this world – and from today's perspective the extent to which they stemmed from unquestioned assumptions about the benefits of European civilisation can be disturbing. Yet for the sincerity of their commitment to their calling, for the high cost to their own physical and mental health, and for the untiring labour they invested in understanding the languages and customs of people so profoundly different from themselves, the missionaries claim a special place in the history of the colony.

The painter Alexander Schramm provides another instance of German interest in indigenous people and their culture, as Janice Lally and I suggest in our contribution. As with so many of the German immigrants, we can only speculate about what drove him to embark on a voyage to the Antipodes, yet we have some cause to be grateful that he did. The few paintings and other works by Schramm available to us in public collections provide an invaluable record of the presence of indigenous people alongside German and other settlers in South Australia. Where British artists tended to ignore the presence of the Kaurna and others, or at best to present them as exotic or picturesque embellishments, Schramm shows a distinctive empathy and an attention to detail.

Other Germans followed in Schramm's footsteps. The botanists Richard Schomburgk and Carl Wilhelmi and the policeman-cum-photographer Paul Foelsche all turned their hands at various points to amateur ethnography. But perhaps the most remarkable of all was not one of the settlers but rather the traveller Erhard Eylmann, the subject of the chapter by his biographer Wilfried

Introduction

Schröder. Eylmann's travels through South Australia and its Northern Territory left a remarkably rich ethnographic legacy. While in many regards Eylmann's observations reveal serious gaps in his understanding of indigenous Australia, the dedication with which he pursued his work, and the multiple privations he endured in performing it, are quite astonishing. His understanding of ethnography might not have been without its deficiencies, but his capacity to gather and interpret evidence is sophisticated. Eylmann had after all received a German scientific training, and it stood him in good stead as he struggled to make sense of the complex human and natural world he confronted in South Australia.

Not only in Eylmann's case are the blessings of a German scientific education evident, as Philip Jones illustrates. His discussion highlights the incalculable advantages to the colony of an array of German-trained scientists, who for various reasons left their homelands behind them and brought their very considerable talents to bear when they got here, commonly with, at best, modest support. Though he stayed in South Australia just five years, Ferdinand von Mueller established a trend which others soon joined. Among them was the little-known figure of Marianne Kreusler, one of the naturalists who found a home at Buchsfelde near Gawler, from where she performed work which garnered international praise. On North Terrace, too, the German scientists made their presence felt, not least in the Museum and in the Botanic Garden.

The latter's debt to Richard Schomburgk – himself one of the Buchsfelde naturalists – is enormous, as one of his descendants, Pauline Payne, records. Like so many other Germans who rose to pre-eminence in their chosen fields – Alexander Schramm, Carl Muecke, Carl Linger, Marianne Kreusler, Otto Schomburgk – Richard Schomburgk arrived in Adelaide on *Princess Louise* in 1849. This was a cohort whose fundamental life experiences had been urban rather than rural, and whose political worldview had been in many cases coloured by both the hopes they had invested in the liberal revolutions of 1848–49 and by the disillusionment which followed the restoration of a conservative order. The 'Forty-Eighters', as they are sometimes called, brought with them an intellectual energy and cosmopolitanism which bestowed huge benefits on what was still a tiny and precarious colony.

Few figures illustrate the cosmopolitanism of mid-century Adelaide better than those who populate Michael Bollen's essay on the German Hospital that never quite came about. On one level it is a story of failure, since the long-debated hospital in the end took at most just one patient. On another, however, it is a noteworthy success story of German integration, of the easy relations that characterised Anglo-German Adelaide, personified in the larger than life characters of the mercurial Dr Bayer and the ebullient Osmond Gilles – the latter technically not German, but a merchant of Hamburg for 17 years and, like many of his day, a fluent speaker of both German and English.

Horst Lücke delves into the sometimes controversial achievements of Ulrich Hübbe in the realm of the law. While all South Australians have heard of the benefits of the Torrens Title system, few have an appreciation of the benefits it brought this and other parts of the world or of the role a somewhat enigmatic German played in introducing it to South Australia.

* * *

At the corner of North Terrace stands a monument commemorating the involvement of South Australians in the Boer War; one of the names inscribed on it is a certain Captain Samuel Grau Hübbe, the son of Ulrich. The very presence of that name hints at how successfully Germans had integrated themselves into South Australia; they had been hugely successful in finding a place in the colony, adopting its language and customs, marrying into its society and achieving prominence. Within a generation another Hübbe – Hermann Fritz, the son of Samuel – was added to the list of Australia's dead in the Great War. What more convincing evidence could be offered of the German settlers' devotion to Australia and the British Empire than the offering of the ultimate sacrifice in distant lands?

Yet the North Terrace monument possesses a Janus quality also, because the Boer War signalled a straining of ties between Britain and Germany. Where relations in the nineteenth century had rested on foundations of admiration, respect and even royal family ties, the Boer War did not bode well for the new century. In international politics the Kaiser's Germany was determined to show that it had arrived as a world power; it could barely do so without provoking the ire of the British Empire, accustomed to having its way in world affairs.

In hindsight that war, in which the German state's sympathies with the Boers came to the fore, appears as little more than a hiccup in German–British relations; the calamity came later. The outbreak of the Great War in 1914 cast a shadow over relations between Germany and Britain, which darkened further in 1933. Inevitably it stretched across the world, reaching South Australia, where Germans and those of German descent, despite an impeccable record of loyalty and industry, fell under suspicion. Thereafter, Germans and their contributions to South Australia were viewed differently; the rose-coloured glasses were laid aside, if not snapped in anger and buried. Indeed, it is hard to overestimate the profundity of the change which came over South Australia's – indeed perhaps the world's – estimation of Germany and the Germans after the multiple catastrophes of 1914 to 1945. Where once they were commonly viewed as industrious, tolerant, creative and open to the broader world, from the perspective of the post-Hitler era they were more likely to be viewed as closed-minded belligerents who collectively had brought the world misery and destruction.

The record of the onset of those soured relations during the Great War is not a happy one; its numerous manifestations – internments, the changing of place names, vitriolic attacks and open violence in communities, the closing of German schools – have been recorded elsewhere. Our attention turns to the period after the Great War, to efforts to restore relations and rebuild confidence, but also to some of the enduring damage of 1914's rupture: the stubborn persistence of distrust and animosity which developed on both sides of the tragic German–British divide.

Angela Heuzenroeder's chapter offers a fascinating, culinary perspective on those relations. The date of the appearance of the first edition of the renowned *Barossa Cookery Book* is by itself momentous – in 1917 relations had truly reached their nadir. Yet the publication of this book as response to a crisis spoke at once of a heightened sense of regional identity and also of a commitment to common efforts and causes transcending the poisoned international politics of the day. Fifteen years later, the next edition of the cookbook similarly attested to the power of culture and community to mend damage which at some moments must have appeared permanent. In a similar vein – albeit with an emphasis on drink rather than wine, but like Angela Heuzenroeder according a central role to the activities of women in the affirmation of a regional identity – Julie Tolley looks to the labour of women in Barossa vineyards. She traces it back to the nineteenth century, when German settlers in the Barossa were sufficiently creative and imaginative to recognise the potential of the budding wine industry, and then follows important lines of continuity which run through not just one but two world wars.

The second edition of the *Barossa Cookery Book* appeared just a few months before Adolf Hitler was appointed to the Chancellorship of Germany. At the time, the import of that event was not immediately obvious, and it was not only among German–Australian communities that the Third Reich found its admirers. This collection tries to present something of the breadth of responses among German Australians. As Barbara Poniewierski demonstrates, there were those whose enthusiasm for Hitler knew no bounds; they proudly adopted the trappings of the new regime. While some came to rue the Nazis' success, particularly after the outbreak of war, there were those who remained unbowed and steadfast. Relatively small in number, they suffered the consequences. For still others, an initial temptation was to welcome the efforts Hitler promoted to overcome the ignominy of the Versailles Treaty, to deal with the Depression and to restore Germany to its proper place in the world. Support for Hitler – to begin with at least – was an expression of respect for German culture in all its guises, a respect which was regarded as entirely compatible with loyalty to Australia. Yet in many cases initial enthusiasm was tempered, loyalties were challenged, strained or even divided. Christine Winter examines the dilemmas created by the competing loyalties facing the German-born women who were brought to Australia from New Guinea mission stations. For them, war posed painful challenges concerning their senses of place, belonging and emotional attachment.

In most cases there was no such ambivalence. Paul Pfeiffer came from a long line of German settlers in a region east of Point Pass straddling the Goyder Line. Such was the durability of his family's

German heritage that he could speak and write in German; he was steeped in both an Anglo and – thanks to level of education rare among his contemporaries – a German cultural tradition. At the same time he felt entirely comfortable in the literary idiom of Australian modernism; indeed he established himself as a seminal figure among the 'Angry Penguins'. With the outbreak of war, there was no question of where he would place his loyalty. As in the First World War, so in the second there were countless Australians of German descent who exhibited their loyalty through armed service, often directed against the land of their origins. Pfeiffer was just one of many who paid the ultimate price.

For German Jews, too, there could be no such ambivalence in those interesting times. My own piece on Jewish refugees explores the efforts in South Australia to lend a helping hand to those whom the Nazis, driven by an unparalleled racial mania, were to slate for extermination. Astonishingly, some of those efforts came from within the Lutheran Churches in South Australia, from people who were upholders and promoters of German culture, but who could not reconcile their love of Germany with the vicious and visceral racism which characterised the Third Reich. The life of one of those who fled the Reich to find a new home in Adelaide, the Lutheran educator Karl Mützelfeldt, is portrayed by Volker Stolle, who follows the course of Mützelfeldt's life from his upbringing, education and work in Germany, through the momentous decision to emigrate (his wife was regarded by the Nazis as a 'Half-Jew'), to his distinguished career in Australia.

* * *

Immediately after the war it was not easy for Germans to follow in the wake of all those who had come earlier; as after the Great War, resentments and suspicions did not die quickly. Yet as they did, many of the features of nineteenth- and early twentieth-century German immigrants revealed themselves once more. Individually there were people of great integrity and achievement among the post-war immigrants, such as the theologian Hermann Sasse. Like many, as Maurice Schild shows, Sasse agonised long and hard over the complicity of his fellow Germans in the horrific crimes committed in the name of the Third Reich. After his arrival in

Adelaide in 1949 he steadily developed through his writings and his teaching the reputation of a Lutheran theologian of international import.

The Germans who followed the same path as Sasse through the 1950s and 1960s, like their counterparts a century earlier, distinguished themselves through their industry and the ease with which they integrated into South Australia. A useful indicator of this process, adopted by Ingrid Münstermann, is the membership of clubs. The abundance of clubs open to those with German heritage or with an interest in things German testifies to the continuity of a German presence from the early years of European settlement. Yet the history of those clubs also illuminates the need felt by many immigrants for a kind of cultural comfort zone, where they could speak their native language and exchange experiences with those of similar backgrounds. In the process of acculturation they were vital and moreover they were successful. As Münstermann shows, the acculturation rate of post-war immigrants was extraordinarily high. It is a sign of that very success that among the crowds one might find at the German Club or the *Schützenfest* are many who have absolutely no need to cultivate some sense of German identity. The surviving trappings of 'symbolic identity' can be enjoyed by all – a sure sign of shared comfort in multiculturalism.

If the German-Australian 'success story' were to be personified, then one might choose any member of the Heysen family. The venerable Hans Heysen was of course born in Germany and was to receive some of his training in Europe, but both his name and the vast majority of his works are inextricably linked to South Australia and its landscapes. His is an example of an adaptation to a radically new world which extends beyond his personal, professional and social life and into every aspect of his art and the multiple genres he mastered. His daughter Nora, whose life and work are portrayed here by Cathy Speck, is of another generation and readily embraces and expands the Australian artistic idiom her father had done so much to establish. With her emphasis on Heysen's work as an official war artist in the Second World War, Speck investigates the sensitive issue of loyalty, one with which Hans Heysen had been confronted in the Great War. Both father and daughter happily had careers which extended long beyond the wars, Hans dying in 1968 and Nora in 2003. As much as any place in South Australia their home, The Cedars, which many a contemporary visitor experiences as a kind of artistic-cum-spiritual retreat, epitomises the rich and easy fusion of generations and of cultures.

Notes

1. Friedrich Gerstäcker, *Reise um die Welt. Bd. 4. Australien*, http://www.lexikus.de/Reisen-4-Band-Australien. Translation by the author.
2. Lesli Bodi, 'Gerstaecker, Friedrich (1816–1872)', *Australian Dictionary of Biography*, vol. 4, Melbourne University Press, Melbourne, 1972, p. 242.

Hermann Koeler's observations on South Australia in 1837 and 1838

Peter Mühlhäusler

Introduction

The important contribution made by German scholars to the exploration and understanding of Aboriginal Australia is widely recognised, but this recognition is not always translated into action.[1] Many published documents have remained underexploited, and the knowledge of unpublished German sources remains patchy, despite the fact that much material is located in Australian archives. Hermann Koeler's observations on South Australia are a case in point – they have remained unknown to Australian scholars until very recently. Neither Rob Foster's comprehensive account of early contact history in South Australia, nor Rob Amery's PhD thesis on the Kaurna language (although this has been remedied in the published version), nor the important article by Jane Simpson on the contact languages of the Adelaide area make mention of them.[2]

The German historian Reinhard Wendt suggests that in the nineteenth century, long before the invention of the internet, there was a highly developed communication network through which European missionaries working at the frontiers of the civilised world transmitted their knowledge to academics in their home countries.[3] This was not a one-way transmission of new facts and findings, but a highly interactive process of communication. There was a second, secular network, which involved educated Europeans residing in or travelling on business to remote parts of the world who communicated their findings back to academics in Europe and who at times engaged in academic debates. One of these debates concerned the intellectual and linguistic status of 'primitive' people.

The question of whether the dark-skinned inhabitants of Africa and Australia were capable of intellectual and spiritual progress was fiercely debated by scholars, colonial administrators and missionaries, and Koeler was well aware of the pertinence of his records to this debate.

Examples of the exchange of information and ideas include the study of languages (philology) and the disciplines of anthropology and geography (in particular, human geography), which emerged in nineteenth-century Germany. While these new disciplines flourished in Germany, there was neither the money nor trained personnel to support the number of expeditions needed to gather information, and there were many armchair academics who relied almost exclusively on reports sent to them from all corners of the globe. Information was obtained from numerous educated Germans in all parts of the world, who either willingly provided information when written to, or who supplied information to scholars back home on their own initiative.

Hermann Koeler

One of the many informants who corresponded with researchers back home in Germany was the German ship's doctor Hermann Koeler. What makes Koeler a particularly interesting figure is that he was one of the first Germans to visit South Australia and to report on the conditions which prevailed in the first years of the colony. When Koeler arrived in October 1837, aged 24 years, there were probably about a dozen Germans in Adelaide, who had arrived on the *Coromandel* and the *South Australian*. His own vessel was the *Solway*, which was under charter to the South Australian Company to take 52 German migrants to the new colony, along with a cargo which included supplies for the company's whaling station at Encounter Bay and boilers and machinery for the company's operations at Kingscote.[4] The German migrants were mainly young single men, agricultural labourers, carpenters and bakers, but a few were married men with families, and none of them appears to have left a written record about the experience of the early days of South Australia.

Who, then, was Hermann Koeler? How did he fit into the scientific internet, and what was his specific contribution to our knowledge of South Australia in the earliest years of the colony? An extensive search for information about Koeler in both Germany and Australia has yielded disappointingly little of any consequence. We know that Koeler was a medical doctor and that he was born on 3 August 1813 in Celle, Germany. His parents were Friederich Ludewig Koeler and Charlotte Wilhelmine Julie Wichmann. Little is known about this family of 10 children. No reliable information about Hermann's studies and employment has been found to date. What is known is that he travelled widely between 1837 and 1848, presumably supported by his income as a ship's doctor. There is no evidence that he was in the employ of a university or a scientific organisation, but he appears to have been in the habit of submitting manuscripts to Professor Carl Ritter, the founder of modern German geography, and one of the founding members of the *Gesellschaft für Erdkunde zu Berlin*. During his travels as a ship's doctor Koeler set foot on all five continents, and he left behind three known publications dealing with diverse topics. The first was in the form of two papers based on his 1837–38 visit to South Australia, printed in a journal in 1842 and 1844,[5] the second a 1848 book on the people and language on the coast of Guinea, and the third a book on the temperature measurements he took during several voyages in the Atlantic, published in 1849.

His reports were read by Professor Ritter and subsequently published by Dieterich in Göttingen, a university town relatively close to Koeler's birthplace, Celle. Kremer, a twentieth-century commentator, notes that Ritter disapproved of the blatant racism in Koeler's work and that he added critical question marks and exclamation marks when using Koeler's information in his own work.[6] We can thus not be sure that the printed versions of the reports he submitted were not edited.

The title of both of Koeler's papers was 'Einige Notizen über die Eingeborenen an der Ostküste des St. Vincent-Golfs, Süd-Australien; 1837 und 1838' ('Some notes on the Aborigines on the East coast of the St Vincent Gulf, South Australia; 1837 and 1838'). Koeler began his visit to Adelaide some time in late 1837, and during a mishap in April or May 1838 he lost his notebook and his collection of plant specimens. He had intended to board the English brig *Lady Wellington* at Encounter Bay in April 1838 to travel to Launceston, but the whaleboat which was to take him to this vessel capsized. He eventually boarded the *Lady Wellington* and arrived in Launceston on 14 May 1838. According to the shipping lists in the *Colonial Times* (Tasmania), he appears as Dr Keller on the passenger list, while a mysterious character named Dr Holdier is listed as a passenger departing from Hobart on 11 December of the same year on the *Brougham*. Given that Koeler was a medical man (a profession notorious for its idiosyncratic handwriting) and that he would have used pre-Suetterlin Gothic script, it seems likely that his name was misinterpreted, and this is one of the causes of his apparent elusiveness. As regards his research in Tasmania, no records have been found.

Another reason for Koeler's elusiveness is that he appears to have avoided contact with officials. In South Australia he did not seek an interview with the Protector of Aborigines or the Governor and does not comment on them in his reports.[7] While avoiding both the influential Europeans and being dismissive of the lower-class Europeans, Koeler spent much of his time in South Australia with Aboriginal people and appears to have made friends among them. The children in particular were fond of him, as he was a source not only of excitement but also of food (1842, p. 54):

> My favourite, little *Williammi* had the crest of a cockatoo at the back of his neck and the end of a dog's tail hanging down to the middle of his back; kangaroo teeth were attached to some of the bunches of his black hair, twisted together in a sausage shape with gum; his scalp was heavily made up with ochre and his neck decorated with a string of red glass beads. His long brownish downy hair looked like a beard on his cheeks and covered his back like a pelt; but the body was not yet deformed by the ugly, thick rope-like scars. Long before I caught sight of him, his cheery '*Tommi, Tommi*' (for I had adopted this name since it was easy to pronounce) rang out to greet me, and he ran to me rejoicing, clasped his arms around my legs – and begged for '*birketti*' (biscuit).

In examining Koeler's two papers on early Adelaide I would like to address three questions. What new information about the early days of the Colony of South Australia and its inhabitants do they contain? What can we learn about the ideological position taken by Koeler? And, finally, is there a particularly German twist to Koeler's tale?

New information

In answering that first question, linguist Heidi Kneebone has suggested that Koeler probably plagiarised Dampier's earlier accounts of Aboriginal people, and it is not always clear whether his account of events in Adelaide represents his own observations or newspaper reports.[8] Tom Gara, by contrast, is of the opinion that Koeler was a pretty accurate recorder of events and that his records both confirm and add to the early first-hand accounts of Henry Watson, William Wyatt, William Williams and Louis Piesse.[9] Koeler's contribution to our understanding of the relations between Aborigines and white settlers in the first years of the colony is significant because he did not represent any official body. Unlike Protector Wyatt, who painted a picture of relative racial harmony, Koeler's account is more disturbing. His observations of an incident taking place on 6 December 1838, when a white settler hunting for quail accidentally wounded two Aboriginal men, indicate that the Aboriginal companions of the wounded men threatened to set all the settlers' huts on fire, an account confirmed later by James Backhouse.[10] Koeler reports other incidents of friction and threats between settlers and Aborigines not reported elsewhere. He comments on the great antipathy of the lower-class colonists towards the 'black brutes' and indicates that the colonists had loaded rifles in their rooms and that they took them even on short journeys.

Koeler also comments on the mistrust the Aboriginal people had for the settlers. None of these tensions surfaces in the official quarterly reports submitted by the Protector to the British Government. Koeler also gives a picture of the negative effects of contact with the whites in two other domains. The spread of white settlers and their animals had a most detrimental effect on the local wildlife, with the reduction of huntable animals resulting in Aboriginal people begging for or stealing the settlers' food. The beginning of a culture of dependency was compounded by the commencement of a dependency on alcohol. The disintegration of Aboriginal society so early in the colony's life also had a medical side, as Koeler emphasises (1844, p. 61), in particular the spread of venereal disease through the Aboriginal community:

> As a gift of the whites, and above all of the sailors who are not very particular, syphilitic illnesses have already manifested themselves here and there, and have also found victims among the whites. One black in fact, who had spent time with the whalers of *Encounter Bay*, killed a sailor through whom his two wives had been infected.

In sum, Koeler regarded the early colonists as neither peaceful nor beneficial to the local Aborigines and he refers to an 'uneducated and brutal' (1844, p. 61) element amongst them.

While Koeler focuses on the Aboriginal community, he also made a significant contribution to our understanding of the living conditions of the about 2000 white settlers in the early years of Adelaide. Conditions were harsh and life was very expensive, as there was an inflation of the price of all basic needs. Milk was virtually unobtainable and beef and mutton were rare, as the grazing industry was still in its infancy. Koeler comments on the lack of a reliable source of drinking water and he complains about the constant smoke pollution caused by the Aborigines' habit of hunting with fire and accidentally starting fires, mentioning an unwelcome side effect (1844, p. 60):

> By far the majority of the immigrants suffer, in the first summer (winter) [Koeler's parenthetical addition is for the benefit of his northern hemisphere readers] that they experience in the colony, inflamed infections of the eyes, principally of the eyelids and the conjunctiva over a period of 3–4 or 6 weeks ... As the causes of this I have already stated that the reflection of the sun off the sandy ground, denuded of its plant cover by fire; the terrible dust; the sudden transition from warmth to cold at sunrise and sunset, the countless swarms of insects and the dense smoke of the resin-rich woods must be stressed above all.

Koeler's own accommodation in Glenelg during his stay was representative of what the early settlers had to put up with (1844, p. 45):

> *Holdfast Bay* (*Port Glenelg*) in 1838 consisted of four reed huts (one of them a warehouse for the South Australian Co.), two tents and

two or three plank sheds, inhabited by a boatbuilder, an innkeeper, a warehouse supervisor and a fisherman; in addition there were two *private gentlemen*, and I had the honour of being one of them for a lengthy period. The huts are located immediately behind the sandy dunes with some bushes growing on them, on the southern side of a small creek, almost dry at ebb-tide. To the north, after the mouth of the *16-mile-creek* and beyond, the beach is bordered only by low dunes, mostly rising as a single wall of 20–30 feet in height [emphasis in original].

Koeler gives extensive details about the physical conditions of the colony, its sparse vegetation cover, its seasons and its geology, observations which are astonishingly perceptive, considering his youth. Many of these physical conditions of the early colony have become altered beyond all recognition. An example is his description of the River Torrens (1842, Appendix 1):

So the *Torrens River*, which divides *Adelaide Town* in a northern and a southern half, comes down from these hills and really deserves the name of river only in the rainy period, when it plunges along, deep and torrential, destroying great sections of its steep banks and often whirling in cascades over gigantic trees which it has torn down from its edge and jammed across its bed at narrower places. But in the dry season it offers the unique spectacle of a river which does not flow but still contains water. For the river bed consists almost exclusively of individual widenings (mostly with steep 15–20 feet high banks) which reach a not inconsiderable depth even in summer, and while varying in length are seldom more than 30–40 feet wide, and often have a far lesser width. These widenings, which form individual reservoirs, are separated from one another by extremely shallow places, which perhaps originated initially when trees torn loose by the torrent became stuck fast and formed dams against which masses of debris and earth were deposited, thus effecting a partial raising of the river bed, with the water of the upper reservoir later re-establishing communication with the lower through narrow clefts. In the hot season the water flows over these places in streams barely a foot wide and only inches deep, and very frequently one finds the water of almost all the small and larger *pools* stagnating, and only a little water seeps perhaps underground through the small pebbles. These shallows vary in length from several feet to 20 or 30 paces. Apart from the fact that one can jump over the river at all these points, a number of trees which have fallen diagonally across the wider places immediately at water level or at some height above it form natural bridges; and only when the rainy season floods the shallower and lower stretches of riverbank is the crossing more difficult. The river can then be followed to the *creek* 6 English *miles* from Adelaide, while it normally disappears in the so-called *reed-beds* only a half hour beyond the town. This is a shallow swampy surface overgrown with high reeds which provides the most welcome material for the first huts of the new arrivals [emphasis in original].

One of the most substantial contributions Koeler made was his notes on the Kaurna language, which predated the missionaries Teichelmann and Schürmann's 1840 account. Apparently they were not aware of Koeler's writings. Koeler was not a trained linguist, and what he recorded was not the Kaurna language as spoken in the Kaurna community, but a greatly simplified version thereof. Indigenous people in many parts of the globe deliberately simplify their language when communicating with Europeans, that is, they create a kind of foreigner talk or pidgin. There can be no doubt that he mistook an impoverished contact jargon for the language of the Adelaide 'tribe'. Mistaking the simplified form of speech used to address outsiders for the real thing was not uncommon in those days and it reinforced the prevailing prejudice that languages spoken by indigenous people were deficient and primitive. As Koeler opines: 'the language of such lowly-ranked people cannot be other than limited and under-developed' (1842, p. 48).

In particular, as the next text demonstrates, Koeler, like numerous contemporaries, accuses the Kaurna people of not being able to manage abstract concepts (1842, p. 48):

Concerning the very small range of this glossary, I cannot refrain from making reference to the difficulties which present themselves to anyone researching the names of nouns, adjectives and verbs which cannot be perceived by the senses. In communicating with people who possess such a dearth of concepts despite the adequacy of their powers of comprehension, one must attempt to abstract the qualities of certain objects, whereby gesticulation is perhaps the only means of clarifying the ideas on both sides, or at the very least as many comparisons and combinations as possible are necessary if one wants to be certain that both sides have clearly understood one another.

The alleged primitiveness of the Kaurna language is illustrated in other ways as well. Koeler seemed not to have been aware of verbal morphology, a point he acknowledged himself when he noted: 'I could not detect any trace of declension or conjugation and the verb exists only in the infinitive form' (1842, p. 49). His failure to record inflections in the language has an interesting consequence. In his descriptions, the distinction between grammatical categories such as nouns and verbs becomes very much attenuated, and this may explain the confusion of 'seawater' and 'drinking' mentioned below, and others such as 'spearpoint' and 'scrape'. To what extent this confusion is Koeler's, and to what extent it exists in pidgin Kaurna, can no longer be ascertained.

Poverty of expression is another stereotype prevalent at the time. Koeler lists about 140 Kaurna words, some of which are simple one-word translations, others are amplified with encyclopedic information. Amery has carried out a thorough examination of this wordlist in the edited texts.[11] He has identified a number of mistranslations such as when he glosses *kopurlo*, 'seawater' as 'he drinks' and *wiltunna*, 'eagles' as 'to fly'. Koeler does not distinguish Kaurna words from words of pidgin English that had spread to South Australia from New South Wales such as *makitti*, 'musket gun' or *waddi*, 'club'. Moreover, the document is not free from printer's errors. Still, Koeler adds a small number of Kaurna words not elicited by Teichelmann and Schürmann and others to our knowledge of the Kaurna language, and he is at his best when he provides encyclopedic information, as in his description of *kúngula* (= *kungurla*), 'yabbies' and how they are caught (1842, p. 52), the first eyewitness account we have of how Kaurna children caught yabbies.

> Often one sees the little blacks stretched out on half washed-out and fallen tree trunks which lean out over the river or are already partly sunken in it, attracting them with a piece of fat or meat stuck on the end of small spears.

Culture change is observed in the names of Koeler's Aboriginal friends and informants (1842, p. 50):

> As far as proper names are concerned, they are sometimes given on the basis of obvious physical conditions, and a blind person is named *Patjútteh* (blind), another is named *Jérko* (calf); others bear in part very euphonious names whose meaning (if they had one at all) I could not ascertain, e.g., *Katanja, Manuto*. The majority now bear English names like *Bob, Gim, Tom, Bill, Peg, Moll, Betty, Jack, Rodney*, and apart from that the most absurd names are often repeated to a ridiculous extent so that one is compelled to add other appellations in order to avoid mistaking identities.

Koeler observes that European naming practices had become deeply entrenched within a short period of time (1842, p. 51):

> The South Australians seem to manage for a very long time without names for their children, and one often receives the answer *'No name'* when one asks after the name. Now the colonists often play the role of godfather, and give one this name, and another that name, and these names are then without questioning adopted and used. Apart from the most popular abbreviations of the most common English Christian names, like *Bob, Bill, Jack, Tom, Poll, Jane, Betty, Peg*, one often sees the names of ships and other things like that in use: so one is called *Captain Jack*, another *Captain Mitchell*, a third *Big Rodney* etc.

The most problematic aspect of Koeler's language work is his etymologies, which are totally haphazard, as when he establishes a similarity between Kaurna *morra*, 'hand' and *burra*, 'hand' in the Bonny language of West Africa, or in his suggestion that *je'sta*, 'earth' (probably a misprint from *yarta*, as Kaurna, like other Aboriginal languages does not have an 's') is related to Germanic *jord*.

Still, given the scarcity of information on the Kaurna language, a careful study of Koeler's remarks can contribute a reasonable amount of new information. Considering that he was a total amateur, his findings are neither better nor worse than those produced by other amateurs at the time, and the effort linguists have to make to extract useful information is of the same order of magnitude. Moreover, Koeler's notes are of interest for other linguistic reasons. At the time of his visit pidgin Kaurna was still the contact medium between the settlers and the local Aboriginal population, but pidgin English had begun to take its place. Koeler produces a number of early examples of this South Australian pidgin English, which developed later into 'cattle station English' in the state's north.[12]

Koeler's ideological stance

Some of Koeler's comments on the Kaurna language should have alerted the reader to his ideological position in the 'primitive races' debate. In his remarks on the local language of Adelaide, his belief that he was dealing with a primitive language prevented him from considering another possibility: that in the 1840s it was generally believed that the languages of indigenous people were deficient in major aspects. However, there were considerable differences over whether such perceived deficiencies could be overcome or not. Koeler, it would appear, believed that the only development of which they were capable was in the realm of morality, whereas their intellectual ability could not progress further. His view of the South Australian Aborigines was that they occupied the bottom rung of the evolutionary ladder (1842, p. 43):

> If one wishes to subsume them under one of the commonly accepted human races, these South Australians (whom one could call the *Adelaide tribe*) have to – like all the original inhabitants of the mainland of New Holland and Van Diemen's Land – be counted among the Ethiopians. And if this entire race occupies the lowest rung of the human race in both physical and intellectual aspects, then these South Australians in turn represent the lowest of them all, and in some ways are backward even in comparison with other New Hollanders.

Such views are elaborated on again in Koeler's condescending concluding remarks (1844, pp. 61–2):

> I will herewith close these brief and fragmentary notes in which I have strived to demonstrate several characteristics by which I have attempted to confirm the view – often challenged by uneducated and brutal European inhabitants of distant continents – that the spirit, with all its inclinations and passions, all its poetry and efforts, is the same in the educated person, who makes his own ego the subject of his studies,

as in the most primitive natural man who views his surroundings with purely material eyes alone and is hardly aware of more than the lowest rung of social interaction (which is the only means permitting the individual to reach the highest level of development available to him), which knows no other goal than the maintenance of his species. But only the heart, in its moral and in its passionate instincts, beats to the same measure across the whole human race. The understanding, while living and creating according to the same laws, moves with greater energy in one race than in another, here it soars up to a safe height which remains vertiginous and beyond reach for another; in one race it plumbs depths which are for another eternally unfathomable chaos. The lessons of history are constantly renewed and constantly reiterated, but they remain nonetheless the same truth. It shows us that the limits to the physical and intellectual power of states as of individuals are given and fixed; in that only the form changes, while the substance remains. It reveals to us not the ideal but the real greatness which man is permitted to attain; it shows us a turning point in the fate of all peoples, which occurs in each instance in the same period of development of that people. It also teaches, in constant change, that there is a 'So far and no further!' for each race, and introduces each one to us at its height: but how different this is in each case! The South Australian will have disappeared before he has had an opportunity to reach his height, and history will tell about him as belonging to those who do not survive their infancy.

History has not borne out Koeler's views, nor were they shared by everyone who visited or settled in South Australia.

There were many who believed that external geographic conditions had prevented non-Europeans from reaching their full potential and that by civilising, christianising, and helping them materially, they would attain the same level of civilisation as Western Europeans. This view was found among the geographers in Berlin to whom Koeler submitted his observations. Advocates of the possibility of moral and medical improvement tended to regard the languages spoken by the members of other races as capable of being used for the translation of the scriptures and for education. Among the German settlers we find assimilationists such as G. Listemann, who in 1851 argued:

Could one but incline the parents through certain inducements which could be introduced for the purpose, to voluntarily send off their children to school, could these be kept from communal life with their tribesmen, then the success of the effort to bring them toward culture would enjoy greater blessing. But another thing: one would not have to limit oneself, as has been the case to date, to keep the pupils to their 14th year (girls often already leave school in their 12th year), but one would have to care for them further, boys perhaps in care of a farmer, a tradesman or as a servant, and similarly the girls, thus placing them in a position where they are not compelled to return to the tribe, where, naturally, soon all the good that they have learnt in school disappears. The children in school easily learn to speak English, and there is plenty of evidence to suggest that the natives do not lack ability to take in instruction and to apply it.[13]

A German perspective

Do the prejudices that pervade Koeler's writings represent a particularly German point of view? The debate about the position of 'primitive' people and their intellectual potential was found in all Western European countries, as were wild generalisations over the intellectual capacity of members of different 'races'. It is important to evaluate the seemingly blatant racism in contemporaneous writing as a reflection of ignorance as well as prejudice. Christian missionaries were keenly interested, for instance, in finding out whether the Bible could be translated into the languages spoken by Indigenous Australians, but in the early nineteenth century they simply did not know. Koeler's views on the limitations of the Kaurna language were not different from those held by many Anglican missionaries, who put a great deal of effort into replacing Indigenous languages with English in order to overcome what they believed were principled limitations of Indigenous languages. It is interesting to note that the Lutheran missionaries Teichelmann and Schürmann, who began to work with the Kaurna people a short time after Koeler's visit, felt that the Kaurna language could be developed to express the concepts of their religion and used for teaching.

Conclusions

We can summarise what has been discussed thus far: firstly, Koeler demonstrates the importance to contemporary researchers of consulting German sources to complete our understanding of the early history of South Australia. That a major published article should be ignored by linguists and historians until so recently is difficult to comprehend.

Secondly, the paper further illustrates the danger of projecting present-day disciplinary boundaries onto the past. Geography in nineteenth-century Germany was a discipline which dealt with numerous other questions of knowledge that nowadays are the domain of historians, anthropologists and linguists. A perusal of the archives of geographical societies could complement the current search in mission archives for information on customs and language.

Thirdly, in relation to the specific contribution that Koeler made to our understanding of the early contact history of South Australia, in my view, his is a major contribution, both because of its early date of publication and because of its scope.

Fourthly, to make sense of a document such as Koeler's requires many skills: an understanding of the intellectual climate prevailing at the time; triangulation with other contemporary documents, technical linguistics and anthropology; a knowledge of German measurements and units of currency; and, of course, a thorough knowledge of the German language.

Finally, there remain several unanswered questions. Above all, the man Koeler remains an enigma. Why is he not mentioned in all sources? Why did he not note any dealings with official bodies or white settlers? Why did he not work as a medical practitioner? Why does he provide conflicting dates for his stay? Are any other of his notes still in existence? A visit to the Geographical Society of Berlin may be a start, a visit to his descendants (if he had any) and his family may also be useful. Now that his work has now finally appeared in translation,[14] it can only be hoped that it will stimulate others to continue investigating these issues.

Notes

1 I am indebted to Rob Amery and Tom Gara, who jointly researched Koeler's visit to South Australia with me. Some of the ideas contained in the present paper are based on suggestions made by these two scholars.

2 Robert Foster, 'An imaginary dominion: The representation and treatment of Aborigines in South Australia 1834–1911', PhD thesis, University of Adelaide, 1993; Rob Amery, *Warrabarna Kaurna! Reclaiming an Australian Language*, Swets & Zeitlinger, Lisse, 2000; Jane Simpson, 'Early language contact varieties in South Australia', *Australian Journal of Linguistics*, vol. 16, no. 2, 1996, pp. 169–207.

3 See especially his collection, *Sammeln, Vernetzen, Auswerten-Missionare und ihr Beitrag zum Wandel europäischer Weltsicht*, Gunter Narr Verlag, Tübingen, 2001.

4 Cosmos Coroneos, *Shipwrecks of Encounter Bay and Backstairs Passage*, South Australian maritime heritage series no. 3, Department of Environment and Natural Resources, Adelaide (Australian Institute for Maritime Archaeology, Special publication, no. 8, Fremantle, WA), 1997, p. 45.

5 Hermann Koeler, 'Einige Notizen über die Eingeborenen an der Ostküste des St. Vincent-Golfs, Süd-Australien; 1837 und 1838' ('Some notes on the Aborigines on the East coast of the St Vincent Gulf, South Australia; 1837 and 1838'), *Monatsberichte ueber die Verhandlungen der Gesellschaft fuer Erdkunde zu Berlin*, pp. 42–57. The second part appeared in the same journal and with the same title in 1844, pp. 33–75. All future references to Koeler are either to the 1842 or 1844 issue of the journal.

6 P. Kremer, 'Carl Ritters Einstellung zu den Afrikanern: Grundlagen für eine philanthropisch orientierte Afrikaforschung', in Karl Lenz (ed.), *Carl Ritter – Geltung und Deutung*, Dietrich Reimer Verlag, Berlin, 1981, p. 149.

7 There are no contemporaneous references to his time in Adelaide. This absence of any official South Australian record of Koeler's visit has an explanation. All public records were destroyed by fire in either 1839 (according to T. Worsnop, *History of the City of Adelaide*, J. Williams, Adelaide, 1878, pp. 14–15) or in 1841 (according to Nathaniel Hailes in his *Recollections: Nathaniel Hailes' Adventurous Life in Colonial South Australia*, Wakefield Press, Adelaide, 1998, pp. 20–1), but a search in the State Library of South Australia for unofficial records continues, including for mentions of variant spellings of his name.

8 Adelaide linguist Dr Heidi Kneebone, pers. comm., 2001.

9 Tom Gara, 'Adelaide at the time of Koeler's visit', in Peter Mühlhäusler (ed.), *Hermann Koeler's Adelaide: Observations on the language and culture of South Australia by the first German visitor*, Australian Humanities Press, Unley, 2006, pp. 7–24; Henry Watson, *A Lecture on South Australia, Including Letters from J.B. Hack, Esq., and other emigrants*, Office of the Colonisation Commissioners for South Australia, London, 1838; William Williams,

A Vocabulary of the Languages of the Aborigines of the Adelaide District, and Other Friendly Tribes, of the Province of South Australia, McDougall, Adelaide, reprinted in *South Australian Colonist,* 1840; William Wyatt, *Report Upon the Expedition to Encounter Bay*, 1837, State Records, GRG 24/1/1837/372; Louis Piesse, Letter to *South Australian Colonist,* July 1840.

10 James Backhouse, *A Narrative of a Visit to the Australian Colonies*, Hamilton, Adams & Co., London, 1843.

11 Rob Amery & Peter Mühlhäusler, 'Koeler's contribution to Kaurna linguistics', in Mühlhäusler (ed.), 2006, pp. 25–48.

12 Robert Foster, Paul Monaghan and Peter Mühlhäusler, *Early Forms of Aboriginal English in South Australia*, Pacific Linguistics, Canberra, 2004.

13 G. Listemann, *Meine Auswanderung nach Süd-Australien und Rückkehr zum Vaterlande: Ein Wort zur Warnung und Belehrung für alle Auswanderungslustige*, Berlin, 1851. Translation is from B. Arnold, 'German Settlers' Accounts of the Australian Aborigines', *Torrens Valley Historical Journal*, 33, 1988, p. 56.

14 In Mühlhäusler (ed.), 2006, pp. 49–126; translation by Lois Zweck.

A vision frustrated
Lutheran missionaries to the Aborigines of South Australia 1838–1853

Christine Lockwood

The first missionaries to the Indigenous people of South Australia arrived with Governor Gawler in October 1838. Christian Gottlob Teichelmann (1807–1888) and Clamor Wilhelm Schürmann (1815–1893), from the Evangelical Lutheran Mission Society in Dresden, came at the request of George Fife Angas, Chairman of the South Australian Company. Heinrich August Eduard Meyer (1813–1862) and Samuel Gottlieb Klose (1802–1889) followed in 1840. By 1853 all had ceased Aboriginal mission work, their mission considered a failure.

This chapter examines this 'failure' and the role of the missionaries' theology in shaping a vision different from that dominant in the colony and influencing relationships with the government, colonists and other churches. To this end, the missionaries' letters and diaries held in Adelaide's Lutheran Archives have proved invaluable.

The missionaries' background

To understand why the Dresden missionaries acted as they did after their arrival in South Australia, we need to know something of their background and of the theological foundations of their thinking. Eighteenth- and early nineteenth-century Germany saw a spiritual reawakening influenced by Pietism, which emphasised the individual's inner response, manifested through Christian living. Pietism found expression in new mission societies that downplayed doctrinal distinctions, one being the Basel Missionary Society, representing both the Lutheran and Reformed faiths. However, Emperor Friedrich Wilhelm's enforcement, from 1830, of a union between Prussia's Lutheran and Reformed congregations, together with the persecution of dissenters, reawakened among Lutherans an appreciation for what was distinctive in Lutheran teaching.[1] Protests centred on the Lutheran teaching of the Real Presence – the oral reception of Christ's body and blood in the Eucharist as opposed to the symbolic understanding of Reformed theology. Lutheran pastors forced to leave Prussia moved to Saxony, where relations between the Dresden Mission Aid Society and the Basel Seminary broke down over the training of Saxon Lutheran students destined for Basel's Evangelical Lutheran Mission in India. Dresden wanted them instructed in the Lutheran Confessions, but Basel said 'Lutheran' must be understood historically, not doctrinally, and insisted on joint Lutheran–Reformed communion services.

Schürmann and Teichelmann studied initially at the Berlin Mission Institute, which supplied Lutheran missionaries to Dutch and English mission societies. However, in 1836 the Anglican Society for the Propagation of the Gospel in Foreign Lands (SPG) decided that missionaries serving the society must be re-ordained as Anglicans and accept the Church of England's Thirty-nine Articles, which deny the Real Presence. Unhappy with this, Schürmann and Teichelmann refused positions offered to them with the SPG in India. Told to expect no other offers, their plight triggered the founding, in 1836, of the Evangelical Lutheran Mission Society in Dresden, then unique in making the Lutheran Confessions foundational to its witness. The Evangelical Lutheran Mission Society opened a seminary, with Schürmann and Teichelmann its first graduates. Instruction in the Scriptures and Lutheran Confessions was given, along with a comprehensive education and the encouragement of practical skills, while Greek and Hebrew instruction helped missionaries to understand and translate the Scriptures and provided the linguistic skills which facilitated indigenous language learning.

The Dresden Society asked the London Missionary Society (LMS) for advice about starting a mission field and was advised to establish a mission where work had already begun and was comparatively close to Germany, not in a new and isolated field. They suggested east India, near an English mission, with at least two missionaries working together.

The Dresden Society began work in India in 1840. In the meantime, in 1837, the Baptist businessman George Fife Angas had asked Dresden to send missionaries to South Australia, agreeing to support them with £100 a year for five years if satisfied with them. The society agreed because no missionaries were working among South Australia's Aborigines, civil and religious freedom in the colony meant free, independent Lutheran congregations could be established, and the South Australian Company chairman's support augured well for the mission's success.

Lutheran theology and its mission implications

Lutheran theology shaped the missionaries' aims. The doctrine of *sola fide* teaches that people cannot attain salvation through their own efforts: they are forgiven and reconciled to God through faith in the atoning life, death and resurrection of Jesus Christ. This has implications for mission work. First, the Lutheran mission task is to offer the Gospel of forgiveness and reconciliation to all people, since everyone needs forgiveness. Second, this emphasis on

Christian Gottlob Teichelmann.
(State Library of South Australia, SLSA: B6501)

justification by grace through faith permits a greater openness to variant cultural expressions of the Christian faith than found in theologies that emphasise sanctified living and sometimes define this in cultural terms. Lutheran theology teaches that faith expresses itself in gratitude to God and love for others, but the believer can add nothing to his salvation and is free in matters not mandated in the New Testament. For example, in Australia the Dresden missionaries opposed polygamy only after being convinced it caused suffering.

Lutheran teaching emphasises the Bible's authority as God's Word, and conversion as the Holy Spirit's work, creating faith through the Word. For Lutheran missionaries this means they must use the local language to reach people's hearts and teach them to read the Scriptures in their mother tongue.

The Lutheran doctrine of the Two Kingdoms distinguishes church from state. God sustains his creation through civil authorities and institutions, and individuals in their vocations (God's 'left hand kingdom'). Through the Gospel, God brings people into his spiritual kingdom (God's 'right hand kingdom'). Each 'kingdom' has its own role – civil authorities are responsible for justice, peace and good order; the church for Gospel proclamation. The Dresden missionaries saw their primary task as Gospel proclamation, with the government responsible for Aboriginal welfare. They could assist the government as long as they were free to follow their convictions.

The missionaries' convictions influenced relations with other churches. Lutherans believe apostolic teaching alone is essential for church unity. Consequently, they resisted the Anglican insistence on 'apostolic succession' and the re-ordination of Lutherans destined for Anglican mission fields.

The mission vision for South Australia

The Dresden Society instructed its missionaries to establish congregations among German immigrants in South Australia who would, it was hoped, provide support for Aboriginal mission work. They were to learn the indigenous language, making their chief aim to 'bear witness to the heathen of the Gospel of the grace of God' through evangelism, literature, preaching and schools. They were to gather converts into Lutheran congregations, training them to assist in evangelism. In addition, the missionaries should undertake scientific research and maintain peaceful relations with the heathen, Angas and other Christians. As funds were limited, the society could support only spiritual work.

Angas outlined broader aims at a banquet for Governor Hindmarsh in 1835:

> Let us send out persons among them to learn their language ... to treat with them for the purchase of those lands which they claim as belonging to their tribes; to make them acquainted with the habits and views of the white people; to construct a written language for them; to publish the Gospels and New Testament in it; to teach them to read; to make them acquainted with the art of raising food from the ground; to instruct them in the mode of fishing from the sea ... in the method of making utensils, raising huts, the use of clothing; and in time they may be induced ... to allow the settlers to take their youths and teach them to work as labourers.[2]

Angas also instructed the missionaries to learn the indigenous language and customs, to establish a school, and to set up a settlement at the Murray–Darling junction, where they could teach the Aborigines civilised living, agriculture and Christianity. Angas had lent money to a group of persecuted Lutherans in Germany to enable them to migrate to South Australia in 1838. He assumed that, together with their pastor, August Kavel, they would settle near the missionaries and provide the material support and skills the Aboriginal mission settlement would need. He believed the government would provide land and considered that the South Australian constitution, Gawler's Christian commitment and the large number of Christians in the colony offered a good chance of success.

While acknowledging Angas's wishes, the missionaries were firstly missionaries of the Dresden Society. Their clear priority was to bring to the Indigenous people 'the Gospel of the grace of God'. Clearly this would transform Indigenous culture, but their goals were not defined in terms of civilisation, Europeanisation, or assimilation. They envisioned land reserved where Aborigines could preserve their communities, language and aspects of their culture, adapting to the invaders' culture and learning English as necessary.

Piltawodli Aboriginal school and chapel used by the Dresden Missionaries; drawing by W.A. Cawthorne.
(Mitchell Library, State Library of New South Wales)

They would be taught to read the Scriptures and catechism in their own language; Indigenous Lutheran congregations would be established.

Vision meets reality

The missionaries' optimism was soon tested. Travelling to South Australia on the same ship as Governor Gawler, they had many conversations with him. Gawler advocated bringing the Aborigines close to towns and assimilating them as servants. Schürmann disagreed, arguing for separate Indigenous communities and the retention of vernacular languages. Other disagreements concerned the legitimacy of England's colonising ambitions. When Schürmann pointed to injustices to Indigenous people, Gawler suggested Schürmann's opinions would *cause* bloodshed. Schürmann wrote to Dresden: 'the English occupation of foreign countries without consideration for their occupants is humanly and morally unjust'.[3] The Dresden Society warned the missionaries their views were dangerous: '[Y]ou will earn yourselves much antagonism and trouble in your mission work, indeed complete prohibition of it and probably even your way out of the Colony and away from the natives who could be inflamed to anger and revenge by your attitude'.[4] Nevertheless, Gawler and the missionaries developed good relations.

Arriving almost penniless, the missionaries worked for three months before receiving Angas's £25 per quarter. Gawler arranged a loan and use of a hut at the Piltawodli Native Location on the Torrens in North Adelaide. Church services for Adelaide Germans soon folded, because most Germans employed by the South Australian Company were indifferent, and Kavel insisted his parishioners attend his Klemzig services.

In order to learn the Kaurna language, customs and beliefs, Teichelmann and Schürmann mixed with the Adelaide Aborigines at every opportunity. In 1839 Schürmann started a school at Piltawodli, although Matthew Moorhouse, the Protector of Aborigines from 1839 to 1856, believed this to be a futile exercise, while Teichelmann considered it premature because the people were nomadic. Teaching in Kaurna, Schürmann delighted in his students' aptitude, as did Samuel Klose, who took over in 1840. Progress varied, as attendance depended on the students' whims and their parents' movements, with frustration decreasing when boarding began in 1843. In 1844 Governor Grey (1841–45) established a government school in Walkerville for children from Murray tribes. Here the children were taught in English rather than in their own languages. At Grey's insistence, Klose began using English, except in religion lessons. In 1845 the two schools were amalgamated into a new Native Training Institute near Government House. Early in 1846 Klose's employment ended, as did government support for the Dresden missionaries.

Attempts at Aboriginal settlement
Dresden's instructions were to concentrate on spiritual matters. But, confronted by a people seriously affected by colonisation, the missionaries felt the need to care also for their physical wellbeing.

Prevailing opinion considered Aborigines little better than animals. The missionaries disagreed, claiming they had the ability of Europeans, with Schürmann, for example, writing: 'One finds a vivacity, intelligence and cleverness among them',[5] their 'busy, restless

Clamor Schürmann. (Lutheran Archives Adelaide)

spirit betrays the image of God in them also',[6] and 'I have admired and been delighted at the bearing and behaviour towards each other of the free and equal aborigines'.[7] However, the missionaries considered Indigenous society blighted by infanticide, fighting, sorcery, pay-back killings, polygamy, wife-sharing, promiscuity, abuse of children and women and the marriage of prepubescent girls to old men. European settlement added dispossession, exploitation, and introduced diseases and vices.

The missionaries believed that reserving land away from European settlement might provide some solution for both missionaries and Aborigines. Schürmann wrote in 1839: 'I am amazed that the natives have not sunk even further because of their constant association with ... the English rabble, rough and ungodly beyond comprehension. Therefore the plan of bringing the natives into active contact with Europeans, indeed, where possible allowing them to be scattered among them ... is highly destructive.'[8]

The missionaries had built huts and planted gardens with the Kaurna on land reserved for them at Piltawodli, but proximity to Europeans had raised complaints from settlers, and from 1839 both the Protector and the Governor discouraged Aborigines from settling there, finally removing them. In 1839 Schürmann reported that wildlife had left the Adelaide area and government rations were inadequate. Dispossession was reducing a once honest and open people to begging and thieving. Believing Aborigines should be left at least enough land for their sustenance, he hounded Moorhouse until the government reserved land near Adelaide, Encounter Bay, Lake Alexandrina and the Murray, although these reserves were later leased to whites.

Deciding that a settlement at the Murray–Darling junction was impractical and that the area around Encounter Bay and the Murray mouth was more suitable, Schürmann accepted Gawler's invitation to move there. However, asked for money for land, implements and draught animals, Dresden replied in 1840: 'It appears questionable to us that missionaries alone should undertake the civilising of the natives since by so doing they become distanced from their actual calling ... we are convinced that you cannot do more towards furthering it than you indirectly do by way of the ... Word and by erecting schools and dispensing good advice'.[9] Furthermore, Dresden suggested that colonial tradesmen settle nearby, support the mission and help Aborigines acquire the skills necessary for sedentary living. It assumed government help with land and housing and admonished: 'You are not to establish a specifically civil community, but rather a religious one ... Do not concern yourselves with the physical dependence or independence of the aborigines but with their spiritual liberation through the spiritual means of grace.'[10]

In 1840, however, Schürmann's plans changed when Gawler asked him to go instead to Port Lincoln as Deputy Protector of Aborigines.

Teichelmann continued evangelistic work in Adelaide. His pleas for government provision for Indigenous people fell on deaf ears. When a member of the Dresden Society provided £100 to purchase land and make the mission more independent, Teichelmann bought land at Happy Valley, south of Adelaide. In 1844 he encouraged Kaurna people to settle and farm with him, promising them the harvest. After clearing, fencing and planting, none returned to harvest the crop. Teichelmann blamed government rations and his neighbours' ability to pay higher wages. Lack of resources frustrated his desire to start a school and to help the needy and elderly who gathered around him.

Meyer and Encounter Bay

Although Heinrich August Eduard Meyer and his wife came to South Australia in 1840 to work with Schürmann at Encounter Bay, Schürmann did not accompany him, instead taking up his missionary work at Port Lincoln. Meyer learnt the Ramindjeri language, established a school using Ramindjeri and English, farmed leased land with Aborigines and ministered to white settlers, teaching their children. Poverty, government indifference, Ramindjeri nomadic habits and the impact of whalers and sealers thwarted his work. The government denied his request to use land reserved for Aborigines, instead leasing it to settlers. Meyer believed that the government, because it wanted to disperse Aborigines as labourers, was ignoring its responsibilities to help them adopt a settled life in their own country. He also believed that, because the Encounter Bay Aborigines were not troublesome, the government thought it could safely ignore their needs.[11]

Schürmann and Port Lincoln

Schürmann reluctantly relinquished his Encounter Bay plans and accepted the Port Lincoln position. He found Aborigines suspicious of whites, largely because Aboriginal women had been abducted by white men. Clashes, thefts and killings hampered his efforts to gain the trust of Aborigines and settlers. Limited ongoing contact made learning the Parnkalla (or Barngalla) language slow. By 1841 he was becoming increasingly convinced he must address the Aborigines' material situation and questioned Dresden's emphasis on spiritual work:

> You warn me wisely and correctly not to place too much emphasis on the outward affairs of the Aborigines, but who can observe their condition without being convinced of the extent to which they are dependent on external influences? ... I am beginning to fear that the otherwise correct basis for missionary activity, which is limited to the spiritual domain only, can scarcely find any application here or that from this alone the physical and spiritual salvation of the Aborigines could proceed.[12]

Convinced that the only hope was to establish an Aboriginal station, with cattle-raising as a step towards sedentary living, Schürmann repeatedly asked the government to reserve land for Aboriginal people. This would enable him to both preach the Gospel to Aboriginal people and accustom them to settled living.

By 1842 Port Lincoln was in a state of siege. Aborigines attacked pastoral stations and police and settlers retaliated indiscriminately. While settlers complained he was not representing their interests, Schürmann found his official position conflicted with his missionary role. Expected to accompany police expeditions as an interpreter, he witnessed unarmed Aborigines being shot. He was pressured to inform on people and then minister to those condemned to death. In April 1842 he left an expedition in protest: the expedition led by the Government Resident, Mr Driver, killed an unarmed, innocent Aboriginal man whom Schürmann had known well. Soon afterwards Schürmann's position was abolished, but Grey offered the Lutheran Mission a £100 subsidy (shared between the four missionaries) on the condition that a missionary remained in Port Lincoln. Schürmann stayed, but under Driver's supervision. He doubted that Aborigines would ever receive justice.

Schürmann begged Dresden for re-assignment to India or to any sedentary people. He advised the society to abandon mission work where little support was provided and where those to whom the missionary efforts were being directed had nomadic habits. Grey, said Schürmann, believed that Aborigines were dying out and money spent on them was wasted. Dresden refused Schürmann's request.

Himself afraid the local people could die out, Schürmann proposed a settlement at least 10 miles from Port Lincoln. In his plan Aborigines would have three options. They could choose between their traditional lifestyle, regular employment with Europeans, or a settled life based on agriculture or cattle-raising. Government rations would only be distributed at the settlement, as a reward for good conduct. Begging, free rations, prostitution, stealing and handouts in return for odd jobs should not be options. Schürmann believed that such a settlement would be self-supporting within two or three years and would reduce conflict with settlers and also government costs. In 1844 a number of Aborigines asked Schürmann to live with them and help them farm at Kunta, 30 miles from Port Lincoln. A settler, Hermann Kook, promised £200 and his services, free, for a year. Dresden offered £100, provided the government matched it. Grey rejected the proposal.

From 1843 to 1845 Schürmann farmed six acres two miles from Port Lincoln. He employed Aborigines, initially using government rations as payment. He explained to Dresden: 'Even though the preoccupation with such external affairs is not the immediate and actual purpose of my mission it nevertheless gives me pleasure, partly because it presents me with the best opportunity of advancing my knowledge of the language, partly also because the natives do not fail to appreciate the good outcome of such care'.[13] The Aborigines worked with a will but lost heart when others demanded a share of food. Grey refused requests for land, tools and further rations. Crop loss from fire, foraging animals and theft, and the repeated burning of fences forced Schurmann to give up.

In 1844 Schürmann requested £100 for an Aboriginal school. Grey refused.

The end of the Lutheran Mission

The missionaries met in January 1846. Grey's refusal to accept or match Dresden's £100 offer toward an Aboriginal settlement near Port Lincoln convinced them the government would never help Aborigines settle. Without substantial change in the social conditions of the Aborigines, the prospects for evangelism were considered to be hopeless. Because they lacked Christian converts, they were reluctant to take money that could better support the society's flourishing Indian work. Consequently, they resolved to concentrate their work in two locations, retaining their association with Dresden but relinquishing its monetary support.

With most Kaurna gone from Adelaide and the mission school closed, Klose and Teichelmann ministered to Germans and English people in Adelaide. Schürmann joined Meyer near Encounter Bay. They bought land and farmed with the Aborigines, supporting themselves while preaching the Gospel.

In 1848 Meyer was called to serve the Bethany congregation in the Barossa Valley. He accepted, citing the Lutheran settlers' needs and the poor prospects for an Aboriginal Lutheran church. The missionaries decided to close the mission in South Australia, but to continue assisting individual Aborigines. Behind this decision lay financial problems, changes in government policy and the Anglican entry into Aboriginal mission work. Meyer suggested Dresden had not done its homework, sending missionaries to the most difficult field on earth without recognising the financial commitments required to first settle the Aborigines; the field, he believed, should have been left to the English churches.

Schürmann returns to Port Lincoln

In 1848 Governor Robe asked Schürmann to return to Port Lincoln as court interpreter. Expected to accompany police on murder investigations, he was distressed as settlers took the law into their own hands and police punished guilty and innocent Aborigines alike.

In 1849 Governor Young offered Schürmann a £50 salary to start an Aboriginal school. 'If not productive of ... permanent and general good,' said Young, it would 'at least have a tendency to generate and maintain kindly feelings between the Natives at Port Lincoln and the European settlers',[14] and if it kept a few children from their parents, it would be worth the cost. Schürmann started a school at Wallala, 12 kilometres from Port Lincoln. Government expenditure was minimal; in 1851 the school still lacked furniture. Winning the confidence of parents and the affection of his students, Schürmann had no trouble with attendance, student numbers being limited only by government rations. He shared the Gospel also with Aboriginal adults. Botanist Charles Wilhelmi, visiting in 1851, reported, 'twenty-four native children attended [Schürmann's] school, and had made considerable progress in reading, writing &c, which was rendered the more easy to them by the advantage that all information was by this most excellent man conveyed to them in their own language'.[15] Schürmann wrote to Meyer: 'The black children in the school are giving us a joyful expectation and on the whole we are very happy'.[16]

However, the venture was short-lived. Anglicans were entering mission work, with a proposal for a Christian settlement. Governor Young favoured his own church's initiatives and soon assisted only Anglican missions. In 1850 he leased Archdeacon Hale 3000 acres of native reserve at Poonindie, three miles from Schürmann's school, advanced him £600 and gave £300 annually for a schoolmaster, matron and labourer. Hale purchased additional land. Students from the Native Training Institute in Adelaide were married at puberty and, to segregate them from both white society and their tribes, brought to Poonindie to work the land. Initially, local Indigenous adults were strictly excluded from Poonindie. Hale approached Schürmann to join him. Alarmed, Schürmann wrote to Meyer in 1851:

> Archdeacon Hale has invited me … to enter into an agreement with the English Church … I have of course answered negatively, because I was inclined by my conscientious convictions to do so … It appears to me that Archdeacon Hale wants to reduce the influence of my school in Port Lincoln … It could be that if I don't join him, he will find some cause to shift my school from my section to Poonindie … One thing I will not change. I will follow … my 'unfamiliar' confession.[17]

In 1852, Lutherans moving to Victoria asked Schürmann to be their pastor. Schürmann could not desert his students. 'I [have] finally found my settled place and made it comfortable', he told Meyer. 'I would be quite wretchedly crucified by the change.'[18]

In 1852 the Adelaide school closed, as students absconded and parents withheld their children to prevent their removal to Poonindie, cutting off Hale's main source of students. Poonindie's high death rate and students absconding forced Hale to look elsewhere for replacements. In 1852 Young decided to close Schürmann's school and gave Hale £1000 a year to accept Schürmann's students and whichever young Aborigines Young sent him. Schürmann moved to Victoria in 1853.

Stumbling blocks to effective mission work

Inadequate support denied the missionaries independence and crippled their efforts as they struggled to support their Aboriginal work with insufficient resources. Faced with demands from its Indian mission and under pressure for its confessional stance, the Dresden Society supplied only a meagre stipend. It believed missionaries should focus on proclaiming the good news about Jesus Christ and, like St Paul, partially support themselves, living near the level of those they worked amongst. The missionaries supplemented their incomes by growing food, and manual and domestic work also limited their time for mission work. Angas, himself overextended financially, ceased support after two years. Lutheran settlers gave occasional foodstuffs, donations and voluntary labour, but little more. Desperately poor, the missionaries faced resettlement costs, repayment of passage money and, as non-British citizens, premium land prices. Tensions between Pastor Kavel and the missionaries over Kavel's insistence on his 'Apostolic Constitution' and strict church discipline also affected support. In 1842 a group of leading Adelaide citizens formed the South Australian Aboriginal Missionary Society in Aid of the German Mission to the Aborigines, but assistance was short-lived. Meyer accepted money; Schürmann, however, declined because of the conditions placed on it. When government support ended, so did the Lutheran Mission in South Australia.

The relationship between Dresden and its missionaries was respectful, even affectionate; yet replies to letters could take a year, and distance led to misunderstandings and inappropriate advice. Dresden opposed marriage unless missionaries were able to support their dependants, but the missionaries believed that their single state hampered their work as the Aborigines suspected their intentions towards Aboriginal women and young men. All eventually married but struggled to support their families. Disagreement also arose over the extent of the missionaries' responsibility for the Aborigines' physical wellbeing, with the Dresden Society considering this a government responsibility. The missionaries on the other hand became increasingly convinced that, with the government negligent, they needed to fill the void for the sake of the Aborigines and to enable their spiritual work to succeed. Schürmann believed they and Dresden had failed the Aborigines, since it was unrealistic to expect missionaries to overcome obstacles with spiritual weapons alone.

The distance between the mission locations hampered cooperation. Meyer and Schürmann both craved a colleague and regretted that they were forced to work singly – the missionaries were working in widely separated locations at the government's request. Had it been possible for missionaries to work together, they may have felt less isolated and might have seen more positive results.

Language learning and evangelism required ongoing contact and so the missionaries considered the people's nomadic lifestyle to be their major obstacle, which was compounded by the smallness of groups and multiplicity of languages. Teichelmann and Schürmann considered roaming with the Aborigines but lacked the resources to do so. The only solution, they believed, was to encourage Aborigines to settle. Schürmann wrote from Port Lincoln:

> [T]o live amongst the natives is what I have wanted ... But how this is to be accomplished other than by allotting the natives a piece of land as their enduring and inalienable property and to assist them in its cultivation[?] ... Of course I visit them but that does not mean living with them ... This, in the present conditions would only be possible if one completely became a wild person, wore a kangaroo skin ... and nourished himself with their meagre diet ... It is a hard task laid upon us.[19]

As early as 1839 Schürmann believed that results from mission work would be minimal because of the denial of land to Aborigines. Thus when attempts at Aboriginal settlement failed, chances for an Indigenous Lutheran church disappeared.

Without ongoing contact, finding linguistic and cultural equivalents for Christian themes such as grace, faith, repentance and salvation was difficult. Schürmann lamented that the Law was easier to communicate than the Gospel, the Ten Commandments easier to translate than the Lord's Prayer. He wrote that most of all it was hard to find an appropriate word for 'forgiveness', lamenting that in his observation the Aborigines never sought forgiveness but tended to resolve wrongs 'either by abuse or with blows'.[20] It is true that the missionaries translated hymns, Bible stories and catechism portions, but not whole biblical books. When their work ended they were still struggling with religious terms.

The missionaries experienced ridicule, apathy, and resistance to their preaching, particularly when they criticised behaviour. Sometimes they seemed to emphasise the Aborigines' moral failings rather than the predominant Lutheran emphasis on God's love. However, two points need to be made. First, the missionaries wanted to warn against the behaviour destroying the Aborigines and this was not simply an attempt to inculcate European culture. Second, Lutheran theology teaches that people must understand their need for forgiveness before they can seek salvation in Christ. This underpinned the missionaries' evangelistic approach, but their ultimate objective was always to share a loving Saviour. Klose wrote: 'When I heard that within a few days the children would leave the Location to go to the new school, I spent considerable time on the first three verses of [Romans 8] in order to make Christianity really clear and sweet to them'.[21] These verses teach that there is 'no condemnation for those who are in Christ Jesus' because Christ has achieved what sinful human nature cannot and has freed believers from the consequences of sin and death.

Although the missionaries reported evidence of faith among children and adults, they were slow to claim conversions, realising that the Aborigines sometimes said what was expected of them, and converts, under tribal pressure, could revert to heathen ways. The missionaries had hoped to form congregations providing support for new believers.

The poor example of some Europeans and their horrendous treatment of Aborigines, along with their derision of the missionary work, undercut efforts towards evangelism – with the unfortunate consequence that all Europeans were discredited in the eyes of Indigenous people – and contributed to the dispersal and rapid decline of that population. This, and the Aborigines' preoccupation with physical survival, impeded evangelism.

In many regards the Dresden missionaries were out of step with colonial ambitions. South Australia's founders had commercial objectives, and the *South Australia Act* of 1834 made no provision for Indigenous people. Under pressure from the British Colonial Office, the Colonization Commissioners outlined their vision in their first annual report in 1836. Aborigines, they believed, would benefit from contact with 'industrious and virtuous' settlers who would respect Aboriginal land rights, where found to exist, with Aborigines receiving permanent 'subsistence' in return for land sold voluntarily. The Commissioners would promote civilisation and Christianity and supply sheds, food and clothing in exchange for Aboriginal labour, and this plan would be implemented 'in such a way as to be beneficial rather than burdensome to settlers' and 'accelerate the prosperity of the Colony, by training the Aborigines to habits of useful industry, and by bringing a supply of native labour to aid the efforts of the settlers'.[22] One-fifth of land was to be reserved for Aborigines. However, in 1834 all land was opened to sale. A belated

1838 Amendment to the *South Australia Act* recognised Aboriginal land rights.

Successive governors hoped to 'civilise' and assimilate Aborigines into colonial society as labourers through contact with settlers and missionaries. Early attempts to encourage Aborigines in settled living and agriculture at the Native Location were soon abandoned. Gawler and Grey, encouraged by the missionaries, the Protectors and Angas, reserved land for Indigenous use, but colonists, without evidence of permanent Aboriginal dwellings or agriculture, dismissed Indigenous land claims. Land reserved for Aborigines was largely leased or sold to Europeans, and the monies used for running the Aborigines Department. After the 1841 *Waste Lands Act* had allocated some of the proceeds from land sales to Aboriginal welfare, policy began to focus on providing rations to the needy and educating children in English.

Grey's and Moorhouse's thinking evolved as disillusionment with civilising efforts set in, a shift reflected in Edward John Eyre's proposals in 1845. He recommended dividing the country into districts, each with an Aboriginal reserve and manager, with rations used to establish authority. Aboriginal traditions should be broken down, with adults concentrated in defined areas, employed as pastoral workers and encouraged to adopt European ways. Civilising efforts should concentrate on educating children and segregating them from Aboriginal adults. Vernacular languages should not be used. On leaving school children should be apprenticed, marry and settle in a village under missionary influence.

In line with these recommendations, Governor Robe developed a general system of ration depots which promoted social control and Aboriginal dependency. Increasingly, government policy focused on control rather than education, with Governor Young attempting a policy of segregating young Aboriginal people both from Europeans and from their tribes at Poonindie. Moorhouse told a Select Committee in 1860 that educating Aborigines to be civilised was hopeless. According to Schürmann, Moorhouse already believed this in 1839.

It has been common to see missionaries as part of the colonisation process. Anne Scrimgeour claims the missionaries were not opposed to colonisation, that they served colonial agendas and used colonial power for their own ends. She sees colonial administrators and missionaries sharing the same Christianising and civilising goals, the government's objective being colonisation facilitated and justified by the 'civilising/Christianising' of Aborigines, while the Lutheran missionaries' aim was to civilise/Europeanise them through Christianity.[23] However, the Lutheran missionaries' discussions with Gawler show that they opposed colonisation and the seizure of Aboriginal land. They disagreed with colonial agendas but were powerless in their opposition. Their emphasis on salvation as God's gift, received through faith, meant bringing Aborigines to faith, not promoting civilisation or a particular lifestyle. Ideally, as Christian people, Aborigines would work out the implications of their faith for their culture. At Piltawodli the missionaries attempted to address community pressures to 'civilise' the Aborigines. They also sought to 'civilise' them to the extent of encouraging them to settle so the missionaries could learn their language and teach them, and because they saw no alternative if Aborigines were to have a future. But 'civilising' the people was not their goal.

As a result of this distinctive theological understanding, the missionaries' approach differed from that of the government in significant ways. They opposed the dispersal and assimilation of Aborigines as servants, believing God had created them a separate people. Recognising Indigenous land ownership, they advocated land reserves and assistance for Aborigines to settle to enable their communities, identity, language and culture to be preserved, the impact of dispossession and European culture minimised and Aboriginal Lutheran congregations established. Christianity, they believed, would free Aborigines from their superstitious fears and transform the destructive aspects of Aboriginal culture. They proposed training on settlements, and the use of vernacular languages in schools, introducing English as necessary. However, after 1838 the government had no interest in preserving Aboriginal society or assisting Aboriginal settlement. The missionaries were left to founder on their own small plots as they attempted to teach Aborigines farming skills.

Another area of tension was the judicial system. The government used the missionaries as interpreters for the police, the Protector and the courts, with the result that their other work suffered. The missionaries criticised the application of 'British justice' and tried to help Aboriginal prisoners. Schürmann argued for the admission of Aboriginal evidence in court, maintaining that they had their own laws and should not be judged by white law. Moorhouse supported Schürmann, but Grey opposed special laws for Aborigines.

As colonial frustration with the slowness of 'civilising' efforts grew, criticism was focused on the mission school's emphasis on religion, arithmetic and reading and writing in the vernacular, with some instruction in general knowledge and English. Colonists debated the school's usefulness. Initial praise turned to criticism, the majority opinion favouring instruction in English, believing that Christianity demanded assimilation into European civilisation. Critics expected greater changes in students' outward appearance and manners, and their training as useful workers. The *Adelaide Examiner* called the German missionaries' efforts a 'disgrace', a 'lamentable waste of public money'.[24] By contrast, it contended, Aborigines employed by Europeans became useful and industrious. Methodism, it proclaimed, would achieve better results than the Lutherans.

The missionaries insisted on using the children's mother tongue, especially in religion classes, and students made much faster progress as a result. Assimilation, however, implied that English would supplant vernacular languages. Grey's focus shifted to the use of English only in government schools, with an emphasis on Europeanisation and practical training. Offered a teaching position at the Walkerville school in 1844, Schürmann declined. Grey's Native Training Institute brought children in from other areas, deliberately separating them from their families.

The missionaries opposed focusing solely on children and forcibly segregating them from their families, although they accepted boarding facilities as necessary to maintain school attendance. They advocated segregation from destructive European influences but wanted schools as part of Aboriginal communities; they shared the Gospel with people of all ages and hoped their students would share the Gospel with their tribes.

Other churches were more in line with government and community thinking, partly because of the different emphasis of Reformed theology. While Lutherans emphasised justification by grace, the Reformed church emphasised Christian living and tended to define this in terms of European civilisation. Angas saw Christian missions in these terms, urging the missionaries to raise the Aborigines 'from barbarism to the highest pitch of refinement'.[25] Methodists teaching religion at the Walkerville school emphasised a disciplined lifestyle and an English education. The South Australian Aboriginal Missionary Society, representing all denominations, opposed perpetuating native languages, favouring 'a more comprehensive' education, teaching English and useful skills, and taking children as young as possible from their parents. The Colonial Chaplain, the Reverend Dean Farrell, endorsed the Aboriginal Missionary Society's policies. The Poonindie Mission was founded on the principle of isolating young Aborigines from their tribes.

The Lutheran missionaries willingly worked with other churches as long as their convictions were respected. However, they came under pressure from Dissenters and Anglicans. Some despised the missionaries' poverty, manual labour and lack of university training; most disagreed with their approach. Moreover, there were some who were offended by the Lutheran teaching on baptismal regeneration and the Real Presence.

Aspirations for the Anglican church to achieve the prominence it held in England finally thwarted the missionaries' hopes. Governors Robe (1845–48) and Young (1848–54) supported these aspirations. With the Piltawodli mission school's closure, Klose wondered whether he could teach in the new school when it was placed under the Anglican Farrell's supervision, but agreed to if the children's religious education remained in his hands. Robe did not agree. With the formation of Adelaide's Anglican diocese in 1847, Bishop Short demanded the right to supervise the missionaries. Accepting a call to Bethany in 1848, Meyer wrote to Dresden:

> [T]he bishop ... encouraged us to continue the mission at his cost, with the stipulation however that if some should be converted to Christianity, they are then to be led to the English Church ... This is indeed no fertile ground for our Lutheran Church.[26]

With this the missionaries asked Dresden to release them, and the mission was closed. Only Schürmann continued working with

Aborigines, as court interpreter in Port Lincoln and then starting a school. This too was closed when an Anglican venture more in line with government policy presented itself. As Schürmann was unwilling to become Anglican, his work ended.

The Dresden men felt disadvantaged dealing with authorities. With humble origins, imperfect English and an unfamiliar creed and nationality, they could not have the same influence as men like the wealthy aristocrat Hale, of familiar nationality and denomination.

The missionaries' contribution

The Dresden missionaries did not establish an Indigenous Lutheran church. However, they left unique linguistic and ethnographic records of the Kaurna, Ramindjeri and Parnkalla people. Meyer, Teichelmann and Schürmann were competent linguists; other linguists and missionaries built on their work, adopting their orthography and methods. Teichelmann and Schürmann published a Kaurna grammar and vocabulary, which Teichelmann later updated, writing also on Kaurna customs. Their work formed the basis, in recent times, for resurrecting the Kaurna language and promoting cultural awareness. Meyer's Ramindjeri vocabulary book and booklet on the customs of Encounter Bay tribes have informed Ngarinndjeri language and culture revival programs. Schürmann also wrote on the culture of the Port Lincoln tribes and prepared a Parnkalla vocabulary.

The missionaries had some influence. They led the way in establishing schools and influenced the government to reserve land for Aborigines, even if it was leased to settlers. Requesting reservations before an 1841 House of Commons Select Committee, Angas quoted the missionaries' claim that Aborigines inherited clearly defined territories. The missionaries also helped to influence authorities to finally allow Aboriginal evidence in court.

Although the Lutheran missionaries baptised no one, some Aboriginal people showed at least the beginnings of Christian faith. Lutheran efforts provided the foundation for Anglican mission work, and at Point McLeay the Congregationalist George Taplin built on Meyer's linguistic work; indeed, he acknowledged harvesting seed sown by Meyer. The people accepted Taplin because they appreciated Meyer and his wife. Later Lutheran missions learnt from the Dresden work: they used vernacular languages, moved far from European settlement, accepted responsibility for both the physical and spiritual wellbeing of the Aborigines and were more realistic about the financial commitments.

For individual Aborigines touched by the Dresden missionaries, their efforts were not pointless. Prisoners were comforted, people befriended, fed and taught to read and write, the sick and dying cared for and a despised people shown many acts of kindness and love. Race relations around Port Lincoln deteriorated after Schürmann left. Encounter Bay Aborigines mourned Meyer's departure and visited his widow annually until she died. John Harris describes their efforts as 'impressive, courageous, selfless, loving and generous. They were powerless to stem the tide of exploitation and oppression. But at least they tried.'[27]

The 1860 Legislative Council Select Committee on the Aborigines did not seek evidence from the Lutheran missionaries. Those from whom the committee requested information about the missionaries' work – including Moorhouse, their supervisor for many years – claimed to know little. Grey failed to mention their involvement in Aboriginal education in dispatches. Unrecognised, they were soon forgotten.

Conclusion

The Dresden missionaries saw their goal as bringing the gift of God's love to the Indigenous inhabitants of Australia. They envisaged Lutheran congregations in Aboriginal communities established on their own land, such that the Aboriginal people retained their language and culture, insofar as this did not conflict with the Christian faith.

This approach did not resonate with settlers who coveted Aboriginal land, favoured assimilating Aborigines as workers, or who believed that missionaries should Europeanise Aborigines as well as bring them to Christ. As German Lutherans out of step with opinion in an English colony, their influence was limited. When Anglicans began Aboriginal mission work, government support was transferred to them. Without the means to work independently and unwilling to become Anglicans, the Dresden missionaries' work with a nomadic, dispossessed people came to an end.

Notes

1. As set out in the Lutheran Confessional writings in the *Book of Concord* of 1580.
2. Edwin Hodder, *George Fife Angas, Father and Founder of South Australia*, Hodder & Stoughton, London, 1891, p. 143.
3. Letter, 10 December 1838, Lutheran Archives Adelaide (hereafter LAA).
4. Committee of the Evangelical Lutheran Mission Society in Dresden to Schürmann and Teichelmann, 1839, LAA.
5. Schürmann diaries, 14 October 1838, LAA.
6. Schürmann letter to Dresden, 10 December 1838, LAA.
7. ibid., 5 November 1839.
8. ibid., 19 June 1839.
9. Dresden to Schürmann and Teichelmann 27 July 1840, LAA.
10. ibid.
11. For a more detailed discussion of Meyer's work at Encounter Bay, see the chapter by Mary-Anne Gale in this volume.
12. Schürmann to Dresden, 1 July 1841, LAA.
13. Schürmann to Dresden, 27 November 1843, LAA.
14. Despatch no. 50, 21 March 1850, State Records SA, GRG 2/6/5.
15. C. Wilhelmi, 'Manners and Customs of the Australian Natives, in particular of the Port Lincoln District', read before the Royal Society, 29 October 1860.
16. Schürmann letter to Meyer, 23 August 1851, LAA.
17. ibid.
18. ibid., 17 January 1852.
19. Schürmann to Dresden, 27 November 1843.
20. ibid., 11 December 1844.
21. Joyce Graetz (ed.), *Missionary to the Kaurna, the Klose Letters*, Friends of the Lutheran Archives, Occasional paper, Adelaide, 2002, p. 42.
22. House of Commons, *Sessional papers*, 1836, no. 426, p. 9.
23. Anne Scrimgeour, 'Colonizers as Civilisers: Aboriginal schools and the mission to 'civilise' in South Australia, 1839–1845', PhD, Charles Darwin University, 2007, p. 125.
24. *Adelaide Examiner*, 28 January 1843, p. 1A.
25. Angas to Schürmann and Teichelmann, 28 May 1838, State Library of South Australia, PRG 174/10.
26. Meyer letter to Dresden, 29 August 1848, LAA.
27. John Harris, *One Blood: 200 years of Aboriginal encounter with Christianity: A story of hope*, Albatross Books, Sutherland, NSW, 1994, p. 354.

The Moravian Church in South Australia

Bill Edwards

Introduction

In 1866, two small parties of German missionaries left the Adelaide area to commence missionary work in the same region in the far north-east of South Australia. One group consisted of Lutherans. Lutheran missionaries were the first to attempt the evangelisation of Aborigines in South Australia.[1] These enterprises in areas of early colonial settlement were short-lived. Later, the South Australian Lutheran Synod requested the Hermannsburg Mission Institute in Hanover to provide staff for mission work in the more remote regions of South Australia, with two graduates from the Hermannsburg Institute, Johann Goessling and Ernst Homann, and a lay helper, Hermann Vogelsang, subsequently being called to South Australia. With a local lay helper, Johann Jacob, they left Langmeil in the Barossa Valley on 9 October 1866. When they arrived at Blanchewater station on 15 December, they met the Sub-Protector of Aborigines, John Buttfield, who surprised them by announcing that another group of German missionaries had already entered the region.[2]

The second group, although German, bore a non-German name, 'Moravian', which reflected the early history of their religious heritage. The Moravian Church had its roots in the fifteenth-century Hussite religious movement in the provinces of Bohemia and Moravia and, through the influence of the German Pietist, Count Nicholas von Zinzendorf, underwent renewal in the eighteenth century in nearby Saxony.[3] In Saxony the preferred name was *Brüdergemeinde* (brotherhood). The name 'Moravian' was used from the eighteenth century when applied to their churches in Great Britain and America. This chapter traces the origins and development of this movement and outlines the brief attempt by these missionaries to evangelise Aborigines in the first outback mission in Australia.

Origins: Jan Hus and the Hussites

Two brothers from the church in Constantinople, Cyril and Methodius, introduced Christianity to Moravia in 863. They created a Slavonic alphabet to enable translation of the scriptures and liturgies into the local language. However, this church increasingly came under the jurisdiction of the Roman Catholic Church with its Latin liturgies.

The Moravian Church traces its heritage to Jan Hus (1369–1415), a peasant's son, who studied at the University of Prague in Bohemia. He lectured in divinity, became Dean of the Philosophical Faculty in 1401 and Rector of the university in 1402. Ordained a priest in 1402, Hus preached in Bethlehem Chapel, built in 1391 as a place for preaching in the Czech language. Influenced by John Wyclif (1324–84), Hus opposed the Roman Catholic practice of selling indulgences. He also urged the use of the Czech language in worship and preaching. In 1412 he was excommunicated and appeared before a general council of the church at Constance in November 1414. Accused of heresy and refusing to recant his beliefs, he was burned at the stake at Constance on 6 July 1415.[4] His followers, the Hussites, continued to meet in fields, led in Bohemia by John Ziska, until he was killed in 1424, and by a former priest, Prokop, who led them to victory over the army of the emperor.[5] Despite this victory, schisms and persecution forced the movement underground.

A monk by the name of Gregory led a group of peasants, farmers, nobles, scholars and priests to the valley of Kunwald in Bohemia, 160 kilometres from Prague, establishing the Brethren Church in 1457.[6] Thus a church exhibiting many features of Protestant churches was founded 60 years before Luther's Reformation. The group called themselves 'Jednota Bratrska' – a Unity of Brethren, with the Latin title, *Unitas Fratrum,* used in legal documents. Membership increased, despite continuing persecution, and in 1464 the first synod of the *Unitas Fratrum* was held in the mountains of Reichenau in Bohemia. In 1468, King George published an edict against the Brethren. Many were thrown into prison, while others fled to forests and lived in caves, thus derisively becoming known as 'caverners' (*Jamnici*). Despite these setbacks, the movement grew in numbers. By 1500, when Luke of Prague was consecrated a bishop, there were 300 churches, with at least 100,000 members in Bohemia alone.[7] When Ferdinand I became king in Bohemia, he sought the Brethren's help to oppose Protestant reformers. Some Brethren refused to fight, while others supported Ferdinand's opponents. Having defeated Frederick of Saxony in 1547, Ferdinand issued an Edict of Banishment against the Brethren, many of whom fled to Poland.

While some freedom was allowed in the late sixteenth century, persecution was renewed during the Thirty Years' War (1618–48), a period of intense religious conflict between Roman Catholics and Protestants in central Europe. Several Brethren noblemen were executed on 'The Day of Blood' – 21 June 1621 – with white crosses on the pavement of the Old Town Square in Prague still marking the place of their execution. The Brethren ceased to exist as an organised church in Bohemia and Moravia and, yet again, several members fled into Poland and other nearby countries.

Persecution of the Brethren continued throughout the seventeenth century. Early in the eighteenth century small groups met in woods in Bohemia and Moravia. In June 1722, a band of 10 people from the families of two brothers, Augustine and Jacob Neisser, led by Christian David, fled at night into Saxony and were welcomed to the estate of Count Nicholas von Zinzendorf by his caretaker, John Heitz.

David was born into a Roman Catholic family in Moravia in December 1690. When employed as a carpenter in the town of Görlitz he had a deep religious experience and subsequently secretly visited his homeland to evangelise his own people. There he found a remnant group, referred to as the 'Hidden Seed', who sought to maintain the fellowship of the *Unitas Fratrum*.[8] Zinzendorf met David in 1722 and offered a place of refuge for David's friends. This meeting of a humble carpenter and a nobleman would have far-reaching consequences that would extend eventually to the distant, as yet uncolonised, land of Australia.

Zinzendorf and the renewed Moravian Church in Saxony

Zinzendorf, descended from a noble family of the Archduchy of Austria, was born in Dresden, Saxony, in 1700. As his father had died when Nicholas was six weeks old, he was raised by his grandmother, Baroness Catherine von Gersdorf, in a castle in Upper Lusatia. He was influenced by German Pietism, a movement in the Lutheran Church led by Philip Spener, who pastored congregations in Frankfurt and Dresden and who acted as godfather at Zinzendorf's baptism on 26 May 1700. Throughout his childhood Zinzendorf exhibited an intense interest in religious experience, being educated at August Francke's school at Halle. Although Zinzendorf wished to pursue theological studies, his guardian Count Otto Christian sent him to the University of Wittenberg, a centre of orthodox Lutheranism, to study law and prepare for service of the state. At Wittenberg he studied the theology of Luther and sought to reconcile Pietists and orthodox Lutherans.

Visiting the art gallery at Dusseldorf in 1719, Zinzendorf underwent a deep spiritual experience when viewing the painting of Domenico Feti, *Ecco Homo,* with its depiction of Christ with the crown of thorns, and the inscription: 'All this I did for thee; what doest thou for Me?'[9] Appointed a king's chancellor in the Court of Augustus, King of Saxony, in Dresden in 1721, Zinzendorf purchased land from his grandmother to form his estate at Berthelsdorf, east of Dresden. He married Countess Erdmuth Dorothea Reuss, and planned a variety of charitable institutions on his estate, following Francke's example at Halle – Francke had established the Danish-Halle Mission in 1705.

The arrival of the Moravian refugees re-shaped Zinzendorf's plans. He warmly welcomed them on his return to the estate in December 1722. The caretaker, John Heitz, climbed a hill named Hutberg to select a site for the new settlement, two kilometres south of Berthelsdorf. It was an area of marshy wasteland and forest on the often muddy road between Löbau and Zittau. The refugees transformed this landscape and a memorial now marks the spot where David felled the first tree on 17 June 1722. Heitz named the place 'Herrnhut', from the phrase *unter des Herrn Hut,* variously translated as 'under the Lord's protection' or 'on watch for the Lord'.[10] Christian David returned to Moravia to lead other Brethren to this refuge.

The population at Herrnhut grew through evangelism, the attraction of exiles from other regions, and the growth in membership of other Christians dissatisfied with the formalism of established churches. Despite Zinzendorf working patiently and persistently to promote unity, the diversity in the members of the new community promoted divisions, the Brethren, for example, resisting attempts by Pastor Rothe of the Berthelsdorf church to impose the Lutheran Confessions. On 13 August 1727, perhaps as a consequence of intense study and prayer, the Moravian community experienced an event during Holy Communion which was described later as a 'realization of the presence of the Lord and a baptism of his Spirit'.[11] The Moravians saw this experience as the birth of the renewed *Unitas Fratrum*, with Zinzendorf guiding the life of this new community, uniting the traditions of Moravian zeal, practical service and simplicity, Pietist devotion and scholarship, and his commitment to worldwide mission.

Zinzendorf's contacts as a count opened the way for Moravians to commence mission work in the West Indies and Greenland. Visiting Copenhagen for the coronation of King Christian IV in 1731, Zinzendorf met Anthony, a West Indian slave who pleaded for Christians to come and share the gospel with his people. As a consequence, in 1732 two missionaries were dispatched to St Thomas in the West Indies, while, in 1733, other Moravians were sent to Greenland. From that time, until Zinzendorf's death in 1760, and within 40 years of the small band of refugees arriving at Herrnhut, the Moravians sent out 226 missionaries to North America, the Virgin Islands, Antigua and Barbados.[12]

Although Zinzendorf saw the movement as a fellowship within the Lutheran Church, there were moves by civil authorities to recognise the independence of the Moravian Church. Zinzendorf was consecrated a bishop on 20 May 1737 and in 1742 King Frederick William approved the official recognition of the Moravian Church in Prussia.[13]

The Moravians had a profound influence on churches throughout Europe, setting some of the foundations for the evangelical revivals of the eighteenth and nineteenth centuries in Great Britain and for the establishment of other missionary societies. While a few congregations were formed through these movements, the Moravians were not concerned with expanding their denomination, but rather with encouraging new converts to remain in existing churches.

Those influenced included John Wesley. Travelling to America in 1735 on the same ship as Moravian missionaries going to Georgia, Wesley was impressed by their faith and calmness during a severe storm. Seemingly, these German brethren 'owned an assurance which the English – including alas himself – lacked'.[14] It was at a Moravian prayer meeting at Aldersgate in London in 1738 that Wesley 'felt his heart strangely warmed'. He visited Germany in June 1738 and met Zinzendorf in Wetteravia and David at Herrnhut.

The Moravians were active in England from 1738. They formed a society there in 1744 before entering Ireland in 1746, later establishing communities in the United States – at Bethlehem, Pennsylvania, in 1742, and at Winston-Salem in North Carolina in 1752. Moravians were active in the anti-slavery movement, with Christian La Trobe, a Moravian minister in London, urging Wilberforce to take up the cause in parliament.[15] By the time the Moravians commenced missionary work in Australia, they had served in regions as varied as North, Central and South America, South Africa, East Africa, the Gold Coast, Tibet and Jerusalem.

The Moravians in Australia
Following the failure of the early Aboriginal missions, several church and colonial leaders invited the Moravians, already experienced missionaries, to undertake this work in Australia. The Moravians had earned a reputation for their willingness to go to distant and difficult situations and to work in cooperation with other churches. The fact that Christian La Trobe's son, Peter, was the Moravian agent in London and another son, Charles, was Superintendent of Port Phillip District may have expedited an invitation to commence work in Victoria. Two Moravians, Rev. Fred Tager and Johann Friedrich Spieseke arrived in Melbourne in 1850. They opened a mission at Lake Boga in October 1851, but opposition from settlers, problems in obtaining secure title to land and disturbances arising from the discovery of gold in the colony led them in 1856 to withdraw. Spieseke returned to Victoria in 1858

with Friedrich August Hagenauer and together they established Ebenezer mission in the Wimmera district in 1859. Hagenauer moved to Gippsland in 1862 and founded Ramahyuck mission in 1863. These missions survived for approximately four decades and were among the first missions in Australia to persist for several decades. From 1891 to 1919, Moravians cooperated with the Presbyterian Church to establish and staff three missions on Cape York in north Queensland.[16]

Intertwined with the history of the Moravian missions in Victoria was the attempt by three Moravians to establish a mission in the far north-east of South Australia. The initial impetus for embarking on this venture was a groundswell of goodwill in Melbourne towards the Diyari Aborigines of this distant region; it was the Diyari who had saved the life of John King, the sole survivor of the ill-fated Burke and Wills expedition.

The annual meeting of the Society for Promoting Moravian Missions to the Aborigines of Victoria, held on 17 August 1863, resolved to send missionaries to this region. The Melbourne *Argus* reported that the Governor of Victoria, Sir Henry Barkly, who chaired the meeting, expressed gratitude towards these Aborigines for what they had done:

> Some two years ago, when the news was received that Mr. Howitt had found King alive among the Blacks at Coopers Creek, and that those Blacks had treated his late companions with kindness and compassion, a strong feeling was expressed in almost every quarter that something ought thoroughly to be done for these people; and that he thought that in using this expression, it was not intended merely that beads, looking glasses, and tomahawks, should be sent to them by the Government as was of course immediately done, but that people who had shown themselves capable of such human conduct – who were so near the Kingdom of God, – deserved that the Gospel of Christ should be sent to them. (Applause)[17]

Having experienced problems in Victoria as a consequence of European settlement, the society saw the opportunity to commence missionary work 'in advance of the march of European colonisation, in the hope of thus securing an influence over the blacks, before they have become yet more-deeply debased by contact with the vices of civilisation'.[18] The Elders' Conference of the Unity in Saxony agreed to this proposal. W.E. Morris, Secretary of the Society in Melbourne, sought advice from Howitt, the explorer and prospector who had found King in 1861. Replying on 11 December 1863, Howitt referred to a report in the Melbourne *Argus* of that day about the 'deprivations of the natives in the far North'.

Four German Moravian 'Brothers', Carl Kramer, Wilhelm Kuehn, Gottlieb Meissel and Heinrich Walder, were chosen for this work. In May 1864, Kramer, while learning English at Fulneck, the Moravian centre in Yorkshire, wrote to Reichel, the Secretary of the Moravian Mission Board in Herrnhut, of the mixed emotions of fear and joy as he looked forward to returning to Saxony to farewell his family before his departure: 'With joy, because I shall see all my dear relations and friends again altho' for the last time for a good while, I dare say, if not for ever'.[19] The Brothers arrived in Melbourne on the *Yorkshire* on 29 November 1864. As the way was not yet open for them to proceed to Cooper's Creek, it was decided that they should gain experience and improve their English at the existing stations. Kramer and Kuehn were assigned to Ramahyuck and Meissel and Walder to Ebenezer.

Walder and Meissel left Ebenezer for Melbourne on 1 April 1865. They took with them an Aboriginal man, Daniel, who had offered to accompany them to the new station. Some questioned the wisdom of taking an Aboriginal man to such a distant tribe, where a stranger might be greeted with hostility but Walder assured them that Daniel would be sent back if he appeared to be in danger.[20] On 28 April 1865, Walder and Meissel met John King in Melbourne. He told them of his 10-week experience living with the Diyari people, of his dependence on them and of their kindness to him. King encouraged the missionaries to proceed and provided information about Aboriginal customs and languages.[21]

Walder and Meissel arrived in Adelaide by ship on 7 May 1865 and were welcomed by members of the Presbyterian and Anglican churches. On 16 May they attended a meeting of the Aborigines' Friends' Association (AFA) and were invited to accompany their missionary, George Taplin, to Point McLeay Mission on Lake Alexandrina near the mouth of the River Murray. The AFA had established Point McLeay Mission in 1859 under the

Congregationalist Taplin, who remained there as superintendent until his death in 1879.[22] Arriving at Point McLeay on 19 May, Walder and Meissel participated in worship services, observed teaching in the school, told the Aborigines about the people and work at Ebenezer and learned about local customs, before departing on 2 June. Kuehn and Daniel joined them in Adelaide on 17 June 1865. They received a promise from the government of a grant of land as an 'aboriginal reserve', but news of continuing drought delayed their departure to the interior. Kramer remained at Ramahyuck to assist Hagenauer.

To encourage interest in the proposed mission, Walder, Meissel and Kuehn visited churches at McLaren Vale, Tanunda, and Bethel near Kapunda. Reports received from northern regions indicated that, while there had been rain in the area of their ultimate destination, the intervening country remained extremely dry, with cattle dying, and Aborigines supposedly attacking flocks and herds. Throughout 1865 there were frequent references in the *Register* to drought in the far north of South Australia, for example, in January: 'All the country to the northward of Port Augusta is in a deplorable condition.'[23] There were reports that Aborigines had killed settlers in the area. Walder wrote from Adelaide in September 1865 advising that Daniel was ill with consumption and not expected to live much longer. Daniel died on 11 October. The missionaries faced further frustration as it was unlikely that they could proceed to Cooper's Creek within the next six months. Meissel assisted Taplin at Point McLeay, Kuehn was improving his English and teaching two Aborigines at McLaren Vale, and Walder worked with a Moravian Brother at Bethel. In a letter from Bethel in January 1866, Walder referred to Thomas Elder, a leading South Australian pastoralist who had obtained a lease on a large property near Cooper's Creek in 1860. Elder reported further outbreaks of violence between Aborigines and settlers in the region. Elder requested the government to station police at Lake Hope to provide protection for settlers in the region.[24]

Meanwhile, a group of Christians in the copper-mining towns of Moonta, Kadina and Wallaroo on upper Yorke Peninsula were concerned about the welfare of Aborigines in the district and had formed a missionary association. They invited Walder and

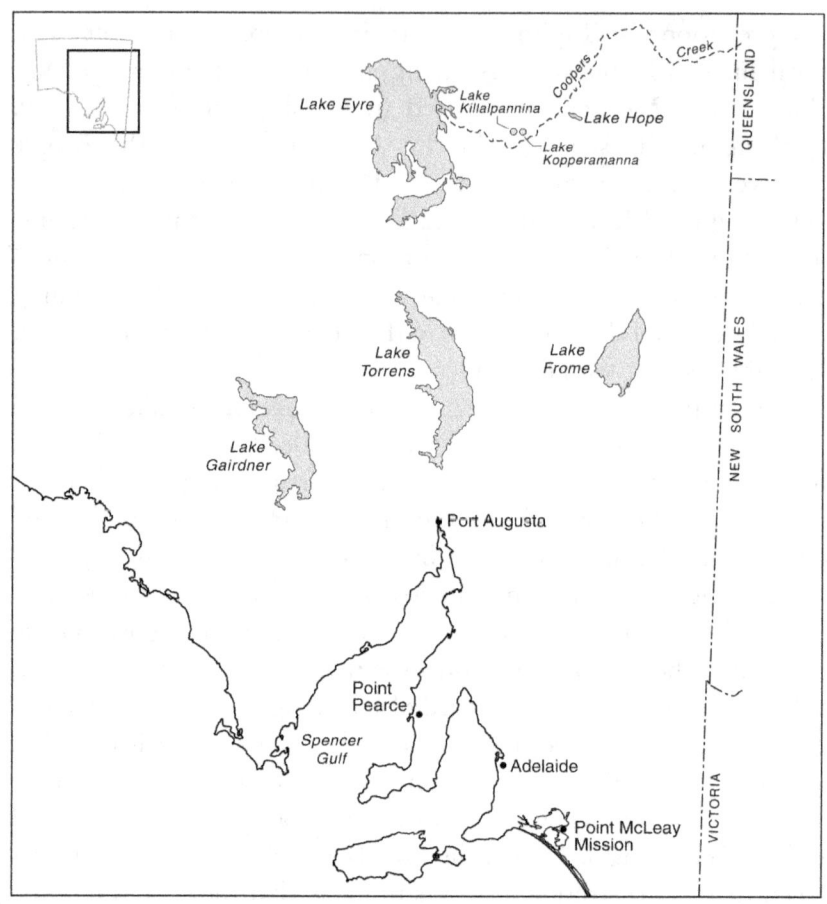

Map of South Australia showing Killalpaninna, Kopperamanna and the Point Pearce and Point McLeay Missions.

Kuehn to visit them in February 1866 and Kuehn remained there to investigate needs. He commenced a school with 20 children, conducted services, provided medical care and distributed rations provided by the government for the 50 Aborigines at Kadina.[25] The Chief Protector of Aborigines in South Australia, Dr Walker, visited Kuehn and recommended Point Pearce, 50 kilometres south of Kadina, as the most suitable site for a mission on Yorke Peninsula.[26]

The delays proved frustrating for the four men, who had set out from Saxony with deep commitment and high hopes. Walder had written to Morris in Melbourne on 31 May 1866. Morris's reply of 12 June reveals that Walder had been critical of the Melbourne committee and questioned their commitment to the enterprise. Walder disagreed with a proposal that an exploratory journey should be made before the whole party became committed to the establishment of a mission. He also opposed the proposal that one of them remain to initiate the work on Yorke Peninsula. Morris enumerated the arguments put forward by Walder and commented on each point. He vehemently denied that the committee lacked commitment to the enterprise: 'The arguments which you have urged and the somewhat strong language of which you have made use appear to me to indicate a feeling on your part that we have virtually abandoned the proposed Mission to Cooper's Creek, or were inclined to do so. But such a feeling, if it did exist, had no foundation.'[27] While expressing the committee's view that the needs of the Aborigines on Yorke Peninsula should not be overlooked and that one of the men should remain there for a while, Morris advised Walder that 'the discussion of the Committee leaves it with you to summon round you your three companions, and if you feel that you can assume this responsibility of taking all away from their present labours to start with them without delay with the view of making permanent settlement at once in the neighbourhood of Cooper's Creek'. Morris requested Walder to advise him of their plans by telegram and informed him that he would instruct Kramer to join them if they decided to proceed.[28]

Meissel left Point McLeay for Adelaide on 27 June 1866. In July, Kramer at Ramahyuck was summoned by telegraph to join the others in Adelaide. Following a meeting on 25 July 1866 attended by representatives from several churches at Chalmers Presbyterian Church in Adelaide, Walder and Meissel left Adelaide on 26 July 1866 driving a four-horse wagon and a spring cart. Kramer was to join them at Bethel, while Kuehn remained at Kadina. Kramer travelled by train to Kapunda, intending to walk to Bethel to meet the others. On the way he met them with their wagon. They had experienced difficulties with the wagon sinking into deep mud and had remained at Bethel until 22 August 1866, exactly two years after their departure from London. The Moravian congregation at Bethel assured them of their support for the new mission.

Kopperamanna

Walder wrote to Morris from Arronie en route on 28 September to advise that they had been joined by a police trooper from Lake Hope who had been to Adelaide to interpret in court. Walder reiterated the wish that Kuehn join them at Lake Hope as soon as possible. Meissel and Kramer also signed the letter to express their united opinion on this matter.[29]

After an arduous journey of 104 days the missionaries reached Lake Hope on 3 December 1866, leaving the wagon stuck fast in sand 40 miles back. They suffered the usual discomforts of travel in the Australian outback – swarms of ants at camping places and flies during daylight, with Walder suffering from inflamed eyes. From Lake Hope they explored the surrounding area, which was at the southern end of the Sturt Stony Desert. Severe erosion in this region had left flat-topped outcrops and wind-smoothed 'gibber' rocks covering the plains. Rainfall is low and variable in this, the driest part of the Australian continent, with the annual rainfall in the Lake Eyre Basin averaging approximately 150 mm.[30] Two possible sites for the mission had been suggested, Lake Kopperamanna, a lake measuring eight by three kilometres, located 72 kilometres west of Lake Hope, and Lake Killalpaninna, a smaller lake 13 kilometres further west. Both lakes were normally dry but filled occasionally with water from Cooper's Creek, when it flowed following heavy rains at the headwaters of the rivers that ran from the north-east.

On a five-day expedition to Lake Kopperamanna the missionaries encountered about 250 Aborigines. Following the recent spearing of a European man at nearby Perigundi, the Aborigines were suspicious of the presence of the missionaries. 'But you are not bringing the whip with you, are you?', they asked.[31] Walder assured them that they would not disturb the Aborigines' possession of the lake and that they had not come to administer punishment, in reply to an inquiry: As a result of Elder's request there were now five policemen stationed at Lake Hope.[32]

Tension between the missionaries and the committee in Melbourne continued. Distance made it difficult to resolve the differences. George Mackie, as chairman of the committee, wrote to Walder on 3 January 1867, noting that it is 'quite plain from the tone of your letter and those of Mr. Kramer, that both of you consider you have suffered injustice from our hands'. The committee had considered the matter and decided there were no good grounds for this view. Walder's reply of 27 February 1867 took up the issues again, as he felt he had been accused of ignoring the committee's advice.[33]

Having selected Kopperamanna as the site for the mission, the Moravians left Lake Hope on 24 January 1867, accompanied by a couple, Frank and Mary, and a youth, Napoleon, who had expressed a desire to learn more English. They arrived at Kopperamanna on the evening of 30 January and attempted to convey their peaceful intentions to the local Aborigines. Some young men assisted them by looking after the horses and carrying water, in return for rations. A school was begun, with nine children attending.

Meanwhile the Lutheran missionaries had reached Lake Hope on 27 December 1866, the Moravians recording in their diary: 'we conversed with them about the places which we should respectively occupy in this neighbourhood, and hope that we shall work together in brotherly love for the Lord's glory'.[34] As the Moravians had selected Kopperamanna as the site for their mission, the Lutherans chose Lake Killalpaninna, where on 31 January 1867 they established Hermannsburg Mission.

The tension which had followed earlier killings of Aborigines by settlers was intensified by the arrival of these two new groups of Europeans. Henry Dean, the manager of Elder's Lake Hope station, had forced a group of Diyari away from waterholes and four Aborigines had been killed. According to a recent study of frontier contact in South Australia, for settlers 'who were a long way from Adelaide and often well beyond the range of police and other government officials, utilitarian concerns prevailed'.[35] The introduction of cattle into the area placed pressure on the limited resources and denied Aborigines access to traditional supplies of food and water. Now the two missionary groups were camped at traditional sites. Soon after the establishment of the missions, a large gathering of Aborigines was held at nearby Perigundi. The missionaries received reports that the Aborigines had resolved to kill all white people in the area. Early in March, an old man known as King John became increasingly demanding of the Moravians, requesting food without offering anything in return. On 11 March

1867 an Aboriginal worker, Mackey, warned the missionaries: 'One sleep, blacks come, kill you'. That night, the Moravians kept their wagon and horses at the ready near their hut, prepared to take flight, although realising that it would be very difficult to escape if attacked. By 14 March the number of Aborigines had increased and the missionaries expected an imminent attack. However, relief came when a police party arrived on its way to Killalpaninna. Within a few days the Moravians were advised by the police to seek refuge at Killalpaninna. The Lutheran, Vogelsang, had been accosted by a party of about 40 Aborigines while travelling on a wagon from Kopperamanna to Killalpaninna and had been forced to fire his revolver into the air to disperse them. The police estimated that there were up to 700 Aborigines near Kopperamanna. Some of the Aborigines feared possible police reprisals against them.

During April 1867 the Lutherans erected their house at Killalpaninna, but the Moravians were uncertain about their future. On 19 April, nine troopers arrived with Sub-Protector Buttfield, although the feelings of the Moravians towards the police were mixed. While they appreciated the protection, they resented attempts by police to encourage the people to hold a corroboree. They were relieved when Buttfield intervened and sent the Aborigines away.[36]

Early in May 1867, the two groups of missionaries heard of renewed threats on their lives. They were placed in an invidious situation, as they took the threats seriously but recognised that any attempt on their part to resist attacks by force would end their hopes of evangelising the Diyari. The Lutherans decided to withdraw and return to the Barossa region of South Australia, leaving Killalpaninna on 9 May 1867, accompanied by the Moravians. They reached Bucaltaninna station, 45 kilometres south-east of Killalpaninna, the following day. The police from Lake Hope joined them there and escorted the Moravians on a return trip to Killalpaninna to collect more of their goods, finding, when they arrived, that nothing had been taken by the Aborigines. The Lutherans left on their journey south, not returning to the region until January 1868. The police wanted the Moravians to settle at Lake Hope under their protection. However, as Aborigines had been driven away from Lake Hope by settlers, the missionaries did not want to be identified with these actions. The Moravians applied to the government for a grant of land at Lake Kopperamanna and requested that the police post be moved there from Lake Hope. By June 1867 they had received positive responses to both petitions, with advice that 100 square miles was to be declared an Aboriginal Reserve. The Moravians again saw the presence of the police as a mixed blessing: on the one hand, they would provide protection, yet on the other, it was noted: 'the men are mostly Roman Catholics, and those whom I have met with unconverted characters. But we must be thankful for the safety from bodily dangers, which their presence will give us.'[37]

The Moravians spent five months at Bucaltaninna, receiving word on 4 October 1867 that the police had moved from Lake Hope to Kopperamanna. The missionaries left Bucaltaninna on 8 October and reached Kopperamanna the following day, with Walder and Kramer erecting a small hut, while Meissel returned to Bucaltaninna to collect their flock of 30 sheep. At first there were few Aborigines in the neighbourhood as they were suspicious of the police presence but, by the end of November, 700 had gathered in the vicinity for ceremonies.[38]

On 24 December the Moravians provided a Christmas dinner for 25 of the Aborigines. They re-opened the school on 30 December with one pupil. The attendance increased to six on the following day. Meissel expressed regret that they had picked up only a few words of the language, as he realised that this would limit the effectiveness of their teaching.[39] The Moravians at Kopperamanna also provided medical care, which included giving medicine to relieve the fever of a woman bitten by a snake.[40]

Conflicts between settlers and Aborigines in the region continued. While the missionaries persevered with their small school, there was uncertainty about the future of the mission, particularly since the message of the Moravians had not produced any responses to encourage them in their work of evangelism. By mid-1868, the lake was drying out and the available water was unsuitable for sheep and horses, the drought also hindering the physical and economic development of the mission. By October 1868, the drought had worsened, with cattle dying and with the Moravians forced to send their wool to Killalpaninna to be washed, as there was insufficient water at Kopperamanna. Meissel wrote in August 1868: 'The country is in a deplorable condition, and the natives reduced to great want'. One of the mission's sheep had disappeared, and it was assumed that Aborigines had killed it because of their hunger.[41]

Withdrawal from Kopperamanna
On 6 November 1868, the Moravians received word that the Directing Board in Berthelsdorf, Saxony, had decided to close Kopperamanna Mission. Kramer was to go to Ramahyuck to assist Hagenauer, while Walder was to help the pastor of the Moravian congregation at Bethel, north of Adelaide.[42] The Moravian Committee in Melbourne had advised that they could no longer accept responsibility for financing the work at Kopperamanna. The title for the Aboriginal reserve at Kopperamanna was transferred by the Commissioner for Crown Lands to the Lutherans to be run as an outstation of Killalpaninna.

Kramer left Kopperamanna to join Hagenauer at Ramahyuck early in 1869, while Walder remained at Kopperamanna to oversee the closure of the mission. He left there on 10 May 1869, accompanied by an Aboriginal man, George, who had been with the missionaries for a year-and-a-half, and who had offered to accompany Walder as far as Blinman in the Flinders Ranges. Walder left South Australia, boarding the *Fire Queen* at Victor Harbor on 19 July 1869. On 6 October, as the ship sailed in the Atlantic Ocean, he wrote a lengthy report, in it describing an accident while driving a team of five horses with a cart to the police post near Kopperamanna. The horses had bolted and the cart was dashed against a bank in a creek. Walder gave thanks for deliverance from a dangerous situation.[43] For his part, Kramer, writing from Ramahyuck on 3 August 1872, reported that he had received news from the Lutheran missionaries at Killalpaninna, where continuing drought caused hardship. He was pleased to hear that the man George, who had been with Walder, was working with the Lutherans.[44]

The three Moravian missionaries who had left Saxony in response to the call to evangelise the Diyari had waited two years before proceeding to their goal and, sadly, were forced to abandon the work within two years of its inception. For the second time in

Australia the Moravians withdrew from a mission station within a few years of its commencement. At Lake Boga, the disruptions caused by the discovery of gold in Victoria and the difficulty of attracting a settled population had led to the departure of the missionaries and the closure of the mission. In contrast to the situation in Victoria, where the numbers of Aborigines were decreasing dramatically, the Moravians at Kopperamanna were in contact with a large Aboriginal population. However, the recent frontier conflict and the Diyari suspicion of any Europeans made it difficult to establish positive relationships with them. Despite the presence of the missionaries, the frontier conflict continued, with the missionaries themselves under threat. At Lake Boga resistance by European settlers contributed to the closure of the mission; at Lake Kopperamanna, however, resistance by the Diyari in response to ill treatment by other Europeans was a major factor leading to the withdrawal of the missionaries. Furthermore, drought at Kopperamanna made the physical conditions very difficult. Although the Moravians conducted school classes for a few children, they saw no response to their message, they had little opportunity to learn the local language, and were unable to build a Christian village community. The Moravians were therefore unable to introduce any of the features of their own tradition to the Diyari and it was left to the Lutherans to carry on the mission work at Killalpaninna until 1915, at the same time producing extensive records of their linguistic and ethnographic studies.[45]

The problems for the Moravians were exacerbated by remoteness, the distance between the missionaries and their supporters in Melbourne, and inter-colonial friction. The Secretary of the Aborigines' Friends' Association in Adelaide, F.W. Cox, wrote to Walder of 6 August 1868:

> There has always been a difficulty in the facts, that you were the agents of a Melbourne Society, & that your entering in upon your work in this colony was not of our proposition, nor were we in any way consulted about it. More than this I do not think that there are many persons here, who would have encouraged the Mission on which you were sent. Though we received you (as I think) with Christian love, there was a general secret mistrust of the wisdom of the step. There were also

some, myself among the number, who greatly mistrusted Melbourne's continuity in well-doing, especially in a distant mission – in another colony – without any promise of speedy or splendid results, to sustain popular enthusiasm. I foresaw exactly, what has come to pass, and foresaw, that at last & before very long, your Mission would be dropped quietly into Adelaide's lap to nurse & care for.[46]

The Moravians had evidently sought financial assistance from the AFA. Cox advised that the association was having difficulty raising funds to support its existing mission at Point McLeay and his committee could not provide the additional £400 a year requested for Kopperamanna.

On 30 March 1868, the new Secretary of the Moravian Committee in Melbourne, J.C. Walter, writing to the Moravian Mission Board in Saxony, identified the following problems at Kopperamanna: the Cooper's Creek missionaries should be married; raising funds was difficult; relations between the committee and missionaries were most unsatisfactory; and the Lutheran mission was not far away.[47] While the withdrawal of the Moravians from the region could be viewed as a failure, they were assured that the work of evangelism would continue among the Diyari through the continuing presence of the Lutheran missionaries.

Of the four men who had set out from Herrnhut in 1864 with high hopes of establishing a mission in this remote area of Australia, Kramer remained in Australia to serve at Ramahyuck and Ebenezer, and Kuehn continued in his role on Yorke Peninsula. Meissel served in Moravian missions in Surinam and Jamaica, while Walder also served in Jamaica.

Moravian churches in South Australia
The missionaries were not the first members of the Moravian Church to arrive in South Australia. Reference has been made earlier to the presence of a Moravian Brother at Bethel. Several Moravians were among the early German settlers in the Barossa district, writing to the Moravian synod in Saxony requesting that a pastor be sent to minister to them. Pastor Cristoph Schondorf arrived in 1854 and preached in a temporary church near Light Pass. He purchased land approximately 10 kilometres north of Kapunda.

Moravians with a variety of trades settled nearby, as Schondorf attempted to build a village modelled on Herrnhut. A church building with a thatched roof was opened on 21 December 1856; Schondorf commenced a school in the same building on 29 April of the following year, also supervising the religious and secular life of this community. In 1876, Pastor L.A. Jacobi arrived to assist him, with Schondorf handing over responsibility to Jacobi at the end of that year. However, he and a few other families separated from the congregation, worshipping in Schondorf's house and establishing their own cemetery on the Bethel property.

Jacobi continued his ministry until his death in 1891. The following year, Pastor Paul Buck arrived from Germany. During his ministry – in 1895 – a new church building was opened. Buck returned to Germany in 1907. As requests to the Moravian Church in Saxony for a replacement were unsuccessful, the congregation applied for membership of the Immanuel Synod of the Lutheran Church and in 1921 became a member of the United Evangelical Lutheran Church in Australia.[48]

In 1872, a small Moravian congregation met in the home of Mr G. Hilbig at South Kilkerran near Maitland on Yorke Peninsula. In 1876, they combined with a local Lutheran church to erect a church building, in which both congregations worshipped. In the early years, the missionary Kuehn visited from the nearby Yorke Peninsula Mission to minister to the Moravian congregation. Later, Schondorf and Buck visited from Bethel. The Lutherans and Moravians erected a new church building, which was dedicated in 1907. The Moravian congregation, membership of which had grown to 70, became part of the Lutheran Church in 1926.[49]

Conclusion

The Moravian tradition continued to have some influence in South Australia through Kuehn's work at Point Pearce. Amongst the supporters of his work was the Superintendent of the Moonta copper mine, Captain Hancock.[50] The Missionary Association formed by residents of towns in the Kadina area on Yorke Peninsula appointed Kuehn as their missionary at Point Pearce, when it was established in 1867.[51] Kuehn remained at Point Pearce until 1880. He later transferred to Perth where he died on 2 July 1913.[52]

Point Pearce continued to operate as an interdenominational mission. In 1882, it was incorporated as the Yorke's Peninsula Aboriginal Mission. In 1916, control of Point Pearce passed to the Government of South Australia.[53] As at Ebenezer and Ramahyuck, Point Pearce enabled the survival of an Aboriginal population in a rural area. Many of the Aboriginal people now residing in the Adelaide region are descended from those who found refuge at Point McLeay and Point Pearce missions in the second half of the nineteenth century. Both settlements remain as Aboriginal communities.

By contrast, no Moravian churches or structures survive in South Australia. However, this temporary presence of Moravian organisations accorded with Zinzendorf's emphasis on the invisible church rather than on visible institutions and his desire to renew existing churches rather than establish a new denomination.

Notes

1   The chapters by Christine Lockwood and Mary-Anne Gale in this volume record the history of these earlier Lutheran mission endeavours.
2   Christine Stevens, *White Man's Dreaming: Killalpaninna Mission 1866–1915,* Oxford University Press, Melbourne, 1994, pp. 45–9.
3   The provinces of Bohemia and Moravia now comprise the Czech Republic.
4   In 1994 a commission of the Roman Catholic Church reviewed the charges against Hus and reversed the original findings (Sophia Coudenhova, '579 Years Later, Hus Gets His Day in Court', *The Prague Post,* 6–12 July 1994, p. 3).
5   Allen W. Schattschneider, *Through Five Hundred Years: A popular history of the Moravian Church,* The Moravian Church in America, Bethlehem, Pa, 1990, p. 19.
6   A.J. Lewis, *Zinzendorf: The ecumenical pioneer: A study in the Moravian contribution to Christian mission and unity,* SCM Press, London, 1962, p. 35.
7   Lewis 1962, p. 38.
8   ibid., p. 34.
9   ibid., p. 28.
10 J. Taylor Hamilton & K.G. Hamilton, *History of the Moravian Church: The renewed Unitas Fratrum, 1722–1957,* 2nd edn, Moravian Church in America, Bethlehem, Pa., 1983, p. 24.
11 ibid., p. 32.

12 David A Schattschneider, 'Pioneers in Mission: Zinzendorf and the Moravians', *International Bulletin of Missionary Research*, vol. 8, no. 2, 1984, p. 64
13 Lewis 1962, p. 150.
14 Stanley Ayling, *John Wesley*, Collins, London, 1979, p. 65.
15 Alan Gross, *Charles Joseph La Trobe*, Melbourne University Press, Melbourne 1956, pp. 5, 44.
16 For an overview of Moravian missions in Australia, see Bill Edwards, *Moravian Aboriginal Missions in Australia 1850–1919*, Uniting Church Historical Society (S.A.), Adelaide, 1999.
17 *Argus*, Melbourne, 18 August 1863.
18 *Periodical Accounts relating to the Missions of the Church of the United Brethren*, Brethren's Society for the Furtherance of the Gospel, London, 25, 1863, p. xvii (hereinafter referred to as PA).
19 Herrnhut Archive, Rubrik 15 V 1A5.
20 *PA*, 25, 1865, pp. 468–9.
21 ibid., pp. 474–5.
22 Graham Jenkin, *Conquest of the Ngarrindjeri*, Rigby, Adelaide, 1979.
23 *Register*, Adelaide, 20 January 1865.
24 *PA*, 26, 1866, pp. 35–8.
25 ibid., pp. 140–1.
26 ibid., p. 201.
27 Herrnhut Archive, Rubrik 15 V 1A5.
28 ibid.
29 ibid.
30 Trevor Griffin & Murray McCaskill (eds), *Atlas of South Australia*, South Australian Government Printing Division, Adelaide, 1986, p. 110.
31 *PA*, 26, 1866, p. 237
32 Stevens 1994, p. 50
33 Herrnhut Archive, Rubrik 15 V 1A5.
34 *PA*, 26, 1867, p. 244.
35 Robert Foster, Rick Hosking & Amanda Nettelbeck, *Fatal Collisions: The South Australia frontier and the violence of memory*, Wakefield Press, Adelaide, 2001, p. 5.
36 *PA*, 26, 1867, pp. 294–7.
37 ibid., pp. 342–3.
38 ibid., pp. 427–8.
39 ibid., pp. 428–9.
40 *PA*, 26, 1868, p. 513.
41 ibid., p. 36.

42 ibid., p. 82.
43 ibid., pp. 294–300.
44 *PA,* 28, 1872, p. 369.
45 Stevens (1994, pp. 202–30) provides an outline of the Lutheran missionaries' linguistic and ethnographic writings.
46 Herrnhut Archive, Rubrik 15 V 1A5.
47 ibid.
48 The Centenary of Bethel Congregation S.A., March 1957, Typescript.
49 St John's Lutheran Church, South Kilkerran, 60th Anniversary, 1967, Typescript.
50 *PA,* 28, 1872, p. 323.
51 T.S. Archibald, *Yorke's Peninsula Aboriginal Mission,* Hussey & Gillingham Ltd, Adelaide, 1915, p. 9.
52 *The Western Congregationalist,* Perth, 1 July 1913.
53 Ian Howie-Willis, 'Point Pearce', in David Horton (ed.), *The Encyclopaedia of Aboriginal Australia,* vol. 2, M–Z, Canberra, Aboriginal Studies Press, 1994, p. 877.

Nothing pleasing to impart?
H.A.E. Meyer at Encounter Bay, 1840–1848

Mary-Anne Gale

Introduction

After eight years of work the Lutheran missionary Heinrich August Eduard Meyer left Encounter Bay in 1848, lamenting: 'I have nothing pleasing to impart ... I could not achieve anything among the blacks.'[1] He was writing to his supporters in his homeland, the Committee of the Evangelical Lutheran Mission Society of Dresden. His disillusionment over his failure to win over a single convert and his perennial lack of funds eventually forced him to become a bullock dray teamster, regularly carting goods and supplies to and from Adelaide. A year later, he finally abandoned his mission to the Aboriginal people of Encounter Bay to accept a call to become the Pastor of a Lutheran congregation at Bethany in the Barossa Valley. And so it was that Meyer left behind his hopes and aspirations of the mission field, believing his effort to learn the local language and to translate the Good News of the Gospel into Raminyeri (or Ramindjeri)[2] had all been in vain.

This chapter seeks to challenge Meyer's own claims of failure by reviewing his significant linguistic heritage. It celebrates the rich legacy of Eduard Meyer (as he was generally known) and the important contribution his work makes to the contemporary study and revival of the Ngarrindjeri language of South Australia. The descendants of the people he sought to convert are now the present-day beneficiaries of his many years of labour, as they draw from Meyer's comprehensive wordlist and grammar.

For eight years Eduard and his wife Friederike lived and worked with the Ramindjeri people of the Encounter Bay region, 85 kilometres south of Adelaide. From the beginning, Meyer was clearly resolved to bring Christianity to the local Aboriginal people in their own language. He was German and a follower of the Lutheran faith, therefore adopting the approach that the best way to bring the word of God to any group of people was through their own language. From day one, Meyer set out to learn the Ramindjeri language and to record its complexities for the benefit of those who might wish to share his desire to communicate with the local Aboriginal people. His legacy today is a remarkably insightful grammar containing many example sentences, as well as a comprehensive wordlist of 1670 entries. Meyer's linguistic work was the basis of further language studies undertaken by the Reverend George Taplin, the founding Congregationalist missionary from 1859 to 1879 at the Point McLeay mission. The first task Taplin undertook on his new mission, on the banks of Lake Alexandrina, was to copy Meyer's Ramindjeri-to-English wordlist and make it his own, converting it from English to Ngarrindjeri.[3] Both lists now inspire current Ngarrindjeri language revival efforts.

Who was Meyer?
Eduard Meyer was born in Berlin on 5 May 1813 to a factory worker Carl Meyer and his wife Charlotte Kunst. Meyer began his mission training in 1833 at the Jänicke Mission Institute in Berlin, later transferring in 1836 to the Dresden Mission Institute in Saxony. He continued his studies in Erlangen, where he learnt Greek, Hebrew and Tamil. The intention was that he would serve as a missionary in India, but it was to the Australian mission field that he was eventually sent. Even back then, Meyer underestimated his language ability and skills, when he quipped in a letter to his 'dearest Pastor' prior to embarking for Australia: 'The little that I have achieved in the Tamil language cannot be taken in account. One equipped with more talents could achieve as much in a shorter time.'[4]

The Evangelical Lutheran Mission Society of Dresden was established in 1836. Support which earlier had gone to the Basel Mission Society was now directed to Dresden's own mission. The first Dresden mission director was Pastor Johann Georg Wermelskirch, who edited the mission journal *Dresdner Missions-Nachrichten*. Meyer sent regular letters and reports back to his beloved director from the time he left Dresden, this important collection of his writings now providing significant insights into Meyer's work with the Ramindjeri people of South Australia. 'The Meyer Letters', comprising well over 100 pages of correspondence, have been recently translated from Old German into English through the diligent and skilled efforts of Heidi Kneebone, the late Cynthia Rathjen, Sandy Marty and Lois Zweck. The letters are particularly interesting today because they give an honest account of Meyer's thoughts, experiences and disillusionment with the mission field. Meyer writes to his director as if to a friend and father figure, and often begins his letters with affection. He invariably starts with 'Most Beloved Pastor', and signs off as 'Your ever loving H.A.E. Meyer'. In 1844 his new correspondent became Dr Graul, who took over as the next director. In his final mission years he reported back to the Committee of the Evangelical Society of Dresden.

On completion of his studies in Germany, Meyer was ordained in the Stadtkirche in Greiz on 26 February 1840. A week later, he married Friederike Wilhelmine Sternicke, just two months before departing on the *Caleb Angas* for the newly formed Colony of South Australia. The young married couple set sail for their new home on 8 April 1840, travelling with their Lutheran colleague Pastor Samuel Klose. They arrived at Port Adelaide on 10 August, the long and tiresome journey taking 'four months, one week and two hours' (correspondence, 12 August 1840).

Meyer's goals
Meyer states that his commission, as assigned by the Dresden Institute, was 'to devote our time truly and diligently to the proclamation of the Gospel among the original inhabitants of South Australia' (correspondence, 30 January 1844). He expected to serve in Encounter Bay with his close colleague Pastor Clamor Schürmann, but Schürmann was instead sent to Port Lincoln to work with the local Barngarla people soon after Meyer's arrival. However, Schürmann made at least four trips to Encounter Bay prior to his departure to the west and began to learn the Ramindjeri language of Encounter Bay. He provided Meyer with a wordlist that compared the Adelaide language with that of Encounter Bay, from which Meyer concluded '[it] appears to be completely different' from Adelaide's Kaurna language (correspondence, 12 August 1840).[5]

Meyer later observed that this difference 'consists not only in the words but also in the formation of the same' (correspondence, 11 December 1840), thus providing the incentive to conduct further language study.

Schürmann had organised a temporary dwelling for Meyer at Policeman Point, or *Poltong*, which is the promontory reaching towards Granite Island. This humble residence, owned by the Governor, was one of several slab huts built for police use, with no glass in the windows. It was meant to suffice until a more permanent dwelling, promised by the Governor, was built closer to the Aboriginal camps in Encounter Bay. From here he was to serve the 'two large tribes living [supposedly] eight miles apart' (correspondence, 12 August 1840). On Meyer's arrival he was to find one group of Aboriginal people living at Rama (alongside the Bluff) four miles west of the mission house (known as Limbnana) and another at Kanjennal (Freeman's Knob) at Port Elliot, eight miles east of his dwelling (correspondence, 11 December 1840). Meyer was soon to wear out his boots tramping from one camp to the other on foot.[6]

Fortunately, Schürmann was able to travel to Encounter Bay, once with Eduard (21 to 26 August), prior to the Meyers settling there permanently on 10 September 1840 to evangelise the Ramindjeri/Ngarrindjeri people. This was very soon after the widely publicised massacre of July 1840, which resulted in a great deal of animosity towards the Coorong 'Blacks', who had killed the survivors of the shipwrecked *Maria*.

The urgent task Meyer set himself was to learn to speak the local Ramindjeri language:

> The first and most necessary thing I had to do was to take a native into our house, in order to acquire the language. The first I procured was a very useful person, for he spoke broken English fairly well. I therefore promised to give him everything he needed so that he might now stay with me; but in vain, he only tolerated it for nine days. I regretted it very much, for in these few days I had collected a good supply of words as well as, more particularly, of phrases. On the 30th of September, as I had been completely deprived of all opportunity of occupying myself with the language, I made my way to *Rama* with a heavy and

downcast heart in order to seek out my Bob. However, I was only able to prevail upon him once more a few days ago to accompany me. On this occasion when he caught sight of me from the hillside, he hastily bound a cloth around his head and excused himself with a headache. (correspondence, 11 December 1840)

In despair he then turned his attention to the children:

As I was now unable to achieve anything with him [Bob], I turned to the men sitting thereabouts and spoke to them somewhat sternly as to why they did not send their children in order to learn. Thereupon they spoke for a long while amongst themselves – of which I of course understood not a word – then they summoned all the children to my house. And how humbled did I stand there now – I had left my cottage in sadness because there was not a soul there with whom I could speak, and now a large and important field of work was opening up for me. My heart stirred with joy, as I saw the children leaping about, who sometimes sprang ahead and called out to passers by: *ruwa, lerefange, ruwa, lerefange,* much paper, much paper (term for school), or sometimes came back in order to walk hand in hand with me. After an hour and a half we had reached our destination; and now the first thing to be done was to prepare some food, for the little ones were tired and hungry.

After I had written the numerals on one piece of paper and the alphabet upon another, I commenced work at three o'clock with my seven pupils in God's name. The broad, expansive sky was the roof of our school house and the warm sand the benches. Several of the lads were very attentive and within two hours afforded me the pleasure of being able to count. And so matters proceeded for eight days – mornings and afternoons for two and a half hours ... now I could write to the Protector in Adelaide[7] that the children were willing to attend school if a building and sufficient provisions were provided ...

These my actions, the reason why I commenced work with this school so early, I can perhaps excuse if justification is necessary, with the old saying: 'One learns by teaching'. If I found the children were tired I induced them to talk, whereby I had good opportunity to collect words ...

(correspondence, 11 December 1840)

Meyer's letters clearly articulate his sole purpose in learning to speak the Ramindjeri language – to communicate the Gospel to the people of Encounter Bay and thus win converts who can be baptised into his Christian faith: '… that the Lord may place us here among the peoples to be a blessing to them in order that His holy name be praised from the rising of the sun until its setting' (correspondence, 23 December 1840). Encounter Bay had long been an important centre for the whaling industry, and Meyer had concerns for the negative influences some of the 'godless whalers' were having on the local Ramindjeri people. He was also worried about their involvement in inter-tribal fighting, particularly against the perpetrators of the *Maria* massacre: 'my blacks have been involved in conflict with the nearest, somewhat ferocious tribe' (correspondence, 10 March 1841). Meyer actually visited the Milmäjerar people from the Coorong, the group accused of killing the 21 survivors of the *Maria*, and writes: 'They were very shy at first, so I went alone to them and spoke to them in a friendly manner in their language … The most peculiar thing was that I was understood by the Milmäjerar man and that he answered me comprehensively. We were not able to discover whether he understands two languages or whether they share one and the same language' (correspondence, 10 March 1841). His conclusion was that nothing could be achieved 'until one of them is truly converted to Jesus Christ', thus justifying his determination to bring the news of Christ to the local Ramindjeri people in their own language (correspondence, 10 March 1841).

Meyer the linguist
Progress on the language was frustratingly slow for the diligent Meyer, who saw the need for great urgency in his language work. However, by July 1841 he could write with satisfaction that he had assembled the most essential elements of the Ramindjeri grammar as well as a comprehensive collection of words. Moreover, he had translated the Commandments and even composed a hymn, although the lack of a school house remained a hindrance to his work in achieving his highest goal, that is, conveying 'an understanding of the eternal truths and the nature of God' (correspondence, 27 July 1841).

At times the impetuous Meyer was dissatisfied with the progress

Pastor H.A.E. (Eduard) Meyer in 1860.
(State Library of South Australia, SLSA: PRG 186/7/10/1, no. 10)

he made in achieving that task and often annoyed the Ramindjeri people when he broke cultural taboos. Meyer's neighbour, Sergeant McFarlane, noted that the 'little Murray' people (presumably those living at Freemans Knob) claimed they came less often to Encounter Bay because '[Meyer asks] too many questions with regard to their death and their ancestors ...' Meyer's zealous justification is that: 'I must often ask, in order to make it clear to them that they too will die' (correspondence, 21 August 1841).

Meyer also faced competition from other white settlers who were better able to entice the Ramindjeri to be cheap labourers. He later lamented to the director of the Dresden Mission that the availability of meat from others – almost certainly whalers – meant that he could not 'induce one of the most useful of the natives to come into my house in order to work with me' (correspondence, 5 September 1841). Wermelskirch responded encouragingly, imploring Meyer to think of earlier instances of conversion among such people as Eskimos and the people of Greenland. The troubles and frustrations were to be expected, and, he reminded Meyer: 'you prepared yourself for this' (correspondence, 25 January 1842).

In January 1842 Meyer was offered a room in 'Government House', a three-roomed brick cottage, which was part of the police station at Policeman Point, in lieu of the promised – but still unbuilt – school house.[8] There he gathered for the first time the people he referred to as 'my natives' for a sermon, which he gave in the local language. His pride in this achievement, and at the same time his awareness that much linguistic work was still to be done, is evident in the correspondence recording that day (12 February 1842):

> Firstly we sing one verse, then the prayer followed by a story from the Bible and then the Ten Commandments; both with a short explanation and illustration, the fourth and seventh Commandments especially for the children and the fifth and sixth for the adults. The conclusion is the same as the beginning ... Oh that this could be done more succinctly, more fluently and more comprehensively. Oh, dear Brothers! May we be remembered in your prayers before the Lord, that we may soon attain complete mastery of the language, that the Word of God might be proclaimed with strength and vigour.

Although it was only 16 months since his arrival at Encounter Bay, Meyer still chastised himself for not being able to preach more fluently in Ramindjeri and solemnly committed himself to learning the local language and customs in the months to come. Laborious though this process was, he recognised it as a necessary foundation for his own goals, but saw also that it could be of use to others. Little did Meyer know then that its usefulness to others would arise in 1859 at Point McLeay mission, and ultimately over 150 years later amongst Ngarrindjeri people from across the southern part of the state. Viewed from that perspective, his contribution has been far from trifling.

Nonetheless, his diligence came at a cost. He received little financial support from the Governor, nor from those in his homeland. Since a great deal of his time was spent walking as he sought out 'his natives', his boots rapidly wore out, Meyer lamenting in a letter from February 1842 that he had not spent more than £1 on clothing and that he was not only in tatters but had little prospect of finding clothing (correspondence, 12 February 1842). Regardless of the state of his clothing, he pushed forward resolutely with his mission, completing both his word collection and his grammar in the first month of 1843. In due course – and just two-and-a-half years after his arrival at Encounter Bay – he was able to send both the grammar and wordlist to Governor Grey in Adelaide. It was a remarkable achievement, not only for the extraordinarily short time in which it had been accomplished, but also for its reliability and its usefulness. Grey and the then Protector of Aborigines, Matthew Moorhouse, pledged £10 and £5 respectively toward its publication (correspondence, 13 May 1843). Yet as Meyer himself noted, his pride in that scholarly achievement was balanced by a sober reality – he had not yet been rewarded with the conversion of a single soul 'through the tedious learning of the language' (correspondence, 24 January 1843).

His work was duly published as an 111-page document with the clumsily descriptive title *Vocabulary of the language spoken by the Aborigines of the southern and eastern portions of the settled districts of South Australia, preceded by a Grammar showing the construction of the language as far as at present known*.[9] Forever humble, Meyer dedicated what he called 'this small contribution' to 'His Excellency George Grey, Esq, Governor and Commander-in-chief of South Australia', and signed off as 'His Excellency's most obedient servant'. In his preface, Meyer acknowledged the difficulties he had with the English language, and thanked a Mr Lindsay who 'readily assisted' him, and assured the readers that because he had reviewed the wordlist with 'different natives', 'the meaning assigned to the words may be relied upon as correct'.[10]

Disillusionment

Although his work was warmly received by the Governor, by the end of the year disillusionment had again set in for Meyer. In November he wrote to his 'revered and deeply beloved brothers' in Dresden, reporting to them the sadness he felt in being unable, as he frankly confessed, 'to perceive anything which could give me a faint glimmer of hope that your wishes and expectations in regard to the eternal salvation of this people will be granted' (correspondence, 9 November 1843). However, he persevered, translating some verses of hymns into Ramindjeri, also continuing to offer worship services to those willing to participate.

Any hope that singing in their own language might persuade the Ramindjeri to convert remain unfulfilled. By the end of 1843 Meyer confessed that there seemed little chance of conversion among the adults. By contrast, among the children there was still some cause for optimism. The building of a day and boarding school, he had concluded, 'is the only way in which we might expect some success with God's blessing' (correspondence, 4 December 1843). From then on he concentrated almost entirely upon the children, hoping to influence his charges more by having them live away from their parents in the school house, which had long been promised to him by the Governor for his mission work. The school was built on 20 acres and was lease-free for 21 years.

Because we rely so heavily on Meyer's own account of his relations with the Ramindjeri adults, the reasons for his failure to convert them are difficult to identify. One of Meyer's records of a conversation he held with one Ramindjeri man might contain some clues about the reluctance of his would-be converts. Meyer had secured the services of his old informant, a man who went by the name of Encounter Bay Bob (also named Kung Knavery), and, as is evident from Meyer's account, he initiated a rigorous and potentially discomforting line of questioning. Encounter Bay Bob was first asked where he thought he would go after death:

> Bob replies: 'I do not know what I should say.'
> Meyer responds: 'There are only two ways, one leads to Jehova and the other to the place of pain and all lamentation.'
> Bob replies: 'I will be going to the Devil.'
> Meyer: 'Yes, Bob, I am afraid if you do not change your life you will go there; but you could do better.'
> Bob: 'Well then I will become a farmer.'
> Meyer: 'This will not suffice Bob, but do it the same, it is a significant step towards your betterment.' (correspondence, 30 January 1844)

Finally, after nearly four years of promises, the Meyers were able to move into their new residence in Encounter Bay, just one mile from Rosetta Head (the Bluff). It was several miles west of his old residence at Policeman Point, which he had found far too close to the police officers (whom he complains were 'more hated than loved'), acting as a deterrent to any possible visitors.

Colonisation and the influx of white settlers in the area was by now having a devastating influence on the day-to-day lives of not only the local Ramindjeri, but also neighbouring Aboriginal groups. They quickly learned that they had to become opportunists to survive, and by the early 1840s, 200 to 300 'Murray' Aboriginal people had come to live in close vicinity of the two operating whaling stations[11] during the whaling season, which lasted seven to eights months (correspondence, 25 July 1844). The Aboriginal people provided much valued labour for the fisheries, carrying blubber to the pots and stirring the boiling contents; they were also excellent lookout scouts.[12]

Despite the distractions, Meyer continued his efforts to evangelise any Aboriginal people within his reach, knowing that the local language he had learnt was similar to others spoken further along the lower reaches of the Murray River. But he was not successful, and continued to lament 'the fact that I have been able to achieve so little up to now for the salvation of eternal souls' (correspondence, 30 January 1844). He tried to remain optimistic, however, especially when on 16 March 1844 the Meyers finally moved into their new mission house with the help of 'our blacks', who willingly assisted, saying 'You are our friend, after all we have the same language' (correspondence, 30 January 1844).

To the Ramindjeri, Eduard's dedication and persistence were mystifying. They were concerned for him and his lack of recreation and rest. One Ramindjeri man went as far as asking Meyer: 'Why do you work? Then you sit down and read or write. You will not live long – come with us if you are hungry catch a fish for yourself, eat and lie down to sleep, if you are hungry again, so the same thing and you will live for a long, long time' (correspondence, 25 July 1844). Others told him to 'Go home and tell Jehova we do not want to hear anything about him; he will throw all of us into the fire when we are dead etc' (correspondence, 25 July 1844).

Rather than heeding their sound advice, Meyer became even more zealous in his evangelical determination and his visits to the local Aboriginal camps. This only led to more despair as, by Meyer's own account, the locals remained stubbornly unimpressed by his warnings of the consequences of turning their backs on God. Some would change the topic or direct their attention elsewhere. Others, Meyer observed with palpable frustration, 'concur with everything I say and declare themselves to be bad, but immediately afterwards ask whether they are to come to work on the next day and what they would receive for this, a shirt or a blanket?' (correspondence, 25 July 1844).

New hope

Despite his efforts being received with indifference, by August 1844 Meyer was rejoicing with new-found hope. Four years after his arrival, the promised school house-cum-chapel was approaching completion and on 27 August 1844 it was finally dedicated and opened (correspondence, 14 January 1845); three months later the first children arrived to commence their studies. Initially 11 children were enrolled, with hope for more, although there was concern that they had enough blankets for only 18. Meyer was sufficiently astute to recognise that 'the blankets have been the only thing which is keeping them there'. He extracted promises from the parents that they would not take their children away, and that, should the children abscond of their own accord, they would drive them back with sticks. As ever, Meyer remained unwaveringly committed to his ultimate goal, 'the salvation of their eternal souls' (correspondence, 14 January 1845).

Happily for Meyer, student numbers steadily rose over the next few months, reaching as many as 16. He wrote of his pupils that they 'have considerable intelligence, are keen, witty and some also have a desire to learn. I frequently encountered them of an evening sitting at the fireside, the alphabet in their hands or heard them reciting what they had learned, counting and the verses of songs.' Although progress in their learning was welcome, progress of a different kind mattered most to him. Observing a nascent interest among the children in his Christian God, as he claims he did in January 1845, was a moment of great emotion and joy: 'That my eyes did not remain dry when for the first time I saw the children standing around the table with folded hands and heard them reciting their table grace or when a hymn to the glory of God would be heard issuing from their room of an evening, hardly deserves mentioning' (correspondence, 14 January 1845).

Later that month, Meyer and his pupils ventured on a long journey to Adelaide, during which Eduard was delighted to witness his students' dedication. At Willunga 'the children had slept the night and astonished the people, because they would not eat without first having said grace'. At Ebenezer[13] the children were rewarded with cake after singing their song, and with flour by another woman after saying the Lord's Prayer (correspondence, 17 March 1845).

Student numbers did not remain high for long, as Meyer was soon forced to dismiss three girls who were 'too advanced in years and hence in vices'. But ten boys and three girls remained and were, in his words, 'sweet and affectionate'. This setback did not deter Meyer from continuing his daily routine and determination with his remaining charges. Each school day comprised one hour of religious instruction, which involved learning prayers by heart, hymns and Commandments in their own language. Then they moved onto reading, writing and arithmetic. On Sundays they attended the regular service, always given by Meyer in the Ramindjeri language: 'The children have very good memories. This is particularly evident when I examine them of a Monday on the content of the Sunday Sermon' (correspondence, 17 March 1845).

Despite his evangelical successes among the children, Meyer did not abandon hope for the adults and was pleased that a number came to the first-year anniversary service of the opening of the chapel. Afterwards he invited Tjirbuk [Sjirbuke], Nakandcanambe and Encounter Bay Bob to lunch, acknowledging that 'every native expects a little flour if he endures the service'. Much to Meyer's delight Nakandcanambe soon undertook to build a cottage alongside Meyer's, with the intention of settling down and farming the land (correspondence, 20 July 1845).

The end
By 7 October 1845 mission funds were getting very low. A letter written in October 1845 gives graphic, almost tragic insight into the penury which Meyer and his family endured: 'I cannot deny that

from time to time the craving for a piece of meat was considerable; thus when the cat used to come in, sometimes two to four times a day with a bird, most similar to a quail, you should have seen us jump up in order to retrieve it from the same, and thus it was that through the cat's skill we enjoyed a delicious meal now and then' (correspondence, 7 October 1845).

Much to Meyer's delight, in 1846 his close friend and colleague Clamor Schürmann returned to Encounter Bay to work with him, after having been with the Barngarla near Port Lincoln. Unfortunately, after a beating from Schürmann for stealing tobacco from a neighbour, seven of the eight boys absconded from the mission school. On 23 September, 11 boys gathered for new suits, but again a number absconded. When this misfortune was recorded in correspondence in the depths of winter of the following year, it was apparent that deep despondency, if not irreversible disillusionment, had set in among the missionaries: 'For the past few months, both the Adelaide and Encounter Bay stations have presented a sorry sight. Almost all of the adults have removed themselves and here the children come and go so frequently, that one all too often loses heart and will to continue with the children' (correspondence, 20 July 1847).

By 1847, with no converts and a severe lack of mission funds, Meyer was forced to consider taking on supplementary work. He became a teamster, carting goods to and from Encounter Bay until 1848. He was, however, eventually compelled to accept a call as Pastor of the Lutheran congregation at Bethany and Hoffnungsthal in the Barossa. He became the first President of the Bethany–Lobethal Synod from 1848, serving in this role until 1861.

In December 1862, Eduard Meyer died suddenly in his sleep at Bethany – from a stroke. He was only 49 years of age. He had always suffered from abnormally high blood pressure, for which there was no medicinal cure in those early days. He was survived by his wife, a son and two daughters. Today there are many descendants.[14]

Meyer's legacy

Meyer may have lamented, in August 1848: 'In reference to the Mission's activity among the natives, I have nothing pleasing to impart ... It goes without saying that I could not achieve anything among the blacks.' I argue, however, that Meyer's work was not in vain, and he did in fact, through his grammar and wordlist, leave behind a considerable linguistic legacy for the Ramindjeri and Ngarrindjeri people. His grammar and wordlist, published just two years after his arrival at Encounter Bay, comprises 1670 words that were thoroughly checked with a number of Aboriginal people, the wordlist forming the basis of that compiled by the Reverend George Taplin at Point McLeay some 16–17 years later.[15] Today, 160 years after Meyer's departure from Encounter Bay, this list is being used by the Ngarrindjeri community in language and cultural revival activities and programs. Although up to 450 Ngarrindjeri words are still in the oral memories of the Elders today, Meyer's and Taplin's more extensive wordlists serve as valued resources that are drawn from, particularly by the younger generation, to meet new and emerging needs.

In addition, Meyer's grammar gives some genuine insights into the language, including an explanation of an anti-passive construction which has been praised by contemporary linguists as being particularly astute.[16] Taplin used Meyer's grammar as the basis of his own grammar, filling in details that Meyer was unable to complete.[17] Although Meyer's grammar adopts considerable technical language, which can be incomprehensible to the lay person, efforts have been made to rewrite his grammar in a more accessible form. In May 2008, *Ngarrindjeri Learners' Guide* was launched at Raukkan.[18] It draws heavily from Meyer's (and Taplin's) work, so it was gratifying to have so many of Meyer's and Taplin's descendants present at the launch.

In part, the value of Meyer's grammar lies in the many sentence examples he included for each of the many different grammatical points he outlines. Because so little Ngarrindjeri grammar remains in the memories and speech of Ngarrindjeri people today, these sentences offer a great deal of guidance for the construction of new and authentic sentences. Until recently, use of the Ngarrindjeri language was restricted to peppering English speech with Ngarrindjeri words, while retaining English word order and grammar. Now that Meyer's traditional grammar has become more accessible, further language opportunities are emerging, as people learn to write and speak whole sentences in Ngarrindjeri.

New functions are therefore arising for the language, particularly through performance, for example, 'welcome speeches', the reading of poems and the composing and singing of songs.

Meyer also wrote an ethnographic contribution, *Manners and Customs of the Aborigines of the Encounter Bay Tribe: South Australia*, in which he explains some of the traditional beliefs and cultural practices of the Ramindjeri people.[19] Although judgemental, it is insightful in its explanations and provides fascinating descriptions of the formation of various geographical landforms in the south coast area, particularly through the actions of the Dreaming ancestor Nurrunduri.[20]

In modern times – in the early 1960s – the Ngarrindjeri language had only been spoken in whole sentences by a handful of Elders, but now Eduard Meyer's linguistic diligence and attention to detail, first applied 160 years ago, is facilitating new opportunities for the Ngarrindjeri language. Nine different schools and kindergartens in the state offer language renewal programs in Ngarrindjeri.[21] Meyer's wordlists are also used by various Aboriginal dance troupes, bands and groups involved in cultural tourism activities. Although some Ngarrindjeri Elders in the recent past have been sceptical of linguists and missionaries and the contents of their books, they are now recognising the value of such resources. They can see that the younger generations are keen to use more than the 450 words still remembered, acknowledging that perhaps the language that only survived in books is useful after all and is worth bringing back for the sake of their own grandchildren. Indeed, 147 years after Eduard Meyer's untimely death we have some very pleasing news to impart regarding the fruits of Meyer's labours during his mission to the Aborigines of Encounter Bay.

Notes

1 The quote continues: '… since my last report'. This letter was dated 29 August 1848, nearly two years since his previous letter. It was written from the settlement of Bethany, north of Adelaide. Meyer's correspondence is held in the Lutheran Archives in Adelaide. All quotations from Meyer's letters are from this source.

2 Early spelling used for this language variety was Raminyeri, but contemporary spelling and pronunciation is Ramindjeri.

3   The term 'Narrinyeri' is used for the language of the Lower Murray, Lakes and Coorong region. It includes many different dialects (one for each of the many clans), such as Yaraldi. Ramindjeri is the northernmost dialect of Narrinyeri. The term Narrinyeri (Ngarrindjeri) was first used by Taplin (1878).
4   Meyer correspondence, 2 July 1839.
5   A contrastive list of five words each appears in Meyer's correspondence, 12 August 1840.
6   One of the last known camping grounds of Aboriginal people within the vicinity of Encounter Bay was Kent Reserve, at the mouth of the Inman River (about halfway between the Bluff and Policeman Point). The local Ramindjeri people probably moved away from the Bluff to Kent Reserve when the whaling industry closed at the Bluff.
7   Dr Matthew Moorhouse.
8   See Rhonda Treager, 'The Encounter Bay Mission 1840–1848', in *Brief Encounters at Victor Harbor*, South Coast Fellowship of Australian Writers, Victor Harbor, 1982.
9   There is also a long subtitle: *by the tribes in the vicinity of Encounter Bay, and (with slight variations) by those extending along the coast to the eastward around Lake Alexandrina and for some distance up the River Murray.*
10 H.A.E. Meyer, *Vocabulary of the language spoken by the Aborigines of the southern and eastern portions of the settled districts of South Australia, preceded by a Grammar showing the construction of the language as far as at present known*, James Allen, Adelaide, 1843, p. vii.
11 At this time, one whaling station was operating at the Bluff, with another based on Granite Island. Previously, a fishery had been operating near the mouth of Hindmarsh River on the mainland, just east of Granite Island, but this was later transferred to Granite Island (see Treager 1982).
12 Anthony Laube, *Settlers Around the Bay: The pioneering families of Encounter Bay and Victor Harbor*, Anthony Laube, Adelaide, 1985, p. 42; Treager 1982, p. 56.
13 Ebenezer was Brother Teichelmann's (Meyer's colleague) property in Happy Valley, south of Adelaide.
14 Of the six children born to the Meyers, three survived to have children of their own: the first-born girl Louise Auguste, second-born Charlotte Friederika and the youngest son Gotthilf Carl. Descendants of Louise include the Hoff family, who are the custodians of several family heirlooms brought out on the ship by the Meyers in 1840.
15 The original handwritten wordlist of Taplin's is held in the Barr Smith Library, University of Adelaide. See George Taplin, 'Vocabulary of the Narrinyeri Language', in G. Taplin (ed.), *The Folklore, Manners, Customs*

and Languages of the South Australian Aborigines, E. Spiller, Acting Government Printer, Adelaide, 1879, pp. 125–41.
16 R.M.W. Dixon, 'Preface', in Marylyce McDonald, *A Study of the Phonetics and Phonology of Yaraldi and Associated Dialects*, Lincom Europa, Munich, 2002, p. 7.
17 Rev. George Taplin, *Grammar of the Narrinyeri Tribe of Australian Aborigines*, W.C. Cox, Government Printers, Adelaide, 1878.
18 See Mary-Anne Gale with Dorothy French, *Ngarrindjeri Learners' Guide*, trial edn, University of South Australia, Adelaide, 2008.
19 Published in Adelaide by George Dehane in 1846.
20 This important Ngarrindjeri Dreaming Ancestor is spelt Ngurunderi today.
21 Department of Education and Children's Services, 'Aboriginal Language Programs in South Australian Government Schools and Centres: Statistics and other data', DECS, Adelaide, 2006.

The Grand Duke, the Town Council and the Bützow Butchers' Guild

The tradesman's plight and Mecklenburg migration to South Australia

Lois Zweck

When I was born into a family of South Australian German farming stock, that phrase was almost a tautology: South Australian Germans were predominantly farmers, and we assumed it had always been so. That was certainly true of my Australian-born forebears, but a little investigation of the immigrant generations of my ancestors revealed a different image. In *Barossa Folk* Noris Ioannou cited the figure of at least one-third craftsmen among nineteenth-century German arrivals to South Australia.[1] In the case of my German-born ancestors, *Handwerker* – including tradesmen as well as craftsmen or artisans – make up over two-thirds of the total. On my father's side I found one cottager, a locksmith, a tailor, a stone mason and a weaver. My maternal ancestors included two farmers, two cabinetmakers, a shoemaker and a butcher's widow. The background of this butcher's widow from the Mecklenburg[2] town of Bützow forms the substance of this chapter. The Bützow Town Hall Archives preserve the correspondence of her husband, her brother-in-law and her son – all butchers – with the Bützow Butchers' Guild, the Grand Duke of Mecklenburg, and the Town Councils of Bützow and Doberan. These documents illuminate, on the one hand, the struggle of the guilds to maintain their privileges and the ensuing restrictions facing the next generation of apprentices and, on the other, the constraints imposed by the prevailing marriage laws and the inadequacies of local social welfare structures. Together, they graphically demonstrate the pressures contributing to the burgeoning emigration rate in the middle of the nineteenth century.

The story of the Luck family butchers in Bützow, as recorded in church and guild registers, begins in 1777, when Carl Luck was registered as an apprentice by the local butchers' guild. To gain admission he had to prove his legitimate birth, but since he could not produce a birth certificate, the guild accepted his parents' marriage certificate instead.[3] His father was neither a butcher nor a citizen: at the time of Carl's birth he was on campaign as a fusilier with the Prussian Army – either illegally recruited or press-ganged during the Seven Years' War. He subsequently settled in Bützow as a night watchman, attracted by the economic upsurge there following the opening of its university in 1760.

On completion of his apprenticeship and journeying, in 1791 Carl Luck was accepted as a 'master of the guild', he married a butcher's daughter from nearby Schwaan, and died before reaching the age of 50.[4]

Of their eight children, only three sons survived infancy, and all three took up apprenticeships as butchers, with the youngest dying a few months after finishing his training. After the closure of the university in 1789, Bützow reverted once more to a sleepy country town, exacerbating the pressures faced by the local guilds, pressures also faced by their European colleagues. When Christian Luck applied for registration as a master butcher in 1825, he faced stiff opposition from the Guild, and the ensuing correspondence involving the Guild, the Town Council and the Grand Duke[5] illustrates the difficulties confronting prospective *Handwerker*.

Christian Luck describes his situation in the following plea to the Grand Duke in November 1825:

> Most illustrious Grand Duke, most gracious Grand Duke and Lord!
>
> My father, the local Master Butcher Luck, died 16 years ago, leaving my mother, myself and two younger brothers in very straitened circumstances. Forced to carry on the trade with outside journeymen, my mother's situation became ever more desolate until in the end she was totally impoverished and had to give up the business. As soon as I had reached the requisite age I took up an apprenticeship with the local Master Butcher Müller, and after I had survived my years

of training, he lent me everything I needed to become a journeyman. As such I stayed on with him another two years, and paid off my debt to my master with my first year's wages. The wages from my second year I used to buy cattle which I slaughtered for my mother, which enabled her to begin plying the trade once more. I have been with her for three years now, and by dint of persistent industry I have succeeded in snatching her from the penury into which she had sunk.

I am now 27 years old, and by fulfilling my filial duty I have been and still am prevented from fulfilling my obligations as a journeyman, because if I left my mother she would relapse into her helpless state once more and become a burden on the town, as she is old and sickly. I requested a meeting with the local Guild of Master Butchers, where I put my case – which they were already sufficiently acquainted with – and formally requested admission as a master, providing your Royal Highness should be graciously inclined to accept my most submissive plea to grant me a royal dispensation from my journeying obligations.

The aforementioned Guild declared that it would in this case have no objection to my admission, as long as my mother did not intend to take the opportunity to conduct the business on her own behalf again with one of my brothers who has also learned the trade. Apart from the fact that neither my mother nor my brothers has the means to set up a new business, since I even had to pay their costs for registering as journeymen, the former is prepared to give a written undertaking assuring the Guild that neither of my brothers is to be taken on by her as a journeyman without having fulfilled his journeying obligations. And I will never leave my mother, as long as I have bread she will never need help from anyone else. I have fulfilled my military obligations, as the most humbly attached exemption certificate testifies, and I now beg with the most profound humility that Your Royal Highness may be most graciously disposed to grant me a most gracious royal dispensation from the obligatory journeying.

Imploring your most favourable attention and the return of the attached document,

I will die as Your Royal Majesty's most submissive subject

Christian Luck

When the Duke's officials forwarded the petition to the Bützow Guild requesting their opinion, they respond with a firm 'no', citing a number of grounds for their unwillingness to admit Luck as a master. They considered him to be too young, he having only recently attained his majority (25 years); he was too fit to be granted dispensation from journeying on medical grounds, as his exemption from military service was due to the ballot rather than to his medical examination. (Each district had to supply a certain number of conscripts, and after the medical examinations, the surplus candidates were chosen for exemption by lot.) In any case, the Town Council was not likely to grant him citizenship, as the town already had too many citizens in proportion to its size, and the two qualifications of citizenship and master status are inseparably linked.

The Guild's major objection, however, was that there were already too many butchers in the town – 16 for a population of 3200 – some of whom were already impoverished, and admitting one more would be detrimental to Luck as well as to others. And finally, the suggestion that his mother might give an undertaking to give up the trade in her son's favour cannot constitute a guarantee: if he should at any future time cease to support his mother, the local Council would be compelled to allow her to carry on the business again with another of her sons so that she would not become dependent on the Poor Fund.

Christian Luck was naturally outraged at the suggestion that he might ever abandon his mother, and in a second petition he refutes all the Guild's objections, asserting also that the Council has promised him citizenship. It would not be practicable, he asserted, for one of his brothers to support his mother, as it was imperative that they undertake their journeying at this time, or they would eventually find themselves in the same predicament he was in now – faced with journeying obligations when it was really time to settle down and establish their own households.

The Duke granted the dispensation and ordered the Guild to instate him when he had fulfilled all other conditions for becoming a master. However, the Guild was not prepared to capitulate so readily: they simply promised to accept him as a master immediately upon the death of his mother, declaring when challenged that this constituted compliance with the Duke's orders. By this time the Duke had lost patience, ordering the Guild to instate the new master forthwith, and the Guild had to be content with the mother's undertaking to cease plying the trade.

Christian Luck, the new master and now citizen, married immediately, with five children born over the following decade. After little more than 10 years, Christian Luck was found frozen to death on the road from the nearby village of Passin, where he had gone to collect some calves for slaughter, leaving a second widow Luck destitute, with five children aged under 10 years to support and no one to carry on the business.

In the meantime, the first widow Luck, just as the Guild had feared, had been permitted to take up business as a butcher once more. From 1831 her second son Johann, having completed his journeying, had been living and working with her, together with his fiancée, whom he had met in Doberan during his time as a journeyman. In 1835 he had received a written assurance from the then Mayor that he would be accepted as a citizen, provided he paid his dues and had been instated as a master by the Butchers' Guild. Since he lacked the funds both to pay his citizenship dues and to establish himself as a Master Butcher, he had done nothing further, subsisting – the Council alleged – partly on his mother's subsidy from the Poor Fund, as well as occasional slaughtering in her name but on his own behalf. Unable to set up a household of his own, he was unable to marry, and by 1838 he and his fiancée had four illegitimate children. But when he requested citizen status once more in order to marry, the Council took drastic action. A wagon was sent to load up mother and children and their effects and transport them to her home town of Doberan. Since she was legally a resident there, the Doberan Council was obliged to support her and her children.

The Bützow Council's response to Johann Luck's request for citizenship was scathing: since he had admitted to owning nothing but his tools of trade, he obviously did not have the funds necessary to establish himself in business, meaning that his whole family would simply become a burden on the town's welfare system as soon as he married. Like his brother, he appealed for the Duke's assistance – in this instance, to command the Council to grant him citizenship and permit his marriage. Ultimately, however, negotiations with the Town Council of Doberan resolved the problem.

By paying Luck's dues to the Bützow Guild for him and providing a guarantee of assistance in case of need, the Doberan Town Council enabled Luck to establish a business and a household in Bützow and become a citizen there, so it was no longer obliged to support his fiancée and her children. This time the Guild apparently offered no resistance: Johann Luck's children were made legitimate by their parents' subsequent marriage and two sons followed their father in the trade, with one becoming guild treasurer and one appointed official supplier to the Duke's court in Schwerin. The last 'Butcher Luck' in Bützow was a young apprentice at the time when the family was visited by a South Australian relative in 1925, and his widow still lives nearby.

The Mecklenburger has no fatherland

The story of Johann Luck is a nice example of the quintessential Mecklenburg predicament expressed melodramatically in the best known of all Mecklenburg literary works, Fritz Reuter's epic poem *Kein Husung* (*No Fixed Abode*).[6] The problem of residence permits and proof of domicile, which were prerequisites for marriage, forms the crux of that narrative, in which the rejection of a farmhand's plea for a cottage so that he can marry his pregnant fiancée leads to catastrophic consequences, including manslaughter, madness and flight to America.

Under the feudal system serfs had been bound to the land, and in the seventeenth century the punishment for attempted emigration was severe, even including the death penalty. But in 1753 Duke Christian Ludwig initiated a more enlightened approach to the perennial problem by opening up deserted farmland for small holdings (*Büdnerei*); however, this provided a solution only for those with some means who were resident within the Duke's own domains. The population growth of the early nineteenth century made rural workers particularly vulnerable to the difficulty of finding a domicile in the territories of the nobility, where the estate owners held all the land and virtually all the available accommodation. From the abolition of serfdom in 1820, farm workers theoretically had the right to move to any area in search of employment, but estate owners were reluctant to take on new households because residential rights implied the right to social welfare. All inhabitants had a right to welfare assistance only in the town or on the estate where they had residence rights, and as Johann Luck's story demonstrates, local authorities were eager to dispose of these responsibilities wherever possible, and this had important ramifications for issues of social mobility and emigration.

In 1865 a progressive nobleman, Bock, summed it up by saying that the Mecklenburger has no fatherland:

> As soon as a Mecklenburger sets foot over the confines of his birthplace, whether it is a town, an estate or a village, he is in a foreign country. No, it is even worse: foreign countries accept him quite willingly – it is the foreign country within his own fatherland which rejects him. According to the law he cannot count on finding a domicile on the next estate or in the next town. The Mecklenburger has a parental home, a home town but no homeland [*ein Vaterhaus, eine Vaterstadt, kein Vaterland*].[7]

Mecklenburg's high illegitimacy rate of 20 per cent was one consequence of the situation, and for many couples faced with a similar predicament, emigration proved the best solution. Couples were granted a dispensation to marry if they renounced all residency rights, had made arrangements to emigrate immediately after marrying, and possessed at least 50 *Thaler* after paying for their passage – a policy which positively encouraged emigration, primarily to America.

This was reflected in the prevailing attitude to mass emigration, which was originally seen as a simple solution to social problems. In 1817 the castle at Güstrow – unused after that line of the ducal family had died out – was turned into a state poorhouse, and when it was filled to overflowing in 1823, the inmates were simply loaded aboard a ship and sent to Brazil. In 1844 Count Rantzau sent a number of his estate workers to take up 2000 acres of land he had purchased in New Zealand, as an investment for himself and as a way to improve their lot. When they were unable to take possession of their unsurveyed land, many families became impoverished and after obtaining passage to Van Diemen's Land took the opportunity to come to South Australia, where they settled in old miners' huts in Glen Osmond and were given assistance by the local German communities.[8]

But when emigration from Mecklenburg peaked at 9450 in 1854 and the number of emigrants exceeded the number of births, the exodus was at last addressed as a problem, with positive steps taken to provide the rural population with housing and cottage blocks and the establishment a system of hereditary leasehold.

From Mecklenburg to South Australia
We left the family of Christian Luck facing life in the Poor House following his untimely death, but the generosity of a friend who bought their house and allowed them to live in it rent-free saved them from that fate. As two of the sons followed their father and grandfather into their traditional trade, the whole family no doubt looked forward to the time when the oldest son, Friedrich, would qualify as a master and take up the business once more.

By 1849 Friedrich had completed his apprenticeship and was working as a journeyman in Doberan, when he was called up for military service. He narrowly passed the height test (5 ft 1 inch) and was also passed medically fit; his number did not turn up in the exemption ballot, and he was instructed to report for duty later that year.[9] However, in February 1851 we find him instead marrying Sophie Helmke in Lyndoch Valley, South Australia. If the family's deductions are correct, Friedrich Luck arrived in Port Adelaide on 31 January 1850 after leaving Hamburg on the *Alfred* on 27 October 1849, together with the Helmke family, consisting of Gottlieb Helmke, his second wife and four daughters. Helmke – from Kröpelin (a small town between Bützow and Doberan) – was another butcher who had been trained under the auspices of the Bützow Butchers' Guild. He had been plying his trade in Doberan for two decades before Friedrich Luck appeared there as a penniless journeyman. Helmke was reputedly a wealthy man, whose emigration was prompted by hopes that the climate would alleviate his tuberculosis, and it is assumed that he paid Friedrich Luck's passage. Once in South Australia, and when he and Sophie were married, Friedrich gave his occupation as butcher, but in December 1852 he and his brother-in-law von Boeckmann (also from Mecklenburg) purchased Sections 3044 and 3045 in the Lyndoch Valley together, and he spent the rest of his life as a prosperous farmer.

Three thousand Bützow residents have been documented as

emigrating during the nineteenth century – from a population of around 4000 – but the overwhelming majority headed for America. (The handful of families who came to Australia instead included the cabinetmaker Wernicke, whose son August was possibly our only German bushranger, and surely one of the shortest-lived, struck down as a teenager at Wantabadgery in New South Wales in his first shoot-out with the police as part of Captain Moonlight's gang.)

The story of Mecklenburg migration to South Australia begins with the arrival of the ship *George Washington* in 1844. The Adelaide *Observer* mentions Mecklenburg as one of the states of origin of the passengers, but the reconstructed passenger list contains only names from Brandenburg and Silesia, leaving 29 passengers unaccounted for.[10] More significantly, Captain Probst of the *George Washington* took a positive interest in the colony, visiting the German settlements, gathering testimonials and soliciting a pamphlet from Pastor Kavel with the intention of promoting the colony as a suitable destination for German migrants.[11]

Captain Probst returned with the *George Washington* two years later, bringing with him about 70 Mecklenburg migrants who, according to the *Register,* were seeking 'a secure retreat from political strife' and intended to establish a settlement of their own. Of the 23 individuals and household heads listed in the joint emigration permit, two are maidservants, 12 are craftsmen or tradesmen (four carpenters, two millers, two butchers, a blacksmith, tailor, weaver, and gardener), with the remainder as rural workers.[12] The leader of the group was Matthias Lange, yet another butcher from Kröpelin, who had completed his apprenticeship and become a master in the Bützow Butchers' Guild one year before Christian Luck.

These Mecklenburg families in fact merged with other German villages in the Adelaide Hills and the Barossa, but their enthusiastic letters home prompted the formation in Kröpelin of a Society for Emigration to South Australia. Its manifesto spoke of:

> ... the general scarcity of business with no prospect of better times, the increasing confusion in our German fatherland which must fill every household head with concern for the future, and on the other hand the favourable reports of the Cröpeliner living in South Australia, Matthias Lange and Johann Rönnfeldt, who express the certainty that

every hardworking individual will make a good living in that free land, which is privileged by nature above all others by its beautiful climate and fertile soil.[13]

A number of shipping agents took up business in the local towns, and in 1849 Dieseldorff, a shipping agent and writer of one of the emigrant guides to South Australia, undertook a lecture tour which also included Doberan. Heinrich Rönnfeldt, Matthias Lange's brother-in-law, left for Adelaide with his family on the *Wolga* (*Ocean*)[14] in May 1849. He was apparently disappointed with what he found in the colony, but by then others like Gottlieb Helmke and Friedrich Luck were already on their way, and more were to follow. Chain migration has been recognised as a major factor in the great population movements of the nineteenth century, and it is noteworthy that the major links of this particular chain – Lange, Helmke and Luck – all involve the Bützow Butchers' Guild.

Several years after Friedrich Luck's emigration, the Grand Duke of Mecklenburg received yet another appeal from a Butcher Luck, Friedrich's younger brother, August.

> To the Grand-Ducal High Ministry of the Interior in Schwerin
>
> I, the apprentice butcher August Luck, have been apprenticed to Master Butcher Kleiss here in Bützow for 3 years. I have, however, no prospect of advancing in the trade because I have not earned any income during this time, and my mother finds herself in the greatest poverty, and is even being supported by the local commune, so my future can only lie in becoming a labourer or farm hand. I do however have a brother who owns a farm in Australia, in Lyndoch Valley near Adelaide. He has now written to ask me to join him and has booked a passage for me to Adelaide through the Amsberg family in Hamburg. Because my entire life's happiness depends on this, I dare to most humbly plead: That the High office of the Grand-Ducal Ministry will graciously give its approval and grant me a passport for this journey and permit my emigration. Because the ship for which my passage has been booked is leaving between the 15th and 18th of this month, I again plead in most submissive obedience: That the High office of the Grand-Ducal Ministry would kindly gratify me by sending me the passport as soon as possible because I have to make some arrangements before joining

the ship. Finally I would like to add that I am the son of the local butcher's widow Luck, my father froze to death on the local country road whilst fetching calves, and I am 18 years old.

I look forward to a favourable hearing of my request and remain in deep devotion as a most submissive and obedient subject of the high Grand Ducal Ministry,

August Luck

Once more the question is referred to the Town Council, and it is hardly surprising that they enthusiastically recommend granting August the permit.

Respectful report of the Town Council in Bützow

Re: the application of the butcher's apprentice Luck to be granted an emigration permit

To the Grand-Ducal Ministry of the Interior of Mecklenburg

The butcher's apprentice A. Luck, 20 years old, is the son of the local Butcher Luck who died many years ago in the greatest wretchedness, and since his father left no capital and his mother is supported by the Poor Fund, he has not had a guardian. He himself possesses nothing and would not be able to carry out his intention of emigrating to Australia except for the fact that his brother, who himself emigrated there several years ago, has made arrangements with a Hamburg trading company for the passage of his mother and siblings by means of an order from Adelaide, which has been shown to us. His mother and sisters however wish to remain here for the present and the applicant alone wishes to make use of the offered opportunity to acquire a fortune in foreign parts. He therefore needs no money other than for the trip to Hamburg, and that will be given to him by his brother who is employed at the local railway station.

The only obstacle which could stand in the way of his application is the fact that he has not yet fulfilled his military service. However, if one takes into account that he has no capital at all and will perhaps never or only very late be in a position to establish himself here and set up his own household, we can only recommend that his application be graciously granted.

Bützow 11 April 1854

The Town Council

The fact that Luck has not fulfilled military service does not prove an insuperable obstacle when compared with the opportunity to dispose of an impecunious subject. The Town Council preferred to leave the issue of August's age rather vague, but when it was determined that he did not have to present himself for military call-up in the current year, his passport was issued, resolving the problem with remarkable speed for a bureaucracy! On 23 April 1854 August Luck set sail for Adelaide on the *Wandrahm*. In South Australia he plied his trade as a butcher in city and country with no great success, although members of his family continued the tradition until one last grandson was employed as a slaughterman at the Gepps Cross abattoirs.

A year after August's departure, his widowed mother and her two daughters also took up Friedrich Luck's offer to bring them to Australia, the younger daughter Sophie accompanied by her husband-to-be, carpenter Fritz Moeller – one of the 500 arriving in South Australia from Germany in the nineteenth century, as documented by Noris Ioannou.[15] After six years in the city, Fritz established himself as a carpenter, undertaker and small farmer in Rosenthal, and three of their seven daughters married sons of the two carpenters who arrived with the *George Washington* group in 1846. The couple's Adelaide years provide a glimpse into a strong network of German craftsmen and tradesmen here, well documented in the Lutheran Church registers kept by the independent Pastor Kappler during his ministry in the city. Since Kappler had no regular church of his own in North Adelaide or the West End of the city where the trades were concentrated, most marriages and baptisms were held in private homes, and those locations reveal connections between German tradesmen spanning their often diverse nationalities. Fritz and Sophie were married in the house of a baker from the Harz (Hanover), where the other witness was a shoemaker from the Duchy of Brunswick. The following year Fritz witnessed August Luck's marriage at the home of his brother-in-law, another baker from the Harz. Fritz and Sophie's first two daughters were baptised together with the children of a Mecklenburg baker, the first in the cottage of a basketmaker from Saxony and the second in their own home.

German migration to South Australia in the nineteenth century is customarily divided unevenly between the rural Old Lutherans from the eastern provinces of Prussia and the small urban intellectual elite whose achievements in the arts, the professions and politics are considered such a significant contribution to the progress of the colony. This characterisation obscures the fact that many among the Prussian rural population were skilled in a trade in their homeland and continued to ply that trade in the German villages here, although many may also have taken up farming. It also ignores the other, less prominent, city dwellers who emigrated from a broad range of German states and practised the full range of trades, although not all of them prospered sufficiently to maintain that status. The political factors which prompted the 'Forty-Eighters' to emigrate may have played a role among the tradesmen too: since their training involved years of journeying, they were considered not only better educated than the majority of the rural population, but they were also more politically aware, and indeed often radical. But the socioeconomic restructuring which occurred throughout Europe during the nineteenth century – exemplified by the Weavers' Revolt in Silesia in 1844 – deserves detailed examination as a significant motivation for emigration. Ioannou has noted the particularly high concentration of carpenters and other wood craftsmen among the German settlers in South Australia, referring to the role played by the expansion of mass production, which, ironically, was no less significant in the new British colony than it had been in their continental homeland.

The chain of migration linked to the Bützow Butchers' Guild stretches from the landing of the first group of Mecklenburg migrants in 1846 to the arrival of the last family members almost 10 years later, and suggests that guild affiliation can play a parallel role to that of the well-established migration chains of the extended family and village or church connections. The documents outlined here point to guild and town records as an untapped potential source of the prehistory of our German families, although the Bützow Archives' holdings and that town's active interest in its nineteenth-century emigrants are admittedly rare finds.

Notes

1. Noris Ioannou, *The Barossa Folk: Germanic furniture and craft traditions in Australia*, Craftsman House, Sydney, 1995, p. 30.
2. The former Grand Duchy of Mecklenburg is now combined with the remnant of its neighbour Pomerania as the federal state of Mecklenburg–Vorpommern on the north-east coast of the Federal Republic of Germany.
3. The Butchers' Guild register, the *Ein und Auß-Schreibbuch der Schlächterlehrjungens,* begun in 1718, is held along with other guild documents by the Heimatmuseum in the Krummes Haus, Bützow.
4. Genealogical records of the Luck family are found in the Bützow church registers held by the Mecklenburgisches Kirchenbuchamt in Schwerin; they are also available on microfilm from the LDS Family History Centres.
5. Correspondence of Christian Luck 1825–26, Sophie Luck 1831, Johann Luck 1838 and August Luck 1854 held by the Bützow Town Hall Archives; copies kindly supplied by local historian Fritz Hossmann.
6. Although similar regulations applied in other German states, the Mecklenburg nobility held a greater proportion of the land and retained more privileges than in comparable states, greatly exacerbating the associated problems.
7. Bock, 'Gedanken über die Ursachen der Entvölkerung Mecklenburgs', *Landwirtschaftliche Annalen,* 1865; see also H. Dietzsch, *Die Bewegung der Mecklenburgischen Bevölkerung von 1850 bis 1910*, Herberger, Schwerin, 1918.
8. See Joyce Graetz, 'Hands across the Tasman' and David Schubert, 'From New Zealand to South Australia', in *Journal of Friends of Lutheran Archives*, 3, 1993.
9. Military call-up documents held by the Bützow Town Hall Archives.
10. H.F.W. Proeve, 'Lutheran Arrivals 1844: *Joseph Albino* and *George Washington*', *Lutheran Yearbook,* Adelaide, 1969.
11. *Observer*, Adelaide, 5 October 1844.
12. *Barossa Historical Bulletin*, vol. 1, no. 2.
13. F. Bergmann, '"Da steht sie nun, die lebendige Fracht": Auswanderer und Auswanderung aus Kröpelin', *Bad Doberaner Jahrbuch*, 1995 p. 175.
14. The German ship *Ocean* succeeded in evading the Danish blockade of Hanseatic ports (during hostilities over Schleswig–Holstein) by adopting a Russian name and sailing under a Russian flag.
15. Ioannou 1995, p. 30.

The hospital that never was

Michael Bollen

Mines of great wealth, real and imaginary, revived the sad body of South Australia in the mid-1840s, and again it began singing across seas. By the turn of the decade, Adelaide was a crush. The town's only hospital, the government-run Adelaide Hospital, was constantly full: the Colonial Surgeon called for tents, while lonely invalids knocked on doors, looking for reception.

The government was tacking on new wards, but had voted the expenditure in 1848 only over protests in the Legislative Council – the day's unelected 'parliament' – from 'non-official' members, magnates keen to seize control from London and its local representatives. The Colonial Secretary, in charge of the hospital, ridiculed the ringleading pair as hypocrites, recalling that they themselves had used the place to get free treatment for humble souls in their retinues.[1]

The *Register* newspaper, friend of the poor and the working man, excoriated the non-official honourables for their heartlessness, but it too was inclined to describe authorities in London and the colony as meddling foreigners, warning of 'open rebellion'[2] unless the Home Government met the colony's just demands. You and whose army, teased the other papers, but with a new constitution promised yet always delayed in coming from London, there was much cargo-cultism in the air.

Time now, muttered some voices, for wealthy citizens to commence a hospital in the grown-up English way by voluntary contributions: 'Could there be a more glorious page in our history than that relating to the foundation of a public hospital that might be under their own eye and own governance, and have the pleasing reflection of having done good in their day and generation?'[3] No move was apparent, however, until an advertisement in German, published among the newspapers only in the Tanunda-based *Deutsche Post*, called '*sämmtliche Deutsche zur Teilnahme an dem Bau eines deutschen Hospitals*' (all the gathered Germans to participate in building a German hospital).[4]

Already, it advised, 'a number of Germans' had taken the opportunity to discuss the need for this endeavour. The ready agreement of most of those present, along with 'other favourable circumstances', made such an institution soon possible 'if there is quick and busy cooperation from noble philanthropists who through word and deed take part in the most beautiful works of human charity'. Signed 'Many members of the German Reading Club [*Deutsche Lesegesellschaft*]', the notice asked 'all German brothers' to assemble for a further discussion in the evening of 4 February 1850 at Mr Pohlmann's place in Adelaide – which, as it did not explain, was the Hamburgh Hotel on the corner of Rundle Street and Gawler Place.

Other mysteries dwelt in this so determinedly German advertisement. It gave no hint, for instance, of what a 'German hospital' or the need for one might be.

Dr Friedrich Carl/Frederick Charles Bayer

Did the promoters really think Germans in the country, and especially the Prussian Old Lutherans who made up perhaps half the colony's German population, would drop prayer book and plough to descend on this meeting with men they did not know? In the city, Germans of different faiths and fatherlands numbered one in seven denizens of the busy eastern part, but many were shy of German causes, because they worried the British might think them separatist, or were just too busy finding their daily bread.

As it was, about 40 brothers turned up, perhaps a usual crowd, all city traders: merchants and shopkeepers, druggists and drapers, metalsmiths and jewellers, hoteliers, an architect and building tradesmen, a physician, a schoolmaster, a journalist, a professor of music.[5] All bar one had arrived since 1846, the year their host from Hamburg, droll Wilhelm or William Pohlmann, took the licence of what had been the Suffolk Inn. Pohlmann had since married a daughter of fellow Rundle Street publican George Ottaway, a native of Kent who had enjoyed his own intimate German moments in the

Dr Bayer in about 1867, the year of his death. 'The head that rose up from his shoulders was massive', wrote 'An Anglo-Australian', 'with the forehead strongly developed; his blue eyes were keen and penetrating under his protruding brow'.
(State Library of South Australia, SLSA: B 929)

colony, Dr Bayer from Bayern (Bavaria) having removed his arm after a quail-shooting accident.[6]

This Dr Bayer, one of the colony's very few southern Germans, was a man of colossal build and presence. According to a letter from 'C. Boehme, Dr Ph., Secretary pro tem' to the *Mercury* newspaper, the meeting itself came about after Bayer had spoken several times to 'his friends' – of whom he had many, including but not only a number of Germans.[7]

He had arrived three years earlier, however, knowing no one and bearing just scanty English. A merchant from Bremen and man about town named Henry Noltenius, a colonist since 1843, took the big medico under wing (so to speak), pitching the press a Bremen journalist's praise of the *'moral firmness'* displayed by the 'excellent, talented and practical' young doctor, who had been barred from the Bavarian state medical system for refusing, even under punishment, to give up the names of participants in a fatal duel, and so headed for New Holland.[8]

Wrapped in this romantic cloak, ambitious Dr Bayer soon met a roadblock in the shape of the South Australian Medical Board: 'They said my diploma was not derived from a University recognised in London; but that I could practise amongst my own countrymen, but not else. I threatened to bring the whole case before Governor Robe, and then I got passed; but they humbugged me for six months and would not examine my papers, and I had no right to demand a personal explanation.'[9] It was nearly two decades later when he told this story, but the memory still roused sudden anger. Dr Bayer had no wish to work only among his 'countrymen', but incentive aplenty to prove the German name and abilities.

His surgical skills, learnt in the 'dead house' with easy access to cadavers, were soon admired, while at the bedside he swapped magnificent gloom for life-restoring cheer. Seizing the day, Dr Benjamin Kent, an English old colonist of 'gentlemanly and exceedingly plausible manners', persuaded the Bavarian into partnership. Six months after his arrival Bayer wielded the knife as Kent administered the gas in the colony's first operation under ether anaesthetic. The Medical Board registered him a few days later, while his marriage in 1848 to Kent's daughter eased his way into society – although the big doctor's only pleasure, thought a friend of that young woman, remained driving about to see his patients.

Late in 1849 the government appointed him one of the six honorary medical officers in charge of patients at the Adelaide Hospital, a duty that had been for years the Colonial Surgeon's alone. This made Bayer the only man of German birth with a position of any prestige in the government establishment.

He had a large house on North Terrace by this time, and other properties besides. As the only registered doctor of German birth working regularly in the city, he had the run of the German-speaking market – which, given his popularity also among 'English' patients, including many leading lights, gave him the largest practice in town. He shared it now with new English-born partners, his theatrical friend the *Mercury* averring:

> Should Atropos, of which we've fears,
> To snip our weazen whet her shears,
> We'd call in Bayer, Cowper, Knott,
> And drive the Fury from the spot –
> Three names which, without using figures,
> Have ruined Adelaide's grave diggers'.[10]

Thumping the tub

Early in 1850, a large Newfoundland dog nearly won the bone merchants their revenge. It rushed on Dr Bayer's horse, which threw him so his massive brow landed on two sharp stones. Grim hours passed, but the doctor's father-in-law and partners were by his side, and he was all right on the night of 4 February, ready to thump the tub before his German brothers.

His powerful speech, wrote secretary Boehme in his letter and 'Gamma' to the *Register*,[11] took as its theme the 'well-known fact here in Adelaide that our Hospital accommodation was insufficient, and the want of it was most severely felt among the German colonists, who, not knowing the English language, were really in a sad position in case of sickness'. This found a ready echo, so funds totalling £180 were pledged on the spot, the first £50 in the joint names of Bayer and Noltenius. The brothers resolved to send subscription sheets to 'all friends, and especially the German clergymen', chose a provisional committee – Dr Bayer president, of course – and decided to hold a further gathering at the same place on 22 February, the day after the Agricultural Show (presumably reckoning some country Germans would then be in town).

And so was the foundation laid, wrote 'Gamma', of a work that would be blessed not only by the patients it healed, but 'many blessings will those reap who assist in carrying it out, from the far off fatherland, from ... parents and relations'.

If patients were from the fatherland, would ones from the 'mother country' be welcome too? Just when Gamma's letter – the German hospital's English-language debut – seemed ready to say this proposed hospital, like London's well-known but curiously unmentioned German Hospital that opened in 1845, would be specifically for patients born in German lands or German-speaking, it stepped out of the evening's events to ask for help from readers on the ground the hospital would be open, 'according to its room, not only to Germans, but to every patient, be his country what it may'.

Precisely the same could be said of the existing Adelaide Hospital. By recent decree at least, the main rule regulating its available room was that destitute patients must have first call on the beds, with any left over (and there were none) available only on payment of a proper fee. How would a patient qualify for admission to the German hospital? What rights of access were on offer for subscribers? The letters gave no detail, leaving the questions hidden behind the institution's German name.

A 'submitted' promotional article in the *Deutsche Post* was cagey – indeed silent – on these issues.[12] It said this *deutsches Krankenhaus* would bring 'blessings to all the Germans of South Australia', but made no mention of the language issue, focusing rather on the town's general lack of sick beds. It neither stated the hospital would be for Germans in particular, nor that other patients would be accommodated. Along with an accompanying advertisement, it implored 'a very large number of Germans' to come for the 'second' meeting. The notice in English-language papers about this 'general' meeting, by contrast, was in tone more an advice than invitation – but it did invite readers to share in the honour: names of subscribers would be 'published in this paper'.

In the event, the 22 February gathering was 'numerously attended' – or so said the town's two most popular newspapers and bitterest of enemies, the godly *Register* and irreligious *Mercury*.[13] Each sent a representative to the Hamburgh Hotel for this meeting, where events were conducted again in German.

Called to the chair was an angular, auburn-haired Catholic clergyman named Henry Backhaus, of Paderborn, Rome, Calcutta, Sydney and, since late 1847, Adelaide, where he had become second-in-charge to Bishop Murphy's mainly Irish congregation, of which Dr Bayer was a weather-permitting type of member, along with a few other Germans. Rev. Dr Backhaus, musically gifted and a noted amateur homoeopath, said how happy he was to be surrounded by so many of his countrymen, mentioned God, made encouraging noises, then asked secretary (*pro tem*) Boehme to report on progress.

Dr Boehme (PhD not MD) had been in the news for his observations on the manufacture of gas in Odessa, but also as

Henry Backhaus in 1852 became the first Catholic priest on the Victorian goldfields. He was a financial wizard, in Bendigo earning the nickname 'Rev. Corner Allotments'.

pro tem president of the new *Deutsche Liedertafel* (German Song Society), a convocation of singing small businessmen who advertised their ambition – in a German-language notice in an English-language paper – as being to enhance the town's musical education along with its feelings of *'gemütlich-geselliges Zusammensein'* ('cosy-sociable togetherness').[14] Until the song society and hospital twins emerged, the German Reading Club had been the Adelaide's lone German secular cultural society – and it barely vegetated, in the words of one disappointed immigrant.

Tonight, however, the secretary channelled glad tidings of German togetherness in noble cause. He had been visiting German settlements in the country, said Boehme, and met everywhere a full determination to help. Now he could show the crowd 'thirteen subscription-sheets out of a hundred, subscribed almost entirely by his German countrymen, on which they could find the sum of 426 pounds', including some promises of work in kind rather than cash. He hoped the English fellow-colonists would assist, 'as their hospital would certainly be a German one, but … no invalid should call at its doors without finding help'.

Soon it was Dr Bayer's turn to loom large amid loud acclamations. He had long cherished, he said, the hope of seeing a hospital erected here 'for his German brethren', and now felt certain it would happen. He reckoned himself able to give hope the government would make

Andreas Kappler later became a well known figure in Mount Gambier. As a boy in Saxony he preferred the manners of the occupying French to those of the liberating Prussians and Russians. (State Library of South Australia, SLSA: B 34567)

a grant of land, and 'had the pleasure to be able to tell them, that several eminent English physicians, in conjunction with himself and some German medical men, had declared their willingness to form a *collegium medicum*. (Hear, hear.)' The doctor did not explain what he meant by that Latin phrase, but historically in Bavaria (and elsewhere in continental Europe) it was the body authorised to control medical licensing and services throughout the state.

Saying he still expected to get a couple more, Bayer displayed two plans for the hospital drawn by local German architects, both admired as 'admirably adapted' for a warm climate. One at least of the architects, young Tilman Gloystein, must have been a fast learner: he had arrived from his home in chilly Bremen only three weeks earlier. The reports gave readers no look at the plans. Nothing was said as to the hospital's proposed size.

After the brothers chorused 'Yes!' to Dr Bayer's call for a declaration of faith, Rev. Dr Backhaus oversaw the election of a committee, becoming himself a chosen one, along with the city's and urban Tanunda's 'freelance' Lutheran minister, Andreas Kappler – or Handrej Kapler, as Wends in the Kingdom of Saxony had known him for 13 years before he sailed in 1848 for South Australia, where he was sometimes Andrew Coppler. Astonished by the colony's Old Lutherans, Kappler had agreed to lead congregations only if they overthrew 'all synodical resolutions, in so far as they restrict liberty of action', a commandment that suited non-Old Lutheran commercial types who did not want to be handed over to the Devil if apparently unrepentant.[15] Kappler and Pastor Kavel, leader of the first Old Lutheran flocks, had been savaging each other recently in the *Deutsche Post*.

City traders made up the rest of the committee. Henry Noltenius's business partnership with Dr Bayer perhaps precluded him from election: chosen instead was his brother Bernhard, a later arrival and less happily anglicised. Together with another merchant from Bremen, the brothers Noltenius were Adelaide agents in a novel scheme of assisted emigration funded by the Kingdom of Hanover, which had decided to disgorge workers from its faltering mines in the Harz region. It looked good business for Noltenius, Meyer & Co., but already after the first ships arrived in 1849 the firm was complaining these newcomers expected too much free help. The Harzers had come from lowly paid but secure state employment that included benefits such as medical insurance.[16] Dr Bayer must have been kept busy on the never never. A hospital with direct access would make management more efficient, and a 'German hospital' might beam a welcoming light to the Harz (and other German places), from where business was expected to grow.

Another Noltenius–Bayer venture centred on a popular Hindley Street pharmacy of which Henry was effective owner. In January of this year he charged the new front men, Nicolaus Kronk (from Schleswig–Holstein) – who was now chosen to the German hospital committee – and Kronk's partner from Hanover a hefty sum for the guarantee of Dr Bayer's patients.

Grocer and alto tenor Louis Rodemann, with a countryman from little Lippe, owned a successful grocery store near the Hamburgh Hotel, well placed to supply familiar foods to German patients at the imagined new hospital. Hard-of-hearing Adolph Wichmann, a Rundle Street draper from Hamburg, was the last of the committee members.

Chosen as treasurer was yet another merchant from Bremen, Frederick William Jansen, who later in the year became the first

Rundle Street in 1872 – the Gerke and Rodemann store became an institution. Rodemann was secretary of the *Deutsche Liedertafel* during 1850. He was normally 'Louis' Rodemann but donned 'Ludwig' for German and British Hospital advertisements. (State Library of South Australia, SLSA: B 2493)

German magistrate of the province – but left for Melbourne after taking an undisciplined spit at a fundamentalist British clergyman who warned against the many 'infidel and dissolute Germans that were now scattered through our population – men who could cite with some keenness of perception and aptitude of argument texts of Scripture in support of perverse and sinful habits'.[17] (Complaints rained from Germans, but none from the Old Lutheran leaders.)

After secretary Boehme explained he would soon be leaving them, the brothers elected a journalist named William Eggers to the post. Eggers, from Braunschweig via four years in England, attended the meeting for the *Register*, which dubbed him for the occasion 'our German reporter'.

Dr Bayer, once again, was elected president by unanimous vote – an 'auspicious omen', thought the *Mercury*.

Square circles

In the enthusiasm of the moment one can glimpse Dr Bayer's grand vision: a prominent building in this bursting town, the German name aloft, saving lives and winning esteem. But its shape keeps changing, like a square circle, a hospital especially for Germans and not especially for Germans. Part of its point, and of reports of these meetings, was to prove that Germans could be enlightened, progressive members of the emerging social polity, not mere juveniles in the sway of pastors here or despots at home.

Propriety in this colony demanded there should be only one people, South Australians, meaning in normal talk the amalgamating English, Scots and Irish (otherwise called British in the colonies), although with Germans often mentioned, especially if any were in the room.[18] But it was a tricky question. How should German language and ways figure in the coming new state: what would be their status, and how far integrated, separately maintained, or discarded as irrelevant? Clashing opinions were possible, among Germans and British alike. This German hospital would need to do a dance of veils, play a game of 'fort/da', to show a pleasing countenance to all.

The *Liedertafel* gathered in force outside Dr Bayer's home one lovely night in March, there to serenade him on his birthday and celebrate the new baby institution. Cracks, though, were soon noticed. Many more Germans chose to attend a ball at the Hamburgh Hotel than the first performance of an Amateur Dramatic Society that promised its profits (there were none) to the German hospital, provoking an editor's ire. Small court reports told how, at Tanunda's Alliance Hotel, one German commercial man assaulted another for saying there were individuals on the hospital's subscription list 'who could not pay and were not willing to pay the amount set aside their names'. The city's new German-language paper, the *Süd-Australische Zeitung*, declined to publish a letter about the hospital because it was 'written unmistakably in no sound spirit', but promised to keep a wary eye on events.[19]

One-armed George Ottaway's German and English Ball, held to encourage a 'union of races', went off well in May, but around this time *Register* proprietor John Stephens – an exemplary religious dissenter and staunch friend of 'the Germans' since he worked in

London with his relative George Fife Angas and Pastor Kavel as they tried to get dissenting flocks out from Prussia – fell mortally ill under the weight of libel suits, leaving the *Mercury*, a blow-in of 1849 that made lampooning the colony's 'Saints' its special mission, as the German hospital's main English-language torch-bearer. This almost guaranteed the disinterest of the names most often associated with South Australia's early German history, those pious dissenting powerhouses the Angas family and the South Australian Company.

Among the mixed messages there was no news for months about any doings of the German hospital committee, no report on subscriptions. After the second meeting, editors had told that a deputation would soon wait on the Governor to request a grant of land, but there was no sign of one. Early in June, however, came rolling to the rescue a round bon vivant and 'decided mad man' named Osmond Gilles. During a meeting of the 'German Musical Society' at the Hamburgh Hotel, 'the great O.G.' promised a town acre as a site for the German hospital, and land also to the *Liedertafel* for a hall.[20]

Perhaps Gilles and Dr Bayer, his friend and physician, snickered over the choice of acre, which was in the east end of town near St John's Anglican Church. The clergyman there had accused the big doctor of running over schoolchildren out the front, provoking a furious response from the German, notionally Catholic medico, while cantankerous O.G., who had given the land for St John's, was annoyed the trustees were creating a burial ground there. Indeed, like many notable Anglicans, Gilles was cranky with the Church of England generally, in particular its recently arrived Bishop for thinking he was boss. To beat the Bishop in founding a prominent charitable institution would have thrilled the mischievous sprite, especially as it cost him virtually nothing and was conducted in the name of sometimes aspersed friends and fellow carousers – and himself 'half a German'.

Gilles, 'in looks and manner a Frenchman', conducted a German/British/Australian trading enterprise long before he arrived in South Australia its first Treasurer and richest resident, and sat barefooted at the Bay selling cigars to new chums. He was born and raised in London, but made his fortune during nearly two decades in Hamburg, of which city–state he became a citizen, and where in 1822 he was (he wrote later) chief 'Conspirator' among the

Osmond Gilles in 1841, as seen by the *Adelaide Independent and Cabinet of Amusement*. Andrew Moore's 'The South Australian Polka, dedicated to Osmond Gilles Esquire' was much danced in 1850.

British merchants who formed a 'Coterie to discuss the Arcadia of Australia'.[21] These discussions soon turned into a profitable venture after his brother and other conspirators, with their families and Saxon sheep, left Hamburg for Tasmania the following year.

O.G. had come to South Australia expecting to be a big noise in a Hamburg-style state, but was soon relieved of any official position. These days he mostly brooded on his Glen Osmond estate, venturing out now in German solidarity.

So the land question was settled. Behind the scenes, Dr Bayer and friends must have been busy also on the money-raising front, if a petition presented the next week to the Legislative Council could be believed. Seeking a grant of money, it vowed that already 'upwards of two thousand pounds' were assured in private subscriptions.

The petition was brought into Council by the same 'non-official' member, Jacob Hagen, who in 1848 had led loud opposition to government spending on the Adelaide Hospital. He hurried in midway through proceedings but, most unusually, his fellows chose to consider the petition straight away. What followed has the scripted feel of a done deal.[22]

Already that day, the Governor (Sir Henry Fox Young) had pushed through a small grant to help the *Süd-Australische Zeitung* publish legal notices in translation, the German paper's editors arguing in their request that South Australia's 'nearly eight thousand' Germans were equally with British colonists 'subjects of our most gracious Majesty', and so deserved to be able to read the laws.

The Registrar-General borrowed this language as he rose to address the German hospital petition in square-circle mode. 'It was not the petition of eight thousand Germans,' he said, 'but eight thousand of Her Majesty's subjects, and was in that view entitled to weight.' The existing hospital needed more beds, but he feared creating an overgrown government establishment if they enlarged it to embrace the 'object desired'. This proposed hospital was fostered by voluntary contributions, and so deserved every encouragement. He moved:

> That this Council recommend the Governor to place on the Estimates the item of £1000, whenever the Colonial Architect shall have reported that an expenditure equal to £2000 has been made from voluntary contributions to the public hospital, to be styled _____, and alluded to in a petition read and received that day.

Members chorused in rare agreement, eulogising the Germans – that 'highly deserving exemplary class of fellow colonists' – and the voluntary principle, even while they supported this motion that declined to endorse the institution's German name. About that, the petitioners could hardly complain: their document did say the title 'German Hospital' was chosen only to distinguish it from the 'sister institution', by which reasoning any title unlike 'Adelaide Hospital' would do as well.

The honourable gents spoke airily of the proposed hospital's 'desired object', but none explained what he took that to be. Who was the hospital for?

Germans, in particular, the petition's first clause appeared to say, but it closed with a highly ambiguous mission statement, forecasting a hospital 'the rules of which, though intended more immediately for the relief of German invalids, in relation to peculiarities of language and custom, will be so comprehensive as to embrace all classes of Her Majesty's subjects within the colony'. In between these bookends, it sketched a hospital whose presumed patients had no specific nationality or language. Mere 'country' would give no applicant priority, while of the four doctors listed – Dr Bayer and his partners and father-in-law – only one was German-speaking.

So how was this 'second, or German' hospital German? Introducing the petition, Hagen had said the 'parties concerned' intended to conduct the institution on 'the Continental principle'. No one asked what he meant, but the answer was tucked away in the petition, dressed in the familiar English vestments of self-help, and not named as German. Asked years later about the workings of hospitals in 'your country' (that is, German hospitals), Dr Bayer said they were owned by governments but: 'Everyone, by paying a certain sum, say sixpence per month, has the right to be admitted as an indoor patient or attended as an outdoor patient'.[23] Now, here in this petition, for the first time Adelaide's nascent German hospital indicated some proposed admission regulations, saying 'it has been resolved that any person paying regularly a small weekly sum, to be fixed by the Committee, should, upon requiring it, be immediately admitted, in preference to applicants merely recommended by subscribers'.

Private hospital insurance is familiar enough to us now, of course, but was very rare in English-speaking places at the time. The second, less-preferred mode of admission, however, was characteristic of an English voluntary hospital, where annual subscribers secured the right to send in deserving humble sufferers. Neither mode was available at the Adelaide Hospital, where in 1849, with immigrants landing by ever more rapid waves, the government had appointed its new Destitute Board as gatekeeper. No longer might a mere note from a respectable citizen or employer (such as Jacob Hagen) secure admission for an invalid.

Far more than the existing hospital, this projected one promised to be a place for 'every patient' – except perhaps those destitute of a patron or regular sixpence. By the petition, a destitute German might have better chance of reception at the Adelaide Hospital, rather than the German one. Viewed from this angle, the promoters' aim appears to have been to create a main 'general' hospital in Adelaide, leaving the government to run one for the destitute. Rather a larger ambition than a hospital for the German minority.

Obviously, the two kinds of voluntary contributions might cause confusion at the new hospital – why, for instance, would a wealthy employer subscribe in annual pounds if the bed he wanted for his worker might be usurped by any sixpenny self-insurer? But the colony, like this hospital, was an inchoate kind of place. Combining the elements of government subsidy and private control with its mixed modes of subscriber funding and admission, the no-name hospital begins to look not German or British, but perhaps uniquely South Australian.

Council members chose to speak as if the petition arose from all the Germans of the colony, but it was titled a 'petition of the subscribers' not a 'petition of Germans'. Unusually, no list of subscribers was demanded or given: for all anyone knew, the honourable gents might have been subscribers, and none of them was considered German. True, the document's seven signatories – Dr Bayer and some friends – were all more or less prominent German-born men of the city, but they did not sign themselves as a committee of Germans or even of the German hospital. Indeed they could not, for the petition promised that management would be trusted to a 'mixed committee' yet to be elected by a public meeting of subscribers yet to be held.

German-Anglo, Anglo-German Adelaide

Two evenings later, reported the *Mercury*, 'several members of the committee' – meaning the February-elected committee of Germans – 'with some other gentlemen, desirous of promoting the objects of the Institution, dined together by invitation at the Royal Exchange Hotel'.[24] So much for a public meeting and open election. More intriguing, though, is the news in this report that it was 'originally intended' the hospital should be governed by an equal number of Germans and English. If this was true, it had been kept hidden – including by the *Mercury*, whose editor William Edward Hammond was one of the newly named members. But presumably these men had been in on plans from the start.

One of them, Joseph Stilling, could hardly have not been involved. He was partner with Henry Noltenius in the merchant firm of Joseph Stilling & Co. Together they signed many Germans' memorials for naturalisation. Stilling's origins are obscure, but his name suggests a Schleswig–Holstein or Nordic heritage. As in the

Joseph Stilling in about 1860. His grave at St Matthew's church in Kensington (Adelaide) looks like a Viking's. (State Library of South Australia, SLSA: B 11147)

case of Osmond Gilles, the line between Briton and German could be pretty tenuous. For the *Mercury*, Henry Noltenius was 'An Anglo-German in whom all may find,/The virtues of both countries well combined'. There were quite a few 'German-Anglos' in town as well.

Henry's pharmacy stood next to his friend and now committee member George Coppin's Royal Exchange Hotel, 'Where bucks and bloods in countless numbers range/Where half the business of the town's transacted' – as perhaps Coppin himself wrote in the *Mercury*, of which hedonistic paper he was a main backer. German custom was good at the hotel, its billiard room painted with a *trompe l'oeil* featuring a German bushman.

'Purveyor-General' Coppin, son in England of a medical student who quit to tramp the boards, is best remembered now as an impresario and genius comic actor, sometimes called the 'father of Australian theatre'. It was probably music that first attracted him to Adelaide's Germans: he built a theatre within weeks of coming to town in 1846, promoting as one of his first shows a one-night-only performance by a brass band of newly arrived German miners. In honour of Dr Bayer, 'The Celebrated Bavarian Buy-a-broom Duet, by Mrs Moore, and her sister Mr G. Coppin' was one of the hits of the mid-century.

Coppin was also, like all Adelaide's commercial men, up to his ears in mining speculations, including as chairman of a fledgling mine at Port Lincoln in need of labour. Noltenius, Meyer & Co. persuaded one of the first boatloads of 'their' Harz miners to try these distant works.[25] When the shareholders at Port Lincoln needed to cash up, Henry Noltenius advertised some of their land – 'suitable for German settlement' – in the *Deutsche Post*.

The value of German-speaking 'clans' as a workforce or, especially, group tenants or purchasers of land was well established in the colony, of course. Around this time the Governor himself had a German intermediary looking out for some 'industrious and modest' German farmers to take on land he had acquired near the coast. The German hospital's appeal for a government grant had been made partly on the basis of the Germans' lack of English – inapplicable in many cases, as no one mentioned – but obviously the maintenance of German language was in the minds of the promoters, and not only German ones. This was all on the quiet: not a word was said in the Legislative Council about the language issue, although from one perspective members were giving a (provisional) legislative stamp to the institutionalising of German language in the colony. The German immigration had been always on the quiet, in the sense it was never officially encouraged by the government in England.

Germans occupied parts of the land owned at Echunga by law-maker Jacob Hagen, whose seventeenth-century ancestor (Jacob Hagen) was a Mennonite refugee from the Low Countries to Hamburg, and whose subsequent paternal forebears – all named Jacob Hagen, and all Quaker merchants based in England – retained close links with German 'Friends'.[26] South Australia's Jacob Hagen – 'that impossibility, a tory Quaker' – joined the dinner and the German hospital committee, meaning two days earlier he had presented a petition from himself to himself.

Hagen's brother-in-law and partner in many enterprises, John Baker, was another of the Englishmen on the committee. Baker was the Mr Big of magnates resident around Adelaide. During 1851 his friends Bayer and Noltenius helped him overcome the Old Lutheran vote to win the seat of Mount Barker in the colony's first partly elected Legislative Council. 'A 'great object' of the proposed hospital, Baker told the Council late that year, was to 'supply a place where masters could send their servants in case of illness or accidents' – rather letting the cat out of the bag.²⁷

Osmond Gilles was named on the committee, of course, while Dr Bayer remained president, no questions asked. Noshing at the dinner with him were the other medicos mentioned in the petition. The German hospital promised to be more doctor-friendly than the existing institution. According to the petition, the new hospital's medical committee would control the 'internal arrangements', already a subject of much dispute at the Adelaide Hospital after the reintroduction of the honorary system at the end of 1849. One of the issues was which, or perhaps whose, drugs the honorary doctors could prescribe. Dr Bayer stuck it out until February 1851, later explaining he was 'compelled to leave' because 'I did not like being dictated to, as to what I should prescribe ... I said I would not be humbugged any longer'.²⁸

The doctor and his collegiate friends, not men to be humbugged, would be able to prescribe their own medicines at the German hospital. Presumably the half-price drugs for 'out patients' (as promised in the petition) would be imported by Noltenius/Stilling and funnelled through the Noltenius/Kronk/Bayer pharmacy, with lost profits made up by hospital subscriptions. Or maybe the 'Dispensary' mentioned in the petition was to be the place of that name recently opened by Drs Kent and Weston in Grenfell Street, or perhaps some division was to be made between German- and English-speaking patients.

In an old doctors' lure, the German hospital would also offer gratis advice to all – like cut-price medicines and any real out-patient service, a boon not available at the Adelaide Hospital. The new hospital would let medical students learn the 'Continental as well as the British system', Hagen had said as he introduced the petition. There was no teaching at the existing hospital, and no formal training anywhere in the colony.

The night after the 'election' dinner, Osmond Gilles was at Dr Bayer's house when 30 German minstrels, each carrying a colourful lamp on his staff, emerged on the terrace, there to honour the O.G. for his donation of land – of which Gilles (aka the 'Ace of Trumps') reminded the mixed committee when it met for business the following week, earning himself a vote of thanks with acclamation.

Now 'English' involvement was in the open, the *Mercury* published minutes of this bustling first (reported) meeting for business.[29] Who knows how many of the decisions recorded were made in fact months earlier? Trustees were elected – Bayer, Backhaus, Stilling – and terms set on which subscribers would be entitled to recommend patients: an annual five guineas, for instance, equalled one 'indoor' and two 'outdoor' referrals. No mention was made of sixpenny self-insurers – perhaps that German system was supposed to kick in later, when money was raised, spent on a building, and the grant secured.

Coppin, of course, would organise a concert next month in aid of funds. Backhaus, young Stilling and Dr Weston ('a gay dog') volunteered to ask a 'certain number of ladies' to organise a bazaar.[30] Each committee member had six subscription sheets for filling. Dr Bayer – apparently referring to the practice in New York of charging a head tax on each newcomer to fund an immigrants' hospital that was populated mainly by Irish and Germans – said he had written to authorities in the Hanse towns of Hamburg, Bremen and Lübeck (the embarkation ports), asking them to 'grant to the German Hospital here a similar benefit ... viz., a subscription towards the expense of each future emigrant'.[31]

As for the hospital's name, on the motion of Gilles, seconded by Bayer, members agreed unanimously not to expunge the title under which the movement was started, settling on 'German Hospital, supported by voluntary contributions'.

That name did not last long. Next week, at the end of June, the committee changed it to 'German and British Hospital', still with the suffix – or, in different reports, 'Deutsch und Britisch Hospital', or 'Deutsch British Hospital', while sometimes it was called the German and English (or vice versa) hospital, or often simply still the German hospital.

Funding and Freemasons

This 'less exclusive' name, wrote one journalist, elicited at once a powerful number of new subscriptions, but that seems unlikely: the list of subscribers published for the first time early in July showed not the £2000 avowed in the petition of three weeks earlier, but more like £1660, including O.G.'s land at a value of £500 and the

dodgy-looking entry 'Other German Subscriptions: about £500'.³²
Obviously, the committee had some work before it – especially as
the *Adelaide Times*, never the German hospital's best friend, now
told potential punters the existing hospital, since its last improvements, was healing patients more quickly, leaving beds available.

Time, then, for an all-in-together 'Monster Concert'. Way back
in January, trusting that 'none of that cold reserve which too often
marks the intercourse of Englishmen with foreigners' would mar
this friendly endeavour, the *Mercury* had reported that the 'German
amateur gentlemen' who met to sing at the Hamburgh Hotel would
soon ask British musicians to join them in a 'grand soiree'.³³ The
hospital's 'Monster Concert' (as in the Burra Monster Mine) of
19 July appears to have been the fulfilment, and George Coppin
barked it loud: 'As a combination of talent, nothing approaching
it has ever been attempted in this Province, and right glad are we
to see all jealousies thrown aside in the promotion of a charitable
object, not a single Performer's name, either English or German,
Vocal or Instrumental, of the slightest eminence being wanting …'³⁴
Hundreds were turned from the door, and it was standing room
only inside, but no one complained, all understanding (wrote the
Register) they were there in aid of a 'far higher object'.

The concert contributed around £130 to the coffers, but by late
September, when the *Mercury* published its last list of amounts
actually received from subscribers, the total take in cash was only
£733. Nevertheless the committee – on one of the occasions when
members remembered to turn up for the regular meeting, and at
which as usual a proposed constitution was shelved for future discussion – decided to go ahead with a building. They advertised to
architects from late in the year, seeking plans and estimates for a
hospital with room for 48 beds and whatever other accommodation
could be afforded for £1000 or less.

Meanwhile in December, the Destitute Board, Colonial
Engineer and Colonial Surgeon decided in an unreported meeting
that the £1500 voted by Legislative Council earlier in the year for a
destitute asylum would be better put toward replacing the 60-bed
Adelaide Hospital with a larger one, leaving the present building
free to become the asylum.³⁵

Architect Gloystein, whose drawings had been shown at the

S.T. Gill's drawing of George Coppin in 1849.
Sometimes remembered as the 'father of Australian theatre', Coppin had fingers
in many pies. After the goldrush, Melbourne became his base.
(State Library of South Australia, SLSA: B 341)

Hamburgh Hotel a year before, won the German hospital job early in 1851, his plans chosen from among 13 submissions, all with the architects' names removed in order to allay any suspicion of 'national partiality' (probably the ones written in German were from Germans).[36] The building contract went to John Schirmer, from Hamburg, later well known as landlord of the infamous Tivoli Hotel in Pirie Street, which to suit German custom dared open on Sundays.

Now that South Australia's new but meagre constitution had arrived among some dirty washing, all talk and acrimony shifted to the forthcoming elections, the virtues or otherwise of state aid for religious purposes emerging as a major theme. Dr Bayer and his German coterie supported the old colonist state-aider James Hurtle Fisher in his candidacy for East Adelaide against his radical German-Anglo opponent Francis Dutton, who was soon speaking their language to humbler German crowds. Rev. Dr Backhaus was asked by a long list of mainly Irish names to run for West Adelaide, but he declined – and would anyway have been ineligible as an alien, even a naturalised one, according to a legalism the Advocate-General plucked from somewhere. The city's now two, opposing German newspapers competed in their fury when this was learnt.[37]

With the bubble economy bursting and electoral vituperation in the air, the German hospital's next events in the cause of itself and social unity allowed even the town's establishment conservatives to show their voluntarist bona fides. There were bazaars aplenty in Adelaide, but they were in aid of church-building or denominational purposes, just as 'subscriptions' normally meant funds individuals gave to churches. The German and British Hospital's bazaar was probably the first devoted to a local, secular cause. It was 'long-delayed', taking place over two days in May 1851, but spectacularly successful. Lady Fox Young ran the best-selling stall, exchanging coin for 'wax dolls, cigar cases, Turkish caps, footstools and every … "polite knick-knackery"'.

But the year's most extraordinary social occasion took place the following day.[38] This was the laying of the hospital's foundation stone, accompanied as it was by a grand procession of the united Freemasons – only the second time the town's Lodges had ventured out together, and the first for a non-church affair – and a dinner with the Governor, Judges, the Anglican Bishop and most of Adelaide's notables in attendance.

The *Mercury* hoped 'proper moderation will be observed in the matter of regalia', but it seems the Masons all frocked up for the day. The German brass band and hospital committee led them through the town to the site, throngs cheering (some no doubt jeering) them all the way. Once at the turf, the Provincial Grand Master arranged the implements of the craft, then read the inscription – 'beautifully engrossed on parchment in German and English, also a Latinised copy by the Rev. Dr Backhaus' – which revealed the stone was being laid 'upon the ground generously presented by Osmond Gilles, Esq., on the 24th day of May, 1851, and the era of Masonry 5851, the day on which Her Majesty attained her 32nd year'.

The *Deutsche Liedertafel* performed 'a piece of sacred music', while Brothers Dr Kent and Dr Nash handled the wine and oil parts of the ceremony. Provincial Grand Master Mildred made a speech in praise of Freemasonry replete with a history of mystical unity since the days of the Chaldean seers. The *Liedertafel* sang again, the band played 'God Save the Queen' while men raised their hats, the procession reformed, and all made a beeline for Dyke's Freemasons' Tavern and a banquet 'prepared with an excellence of culinary art inferior, perhaps, only to the secrets possessed by the Freemasons themselves'.

Toasts were drunk, 'accompanied with German instrumental and vocal music', to among others 'the Daughter of a Mason, Her Majesty Queen Victoria', the royal Grand Masters of the Craft in England, Scotland and Ireland, and the province's 'Citizen-Governor' who, notoriously tight-fisted, was yet to make a subscription, but responded with voice aglow:

> The British and Germans are now honourably joining to erect a fabric to humanity – an Hospital whose portals are to be opened, not alone to natives of this or that country, but to all who bear the common relationship of suffering, sickness and pain. Nationalities, creeds, and tests vanish before the unreserved embrace of catholic humanity. (Great applause.)

Speaking frankly, though, he must admit it would be 'satisfactory to me' – that is, to the representative of the Crown – if rather than carry even 'the semblance of a divided nationality', the institution were named for Prince Albert, 'endeared to the Germans on account of the country of his birth, and to the British as the consort of our Queen'.

The *Liedertafel* sang 'Rule Britannia', the Provincial Grand Master said the 'great object of their desire was universal peace, love, and joy to the whole creation', and soon it was the turn of the Lord Bishop. Asked the previous year for a subscription, he had declined on the ground he disapproved of the institution's title, and took a swipe at Osmond Gilles. Tonight he said mysteriously that he 'cared not for names, for this was an age of analysis'. Still and all, Albert embodied the 'union of those two elements – the Angle and the Saxon – that carried England's prosperity and greatness to its present amazing extent. (Hear, hear.)' He believed the brightest features in the English character could be traced back to that earnest conscientious feeling peculiar to the German people: 'Let us then ... hail the addition of that element which was again being infused into the English blood. (Cheers.) Away then with all petty jealousies. Rather than invoke them let it be called the South Australian Hospital! (Hear, hear.)'

Toasted by Charles Cleve, a wealthy Jewish merchant from Frankfurt, the great O.G. rose diminutively amid the usual cheers and laughter to reveal he was quite overpowered to have his health drunk by this meeting of 'colonists from the banks of the Thames, the Shannon, the Clyde, the Rhine, and the Weser'. He agreed 'all trumpery distinctions ... should be laid aside', especially given that English people were of German extraction. The name was a matter for the committee alone to decide, he thought, but if members should choose to honour Victoria's husband, 'no doubt ... their doing so would be followed by substantial proofs of the Royal approbation. (A laugh.) They were far too independent to care for being called either Britons or Germans,' said the Ace of Trumps, 'they were South Australians, and as such they formed the nucleus of a future empire.'

During the dinner Brother Dr Bayer had been called on to eject a Methodist engraver for hissing the Bishop. Now, toasted by J.H. Fisher, he explained his English was not up to a long speech. When the 'idea of a hospital' had occurred to him a few years ago, he said, 'some thought it would be impossible to establish it; others thought it would be ridiculous to make the attempt. He saw by the proceedings of that day that it was neither impossible nor ridiculous. (Cheers.)'

Dead-end road
Late in July Bayer and Gilles gave editor George Stevenson, O.G.'s partner in havoc from early days, a tour of the beginnings of what promised to be 'not merely one of the most correct architectural buildings of our wide-spreading city, but one of the *cheapest*'.[39] Much cheaper, certainly, than the £14,907, 300-bed new Adelaide Hospital edifice sketched by the Colonial Engineer next month in his report to the Colonial Secretary.

It was not, however, the other fantastic hospital that did the German one in. A second successful concert was held in September, but by this time the town's optimism had burst with its credit economy, and O.G.'s mercantile mates, including Kronk, Noltenius and even Coppin the great, were in prison for debt, being sued for

A woodcut of the proposed hospital, published in the *Mercury* on 26 July 1851.
The building was to have two storeys and twelve rooms, 'plus the requisite offices'.
Only the central portion was built, it seems.

wages, or looking for salvation of insolvency. Too much rain had followed drought, and most mines turned out 'worthless holes'; there was even anxiety about the food supply.

The new, partly elected Legislative Council had proved no great friend of the city's Germans. It rejected Francis Dutton's attempt to have a German interpreter put on the public payroll, and in his other attempts to right injustices accused him of 'playing on the German fiddle'.[40] According to reports, disgusted Germans began leaving the colony forthwith. Adelaide was never so German again – and the possibility of a unique kind of South Australianness went up in smoke.

Late in November, with the German and British Hospital building near completion at a contract price of just £1170, and about a similar sum having been raised, John Baker convinced the Legislative Council to include a grant of £1000 in next year's budget. But fabulous news was coming of gold across the border. Men generally, British and German, began quitting Adelaide in droves.

With revenue diminishing, the Legislative Council would need to cut expenditure. Dutton, whose election Dr Bayer and friends had opposed, thought the grant to the German hospital should be held over in favour of one to a proposed hospital at Port Adelaide, but Baker and others kept the grant on the estimates. The Germans,

Baker said, 'had contributed very largely toward the expense of erecting the German Hospital, or at any rate they would have done if they had been able. (Laughter.) They had completed their part of the bargain and the Government were bound to complete theirs.'[41] The quiet plans for a vast new government hospital – never yet presented to the Legislative Council – were put aside for better days.

The German hospital, too, joined the sick list, and it never recovered. Little was heard of it in the next few years: as men returned and new immigrants (especially English ones) arrived, the building seems to have just stood there in Carrington Street, as promise or reproach. A petition was got up in 1855 asking the Governor to make sure it was opened and put to proper use – later that year the government hired it as a depot for excess-to-needs Irish servant girls. The grant was finally paid over in 1856, new trustees having been found for those who had left the colony, just when a new, large, replacement Adelaide Hospital opened at last.

Meetings of German and British Hospital committees and supporters were reported late in 1858 and again in 1859, with jejune attempts made to open the institution as a user-pays hospital or 'sanitarium' (and no one paying much attention to Dr Bayer's – and new secretary Ulrich Hübbe's – suggestion they should still consider a 'quarterly subscription' model). A source claims it once even took in a patient.[42] By 1862, however, the building was an Anglican home for orphan girls. These days the site – town acre 433 – is forested by townhouses.

Neither the Angas family nor Old Lutherans subscribed more than a pittance to the German hospital, but during the 1850s Angas money and a skilful Old Lutheran family established a hospital in the Barossa Valley that enjoyed a long, successful career. This fee-paying hospital went by the euphonious name of Willows Hospital, and it offered services shunned by regular medicos such as Dr Bayer, in particular 'bone-setting' rather than surgery.

From 1868 attempts were made to turn the Adelaide Hospital into more of a subscriber-based institution, but the first hospital in the city that really captured the voluntary imagination was the Children's Hospital, which opened in 1879. Unlike with the German hospital, women were prime movers from the start, and like the Willows Hospital it enjoyed also the advantage of medical difference, offering

Emmeline Bayer, Dr Bayer's granddaughter, shows her colours in 1887.
(State Library of South Australia. SLSA: B7723/23)

homoeopathic as well as regular medical treatment at a time when Adelaide Hospital doctors had threatened to resign if homoeopathy was allowed in their wards. Money for the Children's Hospital came from the Angas family and other wealthy dissenters in medical as well as religious matters. In a typically Adelaide compromise, and a most unusual one, it was decided three of the doctors – all legally qualified – would be homoeopaths and three 'allopathic' (orthodox) practitioners. Homoeopathy owed its origins early in the century to a German doctor, Samuel Hahnemann.

When Dr Bayer expired on the job in 1867 aged around 50, the *Register* doubted 'if the death of any man amongst us would excite emotions of more universal regret'. The Adelaide Photographic Company, 'only possessors of negatives of Dr Bayer', warned against fake images of this man who was so 'true and real himself', Rev. Canon Russell told an Anglican congregation, that 'there sometimes broke from him a strong invective against things which he saw in religious men'. But 'Ah! how kind he was', continued Canon

Russell as he risked confusing his friend the 'Good Physician' with an even better-known healer.[43]

Not everyone had been so convinced, of course. The *After-glow Memories* of an author writing as 'An Anglo-Australian', daughter of one of Bayer's celebrity partners, told her he was

> an exceedingly shrewd, clever man, but in medical knowledge I have a strong impression that he lacked the experience of my father ... It used to be said of him that in all serious cases he would say .... 'He vill die' or 'she vill die', and those who were not his friends declared that the reason ... was, that he would put himself in a good position whatever occurred.[44]

The *Süd-Australische Zeitung* ran no obituary of its own, preferring to translate the *Register*'s adoring one of 'our countryman and friend', particularly as its praise for Dr Bayer as a connecting link between the English and Germans suggested him worthy of 'the highest honours, municipal or legislative, which the colony can offer'. The German paper added an account of Bayer's finale. He was writing a prescription for an Englishman when, his spirit already assailed, he swapped to German and demanded, as a right of Germans not privilege, there should be a German member of the Destitute Board. Then he fell unconscious and never spoke again.

Partly truth and partly fiction, no doubt. That seems to be the story of Dr Bayer's life, and of the German hospital that never was.

Notes

1. *South Australian Register*, 14 June 1848 (hereafter cited as *Register*).
2. *Register*, 3 January 1850.
3. ibid., 16 August 1848.
4. *Deutsche Post für die Australischen Colonien*, 7 February 1850. (That is, three days after the event. No copies of earlier weeks' issues are available. Correspondents lamented that notice was given out too late.)
5. Forty-odd German names are listed first in subscriber lists published in various papers from July 1850. I have assumed these were the men at the meeting, and used naturalisation records and other sources to establish their occupations and other details.
6. *Adelaide Observer*, 29 April 1848 (hereafter cited as *Observer*).
7. *Mercury and South Australian Sporting Chronicle*, 16 February 1850 (hereafter cited as *Mercury*).
8. *Register*, 24 March 1847; 17 August 1867.

9 Report of Select Committee on Management of Adelaide Hospital, *South Australian Parliamentary Papers* 1866–67, no. 150 (hereafter *SAPP*). In October 1847 Dr Bayer was registered by the Medical Board as an MD of Erlangen, 1842.
10 *Mercury*, 8 June 1850.
11 *Register*, 11 February 1850.
12 *Deutsche Post,* 14 February 1850.
13 *Mercury*, 23 February 1850; *Register*, 25 February 1850. (The quotes from the meeting are from these reports. The tipsy *Mercury*, but not the teetotalling *Register*, revealed that the first non-German subscription was ten guineas from the brewer E.J.F. Crawford, whose beer you drank at the Hamburgh and many city hotels.)
14 *Register*, 26 January 1850.
15 Kappler's letter published in *Zernicka* (in Saxony) 16 November 1851, translated copy held at the Lutheran Archives in Adelaide.
16 Renate Vollmer, *Auswanderungspolitik und soziale Frage im 19. Jahrhundert: staatlich geförderte Auswanderung aus der Berghauptmannschaft Clausthal nach Südaustralien, Nord- und Südamerika 1848–1854*, Peter Lang, Frankfurt, 1995, p. 234. In 1847 Dr Bayer's ship – likely the doctor himself – brought the document appointing Christian Ludwig Meyer (partner with the Noltenius brothers) consul for the Kingdom of Hanover, an appointment needed to facilitate the venture.
17 *Observer*, 20 October 1850, 2 November 1850. Jansen advised his countrymen to treat the Rev. John Baptist Austin's words as 'the contemptible yelping of a village cur'.
18 Both Boehme and 'Gamma' wrote that the first (4 February) meeting was held to consider not just the necessity but the 'propriety' of erecting a German hospital in Adelaide.
19 *Süd-Australische Zeitung*, 2 May 1850. This paper commenced in April thanks to 'some forty of our most wealthy' Germans, with Bayer (president), Backhaus, Henry Noltenius and Kronk named as directors, but its editors – Gustav Dröge, Carl Mücke and Otto Schomburgk, who had quit the *Deutsche Post* in a spat over political censorship – were men of independent hue. During 1850 German organisations mushroomed in Adelaide, including, besides those mentioned, an immigration society that operated a labour exchange and real estate agency, a commercial company and a school.
20 *Mercury*, 8 June 1850.
21 Letter from Osmond Gilles to John Leake, 2 September 1833, copy held by State Library of South Australia.
22 The fullest reports are in the *Register* and *Adelaide Times,* 12 June 1850 – each reproduces the petition. Reports vary, as usual, on who said what.
23 *SAPP* 1866–67, no. 150.
24 *Mercury*, 15 June 1850.

25 Vollmer, *Auswanderungspolitik*, p. 225.
26 Information on the Jacob Hagens from *Biographisch–Bibliographisches Kirchenlexicon*: www.bautz.de/bbkl/. One Jacob Hagen was interpreter for Zinzendorf when he met with English Quakers.
27 *Adelaide Times*, 27 November 1851.
28 *SAPP*, 1866–67, no. 150.
29 *Mercury*, 22 June 1850.
30 When the Nuns of the Ladies Committee in Calcutta asked Backhaus to win them six nuns from Ireland, he returned with a round dozen. John Hussey, *Henry Backhaus, Doctor of Divinity*, St Kilian's Press, Bendigo, 1982, pp. 32–33.
31 *Adelaide Times*, 1 July 1850; *South Australian*, 2 July 1850; *Deutsche Post*, 9 July 1850. The *Mercury*'s report is missing from the existing copy.
32 The subscription lists were published in various newspapers – apparently only English-language ones – from 4 July 1850.
33 *Mercury*, 5 January 1850.
34 ibid., 13 July 1850.
35 Ian L.D. Forbes, *From Colonial Surgeon to Health Commission: The government provision of health services in South Australia 1836–1995*, Openbook, Adelaide, 1996, p. 53.
36 *Mercury*, 18 January 1851.
37 *Adelaide Deutsche Zeitung*, 2 April 1851; *Süd-Australische Zeitung*, 11 April 1851.
38 The fullest reports are in the *Register* and *Adelaide Times*, 26 May 1851 – this account is drawn from these and others. George Coppin, especially, was a prominent Freemason. Probably the idea was his.
39 *South Australian Gazette and Mining Journal*, 26 July 1851.
40 *Register*, 27 August 1851.
41 ibid., 30 December 1851.
42 Charles R.J. Glover, *A History of Freemasonry in South Australia*, Freemason's Hall, Adelaide, 1916, p. 30.
43 Bayer died on 15 August 1867. Meetings thought a hospital or ward should be built in his honour (no one mentioned reviving the German hospital) but funds raised were disappointing, and eventually a committee commisioned the English sculptor Thomas Woolner to create a bust – said in reports to be the first such memorial to a South Australian. It dwells now in the Art Gallery of South Australia's collection.
44 Agnes Grant Hay, *After-glow memories, by Anglo-Australian*, Methuen, London, 1905, p. 216.

With heartfelt thanks to Peter Monteath for his heroic help and patience.

Richard Schomburgk
Explorer, natural scientist and Botanic Garden director

Pauline Payne

Popular accounts of South Australian history, such as those to be found in tourist literature, frequently present a story of German migrants in colonial times coming to South Australia as a result of religious persecution, but rarely is there any mention of that very different group of emigrants from the Germanic states who came from a professional background or were skilled tradesmen. Such a group is exemplified by the passengers who arrived on *Princess Louise* in August 1849.

The three-masted barque *Princess Louise* had been chartered by the Berlin-based South Australian Colonisation Society and brought to South Australia a remarkable group of passengers. The group included people with professional and business training, artists, musicians and skilled craftsmen such as cabinetmakers. Many on board had become disillusioned with the outcome of political reforms promised after the uprisings of 1848. The leaders included Dr Carl Mücke (or Muecke, as he became known in South Australia), an educationist and pastor, and Otto and Richard Schomburgk. The younger Schomburgk brother, Richard, had trained as a gardener in Saxony. From 1840 to 1844 he was a member of an expedition of exploration to British Guiana, and he had survived the expedition and returned to Berlin. Richard Schomburgk's story provides a case study to illustrate the significant contribution in the field of science and technology made to South Australia by people from the Germanic states. His career also demonstrates the important role that exploration could provide in enabling a young man of modest means to enter a career in science in the nineteenth century.

Beginning a career in science

Richard Schomburgk was born on 5 October 1811 at Freyburg on the Unstrut River in Saxony. Baptised as Moritz Richard, he seems to have used Richard as his first name his entire adult life. Richard's father, an assistant Lutheran pastor in Freyburg, about 50 kilometres from Leipzig, was not a wealthy man, but the family had a tradition of civic and legal service. The eldest son Robert went into a family business in Leipzig, the second son Otto was sent to university in Halle, and Richard, as the third son, was apprenticed as a gardener in Merseburg. The German gardening apprenticeship was well regarded in England and continental Europe in those times. During the initial three-and-a-half-year period of the apprenticeship the young men were taught some basic botany and chemistry, and practical skills such as grafting and the care of hot-house plants. One of the great strengths of the system was that they were then expected to spend a further three years travelling and working in different states or regions.

Between 1831 and 1834 Richard undertook military service in the Prussian Royal Guard, following which he worked in Berlin. While in Berlin an extraordinary career opportunity arose for the young man. The eldest Schomburgk brother, Robert, had gone to the United States as part of his commercial career. Travelling on to the West Indies, where he had witnessed the havoc caused by shipwrecks and, aware of the need for better nautical maps, he began surveying and mapping at his own expense. His charts brought him to the notice of both the Royal Geographical Society and the British Admiralty, with the former commissioning him to carry out an expedition of exploration to British Guiana during the years 1835–39. When the British Government asked him to embark on a second expedition to British Guiana, the great German scientist Alexander von Humboldt used his influence at the Prussian court to enable Richard to accompany the expedition as an historian on behalf of the Prussian Government and to collect natural history specimens for institutions in Berlin.

An opportunity such as this enabled a young man of moderate means to gain an entrée into a career in science. Yet it posed considerable threats. Before the Boundary Expedition, as it was called, had left Georgetown in British Guiana, Richard contracted

Louis Tannert's portrait of Richard Schomburgk with his medals. An immigrant from Germany, Tannert became the first curator of the National Gallery of South Australia in 1882. (Botanic Gardens of Adelaide)

yellow fever but was one of the few Europeans there to survive the black-vomit stage of the illness. There were other hazards to come: malaria, insect pests, accidental injuries and limited food supplies and, critically for his later career, he had to adapt to challenging new conditions. Since the expedition was greatly dependent on the help of the local Amerindian tribes for logistical support such as supplies and help with river transport, he learned to work with people of a very different culture from his own.

For all the challenges, he was entranced by the tropical flora, this love of tropical vegetation remaining with him throughout his life. Although his collection of plants and animals suffered considerable damage during the expedition and on the return voyage to Europe, many items did survive. Returning to Berlin in 1844 after four gruelling expedition years, Richard began his three-volume *Reisen in Britisch-Guiana*, which was published in 1847–48.[1] At the time he was living with the second oldest brother Otto. Humboldt had helped to organise the release of Otto from the citadel in Madgeburg, where he had been imprisoned in 1837 as a 'demagogue' and a member of a *Burschenschaft*, a progressive student fraternity. After the revolutionary uprising of 1848, the brothers were 'black sheep', as Richard wrote in later years. With Dr C.W. Muecke, the school teacher G. Listemann and others, the brothers formed a South Australian Colonisation Society, originally the Berlin Emigration Society. The group had first planned to go to the Swan River settlement in Western Australia but apparently decided that economic conditions were more promising in South Australia.

The Schomburgk brothers, along with a number of other passengers on the *Princess Louise*, chose land near Gawler, forming a settlement they called Buchsfelde, after the famous German geologist, Leopold von Buch, a wealthy friend of Alexander von Humboldt, who had given the brothers enough money to fund building a house. Here the brothers had a farm of about 63 acres with cereal crops and cattle, gradually developing an orchard and vineyard. Carl Muecke became pastor of the Tabor Lutheran Church at Tanunda and for 40 years was involved with the German press as newspaper journalist, editor and proprietor. He was closely associated with another of the German intellectuals, M.P.F. (Friedrich) Basedow; all three families were connected by marriage. Following the death of his first wife, Muecke married Schomburgk's sister Linna, who, along with the younger Schomburgk brother, Julius, had come to South Australia in 1851. Julius (1819–93) had trained as a goldsmith and silversmith. German silversmiths were renowned for their work in colonial Australia, and Julius was one of the finest silversmiths in Australia in his time.[2]

Richard and Otto were only four miles from Gawler and actively involved in a number of community groups. They were regarded as men of substance and authority in the district and were appointed to the local magistracy. Otto acted as local obstetrician and veterinarian and pastor; he wrote for the German newspaper and became Master of the Lodge of Fidelity. Both brothers became involved in local government. The first meeting of the Muddla Wirra Council was held in Otto Schomburgk's home, and Otto subsequently became chairman of this council.

Richard collected zoological specimens during these years and carried out meteorological work with Otto. The brothers had been

Portrait of Richard Schomburgk's brother Otto. (Schomburgk family)

given meteorological instruments by colleagues in Berlin and had what they described as the first meteorological station in South Australia, keeping a wider range of records than those kept at West Terrace.[3] They were active members of the Gawler Institute, and in around 1860 Richard became curator of the small museum established under the auspices of the institute. The Schomburgks had as a neighbour their fellow *Princess Louise* passenger, Marianne Kreusler, a keen entomologist.

Otto lived to see the first election of the South Australian Parliament in March 1857, under what was at the time one of the most democratic constitutions in the world. With Otto's death later that year, Richard became more prominent in local affairs, increasingly experienced in the customs of Anglo-Australian society. However, he now ran the farm single-handed and must have realised that the Buchsfelde farm life could provide only limited opportunities for the children of the two families. In 1865 the position of Director of Adelaide Botanic Garden was advertised, following the death of the founding director, George William Francis (1800–65). There had been earlier attempts to establish a botanic garden, but the selection of the site on which the present botanic garden is located was finalised in 1855, and Adelaide Botanic Garden opened its gates to the public in 1857.[4]

The 'diplomatic gardener' at Adelaide Botanic Garden

Richard Schomburgk was in a strong position when he took up the position of Director of the Adelaide Botanic Garden at the age of 54 years. He had an international reputation from his publication of *Reisen in Britisch-Guiana*; moreover, he had experience of agriculture, horticulture and viticulture under South Australian conditions, and he had worked with community organisations, such as civic and church groups. The proposals that he put to his Board soon after his appointment demonstrated the balanced approach that was to be his trademark.

He was suggesting re-arrangement of the Herbarium, the provision of better labels and a system garden. These were all part of the scientific and educational role of the Botanic Garden, as was the development of an experimental garden for 'medicinal, industrial and fodder plants'. Plans for better animal houses would appeal to family groups. Keen gardeners would appreciate his new rose garden, the new heating system for glasshouses, an 'aquarium' for *Nymphaeaceae* and other aquatic plants, and the development of an orchid house for a valuable and steadily increasing orchid collection. His first recorded outward letter was to the City Corporation to purchase manure from the city streets, indicating a very practical approach and a certain lack of self-consciousness.[5]

The Adelaide Botanic Garden site was relatively flat. It did not have the natural advantages of the botanic garden in Sydney with its harbour views, of Hobart with the Derwent River and hillside backdrop, or of Melbourne, a large site adjoining the Yarra River. With a limited area, he needed to break the site up into smaller areas. One way of achieving this was to plant avenues of trees, very much in the gardening tradition of his earlier years in Prussia. The most striking of the avenues was that of the Moreton Bay figs planted in 1866, soon after his arrival. Here he was combining indigenous Australian trees with a European design tradition that went back for centuries. Another striking avenue of *Sterculia* or Kurrajong has not survived, but that of *Araucaria* species, such as Norfolk Island pines, remains today.

Photo taken from the Palm House showing one of the statues imported from Berlin and the Adelaide Hospital to the right. (The author)

Although some plants originated from commercial nurserymen, as was the case with the Moreton Bay fig trees, it was the practice of botanic garden directors to establish an exchange system with kindred organisations in order to add to their collection. It might be assumed that the exchange system for a British colonial botanic garden would centre on the Royal Botanic Gardens at Kew in England. While it is true that Schomburgk received a large amount of plant material from Kew and the British Empire network, the records show that he also received a significant amount of material from two non-British sources. One was Bogor or Buitenzorg botanic garden in Java, where there was great interest in both utilitarian and ornamental plants, and a strong contingent of scientific staff, and the other was St Petersburg in Russia. Schomburgk's exchanges with St Petersburg were with his German compatriot Dr E.L. Regel, influential in the world of botany and someone whose worldwide network of contacts complemented those of Schomburgk.[6]

Of the Australasian network, the Botanic Garden in Sydney was an important source of exchanges, and Schomburgk greatly valued his friendship with its director Charles Moore. Contact with the Royal Botanic Garden in Melbourne fluctuated over the years. It began well when Schomburgk visited his compatriot Dr Ferdinand von Mueller. Gifts from Mueller included what was then known as *Pinus insignis*, now *Pinus radiata*, which Mueller planted as an avenue tree, and which Schomburgk promoted as being suitable for local conditions. This species was to become a very important source of softwood timber for South Australia.

Avenues of trees provided a valuable landscape design feature, as did statues, several of which were imported from Berlin. The use of statues in a garden was something with which Schomburgk was very familiar from his German training. Statuary helped provide the atmosphere of a more mature garden while trees and shrubs were growing, and Schomburgk believed they helped cultivate 'public taste for the fine arts'. The statues were complemented by parterre planting and ribbon borders, where hard-edged flower beds were planted in a geometric pattern. Annual flower seedlings were used to make elaborate patterns, along with hardy perennials such as succulents and pelargoniums, both of which grew readily under South Australian conditions and were very suitable for home gardens. This kind of display was popular in Victorian times, but preparation was labour-intensive, and not all nineteenth-century botanic garden directors were prepared to devote the resources needed for such an enterprise. Sir Joseph Hooker when director of the Royal Botanic Gardens at Kew is known to have resented the pressure to provide ornamental displays and ornamental features, arguing that it was not appropriate for a scientific institution to devote significant resources to such activities, a view shared by Ferdinand von Mueller in Melbourne.[7]

Schomburgk was more pragmatic. His early training, practical rather than academic, taught him how to work for a client. Having the ability to balance the different roles of the Botanic Garden, to cope with the demands of the Board and local politicians and to communicate with the public were crucial areas in which he would shine. Adelaide Botanic Garden was from the very beginning to be a 'people's garden'.

One display that was immensely popular with visitors was provided by the new rosary. There was an extensive collection of roses in Potsdam where Schomburgk had worked, but the flowering season in Adelaide was longer than that in Europe, and varieties that had to be grown in glasshouses in Germany could be grown outdoors in the favourable South Australian conditions. The design of the new rosary featured gravelled walks, an important feature for women visitors who had to manage their long skirts as they walked around the garden paths.

Although roses enjoyed great popularity, it was nothing compared with that of the water lily then known as the *Victoria regia*, now *Victoria amazonica,* and closely associated with the Schomburgks. Robert and Richard had seen it growing in British Guiana, and Robert had taken seed back to Britain after his first Guiana expedition. It took until 1849 for people in England to have success in growing the Victoria, but the event brought immense public interest. Early in 1868 Richard Schomburgk and his Board developed plans to grow the Victoria in Adelaide. This would require a special glasshouse, and Schomburgk admitted that the venture was quite risky, as some members of the government considered it an extravagance.[8] He had no practical experience of propagating the water lily, which had not been grown in Europe before he left. However, he could argue that his existing glasshouses were already overcrowded, threatening the safety of their prestigious and ever-increasing collection of tropical plants; the new one would help to accommodate the collection of orchids and other species. Heating equipment was provided by a local firm in Rundle Street owned by Hakan Linde, a Swedish coppersmith.

Risky the venture might have been, but it proved a huge success. Excitement about the flowering of the Victoria saw a proliferation of newspaper accounts, with hour-by-hour descriptions of the opening of the flower buds. In 1868 people would go down to the Victoria House during their lunch breaks in the way that cricket enthusiasts went to the Adelaide Oval to see Bradman bat in the 1930s. Nearly 6000 visitors came one Sunday. Attendances grew to 300,000 for the year, a remarkable figure, given that the 1866 census showed a population of 163,000 for the whole of South Australia. The growing of a Victoria lily was a matter of prestige – rivalry among botanical institutions in Britain and the Continent flourished at this time – and the success in Adelaide helped to build the prestige of Adelaide Botanic Garden and with it Schomburgk's own reputation.[9]

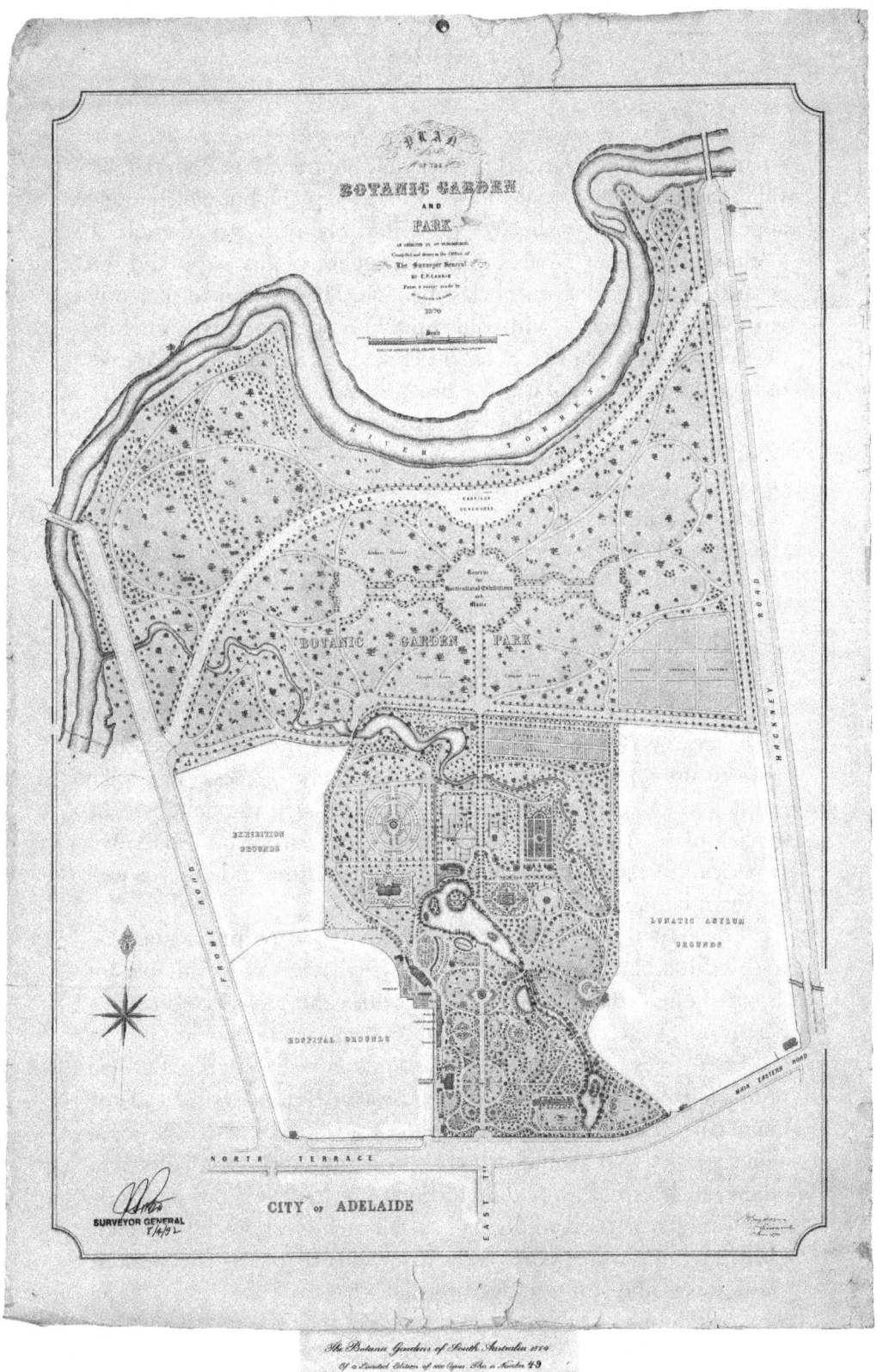

Plan of the Botanic Garden & Park as designed by Dr Schomburgk, Office of the Surveyor General 1874 (facsimile 1986). (State Library of South Australia)

Popular success in hand, the Director could afford to give some attention to a long-planned project that he knew had considerable value from an educational and scientific viewpoint, but which might appear a little dull to the average visitor. His plan was to establish a 'class ground' or 'system ground', where plants were laid out according to their botanical classification. He had waited patiently, working on projects with more public appeal and, meanwhile, developing avenues of trees on either side, using Australian species of brush box, jarrah, marri and black kurrajong.

With such plantings it was a matter of trial and error to see what would thrive and what would not. A number of native trees and shrubs grew well at first but might only survive for 10 years. Experiments with lawn grasses were valuable, not only for the grassed areas of the botanic gardens but also for domestic and civic gardens, with couch and buffalo grass surviving the long, hot Adelaide summers. For example, Schomburgk reported that three acres (1.2 ha) of couch grass planted in 1871–72 withstood what he described as 'the scorching heat of the summer months'. When an extra 84 acres were made available to the Botanic Gardens for what became Botanic Park, the plantings in 1873–74 provided an opportunity for significant trials of trees. Some of these trees, such as fine old Moreton Bay figs, have survived to the present day. The species planted covered a wide variety of European and North American forest trees such as ash, oak, birch, lime and pine, as well as Australian native trees.

Trees such as conifers and eucalypts were propagated in the Botanic Garden nursery so that they would be available for distribution to civic bodies, local authorities and private landowners. Schomburgk actively promoted trees that would be suitable as specimen trees and for avenue planting, as well as trees that had utilitarian or commercial use. As trees in Botanic Park and the main part of Adelaide Botanic Garden grew, visitors could learn about species that would grow well on the Adelaide Plains, and others, such as oak, lime, birch, horse-chestnut, maples or beech, which might be tried in higher rainfall areas such as the Adelaide Hills. An important part of the educational role of the Botanic Garden was and still is to demonstrate what could be grown under local conditions.[10]

Nevertheless, while trees in Botanic Park were chosen with a view to their surviving the Adelaide Plains climate, many of the rapidly expanding collection of plants needed glasshouse conditions. In 1873 Schomburgk once more used the arguments adopted when he was campaigning for the Victoria House. Their fine collection of tropical plants, 'undoubtedly the most numerous and valuable collection in the Southern Hemisphere', was at risk because of over-crowding. They needed a new glasshouse, and he had heard 'very favourable reports of a palm house built of iron in Bremen which is considered one of the finest structures of its kind in Germany, for its tasteful and elegant proportions and general suitableness'.[11] This palm house, owned by a man named Rothermundt, had been designed by the architect Gustav Runge. It was estimated that such a palm house would cost about £1400, necessitating a special government grant. With the additional costs of preparing the raised terrace, the flight of steps and statuary, the total cost was £3800. The 1870s was a very prosperous decade; South Australia had become the granary for Australia, as farms extended to the mid-north region and beyond. Had these been times of economic recession, such as the 1890s, such a proposal might have been doomed to failure, but in 1874 Schomburgk and the Board received approval for the project, and an order was placed with the manufacturer, Johann Höper in Bremen.

The prefabricated iron and glass structure arrived in September 1875, with the Palm House opening in January 1877. Its design was sophisticated and in many ways ahead of its time, combining both wrought and cast iron. Runge used 'curtain walls' similar to glass cladding in modern town blocks and incorporated good ventilation techniques. In the previous 30 years there had been improved production techniques for iron and glass and pioneering work in design, including the technical virtuosity of Joseph Paxton's 1851 Crystal Palace. In Germany the popularity of glasshouses saw new structures being built after the 1860s in the botanic gardens of Berlin, Karlsruhe, Schönbrunn, Strasbourg and Würzburg. The size of Adelaide's Palm House was on a par with those in European cities of the day, and today the old Palm House in Adelaide Botanic Garden is the finest Victorian glasshouse remaining in Australia and appears to be the only remaining example in the world of this type of German cast- and wrought-iron conservatory architecture of its period,[12] many nineteenth-century glasshouses having been destroyed by fire or demolished during the twentieth century.

Schomburgk could now turn to his next major project, plans for a museum of economic botany. The name might seem a little puzzling to many people today, but in the nineteenth century a museum of economic botany could provide an important adjunct to the scientific and educational role of a botanic garden. The aim was to help people understand how plant products were used in daily life, and the Adelaide Botanic Garden already housed a wood pavilion, a small museum containing wood specimens. As early as 1870 the Director proposed that a new museum be constructed, 'a kind of technical one', where commercial and economic plants could be exhibited both in their raw state and in various stages of manufacture. His proposal was accepted, and the Museum of Economic Botany was finally built in 1880–81.

Displays demonstrated how plant products were used as foodstuffs and medicines, and in technology and construction. This was the period before the petrochemical era, and a wide variety of plant products were used for such items as clothes, dyes, glues, resins, storage containers, tools, musical instruments and toys. The toxicological collections included the arrow poison (curare) that Schomburgk had collected on the British Guiana expedition. Paul Foelsche, head of police in the Northern Territory, provided plants used by Aboriginal people near Darwin for medicines, fruit and drink; this was at a time when ethnological displays at the South Australian Museum were very limited. The Museum of Economic Botany also became the home of Schomburgk's growing herbarium collection. Here plant specimens, dried and pressed, were stored between sheets of papers. Just as there was a worldwide exchange system for live plant specimens, botanists from around the world also exchanged dried botanical specimens to build up their collections.

Interested as he was in the herbarium, Schomburgk was by no means a taxonomic botanist of the calibre of von Mueller in Melbourne. His interests and skills lay more in the field of applied botany – horticulture, agriculture and forestry – than in collection and classification of botanical specimens. And in a settler society such concerns made sense to the local citizens. This was a society that supported utilitarian science.

Schomburgk's concern with forestry matters saw him giving papers to the local Philosophical Society (later the Royal Society) on the topic. The society, established in 1853, provided a place where those interested in scientific matters could meet regularly, discuss issues of common interest and share journal articles. In time they met at the Institute Building on North Terrace, built in 1860. Schomburgk and his friends from the Germanic states were familiar with good forestry practice and forestry training, traditions that went back centuries. South Australia had limited resources of timber suitable for building construction, a further problem being the indiscriminate clearing by settlers, which had produced significant destruction of these limited resources. Schomburgk's concern with the destruction of native forests was shared by his German compatriots F.E.H.W. Krichauff and M.P.F. Basedow, both members of parliament. Krichauff proposed in the South Australian Parliament that a survey be carried out to assess existing stands of timber and to determine ways that timber resources could be preserved. Recommendations were also sought about the potential for planting forest trees. This was followed in 1873 by an *Act to Encourage the Planting of Forest Trees*. In 1875 the South Australian Parliament took the further step of establishing a board to protect and regenerate native vegetation and to establish commercial forests. When the first Forest Board was set up in 1875, Schomburgk was one of its members. South Australia's State Forest Service can be said to have been established in 1875, because the legislation provided for a properly staffed forest service. It was one of the first in the British Empire and the first of its kind in Australia. Forest tree nurseries and plantations were established, and trees were distributed to landowners.

Adelaide provided a cultural milieu that also produced an agricultural college at Roseworthy in 1882.[13] Like the *Forestry Act*, it was the first of its kind in Australia, and in both cases the German-born settlers played a significant role, with Basedow actively promoting its establishment. Meanwhile Carl Muecke continued to support the principles and practice of a scientific approach to agriculture through talks and newspaper articles.

Until the establishment of the Roseworthy Agricultural College, the Botanic Garden provided the main institution where crop research was carried out. Australia is a continent remarkable for the fact that virtually all crop plants, except for a few species such as macadamia nuts and quandongs, are introduced plants. Crop plants such as wheat species, vegetables and fruit trees were brought to this country with the very first European settlers. Like Francis before him, and like his colleagues in other Australian botanic gardens of the colonial era, Schomburgk had sections of the Botanic Garden devoted to utilitarian plant species used for food, beverages and medicinal purposes.

As with the decorative plants, material was obtained from sources from around the world, from botanic gardens and agricultural societies, acclimatisation societies, commercial firms and from private individuals. The growing network of agricultural colleges and agricultural stations in the United States played its part, and, as noted above, Schomburgk also had significant exchanges with his Dutch colleagues at Bogor in Java and with Dr E.L. Regel at St Petersburg in Russia. Regel had his own network of exchanges, some of which were in Central Asia, South America and the Far East, which complemented Schomburgk's contacts in the British Empire and Java. Part of Schomburgk's contribution to the Botanic Gardens' development and to his vital role in plant introduction in Australia was that he brought together plants and ideas, not only from British sources but from many other parts of the globe.

While it is true that communications between South Australia and other continents were slow by contemporary standards, there was a lively exchange of information and plant material, and a very pragmatic approach was taken to the sourcing of material. On one occasion Schomburgk contacted a German botanical colleague, Professor R.A. Phillipi in Santiago in Chile, to try to source an elusive Falklands Island pasture grass, and Phillipi in turn contacted colleagues in Central Europe on Schomburgk's behalf. Many South Australian residents were energetic in writing to newspapers with snippets of information about possible crop plants, also using Schomburgk as a central contact point for exchange of plant material, information and advice.

There is no reason to think that Richard Schomburgk was disadvantaged by being of German upbringing and training. In the Victorian era, reformers looked to Germany and France for ideas about the teaching of science and technology. By the mid-nineteenth century, Germany, with its well-equipped laboratories and research institutes, was leading the world in scientific education, while important works of German scientific scholarship were being translated into English. In a social and cultural context, many of those who, like Schomburgk were from a professional or business background, joined what we might term 'mainstream organisations' such as churches, lodges, and groups with an intellectual or scholarly orientation. The Schomburgk family joined the congregation of the Church of England church of St Paul's in Pulteney Street, the son, Otto, attended the leading Church of England school, the Collegiate School of St Peter's, and Richard Schomburgk was a Masonic Lodge member.

In the period 1884–90, the elderly Schomburgk continued to work in the Botanic Garden, spending a considerable amount of time in the Herbarium. After his wife Pauline died in 1879, his younger brother, the silversmith Julius, lived with him in the Director's residence at the Botanic Garden. His son Otto began a successful career in the public service, becoming Sheriff and Comptroller of Prisons, and his surviving four daughters married professional men. Typhoid fever claimed the life of one of his daughters; he survived typhoid fever himself.

Although the entrance gates on North Terrace were added during this period, no major new projects were undertaken. By now Roseworthy College was established and the Forestry Board operational, so that some tasks previously undertaken by the Botanic Garden could now be performed by specialist institutions. With the establishment of the Zoological Gardens in 1883, the animals and birds formerly housed in the Botanic Garden were transferred to their new home nearer the River Torrens. Although some botanic gardens in the world, such as that in Frankfurt, have a zoological collection, the trend was to have a separate organisation.

The 1880s were significantly less prosperous years than the 1870s. Schomburgk's successor was also a German, who went by the name of Maurice (Waldemar) William Holtze (1840–1923). A native of Hanover and graduate in botany of the Imperial Gardens in St Petersburg, Holtze would begin his term of office in a period of economic recession and in time would reduce the scope of scientific work at the Botanic Garden significantly. Lucky to have been appointed at a time when the South Australian economy was about to expand dramatically, Schomburgk was also fortunate that his training and experience enabled him to take advantage of the opportunities available. In his fifties when he was appointed, he had the advantage of life experience that included learning to deal with people from very different backgrounds from his own, and confronting the challenges of farming and gardening under Australian conditions. He was also familiar with the institutions and customs of Anglo-Australian society, enabling him to work cooperatively with colleagues.

Schomburgk's practical approach to problem-solving suited the colonial setting, where utilitarian science was favoured – the approach of the practical person was respected. He was prepared to pace his program development to fit in with the realities of funding exigencies and community expectations. He made sustained efforts to communicate his ideas – through informative annual reports and through papers to professional and business organisations. Schomburgk was Director at a time when people from all walks of life shared his enthusiasm for the introduction of new plants to South Australia, becoming, as a consequence of his worldwide network of contacts, one of the most notable figures in the field of utilitarian and ornamental plant introduction in Australia. Awards from the Grand Duchy of Hesse, the King of Italy and the King of Prussia acknowledged his scientific research. Interested in the broader economic aspects of new crops and the need for crop diversification, he was also concerned with issues that we would today regard as environmental issues, such as deforestation, problems of noxious weeds and sanitation.

Schomburgk was rewarded with political and community support. The Botanic Gardens became known as 'Dr Schomburgk's Gardens', and he gained more funding per head of population than any other Australasian botanic garden director in colonial times. He had been responsible for a period of expansion that saw the Botanic Garden in its heyday, its fine reputation a source of great pride to local citizens. With his children well established in Anglo-Australian society, he continued to work until his eightieth year, dying at his house in Adelaide Botanic Garden in March 1891.

Notes

1. Two volumes of this illustrated three-volume account of the expedition *Reisen in Britisch Guiana* (but not the third on the flora and fauna of British Guiana) were translated by Walter E. Roth as *Travels in British Guiana*, Daily Chronicle Office, Georgetown, 1922–23. A number of the engravings from the *Reisen in Britisch Guiana* as well as some coloured images from *Twelve views in the interior of Guiana*, Ackerman, London, 1841, are reproduced in Pauline Payne, *The Diplomatic Gardener: Richard Schomburgk: Explorer and botanic garden director*, Jeffcott Press, Adelaide, 2007.
2. J.B. Hawkins, *Nineteenth Century Australian Silver*, vol. 2, Antique Collectors Club, Suffolk, England, 1990, pp. 40–5.
3. Unfortunately the meteorological records, sent back to Berlin, did not survive the Second World War. We would like to acknowledge the research of Dr Mark Hutchinson, Dr Engelhard Weigl, Ms Lee Kersten and Prof. Mike Tyler on the Schomburgks' life and work during this period.
4. For an account of the early years of Adelaide Botanic Garden see Richard Aitken, *Seeds of Change: An illustrated history of Adelaide Botanic Garden*, Board of the Botanic Gardens and State Herbarium, Adelaide, 2006.
5. Schomburgk's account of his first year's work is recorded in his first annual report, that of 1866, written in January 1867. Reports will be cited as *Report* together with the year; the exact title varied over the years.
6. Details of these exchanges can be found in Payne 2007, pp. 116, 148–54.
7. Anthony Blunt, *In For a Penny: A prospect of Kew Gardens: Their flora, fauna and falbalas*, Hamish Hamilton, London, 1978, pp. 160–3.
8. Schomburgk writing to Hooker, 2 May 1869, Royal Botanic Gardens, Kew, archival collection.
9. *Express and Daily Telegraph*, 19 September, 1868; Payne 2007, pp. 96–7.
10. Payne 2007, p. 145.
11. *Report* 1874, p. 7.
12. LeMessurier Architects, *The Palm House, Adelaide Botanic Garden: Draft conservation plan*, Adelaide, 1991.
13. The Act to establish Roseworthy was passed in 1879. Professor J.D. Custance was appointed as Professor of Agriculture in 1882 and that same year the property for the college was acquired before formal establishment in 1883.

'Essentially South Australian'
The artist Alexander Schramm

Janice Lally and Peter Monteath

The first European artists to gaze on the territory that was to become South Australia were an Austrian, Ferdinand Bauer, and an Englishman, William Westall, both of them members of Matthew Flinders's expedition to circumnavigate Australia. Bauer, already a very experienced botanical draughtsman, was untiringly dedicated to his task and was impressively productive. On his return to England he could count over 2000 sketches, most of Australian plants and animals. From those meticulously colour-coded sketches he then painted some 300 watercolours, regarded by many as the pinnacle of botanic art of the time.

The landscape artist Westall, by contrast, established quite a different record. He was a young man – just 19 when the *Investigator* left England – with unquestionable talent, but like other British artists of his time appears to have been underwhelmed by the distinctive qualities of the Australian landscape. Its subjects, he complained, could neither 'afford pleasure from exhibiting the face of a beautiful country, nor curiosity from their singularity'. By comparison with his more experienced Austrian colleague, Westall's output was risible – a mere 140 watercolour and sketches. Nonetheless, posterity can at least be grateful to him for his contribution: recording not just some significant landscapes but a number of portraits of Indigenous Australians. They are invaluable documents illustrating how Europeans viewed Aborigines during the contact period in the early decades after settlement, his portraits being remarkably sympathetic and firmly grounded in the tradition of the 'noble savage'.

By the time South Australia was settled in the 1830s – and

thus by the beginning of significant German settlement – things had changed. The landscape which Westall had found so lacking in interest and pleasure as to barely warrant his artistic efforts was, decades later, viewed as much more desirable. What once might have seemed dull and barren was now depicted as rich and bountiful. In part this reflects the European colonisers' adaptation over time to the qualities and potential of the terrain and flora of a country so unlike their own. But it also reflects the need to present to prospective settlers an enticing image of abundance, whereby any consoling similarity with the verdant fields, vales and rolling hills of home would be highlighted.

In the depiction of Indigenous Australians, however, trends moved in the opposite direction. As settlement expanded, the established trope of the 'noble savage' became less useful. While agricultural and pastoral activity pushed further away from the first settlements, little was to be gained from emphasising the existence of proud warriors who might offer resistance to the march of civilisation. It was altogether more amenable to the colonial project, and easier on the European conscience, to paint landscapes devoid of those humans who had already been inhabiting them for millennia. As the art historian Bernard Smith puts it, 'The European control of the world required a landscape practice that could first survey and describe, then evoke in new settlers an emotional engagement with the land that they had alienated from its aboriginal occupants'.[1] Where Aboriginal Australians were not omitted altogether, they were at best marginal or ornamental figures, devoid of individuality or even humanity. As embellishments to sweeping vistas, their function was comparable with an exotic piece of flora or fauna. However, in some cases, one of the central assumptions of the day was difficult to overlook – that they were headed meekly and inexorably towards their extinction.

Perhaps better than any other artist, the career of Westall illustrates these contrary trends. His interest in Indigenous subjects evaporated after his return to England, while his earlier disdain for the Australian landscape gave way to visions possessing an almost Arcadian quality. These later works, produced in the comfort of a studio on the other side of the world, played their role in promoting Australia as a land of abundance, ripe for the colonial picking. Indeed, one early South Australian colonist, a certain John Newcome, happened to record his exposure to a Westall image which had been published in Matthew Flinders's *Voyage to Terra Australis*. Most interesting, however, is Newcome's response to the sobering recognition of the difference between Westall's image of staged tranquillity and the harsher reality he and others confronted:

> The absence of seals, kangaroos and emus, that enliven the views in Flinders' work, and were consequently mixed up in my mind with all sea-side scenery in this part of the world, took from it in my opinion its Australian character, the more so, as no black men or women were gazing in wonder at our noble vessel as she sailed majestically along, nor could I detect any columns of smoke rising from their fires, over the thickly hills.[2]

Westall was British; his work on Flinders's expedition and in the years that followed was integral to the process of exploring, recording, understanding and ultimately settling Australia. But what about German settlers and artists? On the one hand they were complicit in the process of colonisation of Australia: they implicitly accepted the myth of *terra nullius*, they claimed and worked land from which the Indigenous inhabitants had been 'dispersed', and by and large they shared the spoken and unspoken assumptions about the superiority of European civilisation. Yet the Germans' position was also an ambivalent one. They were themselves obliged to adapt to the dictates of British rule, since they formed a minority within an increasingly hegemonic British presence, and it was not their role to promote the material interests of the British Empire and the ideological assumptions which underpinned it.

This chapter explores the essential ambivalence of the German colonial experience in South Australia through the career and work of one German painter, namely, Alexander Schramm. Like British painters before him and during his own time, he came to Australia steeped in European aesthetic traditions. For Schramm – as for Westall – the landscapes and the Indigenous people he encountered were entirely removed from the realm of his experience. In many ways his work is deeply indebted to European conventions and sensibilities. Yet one can detect also clear differences between Schramm's work and that of British painters who sought to depict

South Australian colonisation during its crucial mid-nineteenth century phase. Nowhere are those differences clearer than in his interest in Indigenous people as subjects.

Berlin to Adelaide

Schramm is an enigmatic figure – we know little about him before he arrived in Adelaide and not a great deal more about him thereafter. Although his year of birth is often given as 1814, in reality he was born on 18 December of the previous year and was baptised in St Peters Church in Berlin on 13 February 1814.[3] His father was a bookseller in Berlin, where Schramm spent his early years, including a period of study at the Academy of the Arts. With that period of training behind him, Schramm was able to establish himself as a painter devoted at least in part to local subjects. One of his surviving works from that period, held in Berlin's *Stadtmuseum* (or City Museum, formerly the renowned *Märkisches Museum*), depicts a party of artists gathered in a riverside setting in Berlin. Bearing the title *Boating Party of Berlin Artists near Treptow*, it was painted when Schramm was at the tender age of just 24 or 25 years and, in its skilful execution, provides evidence of a budding prodigious talent. In at least one respect it anticipates his later work in Adelaide – Schramm's preferred subjects are groups of figures against landscape backgrounds.

Schramm's Berlin links are strong and uncontested. A number of German reference works also link him with Stuttgart, Warsaw and Italy, although details are sketchy. It is speculated that his Warsaw sojourn might have covered the years 1838 to 1844; certainly a number of his subjects in the following period are identifiably Polish. The reference 'Bible' of German art historians classifies him as a 'genre and portrait painter' and suggests that he worked in Berlin and Stuttgart in the period 1834 to 1848.[4] If there was a visit to Italy at some time in this period, then it might help to explain Schramm's apparent indebtedness to the Nazarene school, discussed below.

Whether Schramm's travels through Europe were professionally motivated is not known. Youthful *Wanderlust* or health needs might equally have played a role. More important for our purposes is the mystery surrounding his emigration to the Antipodes. Here too, a desire to experience and work in foreign cultural environments might have provided the impulse, but that is not at all clear. It is however tempting to speculate on the reasons for his departure from Germany, given that he emigrated aboard the *Princess Louise*, which departed Hamburg in March of 1849 and arrived in Adelaide on 7 August. Collectively, the 162 passengers aboard the vessel are sometimes referred to as 'Forty-Eighters', because their liberal political convictions persuaded many of them to leave the German states in the repressive wake of the failed revolutions of 1848. They were overwhelmingly of urban middle-class backgrounds, albeit from a variety of walks of life. The passenger list of the *Princess Louise* reads something like a kind of 'Who's Who' of mid-nineteenth-century German migration to Australia. Apart from the 35-year-old Schramm, who by then had a well-established reputation as a landscape and portrait painter, lithographic draughtsman and sculptor, were Richard Schomburgk, the botanist who became Director of the Adelaide Botanic Garden, Carl Linger, the conductor and composer who established Adelaide's first philharmonic orchestra and composed the 'Song of Australia', Hermann Büring, a seminal figure in the history of Australian wine making, and Carl Mücke, who influenced South Australia's education system. Not all of the passengers were to make their futures in Australia. Among them was a certain Gustav Listemann, who was not impressed with the conditions and opportunities the young colony of Adelaide offered. Sorely disappointed, he returned to Germany and published a report designed to warn his countrymen of the vast discrepancies between rosy views broadcast about the attractions of Australia and the bleaker realities.[5]

Whether Schramm should be counted among those whose expectations remained unmet is unclear. A town of some 10,000 at that time could barely match the cultural and intellectual wealth of the Prussian capital in a period of its ascendancy. Similarly, if Schramm had been motivated by some prospect of acquiring material wealth through his art, Adelaide could only disappoint. There is no evidence to suggest that the pursuit of his profession enabled him to lead a life free of financial concerns. In November 1864, some 15 years after his arrival, he died in the Adelaide Hospital of phthisis, a progressive wasting disease commonly in the form of pulmonary tuberculosis, aged just 50. He had neither wife nor children. On the day after his death, 7 November, he was given a 'government burial' in West Terrace Cemetery.[6] A late nineteenth-century assessment of Schramm by the art critic Mary Overbury lends weight to the view that he lived a very modest existence. He was 'small in stature, dark, and somewhat retiring in disposition, he made but few intimates. [He lived] on the proceeds of his brush, often disposed of far beneath their real value, and died some years ago as he had lived, extremely poor.'[7]

On the other hand, if Schramm's motives for emigration were political – like those of so many others aboard the *Princess Louise* – then Adelaide might have brought contentment. The colony, with its already established reputation as a 'paradise of dissent', might have offered welcome relief from the stiflingly authoritarian rule he experienced in his homeland during his youth. One might even speculate that, had he possessed the kind of liberal political leanings that might have driven him to leave Berlin, and which would have been consistent with his middle-class origins, then these might have found expression in his apparent sympathy with the Indigenous habitants of his adopted homeland. And if his artistic pursuits did not make him wealthy, he nonetheless managed to practise his profession for the full duration of his Australian life, a rare achievement and also a tribute to his very considerable artistic talents.

The extent to which he had managed to establish himself as an artist is perhaps best conveyed through a report on the eighth annual exhibition of the South Australian Society of Arts, published in the *Register* on 25 January 1865 – just a few weeks after Schramm's death. It noted that Schramm's works had been prominent among the society's exhibitions for many years. He had attracted widespread patronage, beginning with Mr J.F. Ross, who had bought Schramm's first Australian painting. Among the subjects of his portraits were Edward Stephens of the South Australian Banking Company and a certain Captain Allen. The report specifically mentioned a large picture 'representing a favourite spot on the estate of a South Australian gentleman, with figures of the proprietor and his family, with favourite horses, dogs, etc.' Almost certainly this is a reference to Schramm's portrait of the Gilbert family on the family property at Pewsey Vale. The placement of the family members and their entourage in a finely recorded rural setting was typical of Schramm. Apart from its aesthetic merits, the painting, which will be familiar to regular visitors to the Art Gallery of South Australia, enjoyed the dubious distinction of being the colony's largest painting for a period. Arguably, however, the most telling observation made in the Society of Arts report was that two subjects stood out in Schramm's oeuvre; one was the Australian scenery, the other, 'the manners and customs of the aborigines'. The evident implication was that the latter topic in particular was much more for Schramm than simply one area of artistic endeavour among others; rather, it stemmed from a passionate interest and engagement: 'He was particularly happy in his groups of natives, corroborees, and other subjects in which the scenes and actions represented were essentially South Australian'. This was high praise indeed – the work of a German artist who was brought up and trained in Europe and who spent less than the final third of his life in Australia was regarded by his contemporaries as 'essentially South Australian'.

Schramm the artist

The full scope of Schramm's artistic endeavours will probably never be known, although the librarian Keith Borrow once made an earnest attempt to track as many works across all genres as he could, reaching a grand total of 54.[8] The lists of paintings and drawings by Schramm in public collections are sadly short. Apart from *Boating Party of Berlin Artists near Treptow*, Berlin's City Museum has just six lithographs, most of them portraits. The National Library of Australia in Canberra has two oils by Schramm among its collection, and there is a small number of works in other public collections in Australia. By far the largest number in a public collection is in the Art Gallery of South Australia, which possesses 19 works in various media. There is no evidence that Schramm travelled or worked outside South Australia after his arrival here, but he clearly travelled within the state to practise his profession.

Just how many of Schramm's works might remain in private hands in Australia or Europe is a matter of guesswork, although records of exhibitions offer some gauge of his productivity. He exhibited regularly in the biennial exhibitions staged by the

Berlin Academy of Arts during the period 1834 to the year of his emigration, with the exception of 1840 and 1842, when he was probably in Warsaw. Catalogues of the Berlin exhibitions list some 25 works in a variety of media. In Australia, the South Australian Society of Arts staged exhibitions at which Schramm was generously represented, especially in 1859, 1861 and 1863. On two occasions – in November 1861 and again in January 1863 – Schramm was awarded the prize for the best picture or drawing of any description.[9]

The works preserved for public viewing in South Australia today are few in number, yet they illustrate, both in his technique and his devotion to South Australian subjects, Schramm's indebtedness to European aesthetic traditions as well as a remarkable facility to adjust to the radically new environment of the Antipodes in the mid-nineteenth century.

The indebtedness to his European training is evident in one of his earliest Australian works, namely *Madonna and Child*. The strong graphic outlines of the figures and intensely hued colours of the Madonna's clothing echo the keynote features of the Nazarene painters. These were German-born artists, including Friedrich Overbeck (1789–1869), Peter von Cornelius (1783–1867) and Wilhelm Schadow (1789–1862), who embraced Catholicism and based themselves or worked in Rome for a period.[10] They looked to the medieval past and Christian values, with the aim of revitalising art through a focus on Christian themes and virtues. Characteristically, they used bright clear colours and depicted scenes from the Bible, taking inspiration also from Italian Renaissance artists such as Perugino and Raphael.

Schramm's treatment of the female form with the slight inclination of the head, downcast eyes in a smoothly modelled face, and the gentle yet firm gesture of the hand holding the infant by the ankles, echoes the work of Raphael. The darkened background is simple. Gothic-style detail appears in the carved timber frame of the throne, and a dark-green curtain of drapery is set behind the throne. These deep tones serve to accent the brightness of the foreground figures. The warm pink flush on the infant's rounded face and the robustness of the exposed plump arm support a reading of this image as a celebration of a birth rather than of the passing of an infant, despite its prefiguring the pieta, in which an

Alexander Schramm 1813–1864, *Madonna and Child*, 1851, Adelaide,
oil on canvas 113.5 x 88.4 cm. Mrs Mary Overton Gift Fund 1991.
(Art Gallery of South Australia, 917P14)

adult dead Christ is laid across his mother's lap. The painting was commissioned and painted in 1851, within just 18 months of his arrival in the colony, with some commentators claiming that its production was connected to the German Catholic cleric Dr George Henry Backhaus of St Patrick's Church, Grote Street, Adelaide.[11]

From a very similar period – around 1850 – comes another painting by Schramm which, in its formal aspects at least, evinces a similar indebtedness to a distinctly European tradition. Titled *A Scene in South Australia*, c.1850,[12] it is a finely painted image of a settler family and Aborigines. The brightness, even gaudiness, of the colours places the work firmly in the Nazarene tradition, yet the choice of subject suggests that the artist was coming to terms with a new environment. Collective portraits were not new to him – this was a genre he had practised in Germany – but the depiction of Indigenous Australians was a significant departure. The settlers, in all likelihood Germans, stand before their freshly whitewashed house[13] on a clear, bright-blue-sky morning while in conversation with a visiting group of Aborigines. The scene is imbued with cooperation and harmony. The lady of the house, wearing a crisp white apron, tends a washtub while talking with two female Aborigines, one carrying a child in a sling on her back, the other comfortably leaning against a small tree. The conversation is apparently animated, as indicated by the tilt of the white woman's head as she turns to engage with the woman carrying the child. Another female Aborigine, clad in a blue and brown blanket, sits by a fire in the foreground, tending a large pot while smoking a pipe. The Aborigines are clothed in a disparate array of draped blankets,

Alexander Schramm, 1813–1864, *A scene in South Australia*, c.1850, Adelaide, oil on canvas, 25.7 x 31.8 cm. South Australian Government Grant 1982. (Art Gallery of South Australia, 8212P30)

a fur skirt, or a long white shirt in the case of the adult male with a shock of white hair and beard, yet they are at ease in the presence of the fully clothed settler family. Schramm's acute observation of Aboriginal life is evident in the inclusion of the host of dogs of mixed breeds that accompanies the visitors.

Given the vexed state of race relations in the young colony at this time, the harmony bordering on conviviality might appear to strain the limits of credibility. Yet if the Europeans depicted are indeed German settlers, Schramm might be implying that, when compared with their British counterparts, the Germans exhibited a greater tolerance and forbearance. Moreover, the scene is not entirely devoid of tension – the confrontation of 'civilisation versus nature' is implied in the hissing, raised fur and arched back of the family cat and the defensive barking of the settlers' family dog, restrained by collar and chain, although, by contrast, the Aborigines' dogs appear undaunted. Nonetheless, the theme of peaceful relations was to recur in later work in which Schramm explicitly addressed the civilisation versus nature trope.

Schramm's desire to document the people of the Adelaide region resulted in a number of works, the earliest of which include *The encampment, Adelaide Plains* (1850s, Adelaide) and *Landscape with Aboriginal hunters* (1850s, Adelaide),[14] but his commitment to the task and his empathy with his subject are most apparent in his large oil on canvas, *An Aboriginal Encampment, near the Adelaide foothills*, dating from 1854. In this work Schramm has moved more fully to an Australian idiom, not only in his choice of subject, which excludes a European presence (although not a European influence), but also in his painting style, which in technique and use of colour is distinct from his earlier work in the Nazarene tradition. The very scale of this painting – 89 x 132 cm unframed – entailing cost in time and materials, together with the refined rendering of its subject, indicates a significant evolution of Schramm's interest in and attention to Indigenous themes and the distinctive qualities of the Australian landscape.

The brushwork is handled with delicacy across the full canvas. While the subject is clearly observed out of doors, the quality and evenness of touch indicates that it was finished in the studio. The scene is one of quiet harmony, with extended family groups

Alexander Schramm, 1813–1864, *An Aboriginal encampment, near the Adelaide foothills*, 1854, Adelaide, oil on canvas, 89.0 x 132.0 cm.
South Australian Government Grant 1976. (Art Gallery of South Australia, 761HP1)

assembled in the early twilight in various stages of relaxation or simple activity. Spread across a lightly wooded area beneath the scraggly leaves of tall eucalypt trees are groups of Aborigines variously gathered about campfires, some before bark shelters – *wurlies* – while others are settled on the open ground.

Over 60 figures of men, women and children are depicted, some reclining, others seated, many conversing, some playing a game, perhaps dice. Many individuals are smoking clay pipes, others tend the fire. Children are shown playing freely, some are seated together a little distance from the campfire groups of adults. The painting is dominated by a large number of dogs – more than 50 – which are dispersed throughout the encampment, variously frolicking, feeding their young or sitting beside the family groups.

The closely observed detail offers evidence in an almost documentary scientific sense of accoutrements, clothing and activities indicative of the circumstances of daily life. At the same time, Schramm's empathy with the people is evident in the soft-edged rendering used in his depiction of this tranquil encampment of extended families in harmony with each other and their environment, also sympathetically conveyed through the delicacy of light that pervades this early evening scene. One reading of this low light level, however, is that early evening twilight is symbolic of the twilight of the existence of this group of Aborigines; the shadows also serve to disguise the raggedness and wretchedness of these remnants of the Kaurna people living during this period of white settlement, and which was noted by other observers.[15]

Various figures are partially clothed in Western style, wearing shirts of white or red. Some wear broad-brimmed hats with red ribbons, a few wear trousers, a red ribbon serves as a belt in the case of one man; another wears a white shirt and brown waistcoat but has bare legs. Yet others are naked or wear animal skin cloaks or skirts, and some wear draped blankets, with a few women carrying children in slings across their backs. Schramm's close observation singles out a few identifiable figures. These may have been dominant characters in the group. One, a male, is seated alone by a small fire in the right foreground and looks directly out at the viewer. He wears a finely defined feather cockaded headdress[16] with a grey (perhaps braided possum or kangaroo fur, or braided human hair) headband. His facial features and his feet are both well delineated, his chest is bare and he wears a fur cloak as a skirt. In his right hand, with his arm outstretched toward the fire, he holds an object with a spear-shaped head, perhaps a *wirri*.[17]

In the group gathered about the fire behind him, an older woman sits, her sagging breasts visible as she stretches towards the fire, while the man beside her, who is shrouded in a cloak, holds something small, perhaps a dead bird, towards the fire. In this group a younger woman wears a distinctive headband with a white diadem (perhaps a shell or animal tooth). Flicks of white paint indicate her lively eyes. Two males in this group leisurely smoke their clay pipes, one naked and reclining, the other seated by the fire. Schramm's close observation notes the free expression of the tiny naked child in the right hand foreground as he gestures and raises a stick in his right arm. While his little legs are thin yet shapely, his belly is distended, a symptom of malnourishment.

This scene captures and records the simple shelters, open campfires, communal style of living, the motley array of adopted clothing mixed with traditional coverings and a mixture of adopted accoutrements and tools – billy cans, pannikins, an axe, together with spears and other items.

The landscape of gently enfolding grassy hills stretches beyond this encampment; distant hilltops are darker, with scrubby forest. The sunlight on a distant hillside picks out the dark-coloured bracken fern of this region. The encampment is assembled on a brown-soil flood plain beneath an open tracery of tall trees. The foliage is depicted with characteristically smudgy grey-green marks, and brighter yellow-greens appear in the higher foliage, where the last of the sunlight plays. Filigree branch forms pick out the twisted branches in graphic detail.

Good humour is evident in the small gathering of figures observing a game being played by two men, one squatting, the other throwing something, perhaps dice, to the ground.[18] A nearby standing figure turns to another with his hand raised in a conversational gesture. The only group more actively engaged is a man chopping a dead tree with an axe, observed by two women who collect the wood in the left foreground. One carries a pile of sticks on her head. Schramm depicts the grimace of the axeman's effort by highlighting his white teeth. Nearby, a seated older woman wears a white cloth cap draped over her head.

In this attention to human detail Schramm distinguishes his work from the British depictions of Indigenous Australians at that time. His Aborigines are much more than marginal, picturesque embellishments. The image is of a collective, but one in which the figures possess distinctive identities. Schramm's art combines an obvious concern for the plight of Adelaide's Indigenous population, forced to the foothill outskirts of the settlement, with a highly developed interest in recording in fine and faithful detail the people, their living circumstances and their activities. For that reason his achievement is more than an artistic one; it is a manifestation of a kind of layperson's anthropological interest, not uncommon among other German settlers and visitors.

In contrast to Schramm's work, images produced soon after the establishment of the colony by British-born artists tended to portray the Indigenous inhabitants as diminished figures or alien to the settlers' way of life. The immensely talented George French Angas was admittedly a rare and very notable exception. For the most part British artists evinced little interest in Indigenous people that extended beyond the recording of familiar colonial stereotypes. The Englishman Charles Hill, for example, who arrived in Australia in 1854, painted *The First Lesson* three years later, in which an Aboriginal woman clothed in a blanket is shown mendicant, stooping to accept gratefully a slice of white bread from a young child supervised by her well-dressed mother at the open door of their home.[19] Similarly, John Michael Skipper, a native of Norwich who had arrived in Adelaide as early as 1836, in his painting *Artist and his wife Frances Amelia (neé Thomas) on horses*, c.1840, portrayed himself and his wife as well-dressed figures on horseback, towering above a cowering seated male Aboriginal.[20] In another image of about the same time, *Corroboree*, four figures on horseback witness the spectacle of a dramatic fire-lit night-time scene of a large group of body-painted Aboriginal performers from their vantage point on horseback.[21]

While *An Aboriginal Encampment* functions as an informative yet sympathetically rendered document of Aborigines in their daily life at this time of their displacement, Schramm also recorded the encounter of black with white in more directly philosophical terms. His image titled *Civilization versus Nature*, 1859,[22] was sufficiently archetypal to be repeated in several forms. One of these, a small oil on canvas, portrays a finely rendered image of a prospector dressed in hat, shirt and trousers, kneeling before a small pile of rocks in a creek bed with his tool of trade, a small pick hammer in his hand and smoking a pipe. Silhouetted against the pink blush of the sunset and standing before him in quiet observation are an Aboriginal man and woman and their dog. They wear simple draped blankets as cloaks, the man carries a spear, the woman holds a long stick and also a shoulder swag. A variation on this theme produced by Schramm, indeed bearing an identical title, is likely to date from the very same year.[23] A pencil and watercolour on scraper board, this is less refined in its rendition, but valued as a document in its symbolic confrontation of that time, and also finding its way into the public collection at the Art Gallery of South Australia.

The developed Western world, embodied by a fully clothed white man engaged in mining exploration, confronting the wandering, barefooted natives of the land, representing unspoilt

Alexander Schramm, 1813–1864, *Civilization versus Nature*, 1859, Adelaide, oil on canvas, 17.8 x 24.3 cm (sight). South Australian Government Grant 1952. (Art Gallery of South Australia, 0.1499)

nature, takes the form of a simple tableau. It pays homage to the prevailing view of that time, that 'civilising' forces had arrived with colonisation. The Aborigines of the land, synonymous with 'nature', were inevitably to be subdued as they gave way to the greater force of 'civilisation'. For many, this view equated with a belief that Aborigines were doomed to extinction. Yet in paying homage to a familiar trope, Schramm is also implicitly questioning it. Schramm compares the lot of the two very different figures; however, it is not at all apparent that the European is the more fortunate. Moreover, in this work, as in his earlier *A Scene in South Australia*, there is no sense that the meeting of 'nature' and 'civilisation' might provoke tension or conflict, or might inexorably lead to the triumph of one over the other. On the contrary, a good-humoured coexistence and acceptance of difference prevails. The sense of doom or foreboding which so frequently accompanied the nineteenth-century depiction of Aborigines is absent here.

This holds true for the last of Schramm's known works, the group portrait, *The Gilbert Family*, painted in the year of the artist's death and mentioned earlier.[24] It portrays an Aboriginal groom as an integral part of the group, indeed a member of staff of Mr Gilbert, a prosperous landowner of Pewsey Vale, north of Gawler. Painted in the style of society landowner portraits made famous by Sir Joshua Reynolds (1723–92) and Thomas Gainsborough (1727–88), this work is more formal than the earlier image of daily life of the German settlers engaged in amiable conversation with passing Aborigines. Rather, the scene of the family posed in fine attire, Mr Gilbert's thoroughbred mount, the ponies and dogs, the attendance of a governess and the well-presented Aboriginal groom, all set in a pastoral landscape, provides a marker of the development of the colony, including the class hierarchy already embedded in the colony. A commissioned work, the painting implies a ready integration of the Aboriginal groom into a European class and economic structure, albeit at its bottom rung. Yet Schramm by this time had witnessed enough of the fate of Indigenous South Australians to know that the lot of the young man depicted here was the exception rather than the rule.

Conclusions

It is tempting to compare Schramm with his contemporary, Eugène von Guérard. The latter was a couple of years older than Schramm and arrived in Australia just three years later, in 1852. Born in Vienna, he, like Schramm, received some of his artistic training in Prussia – in Düsseldorf – where for a decade he studied landscape under Johann Wilhelm Schirmer.[25] Guérard undoubtedly did visit Rome, and was certainly exposed there to the influence of the Nazarenes, who, as we have seen, also left their mark on Schramm. Guérard tried his hand at gold-mining for a year or so after his arrival in Australia but then devoted himself to painting and, like Schramm, was able to make a living from his art. Based in Melbourne, he travelled much more widely than Schramm, undertaking a number of productive tours to other colonies, including South Australia. His visits were brief – he was in South Australia just twice, in the middle of 1855 in and around Adelaide, and then in late 1857. It is not known whether he made contact with Schramm, although clearly they would have had much in common.

Like Schramm, Guérard evinced a good deal of sympathy for

Eugène von Guérard, *Winter Encampments in Wurlies of divisions of the Tribes from Lake Bonney & Lake Victoria in the Parkland near Adelaide*, 1858 (original sketch 1855); pen, Indian ink and wash on paper.
(National Gallery of Victoria, Felton Bequest, 1960)

those whose dispossession he witnessed at first hand. In a journal kept while visiting the Victorian goldfields in March 1854, he wrote that he had seen 'a miserable group of eight Aborigines, clad in the most ludicrous odds-and-ends of European wearing apparel, and nearly all in a drunken condition. It is sad to see how the poor creatures are demoralised by the white man's influence.'[26] And in one of his drawings, engraved in the *Illustrated London News* in 1856, he wrote that Aborigines are 'miserable remnants of a once numerous and powerful race'.[27] His attitudes are similarly evident in some of the work stemming from his first visit to South Australia, when he sketched, among many landscapes, individual portraits of Indigenous people as well as depictions of their camps in the Adelaide area. As in Schramm's work, the Aborigines are acutely observed; they are not 'noble savages' but human inhabitants, enduring the privations of provisional wet-season encampments. In their composition, and in the sensibility that informed them, the similarities between Guérard's sketches of Aborigines and those of Schramm are hard to overlook.

In the luscious landscapes in oil for which he became renowned, however, Guérard followed the British lead of the day much more closely than did Schramm. His patrons, many of them landowners, were attracted above all to the Arcadian qualities in these works. Whether pastoral scenes from South Australia or visions of rich fields ripe for harvest in other colonies, Guérard's landscapes appear fecund and enticing. He belonged to a German romantic tradition which held nature in awe; yet, as his patrons required, he could comfortably accommodate a European presence. Among the most popular of his subjects – and one which brought him an impressive number of commissions as well as a healthy income – was the Australian homestead. Typically, the homesteads he painted were dwarfed by the surrounding countryside; although that natural environment was benign, the European presence was not threatened by a hostile or barren landscape. If human figures were present at all – whether European or Indigenous – they were at best peripheral.

Schramm, thankfully, was different. Although not great in number, his extant works – oils and other media – reveal an interest and curiosity in Indigenous Australians that remained with him until his tragically premature death. Its artistic merits aside, the legacy of Schramm's work is an invaluable recording of the presence of Aborigines in colonial South Australia during a crucial and vexed period in the development of race relations. In this achievement, Schramm, the painter of 'essentially South Australian' subjects, neatly complements the meticulous work of so many other Germans with other skills who were active in other disciplines. Together with the likes of people such as Hermann Koeler, Christian Teichelmann, Clamor Schürmann, Eduard Meyer. Erhard Eylmann or Carl Strehlow, Schramm documented and engaged with the lives of Indigenous Australians, even as other Europeans, in life as in art, pushed them to the margins.[28]

Notes

1   Bernard Smith, *European Visions and the South Pacific*, 2nd edn, Harper and Row, Sydney, 1985, p. ix.
2   John Newcome, 'My Colonial Experience', *Adelaide Miscellany of Useful and Entertaining Knowledge*, 9 September 1848, p. 88, cited in Tim Bonyhady,

Images in Opposition: Australian landscape painting 1801–1890, OUP, Melbourne, 1985, p. 87.

3   Schramm's baptised name was Carl Friedrich Alexander Schramm. His parents were the bookseller Carl Friedrich Schramm (who had remarried in 1805 after the death of his first wife) and Carolina Friedericke, née Dippe; they lived at Breitenstrasse 9. Alexander was the third of six children from that union. Information provided by Jean-Baptiste Piggin in a letter to Ron Appleyard, 17 October 1998, contained in Schramm papers, Library of the Art Gallery of South Australia.

4   Ulrich Thieme & Felix Becker, *Allgemeines Lexikon der bildenden Künstler von der Antike bis zur Gegenwart*, vol. XXX, Leipzig, 1936, p. 275.

5   G. Listemann, *Meine Auswanderung nach Süd-Australien und Rückkehr zum Vaterlande: Ein Wort zur Warnung und Belehrung für alle Auswanderungslustige*, A.W. Hayne, Berlin, 1851.

6   Records of the West Terrace Cemetery, cited by R.G. Appleyard in his very useful article, 'Alexander Schramm, Painter', *Bulletin of the Art Gallery of South Australia*, vol. 37, 1979, pp. 26–41.

7   Mary Overbury, 'Early Colonial Art and Artists', *Adelaide Observer*, 12 November 1898.

8   Flinders University Library Borrow Collection, B005/02/02.

9   Altogether 41 works by Schramm are listed (see Appleyard 1979, pp. 38–41).

10 Keith Andrews, *The Nazarenes: A brotherhood of German painters in Rome*, Clarendon Press, Oxford, 1964.

11 Ron Radford & Jane Hylton, *Australian Colonial Art 1800–1900*, Art Gallery Board of South Australia, Adelaide, 1995, p. 28.

12 Alexander Schramm, *A scene in South Australia*, c 1850, oil on canvas 25.7 x 31.8 cm, 40.9 x 46.8 x 5.8 cm (frame) South Australian Government Grant 1982.

13 George French Angas depicted the German settlements of Klemzig, Angaston and Bethany, clearly documenting the rows of whitewashed, thatched cottages, the nature of the women's clothing and the activities and accoutrements of the communities. In Plate XII titled *Klemsic, Village of German Settlers*, one sees a woman with a head scarf, a full blue skirt, white apron and red shawl crossed at the bodice. Angas described the people as having a 'picturesque style of dress' and 'simplicity of manners'. Another Plate LX, depicts Bethany. It includes a tree beside the door of a barn. The wooden barrel at its base and the large plank of timber resting between a tree branch and the ground and the image of two women tending a fire on open ground, on which is a metal pot with steam rising, have echoes in the image of Schramm (George French Angas, *South Australia Illustrated*, published in 10 parts by Thomas McLean, Haymarket, London, 1847; facsimile edition A.H. & A.W. Read, Sydney, 1967).

14 *The encampment, Adelaide Plains* 1850s, Adelaide, watercolour, charcoal and pencil on paper, 16.5 x 23cm (sight), 43.8 x 59.3 x 4 cm (frame); Art Gallery of South Australia; gift of M.J.M. Carter AO through the Art Gallery of South Australia Foundation 2004 and *Landscape with Aboriginal hunters* 1850s, Adelaide, oil on canvas 35.4 x 44 cm, Art Gallery of South Australia; South Australian Government Grant 1954. The majority of the 19 works held by the Art Gallery of South Australia that depict figures in the landscape incorporate Aborigines as integral figures or have Aborigines as the main motif.

15 Edward Snell, *The Life and Adventures of Edward Snell; the Illustrated Diary of an Artist, Engineer and Adventurer in the Australian Colonies,* 1849–1859, State Library of Victoria, Melbourne, 1988, cited in Derek Whitelock, *Gawler – Colonel Light's Country Town: A history of Gawler and its regions, the hills, the plains and the Barossa Valley*, Corporation of the Town of Gawler, Gawler, 1989, pp. 14–15.

16 George French Angas described and illustrated an ornament of this type. Named a *witto witto*, it is 'a bunch of tail feathers of the hawk and cockatoo, split up and tied on a stick worn as a head ornament stuck into the *mangna*'. The *mangna* is a 'bandage worn around the head by men, formed of opossum fur spun into a kind of string', or it may consist of tresses of human hair spun together (see Angas 1847, Item 12, Plate XXVII).

17 Angas 1847, Plate VI, Native Weapons and Implements.

18 Schramm documented this game also in his work *A group of Aborigines*, 1859, black and white chalks on paper, 25.0 x 37.6 cm (sheet); Art Gallery of South Australia accession no. 267D2; gift of Mrs H. Simpson Newland 1926.

19 Charles Hill (1824–1915, arrived Australia 1854), *The First Lesson* 1857, Adelaide, oil on canvas; Art Gallery of South Australia; gift of Mrs I. Rusk 1966.

20 John Michael Skipper (1815–1883, arrived Adelaide 1836), *Artist and his wife Frances Amelia (neé Thomas) on horses* c.1840, oil on canvas mounted on masonite; Art Gallery of South Australia; gift of Maughan Family 2007.

21 John Michael Skipper, *Corroboree* c. 1840, oil on canvas masonite; Art Gallery of South Australia; on loan from South Australian Museum.

22 Alexander Schramm, *Civilisation versus Nature*, 1859, oil on canvas; Art Gallery of South Australia accession no. 0.1499; South Australian Government Grant 1952.

23 Attributed to Alexander Schramm, *Civilisation versus nature*, c.1859, pencil, watercolour on scraper board, 13.9 x 22.5 cm (sheet); Art Gallery of South Australia accession no. 267D4; gift of Mrs H. Simpson Newland 1926.

24 Joseph Gilbert was a son of a prosperous wheat and sheep farming and fox-hunting family of Pewsey Vale, Wiltshire, England. In December 1839 he sailed on the *Buckinghamshire* to South Australia, where he established one of the first viticulture centres, ran sheep for wool and bred thoroughbred horses.
25 Alison Carroll, 'Eugene von Guérard, the Draughtsman and His Views of South Australia', in Alison Carroll & John Tregenza, *Eugene von Guérard's South Australia: Drawings, paintings and lithographs from journeys in South Australia in 1855 and 1857*, Art Gallery of SA, Adelaide, 1986, p. 1.
26 Marjorie Tipping (ed.), *An Artist on the Goldfields: The diary of Eugène von Guérard*, Curry, O'Neil, Melbourne, 1982, p. 72 (cited in Bonyhady 1985, p. 34).
27 *Illustrated London News*, 15 November 1856, p. 491 (cited in Bonyhady 1985, p. 35).
28 With thanks to Georgia Hale of the Art Gallery of SA, Angelika Reimer of the *Stadtmuseum Berlin* and Anke Matelowski of the *Akademie der Künste, Archiv Bildende Kunst Berlin*.

The man of the law
Ulrich Hübbe

Horst K. Lücke[1]

Introduction

Ulrich Hübbe was born in Hamburg on 1 June 1805. On 13 October 1842 he arrived in Port Adelaide, having sailed from London on the barque *Taglione*. He was then 37 years old. After almost 50 years in South Australia, he died at Mount Barker on 9 February 1892, aged 86, and was buried two days later in the Hahndorf cemetery.

Hübbe was an important figure in early South Australia. He made a varied, significant and largely unremunerated contribution to the early life of the province, particularly to the development of the legal system. He is still remembered for the role he played in the most important of the early law reform measures, the introduction of the Torrens System for the registration of real estate transactions, enacted in 1858.

The English legal system which South Australia had inherited was based on transfer by private agreement. To be certain of a legally effective purchase, a purchaser of land had to establish that the vendor was in fact the owner, that is, the last in a chain of genuine vendors and purchasers, all documented as such by valid deeds of transfer. This required so-called title searches, which were time-consuming and cumbersome. To be reliable, they had to be carried out by lawyers, for whom they were a valuable source of income. In England, land was in relatively few hands and transfers were few, so the defects of the system were less serious than they were bound to be in the new colony, where many aspired to land ownership, and where land was soon to become an article of commerce and speculation. J.H. Fisher, the first Resident Commissioner, had anticipated the need for a central register and had prepared legislation to establish it. Governor Hindmarsh resented Fisher, with whom he had to share power, and refused to enact Fisher's bills.[2] As a result, uncertainty of ownership became a problem, for transfer deeds were in private hands and often difficult to find.

Legislation enacted in 1841, more than four years after the foundation of the Province of South Australia, introduced an obligation to register transfer deeds in a central register. It was a useful reform, but it failed to deal with all the problems. Transfer by deed had been retained and remained legally effective, with title searches being very expensive. What was needed was a system which made registration a precondition for a legally effective transfer, so that the register would immediately disclose ownership as well as any encumbrances. Amidst much popular disquiet about expensive legal services, Robert R. Torrens, Registrar-General of Deeds in the early 1850s, began to develop such a system, basing his first efforts on the British *Merchant Shipping Act 1854*, which governed the transfer of ownership in ships.[3] He was not a lawyer and needed a good deal of legal help. He enlisted Hübbe's assistance in early 1857 after he had read letters to the *Register*, in which Hübbe had informed the public that Hamburg and other towns of the Hanse League had maintained inexpensive and reliable registration systems for centuries. Hübbe advised Torrens about draft bills which Torrens had already prepared. No one has questioned that Hübbe played some role in the introduction and defence of the Torrens System, but the extent of that role is controversial.

In 1884 Hübbe dictated a statement to his grandson concerning his contribution to the introduction of the Torrens System, which by then had proved very successful and had been adopted in other Australian colonies. Hübbe claimed in his statement:

- that early in 1857 Robert R. Torrens had discussed with him the 'embryonic' bill then before the general public (which had been prepared by Torrens and some of his helpers);
- that it had been based on the 'British Shipping Transfer Act' (the British *Merchant Shipping Act 1854*);
- that he, Hübbe, had given Torrens an account of the history of the various continental systems, especially the French and German;

- that, at Torrens's request, he had published this account in the form of a book which had later helped to persuade members of the House of Assembly and the public of the good sense of enacting reforming legislation;
- that the idea of adopting the *Merchant Shipping Act* as a model had been found unworkable and had been dropped;
- that he, Hübbe, had translated the system used in Hamburg and other Hanseatic cities;
- that Torrens had adopted this system; and
- that he, Hübbe, had 'drafted the Bill finally on those lines which Mr. Torrens piloted through the House of Assembly and it was taken through the Legislative Council and became the law of the land'.

It has never been doubted that Torrens provided the initiative, energy, political skill and the influence needed for the revolutionary *Real Property Act 1858* (SA) to be enacted. Ulrich Hübbe's statement and other indicators have persuaded some scholars that he, Hübbe, contributed the essential ideas and that he did much of the actual drafting. Others have seen his contribution to the introduction of the system as 'minimal' and his contribution to its subsequent defence and further development as 'moderate'. The controversy would hardly be pursued with such zeal had it involved nothing more than the respective merits and reputations of persons who died long ago. Of greater interest, particularly to comparative lawyers, is the closely related question of whether the South Australian system is a transplant of the Hamburg legal precedent.

Hübbe's life in Germany

Ulrich Hübbe's paternal grandfather, a wigmaker from Mecklenburg, had settled in Hamburg. In our modern jargon, the Hübbes were 'upwardly mobile'. One son, Karl, became a Lutheran theologian and successful author of books (copies of one of these still command high prices) and essays on a wide variety of subjects. Karl's brother, Johann Heinrich Hübbe, Ulrich's father, studied in Erlangen, served briefly as an assistant to a Professor Johann Georg Büsch in Hamburg and, on Büsch's recommendation, was appointed as *Schiffsregistrator* in 1795, at the age of 24 years. This involved keeping records of inquiries into maritime accidents by the court of the Hamburg Admiralty. In 1797 Johann Heinrich married Maria Christine Heyer and also became an Imperial Notary, hoping thereby to earn a little additional money from certifying documentation required for shipping. Though notaries were not well remunerated at the time, this must have been a growing source of income for Johann Heinrich because, following the war between France and Britain and the resulting shutdown of Dutch shipping, Hamburg became the most important harbour on the Continent. Johann Heinrich remained a notary until his death in 1847. He is well remembered to this day as one of the founding fathers of one of Hamburg's most prominent firms of notaries.

Johann Heinrich and Maria Christine Hübbe had eight children: Hans (1800), Wilhelmine (1801), Heinrich (1803), Ulrich (1805), Agathe (1807), Mathilde (1809), Amalia (1811), and Hugo (1813). The family appears to have been fairly well off, for they were able to give their children good educations, and in the 1840s Ulrich received £25 from his father when he was in financial difficulties in Adelaide. Ulrich's brother Hans became a medical practitioner. Heinrich, probably the most successful of the Hübbe boys, graduated from a school of architecture in Berlin and became a hydraulic engineer, a field in which he published and achieved professional success and national and international prominence. Ulrich chose the law and had made a promising start as a writer, when his German career was cut short by his migration to South Australia. Of the girls, at least Wilhelmine and Amalia were married, had families and are remembered to this day.

Their moderate prosperity gave the family no immunity from the dramatic political events of the time. In December 1813 the city of Hamburg, still occupied by Napoleon's army, was under siege by German, Swedish and Russian forces. Marshal Davout, the French Commander, appointed Ulrich's father to a commission which was to draw up a list of persons to be expelled from the city on the ground that they lacked provisions and were in danger of starving. Johann Heinrich is said to have done his best to undermine these plans and to truly assist the needy in other ways. This must have taken great courage, for Davout was a stern disciplinarian. Ulrich, only eight years old at the time, could not have remained untouched by the anguish the family must have felt when his father was exposed to this dangerous predicament.

Young Ulrich received his schooling at Hamburg's renowned humanistic school, the Johanneum, which had been founded in 1529 by Johannes Bugenhagen, an associate of Martin Luther. The fame of the school, where well-known Enlightenment scholars taught, and where Telemann und Carl Philipp Emanuel Bach were cantors, had spread to England. Young Thomas Wilson, in later life the second of Adelaide's Lord Mayors, was a pupil in Hamburg for a number of years, almost certainly at the Johanneum, studying Latin and other foreign languages. Wilson, although 13 years older than Hübbe, is said to have become one of his friends in Adelaide.[4] The Johanneum must have paid much attention to the employment of truly competent language teachers. Edward Sinnett, the father of Adelaide author Frederick Sinnett (*An Account of the Colony of South Australia*, published in 1862), was an English journalist associated with the *Hamburg Reporter* and the *Gleaner*. He taught English at the Johanneum in the 1830s. Ulrich Hübbe's command of English left little to be desired, as is shown by his English-language publications. He also knew Latin and acquired a (probably exaggerated) reputation in Adelaide for being fluent in 11 languages.

Growing up in Hamburg, Ulrich Hübbe would have been exposed to a cosmopolitan and anglophile environment. Hamburg had been a free city republic since the Middle Ages. English merchants, Huguenot refugees, Dutch Calvinists and Mennonites, Sephardic Jews and others had been welcomed in Hamburg and had found it a place in which to live, work and prosper. One of the great shipping companies had been founded by Johan Cesar Godeffroy, an entrepreneur of Huguenot extraction. Another shipping company, which like the Godeffroys was heavily engaged in the Australian trade, had been established by William Sloman, an Englishman. The English influence in Hamburg had been particularly strong. As early as during the late Middle Ages, there were English Merchant Adventurers trading and living in Hamburg, and the English Church, founded in 1611, still flourishes there.

Unlike his two older brothers who had chosen medicine and engineering, Ulrich Hübbe, having decided on a legal career, enrolled at the Christian-Albrechts-Universität in Kiel in 1826.

One of his teachers there would have been Professor Niels Nikolaus Falck, the very same jurist whom William Jethro Brown, Professor of Law in the University of Adelaide from 1906 to 1916, described as one of his favourite German authors. It is a German academic tradition for students to attend lectures outside their own discipline given by scholars of renown. Hübbe seems to have been profoundly influenced by the historian Friedrich Christoph Dahlmann, who taught at Kiel before his call to Göttingen in about 1829. Dahlmann's impact on his students is hardly surprising, for he was a formidable scholar, whose works are still extant in modern editions, and he was also an influential and courageous liberal politician.

In the winter semester of 1826 Professor Dahlmann offered a course of lectures on the history of the Dithmarschen republic. The fascination of Dithmarschen for intellectuals of the post-Napoleonic era is easy to understand. The medieval citizens of Dithmarschen had bravely fought domination by the Princes of Holstein and the Kings of Denmark, and Dithmarschen had, until the mid-sixteenth century, been an independent, democratically organised yeoman republic. These were ideals enthusiastically embraced in various ways by academics and students alike. Liberals like Falck and Dahlmann agitated for a new political order based on some of the principles of the English constitution. Some of the students had fought Napoleon in the Royal Prussian Free Corps von Lützow.[5] Upon their return to their universities they joined the *Burschenschaften*, groups of students who were unhappy with some of the semi-absolutist German principalities and kingdoms, and demanded freedom of thought and of the press, democratic reforms and the unity of the German fatherland. They harked back with a sense of nostalgia to the supposedly proud, freedom-loving and valiant Germans of medieval times and even to ancient Germanic heroes like Hermann the Cheruscan who had defeated the legions of Augustus.[6] People of all shades of opinion were able to look back with approval to the brave people of the tiny republic of Dithmarschen. Although Kiel was Danish, many of the students and teachers were German and it was German affairs, including particularly political affairs, which captured their attention.

It was almost certainly under Dahlmann's influence that Ulrich Hübbe wrote an essay, 'Relations between Dithmarschen and Hamburg – 1265 to 1316, based on documents',[7] which was published in *The Dithmarschen Neocorus*,[8] a book first edited by Dahlmann in 1818. Hübbe's essay must have been included in the further Dahlmann edition of 1827.[9] Hübbe seems to have distilled from the cauldron of patriotic and political agitation which surrounded him an abiding interest in the legal and general history of the German Middle Ages, for he chose – probably inspired if not guided by Dahlmann – the legal history of the ancient Margraviate of Brandenburg as the theme for his doctoral dissertation. He may not have been able to start work on this until he had completed his undergraduate studies in Jena and then Berlin. In an entry concerning Ulrich Hübbe a lexicon of Hamburg writers (1857)[10] includes among his publications '*Recensionen*' (literary reviews) published in the *Literary and Critical Pages of the Stock Exchange*,[11] a respected literary journal of the period.

German students have tended to study at a number of universities in order to benefit from more than just one kind of intellectual stimulation. Hübbe changed from Kiel to Jena University, which was at the time one of Germany's best tertiary institutions and another centre of political agitation. After his move to Berlin, he heard lectures given by Friedrich Carl von Savigny, the famous nineteenth-century German legal scholar who also made a significant impact in Britain. Thereafter Hübbe entered the Prussian judicial service as a trainee-in-law (*Referendar*, then called *Auskultator*) at the *Kammergericht* (the highest Prussian court in Berlin).

His duties at the *Kammergericht* are likely to have been light enough to allow him sufficient time to advance his doctoral thesis substantially. It was entitled, in his own translation, 'The Customary Holdings in the Ancient Marquisate'.[12] A fuller translation would be 'Yeomen's Laws and Court Systems in the Old Margraviate Brandenburg: A resolution of the Representative Assembly of 1531; with annotations and a summary of the court system from 1100–1806',[13] an article of 90 pages (including 30 pages of statutory text). This article was published in volume 45, issue 98, of the *Year-Books of Prussian Legislation, Legal Science and Legal Administration*.[14] It was also printed as a separate booklet. There appears to be no copy of his thesis, nor a record of its German title in the Schleswig–Holstein Archives,[15] which makes it likely that he was awarded his doctorate on the strength of the article/booklet. Dr Greg Taylor of Monash University has kindly supplied me with a copy of the relevant pages of Dahlmann's *Politics in the Light of the Reasons for and the Measure of Existing Conditions*.[16] In this book Dahlmann complimented Hübbe on having made accessible a previously unknown source: 'This previously unknown document ... shows how benign were the protective institutions of the ancient Brandenburg yeomen family law ... until the Thirty Years War'.[17] Dahlmann's comments also called Hübbe's commentary 'scholarly and, more importantly, showing understanding of the living reality of the time'.[18] Coming from a man of Dahlmann's stature, this was high praise indeed. Although Dahlmann had left Kiel in 1829, the positive impression he gained of Hübbe's work might still have contributed to the acceptance of it for the doctorate. The *Doctor Utriusque Juris* was conferred on Hübbe on 10 March 1837 at the University of Kiel. Professor Falck was then Dean of the Law Faculty and participated in the ceremony.

After completion of his practical training at the *Kammergericht*, Hübbe became a legal practitioner in Hamburg. Representing

Julius Oldach, *Der Freund Ulrich Hübbe*. Oil on canvas, 16.1 cm x 15 cm.
(Bildarchiv Preussischer Kulturbesitz/Hamburger Kunsthalle/Elke Walford)

ordinary Hamburg clients could not have taken too much of his time, for he was busy with non-legal activities and with publishing ventures, some with a religious rather than a legal orientation.

In Hamburg Hübbe came into contact with groups of Lutherans from eastern Germany who were seeking to find a new home overseas where they were hoping to be able to practise their faith freely. In 1840 he assisted Pastor Gotthard Daniel Fritzsche to obtain a police permit for his stay in Hamburg and then travelled to England with him to arrange for Fritzsche's group of some 270 German migrants from Posen and Silesia (the Lobethal Germans) to migrate to Adelaide. In England he conferred with George Fife Angas, the 'father of South Australia'. In the dedication to Angas of a book he published in 1857, Ulrich Hübbe spoke of the 'debt of gratitude' of 'those whom you first invited and enabled to come here [to South Australia]'[19] and one might conclude that Angas's persuasive powers played a part in Ulrich Hübbe's decision to follow the Lutheran migrants to South Australia. The Lobethal Germans left Altona on the Danish ship, the *Skjold*, on 3 July 1841 and arrived at Holdfast Bay on 27 October, having tragically lost 41 passengers, mostly children, to dysentery.

It seems likely that Hübbe's interest in German emigrants, their quest for religious freedom, and also his interest in overseas missionary ventures preceded his involvement with the Lobethal Germans. George Fife Angas took a keen interest in the spiritual wellbeing of the migrants who went to South Australia and also felt a deep concern for the welfare of the Indigenous Australians. In 1836 or 1837 Angas and Pastor Ludwig Christian August Kavel approached the Evangelical Lutheran Mission Society of Dresden[20] to recruit missionaries for this purpose. It is not unlikely that Hübbe was involved in these negotiations, for he is mentioned in German literature as the secretary of the Hamburg Association of Lutheran Friends of Missionary Activities,[21] although there is no indication of when and for how long he served. It was in this capacity that he arranged for the publication of *The Lutheran Pilgrim from the North in Defence of Truth and Justice*,[22] which appeared in 1841. This was accompanied by *News of Missionary Activities from Foreign Parishes and Colonies, Collected in Hamburg*.[23] The Mission Society of Dresden sent two recently ordained Lutheran pastors to Adelaide,

Christian Gottlob Teichelmann and Clamor Wilhelm Schürmann, who arrived there on 12 October 1838 from London in the *Pestonjee Bomanjee*, which also carried Governor Gawler.

Yet another indication of Hübbe's early contact with migration to South Australia is his assistance, while still in Hamburg, to a Captain Hahn who was attempting to have an account of his experiences in South Australia printed. The captain had taken the Hahndorf Germans to South Australia in 1838 on his Danish ship, the *Zebra*, and had returned to Hamburg on 11 September 1839. His story proved very popular in Hamburg. Hahn would have told Hübbe of his impressions and might have passed on some of his enthusiasm for the beauty of the Adelaide Hills, so vividly described in Hahn's book.

Emigration and life in South Australia

Emigration was by no means inconceivable to the cosmopolitan citizens of Hamburg, even if it inevitably meant great upheaval. Exactly what motivated Ulrich Hübbe to leave his hometown for Adelaide is not clear, since he left no accessible written account of his reasons, although we can speculate. We know little of Hübbe's political outlook, but it is conceivable that he viewed with unease the deep tensions between conservatives and liberals in the so-called *Vormärz* period, which led to the revolution of 1848. The British Empire and its constitution might have offered the attraction of stability and a more tender concern for the rights of the individual. To this advantage might be added his familiarity with the colony's language and with existing migration links. As Hübbe knew, Danish ships from nearby Altona were already successfully transporting significant numbers of German migrants to South Australia. Hübbe had met George Fife Angas, who must have struck him as commercially successful, trustworthy, and respectful of the principle of religious freedom so prized at that time by Lutherans like Hübbe. Angas may well have told him of the plans being made by his fellow Hamburgers of British nationaliy, led by Osmond Gilles, to migrate to the new colony,[24] thus adding further encouragement.

To these factors perhaps one more might be added. It seems that Hübbe had planned an ambitious publishing project, an almost encyclopaedic history of Brandenburg, with the support of a Berlin publishing house. For reasons not known the project did not come to fruition. This severe disappointment, combined with the factors listed above, might have persuaded Hübbe to seek his future in the Antipodes.

When Hübbe arrived in Adelaide the colony was barely six years old. The early German migrants, farmers and craftsmen, built their simple hamlets on the model of rural Prussian villages of the pre-industrial age and gave them German names such as Klemzig, Hahndorf, Bethanien (now Bethany) or Lobethal. It was only after 1848 that significant numbers of Germans with academic training arrived, often disaffected by the failure of the liberal revolution. Intellectuals who were part of the first wave of German migrants, like Johannes Menge, a German geologist and linguist employed by the South Australian Company, the Lutheran pastors Kavel and Fritzsche or the early missionaries were exceptions. Ulrich Hübbe was yet another such exception, but, unlike the others, he came with neither a clearly defined function, nor an appropriate means of making at least a modest living.

At a meeting with Mr Justice Cooper, arranged by Advocate-General Smillie, Hübbe presented his Doctor of Laws diploma from Kiel, no doubt in the hope of attracting legal employment. The judge would have read it with interest and courtesy, which, however, remained Hübbe's only reward. He had to accept that the British settlers had no use for his exotic legal talents. To say that he was stranded is no exaggeration; he should have asked George Fife Angas for employment before he departed for South Australia. Perhaps he failed to do so because he could not see himself in the role of a humble clerk in the South Australian Company, and he paid for his failure to do so with setbacks, misfortunes and financial difficulties. As the *Australian Dictionary of Biography* states: 'he never freed himself from the financial difficulties which plagued him from his earliest years in the colony'.

Hübbe arrived in the colony, probably with a little capital, at a time when land speculation was making some of the early arrivals rich, while ruining others. His academic achievements were useless in the rough and tumble of the colony. Ruthlessness in business dealings, a quick eye for personal advantage, the commercial experience of an Osmond Gilles, and perhaps even readiness to use one's fists if necessary were prerequisites for financial success. If, in addition, connections like those of Robert R. Torrens could be claimed, success was assured. Hübbe was not equipped to cope with a world dominated by men of this calibre. Only eight months after his arrival, unsuccessful land dealings in the Barossa Valley landed Hübbe in the debtors' prison. He was forced to surrender, in legal fees to the government, his last £25, which had been sent by his father, even though his more merciful creditors had agreed that he should keep this money for his own use. The Adelaide Goal, now a museum, had already been built at this time and one can only imagine Hübbe's anguish in that dismal place and the intensity of his regret at having left the relative certainty and comfort of his home town.

After Hübbe's release from prison, Charles Flaxman, Angas's South Australian agent, made a section of Angas Park land available to him for farming purposes. Unaccustomed to the hard life of a farmer, he lived in what he called a 'hut'. In 1843, this humble abode caught fire and he lost his papers, including his doctoral certificate as well as the library of classic legal, and historical standard works he had brought with him from Hamburg. One of his letters tells us that he 'lamented the loss'. The pain he felt at losing part of his identity through this loss of these beloved objects must have been intense, but he may also have wondered what earthly use they could have been to him in this hostile new environment. There is no indication that he pleaded with his father to help him return to Hamburg. With Angas as his champion, he might have hoped for better things.

The difficulties of his first five years in South Australia had obviously not deprived him of all hope and courage, for on 18 November 1847 he married Martha Grey of Glasgow in the Congregational Chapel in Adelaide. The Hübbes had four children. One of their sons, a captain in the South Australian forces, was killed in action in the Boer War in 1899. The marriage had infringed the ban on mixed marriages imposed by the Old Lutherans in the colony, and Hübbe was unable for some years to join a Lutheran congregation. Eventually he became one of the leading parishioners of the Bethlehem Lutheran Church in Adelaide.

Hübbe had some experience in publishing, and it comes

as no surprise that reporting for the *Register* was one of the first ventures he tried, albeit without lasting success. In the early 1850s he reported for the *Observer* and in 1874 he became the editor of the *Neue Deutsche Zeitung*, but left almost immediately because of political and religious differences with the proprietors. None of these occupations gave him more than very temporary satisfaction, and they did not solve his financial dilemma.

Had Hübbe been able to build a legal career, it would have given him an acceptable living and also a sense of self-worth, just as important as money. In 1846, when living in Grenfell Street, he found quasi-legal employment as a law clerk in the chambers of the barrister John Warner Nicholls of Gawler Place. This must have been poorly paid, and it did not last long.

School teaching would not have been too painfully distant from his chosen calling. He opened a German school in Kensington in 1847 and another in Buchsfelde (the name changed to 'Loos' in 1917), which he had to close when the Wesleyans set up a rival school there. His hope that he might find employment as a teacher in Hoffnungsthal (changed to Karawirra in 1917, and then again to Hoffnungsthal in 1975) was disappointed. His wife became a school teacher, too, and both may have found some success and satisfaction in instructing the young.

In 1857 he was appointed by Attorney-General Richard Hanson to the government position of German interpreter. His annual salary of £100 would have sustained him and his family, if only just. He tried to earn a little extra money by seeking occasional legal jobs. An advertisement by Hübbe in the *Adelaider Deutsche Zeitung* of 27 July 1860, in which he offered consultation on contracts, wills, naturalisations, powers of attorney and mortgages, shows that he tried, perhaps on other occasions as well, to attract legal business from the German community.[25] The Law Society, which had been established in 1851, must have seen this as an infringement of the monopoly of the legal profession and may well have forced him to stop. At any rate, revenue from this source would not have been sufficient to maintain him and his family. It must have come as a blow when the government abolished his position as an interpreter in 1866. One wonders why such a step was considered necessary. German–English interpreters had been needed from the very beginning of the colony and were no less needed in 1866 when the German population exceeded 11,000.

Hübbe's last attempt to achieve employment appropriate to his academic and professional achievements occurred in December 1874, when he applied to the Council of the recently founded University of Adelaide for the position of 'Professor or Lecturer docens in the Faculty of Law', emphasising his knowledge of 'the ancient Saxon and Feudal laws, the true foundations of English jurisprudence'. Alas, no one had ever heard of Dithmarschen or of sixteenth-century Brandenburg laws, and Hübbe, the legal historian, was of even less interest to the university or to any other potential employer than was Hübbe the lawyer. When, in 1883, the Faculty of Law was established, the University Council appointed a Cambridge graduate, Walter Ross Phillips, as lecturer in charge. Hübbe's approach, made eight years previously, had been forgotten.

During the elections for the House of Assembly in 1875 Hübbe stood as a candidate for the Barossa district but was unsuccessful. Before 1887 a seat in parliament was unremunerated, but it might have opened doors. Again, this was not to be.

Hübbe and the Torrens System

In Germany, Hübbe may have fallen short of his own expectations, but he had shown unusual skill as a lawyer, historian, publicist and perhaps also as a negotiator. His failure to achieve a suitable position in South Australia must have been a source of frustration and self-doubt. Once he began to involve himself by letters to the editors of South Australian newspapers and in other ways in matters of law reform, he had found an outlet for his creative energy, a way of making his knowledge and his skills useful to the community. He deserves credit for having become, in modern parlance, a 'public citizen'. It turned out to be the way to lasting fame, if not fortune.

By early 1857 Robert R. Torrens had been working for some time seeking to bring about the reform of the cumbersome and very expensive system used in the colony for real estate transactions. Hübbe's letters to the *Register*, published in early 1857, supported law reform in this area and suggested that the laws in force in Hamburg and in other Hanse towns were superior to the South Australian system. Having read the letters, Torrens sought discussions with

Hübbe and tried to enlist his assistance. Hübbe did not need much prompting and involved himself with great energy and enthusiasm, assisting Torrens wherever he could. He sought information about the Hamburg system by corresponding with his brother-in-law, Johann Friedrich Voigt, Amalia's husband, a successful Hamburg lawyer who eventually rose to great prominence in the German judicial service. There is also correspondence, still preserved in part in the Hamburg city archives, with his cousin Wilhelm, Karl Hübbe's son, who had been Ulrich's fellow law student in Jena and Berlin.

In 1857 Hübbe published, at the request of Torrens and at the expense of the ever-helpful George Fife Angas, the book mentioned earlier in support of the Torrens reform plans.[26] He considered that the book (or 'pamphlet', as he modestly called it) had been pivotal to the success of the reform measure:

> A copy of the pamphlet was laid on the table of each member of the House of Assembly while the principles of the Bill were pending before the House. The pamphlet was eagerly perused by members as well as by the outside public, all of which did much to strengthen the belief in the safety of the proposed measure. I received ample proof that even the legal profession found themselves at a loss to resist the overwhelming weight of evidence adduced.

Hübbe must also have been very pleased that, after a break of 15 years, this project gave him a chance to advance his literary ambitions. Although it was of only marginal relevance to the reform plans, he even indulged his love of ancient law by including a brief account of the ancient Saxon law of landed property.

Hübbe played a role not only in the preparation of the draft legislation but also in the parliamentary process itself. It appears that when Torrens was steering the Bill through the House of Assembly, Hübbe held himself in readiness, and Torrens consulted him on a number of occasions. The *Real Property Act 1858*, which established the Torrens System of land registration, came into effect on 1 July 1858. This event did not mark the end of Hübbe's involvement with the new system, his daughter Isabella later explaining that he became its 'watchdog'. In his 1884 petition to the South Australian Parliament for a pension, Hübbe explained that Torrens had persuaded him to assist without recompense with the drafting of the legislation and had promised that he would later be appointed to a position in the Registry Office. For reasons we do not know, this did not occur, but Torrens arranged for Hübbe to be given a desk in the Registry Office. From this vantage point he followed the progress of the new system and perhaps continued to offer advice to Torrens, who had become the Registrar-General. In early January 1861 the Attorney-General withdrew this minor privilege. Hübbe's expulsion from the office caused great indignation in the German community. Torrens was favourably inclined towards Germans and was not responsible for what must have seemed like a mean-spirited act.[27] According to the *Süd-Australische Zeitung* of 12 January 1861, the Attorney-General had expected opposition from Torrens and had used the opportunity of his absence from South Australia to expel Hübbe. Perhaps Hübbe had been too forthright in his criticism of leading personalities of the period. In 1857, he had publicly criticised Richard Hanson, who was then Attorney-General. In a parliamentary debate about the land fund, Hanson had opposed its future use for the support of German migration, with the argument that limiting it to migrants from the British Isles did not involve inequality, for those Germans who could not bring over their relatives were in the same position as British colonists like himself, who had no relatives to bring over. Hübbe regarded the argument as rather cynical and, in a letter published in the *Register* of 6 June 1857, he accused Hanson of 'marble-hearted coldness': '... a most essential ingredient of [true sound-hearted liberality] is humanity; and humanity is not the character of the sentiments thus expressed determinedly by the Attorney-General this night. *Dixi et animam salvavi* ("I have spoken and have saved my soul").'

It was not Hanson who caused Hübbe to lose his place in the Registry Office, for he had been deposed as Premier and Attorney-General in May 1860 and had become Leader of the Opposition, so it would seem that the reasons for Hübbe's expulsion will remain unknown.

Not surprisingly, there were difficulties with the administration of the legislation and amendments became necessary. The Real Property Law Commission, established in 1861 to examine the shortcomings of the system, had been told by a witness who knew the Hamburg system that it was less productive of litigation than its South Australian counterpart. The commission requested Hübbe to provide information. Hübbe's detailed response was printed as a parliamentary paper and was no doubt helpful when amendments were formulated.

In 1872 a further commission was established to consider the need for further amendments.[28] Hübbe prepared another opinion and was questioned extensively by the commission at three sittings during the period from February to April 1873.

The legal profession was hostile to the new system, and many lawyers, including James Hurtle Fisher, one of South Australia's most prominent lawyers who had initially supported Torrens, considered that it was repugnant to the law of England and thus null and void under imperial legislation. This became a serious problem when the same view was voiced by Justices of the Supreme Court. Hübbe reacted to these ominous developments by establishing an association for the defence of the *Real Property Act*, with a view to bringing pressure to bear upon politicians to come to its rescue if necessary.

Hübbe's contribution to the debate on the reform of the conveyancing system was not the only law reform measure which engaged his interest. As Frederick Sinnett had pointed out in his 1862 account of the progress of the colony, although the population only numbered 135,000 people, the parliament was responsible for a complete legal system, many facets of which needed reform. Hübbe argued for the abolition of primogeniture (achieved in 1869), gave evidence before a royal commission on the reform of inheritance law and drafted a Bill on this subject, proposed a consolidation of statute law, and formulated a plan for an index of all the laws of the colony. His success with such proposals was very modest, partly because the time for such useful measures had not yet come; there were more pressing problems.

Although Hübbe's 1884 petition did not result in his being awarded a pension, the parliament decided that a once-only payment of £200, a considerable sum, be made. One wonders whether the recognition of his services which this implied would not have been even more important to him than the financial help, although the payment must have been more than welcome in view of his modest circumstances. In the same year or even earlier, Hübbe lost his eyesight and during the last few years of his life he lived with his daughter, Mrs F.C. May. His mind remained clear to the end. He is said to have tried to learn the Gaelic language and taught himself to read Dr Moon's raised script and acquired the four gospels and the psalms in Moon script for his own use and that of his blind fellow Lutherans.

Conclusion

Two questions have been controversial for many decades: whether Ulrich Hübbe or Robert R. Torrens was the author of the Torrens System, and whether the system is a legal transplant of the law of Hamburg. Never have they been debated with such intensity and with such careful attention to all the relevant detail, as during the last 20 years. There may never be conclusive answers, but the most plausible answers are surely to be found by comparing the major features of the Bill passed by the House of Assembly on 15 December 1857 and by the Legislative Council on 26 January 1858 with the draft as it was before Torrens made contact with Hübbe. Antonio K. Esposito and Murray Raff on the one hand, and Greg Taylor on the other, have subjected these differences and innumerable surrounding circumstances and events to detailed analyses and have arrived at contrary conclusions, the former regarding Hübbe, the latter Torrens, as the true author.

This account of Hübbe's life will not resolve these issues. However, the contribution which can be made by comparing the lives and the personalities of the two candidates for the ultimate honour, although inevitably somewhat peripheral, is not without its own significance. Apart from illuminating an important aspect of the history of South Australia, it may help to throw new light on Hübbe's own account as summarised at the beginning of this contribution, which implies that he persuaded Torrens of the futility of proceeding with the use of the British *Merchant Shipping Act 1854* as the decisive model, and that Torrens thereafter handed over to him responsibility for a new draft based on the Hamburg model. It is submitted that this version of the story (1) had grown in Hübbe's mind for understandable (and entirely forgivable) reasons, and (2) cannot reflect in every respect the events as they in fact unfolded.

Who does not crave recognition and who does not see his or her own achievements in a golden glow? Who, when giving a serious account of such achievements (as distinct from one meant to be self-deprecating and ironic) will understate their significance? If Hübbe, during the last years of his life, suffered from this common human weakness, who would throw the first stone? The society in which he had chosen to live had denied him material rewards for the hard work invested in his study and training for a higher calling. He had salvaged his self-esteem by becoming a hard-working and unpaid public citizen. How reasonable is it to expect from him a coldly objective account of the impact he had made?

The element of exaggeration in Hübbe's account is easy to identify. Egalitarianism was hardly the hallmark of the colonial society of the period. Torrens and Hübbe were not at the same end of the societal spectrum: Ulrich Hübbe was eking out a meagre living and occupying a humble abode, probably in Freeman Street (now part of Gawler Place).[29] In 1854 Robert R. Torrens, nicknamed the 'Crown Prince of the colony' and by then a wealthy man, had completed the building of Torrens House, still one of the grand houses of Adelaide. It is easy to imagine the impression which it must have made on Hübbe, when Torrens, in early 1847, took him there in his own carriage for discussions about the reform plans. One wonders whether it reminded Hübbe of an encounter, years before in Berlin, when he was still a humble *Auskultator*, with Baron Karl Albert von Kamptz. Torrens emerges from the literature as disrespectful of authority, ambitious and aggressive. If there was one capacity which he altogether lacked, it was that of ever accepting the futility of anything which he had been doing for a sustained period. Torrens had the bit between his teeth and, although he had many helpers (whom he needed because he was not a lawyer), he was the leader of the pack in all respects and, in his eyes, Hübbe was nothing more than just another helper, albeit a particularly useful one. All of Hübbe's pronouncements at the time indicate that he admired Torrens for his initiative and that he was willing to play the role of assistant. It is surely fantasy to suggest that Torrens might have uttered a sentence such as: 'Ulrich, I have failed, please take over the drafting'.

That Hübbe's help with the draft could have been important is shown by the mortgage example given in Hübbe's book, for Hübbe seems to have persuaded Torrens to return to the concept of his (Torrens's) 1856 draft, that is, that a mortgage should merely be a charge rather than an all-out transfer. Whatever else might have changed in the draft Bill as a result of Hübbe's intervention, I must leave for others to judge.

Although Torrens deserves the credit for promoting the legislation politically, Hübbe's intervention was helpful at that level as well, for it enabled Torrens to argue in the House of Assembly: 'No one in this House will assert that this which is accomplished by Germans in Hamburg cannot be accomplished by German and English colonists in South Australia'. Who knows whether the determined opposition of the legal profession to the reform project could have been overcome without the demonstration that there was a living example of a successful registration system in Hamburg? Whether or not the law of Hamburg was transplanted to South Australia, it certainly played an important role in the development of the Torrens System. As for the *dramatis personae*, may they rest in peace.

Notes

1 Professor Emeritus, the University of Adelaide. The author is grateful to Ms Lee Kersten of the University of Adelaide and to Dr Greg Taylor of Monash University for having supplied important information.

2 J.H. Fisher, *A Sketch of Three Colonial Acts: Suggested for adoption in the new Province of South Australia, with a view to ensure the most perfect security of title to property, to simplify and facilitate the mode, and moderate the expense of its transfer: with proposed forms of deeds*, 1836. Ralph Hague has described the problems which arose between Fisher and the Governor in the first chapter of his book (R.M. Hague, *Hague's History of the Law in South Australia 1837–1867*, Barr Smith Press, 2005 [1936]).

3 R.R. Torrens, *The South Australian System of Conveyancing by Registration of Title with Instructions for the Guidance of Parties Dealing, Illustrated by Copies of the Books and Forms in Use in the Land Titles Office*, Register and Observer Printing Office, Adelaide, 1859.

4 S.C. Wilson & K.T. Borrow, *The Bridge over the Ocean*, Adelaide, 1973, p. 233.

5 *Königlich Preußisches Freikorps von Lützow* – a kind of light infantry, which consisted of self-financing volunteers who had banded together to fight in the wars of liberation.

6 Immortalised in *Die Hermannsschlacht* by Heinrich von Kleist, written in 1809.
7 *Verhältnisse der Dithmarschen mit den Hamburgern, vom Jahre Christi 1265 bis 1316.*
8 *Der Dithmarsche Neocorus.*
9 The full title of this work is: *Johann Adolfi's, genannt Neocorus, Chronik des Landes Dithmarschen, aus der Urschrift hrsg. von F.C. Dahlmann.* This edition is available in the Göttingen University Library.
10 Hans Schröder, *Lexikon der hamburgischen Schriftsteller bis zur Gegenwart* (*Lexicon of Hamburg writers to the present*), vol. 3, 1857, pp. 408–9.
11 *Litterarische und kritische Blätter der Börsenhalle.* The Börsenhalle in Hamburg housed the Chamber of Commerce. From there a number of political, economic and literary journals were published in the early part of the nineteenth century.
12 'Marquisate' is acceptable, although 'Margraviate' seems preferable.
13 *Bauernrechts- u. Gerichtsordnung der Alten Mark-Brandenburg; ein Landtagsschluß vom Jahre 1531. Mit Anmerkungen u. einer Übersicht des altmärkischen Gerichtswesens vom Jahre 1100 bis 1806.*
14 *Jahrbücher der Preußischen Gesetzgebung, Rechtswissenschaft und Rechtsverwaltung.*
15 *Landesarchiv Schleswig–Holstein.*
16 *Die Politik auf den Grund und das Maß der gegebenen Zustände zurückgeführt,* vol. 1, 3rd edn, 1847.
17 'Die früher unbekannte Urkunde ... zeigt, welche schützende Ordnungen des altmärkischen bäuerlichen Familienrechtes ... noch bis zum dreißigjährigen Kriege walteten.'
18 'gelehrt und was mehr ist mit Einsicht in das Leben der Dinge erörtert'. These comments would have thrilled a young man with Hübbe's academic aspirations. That Dahlmann and Hübbe were in communication is apparent from Hübbe's essay in the *Neocorus*, but it is difficult to determine whether the comments were published before or after Hübbe's departure in 1842 for the Antipodes. The text to which I have had access appears in volume I, p. 267 of the third edition of Dahlmann's book, published in 1847. The page number given in Schröder's Lexicon is 244, a reference either to the first edition of 1835 or to the second, which, oddly, appeared in 1847, the same year as the third.
19 *The Voice of Reason and History Brought to Bear Against the Present Absurd and Expensive Method of Transferring and Encumbering Immoveable Property,* Adelaide, 1857, p. 1.
20 *Evangelisch-Lutherische Missionsgesellschaft zu Dresden.*
21 *Verein lutherischer Missionsfreunde.*
22 *Der lutherische Pilger aus dem Norden für Wahrheit und Recht.*

23 *Missions-Nachrichten nebst Berichten von auswärtigen Gemeinden u. Colonieen, Gesammelt in Hamburg.*

24 Many Adelaide suburbs or streets bear the names of these prominent early English settlers, some of whom arrived later than Ulrich Hübbe. A probably incomplete list reads as follows: Osmond Gilles (first treasurer of the colony, had made his fortune in Hamburg); Philip Oakden (Gilles's brother-in-law, landholdings in South Australia); Robert Leake (large-scale grazier); John Hector (manager of the first Savings Bank); Frederick Sinnett (son of Edward Sinnett, teacher at the Johanneum); Thomas Wilson (solicitor, poet, linguist, art connoisseur and organ builder, second Lord Mayor of Adelaide); Francis Stacker Dutton (member of the Legislative Assembly); William Dutton (landholdings in South Australia); Frederick Hansborough Dutton (grazier in Kapunda); Alfred Swaine (employee of the South Australian Company).

25 The author is grateful to Ms Lee Kersten for having drawn this advertisement to his attention.

26 See note 19.

27 Torrens is reported as having stated on one occasion in the House of Assembly: 'The German race [is] congenital with ourselves, and their habits [are] similar to those of the Anglo-Saxon'.

28 Commission Appointed to Inquire into the Intestacy, Real Property and Testamentary Causes Acts.

29 That is where he had his office as a government-appointed interpreter. He may well have lived there or nearby.

Erhard Eylmann
Ethnographer and explorer

Wilfried Schröder

Few scholars of Aboriginal Australia would be familiar with the contribution made by the German ethnographer Erhard Eylmann (1860–1926), who travelled widely in Australia during the late nineteenth and early twentieth centuries, studying and recording the culture of many Aboriginal tribal groups in the centre and north of the continent.[1] He collected much detailed information about their physical appearance, anthropometry, language structure and grammar, sign language, smoke signals, details of ritual and non-ritual scarification, tooth avulsion, medicine, rituals and behaviour, social organisation, population density, totemism, age grouping, and so on. Eylmann also made a detailed study on begging in South Australia and provided data on fire-making. In 1908, he published his major work on Australian ethnography in German titled *Die Eingeborenen der Kolonie Südaustralien* (*The Natives of the Colony of South Australia*). Translated only in part into English, this work and Eylmann's contribution to Australian ethnography remain largely unknown to this day, especially outside the German-speaking world.[2]

Life and studies
By the second half of the nineteenth century, the geography of the earth was becoming more precisely known, largely due to new discoveries made on expeditions exploring the regions of South America, Africa and Asia, and by voyagers who journeyed to the Arctic and Antarctic waters and the Pacific Ocean, with its countless archipelagos. Australia, however, was referred to as the 'fifth continent' and its desert interior especially remained largely unexplored by Europeans.

Erhard Eylmann was born in 1860 in Krautsand, northern Germany. He spent his childhood in a harmonious family. At school he was very much interested in the natural sciences; a keen amateur astronomer, he was also greatly attracted to geography and geology. Thus it is not surprising that during his university years in Freiburg, Leipzig, Heidelberg and Würzburg he studied both the natural sciences and medicine. He obtained two doctorates, one in philosophy and the other in medicine.

It was in Freiburg in south-western Germany that he met his future wife, Beate Ruh, and theirs was a deep relationship, marked by strong common interests. Although of different faiths (Eylmann was Lutheran, Beate a Roman Catholic), they were able to marry without delay or complications in Helgoland. They then set out for Cairo, where Eylmann took up his first and only job as a medical doctor. He chose Egypt for its climate, as his wife was ailing, and he hoped that she would benefit from living in an arid climate. Tragically, the newly-weds enjoyed only three years of marriage before Beate Eylmann died. She left behind a distraught husband, who after her death left his medical post and completely renounced medicine, never again even mentioning that he was a medical doctor. He could not forgive himself his failure to save his beloved wife. His sense of guilt was impervious to any logical arguments. Embittered, he shut himself off and then returned to Germany, where he lived on his parents' farm.

After reappraising his situation for some time, Eylmann decided to change the direction of his life. He left in 1894 for Berlin, the metropolis of science, and enrolled at the Wilhelm University, where he took courses in ethnography, geography, and geology, all of which included much practical work. During his spare time he attended lectures at the Berlin Society of Anthropology, Ethnology and Prehistory. At these gatherings he met the co-founder of the Berlin Society Rudolf Virchow, the ethnographer Adolf Bastian and other leaders of science, who persuaded him to take advantage of the wealth of scientific institutions in Berlin. He often visited the Museum of Ethnography, the Museum of Natural Sciences and other museums there. Eylmann was thus more and more inclined to move his life in a new direction. He learned about the many voyages of explorers, who included Heinrich Barth, Ludwig Leichhardt,

Ferdinand von Mueller, Eduard Dallmann and Gerhard Rohlfs – the last two from his own Weser–Elbe homeland. He thought that he would find a new aim in life via such enterprises, and from them new perspectives might emerge. At that time many expeditions were being organised from Berlin, partly supported by the Academy of Sciences, partly by other organisations. The exploration of the German colonies at this time had not only a scientific but also an economic dimension.[3]

It is likely that his meetings with Virchow and others led him to develop a plan for an expedition to Australia, since this was a time when Europeans considered the 'fifth continent' rich terrain for ethnographic fieldwork. Eylmann clearly considered Australia to be the most suitable continent to carry out his own scientific investigations. Following detailed discussions in Berlin, he returned home, and then in 1896 he began the first of his Australian expeditions.

Eylmann the explorer
Eylmann arrived in Adelaide in February of 1896. As he later recorded in his *magnum opus*, he spent the first four weeks learning what he could about Australia in the library, in the zoo, in the Adelaide Botanic Garden and in various museums, including the South Australian Museum. With that preparation behind him, he commenced the first stage of his solo journey on the first day of March – it was a train journey to Oodnadatta, where he was to make the preparations for the expedition proper.[4] He then travelled primarily by horse or on foot north across the continent to Palmerston on Port Darwin, and then all the way back, only stopping for rest and to carry out his work along the way. He also made numerous excursions to the east and the west of the main track in search of Aboriginal people he could investigate. In early 1898 he was back in Adelaide.

The main purpose of that first great expedition was to visit Aboriginal tribes and to record as exactly as possible details about their lifestyles in order to ensure a solid basis for future investigations. In Adelaide he had been lucky enough to meet Amandus Zietz, Director of the South Australian Museum of Natural History, who became his friend and supporter. Thanks largely to Zietz, who familiarised him with the local situation and alerted him to potential problems he might encounter, as well as introducing him to the relevant literature on Aboriginal people, geography and so on, Eylmann became well acquainted with the prevailing conditions in Australia. Moreover, Zietz assisted him by making some practical preparations for his expedition. He wrote letters of introduction to different institutions and people, thereby making known Eylmann's impending arrival, which was crucial for Eylmann as a lone traveller.

Apart from his rail journey to Oodnadatta, Eylmann also travelled by camel, but mostly by horse, with long sections also covered on foot. He travelled like a simple 'bushman', as he described himself, accompanied only by the horses which carried his provisions, his scientific diaries and his notebooks. Colt pistol and rifle were always at hand, as he encountered many adventurous situations, and he shot game to feed himself as it became more and more difficult with passing time to locate and transport provisions.

Eylmann met many fascinating people from different walks of life along the way. In Alice Springs, for example, he met Francis James Gillen, who was to become famous for his studies of Aborigines, and he stayed at Gillen's home for some time. Eylmann consulted with his host, who did much to support Eylmann's journey by giving him letters of introduction to valuable contacts, and so on. Later Eylmann was to return the favour. Spencer and Gillen report in their own ethnographic masterpiece *The Native Tribes of Central Australia* that Eylmann – by their account at some considerable trouble to himself – had gone to a small cave in the Crawford Range to make a careful record of indigenous artwork there. His sketches of the designs are reproduced in their book.[5]

The main locations along the route that Eylmann followed were the Lutheran Hermannsburg mission station on the Finke River, Lady Charlotte Waters, Lake Woods and Palmerston. At these locations and elsewhere Eylmann lived for periods in the world of the Aborigines. He joined in with them whenever he could, eating, drinking and sleeping in their camps. During this time he made many photographs and sketches while recording in his notebooks meticulous descriptions of everything he observed in the social structures of the various indigenous groups he encountered – among them the Ngarrindjeri, Arabana, Diyari, Arrernte, Luritja, Wagait, Waramungu, and others. From these interactions he garnered a great deal of information on all aspects of Aboriginal social life, observing and recording the details of Aboriginal people's physical appearance, their polysyllabic language and sign language, the state of their health and much more.

Moreover, like many ethnographers of his time he was interested

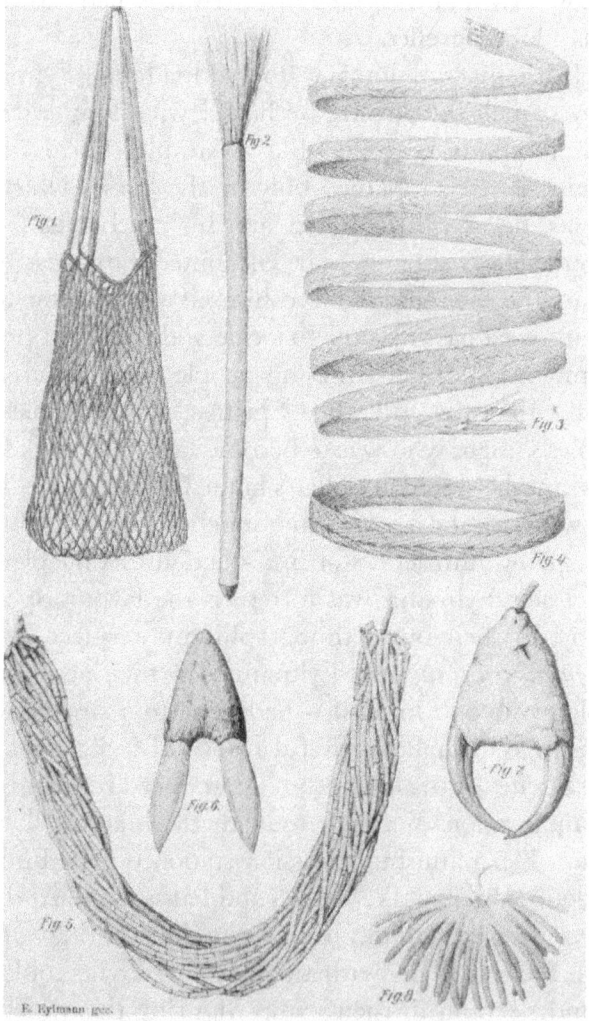

Some of Eylmann's detailed sketches of Aboriginal artefacts. (From his book *Die Eingeborenen der Kolonie Südaustralien*, Dietrich Reimer, Berlin, 1908, Table xxxvi)

in indigenous kinship systems, communal property, trade and gift exchange, religious beliefs, mythology, magical practices – including the use of magic in ceremonies, for example, in the rainmaking ceremony of the Arrernte. He examined the significance of dreams, spiritual beliefs, burial ceremonies, including cremation, cannibalism, the role of women, and initiation ceremonies. He observed fire-making practices, gaining insight into the myth of its origin and its methods. The further he travelled, the greater the knowledge he gained of hunting and fishing, the types of food eaten and thei cooking, tobacco and the narcotic plant known as *pitjuri*. He compared regional variations in such things as campsites, shelter, clothing, adhesives and weapons. Eylmann studied implements, basket-making, weaving, meshwork, ornaments, body decoration, music, corroborees, rock art and medical practices.

Not only did he observe and record, Eylmann also collected artefacts from Aborigines, such as boomerangs, clubs, spears, nets and others items, forming the foundation of an impressive ethnographic collection, which by the time of his death contained 263 objects – excluding rock samples. These objects he obtained by purchase, by exchange, or as gifts from many different tribes.

His interests extended beyond the indigenous people to their relations with others who had entered into their world. Encounters with missionaries, European settlers and the Chinese, along with many discussions around evening campfires, helped him to fill a significant number of diaries and notebooks. Among the missions he visited was Hermannsburg, where both Carl Strehlow and Johann M. Bogner supported him in his work. Eylmann spent some three months there in 1897.

Moreover, Eylmann developed an interest in the natural world, enabling him to publish scholarly work in this area as well. Of particular note is the expertise he developed in the area of ornithology. It took some time, but eventually he wrote two significant works on the birdlife of South Australia. The detailed results of his research in the field of ornithology are an indicator of the extraordinary breadth of his scientific knowledge and skill. Alas, his timing was poor; his work on birds was published on the eve of the Great War, with the result that it, too, did not gain the readership it deserved beyond the German-speaking world.[6]

As he travelled and explored, Eylmann lived in the simplest possible circumstances. He crossed bush and desert areas, sometimes in metre-high grass, fording streams and wild rivers as he made his way through seemingly impenetrable scrub. Eylmann's first great expedition to Palmerston and back in the years 1896 to 1898 was soon followed by a shorter expedition, this time to the south-east of Adelaide. Proceeding through Hahndorf, where of course he observed that the majority of the inhabitants were fellow Germans, he made his way to the Coorong and then proceeded as far as Cape Otway in Victoria. By that time he had covered a distance of some 800 kilometres, all of it on foot. He returned by another route, which took him through the Grampians and Bordertown back to Adelaide. In all this time he saw relatively few Aboriginal people – the difference from his experience in northern Australia was striking.

He was back in Adelaide for just two weeks before boarding a steamer bound for Germany. Yet his thirst for knowledge about Australia was still not fully quenched. In the middle of 1900 he was back in Adelaide, from where he made a further two shorter expeditions. One was very brief – just eight days to the mission station at Point McLeay on Lake Alexandrina. And then he headed north to Lake Killalpaninna – on the eastern edge of the Lake Eyre region – where the Lutheran missionaries had established the Bethesda mission and which became Eylmann's home for some six weeks. Thereafter he returned to Adelaide to await departure from Australia again at the end of August. Back in Germany he devoted himself to his ethnographic work towards the publication of his great study, but his thoughts turned to a renewed expedition in Australia, which he was able to complete in the period 1912–13. On that occasion, too, he journeyed extensively through the south-east of South Australia. After that expedition any thought of further travels in Australia were quashed by the intervention of the Great War and of Eylmann's descent into poverty.

Eylmann the ethnographer
Through all the travails, perils and privations of travel in the Australian outback, Eylmann never lost sight of the overriding mission he had set himself. He was determined to publish a book

A rare photograph of Eylmann in Australia. The identities of the two indigenous men and of the photographer are unknown. (Private archive of the author)

on Australia and on its Aboriginal peoples, a contribution to the cultural history of the continent.

After 1900 Eylmann's main activity was the preparation of that great work, which was finally published in 1908 and which included some 500 pages, 36 photos, eight other illustrations, one table and a map and index.[7] As far as content was concerned, Eylmann attempted an exhaustive presentation of the lives and cultures of Aboriginal Australians. He described their bodily and spiritual characteristics, spoken languages, pictorial languages, ceremonies, sexual life, social institutions, religion and the cult of death. He gave accounts of the alleged killing of children and sacrifice of men, fire-making, hunting and fishing, food and cooking, tools, toys, camps, shelter and camp fire, the use of clothing, colours, weapons, tools and utensils, spinning, weaving and pleating, jewellery, entertainment, primitive arts, maladies and treatment of the sick.

The greatest part of his work is related to this close observation of Aboriginal life and culture. It shows Eylmann to be deeply indebted to a German ethnographic tradition which valued above all else an empirical approach. Eylmann wanted to record and show his subjects exactly as they were in real life. His attention to detail is very impressive and indeed is the most valuable characteristic of his work. A helpful insight into what Eylmann himself hoped to achieve with his work is to be found in his foreword, where he writes:

> In this study I have attempted to describe in as much detail as possible the physical and spiritual nature of the indigenous population of the colony of South Australia. In this task of mine it has been my intention to remain purely objective in every regard and not to allow my judgment to be influenced by any prejudices or opinions expressed elsewhere. I am sure I do not need to stress too strongly that in my research I have applied the greatest care and conscientiousness.[8]

His indebtedness to German writing and thinking is evident in one area in particular. A very detailed table in his book contains precise measurements of 11 adult Aborigines taken at Killalpaninna. There are 40 measurements altogether, beginning with the exact distance from the top of the skull down to the soles of the feet, through to the size of the nostrils. In a note to his table Eylmann acknowledged that he was indebted to the physical anthropologist Rudolf Virchow in Berlin for the detailed scheme of measurements he applied.

Yet it is also clear from his book that he was well aware of English-language sources on Australian ethnography, with which he had the chance to familiarise himself in Adelaide before heading north. Thus, alongside the German ethnographic and even philosophical literature of the day, he cites such sources as the *Transactions, Proceedings and Reports of the Royal Society of South Australia*, along with Brough Smith's *The Aborigines of Victoria*, George Taplin's *The Narrinyeri*, David Lindsay's *An Expedition across Australia from South to North*, E.M. Carr's *The Australian Race*, Baldwin Spencer's *Report on the Work of the Horn Scientific Expedition to Central Australia* (the report was published in 1896, the year of Eylmann's arrival in Australia), and of course – more than any other single source – the standard work of Spencer and Gillen, *The Native Tribes of Central Australia*.

Whether in a German or an Anglo-Saxon tradition, and whatever the claims to pure objectivity made by Eylmann and many other ethnographers, nineteenth-century ethnography was of course anything but free of European values, judgments and perspectives, even if practitioners were not necessarily conscious of them. Indeed, Eylmann's writing is for the greatest part descriptive, and herein lies much of its value, but he does not stop short of making explicit judgment. In doing so he shows himself to be both a man of his time, heavily influenced by the ethnographic thinking of his age – and above all its 'Social Darwinism' – but he was also a very thoughtful observer, capable of compelling insights and indeed even criticism of European practices.

This is particularly evident in the concluding chapter of his book, where he discusses the role of missions. Having spent time at such places as the Catholic Mission at Daly River, the Lutheran Missions at Killalpaninna and Hermannsburg as well as the Point McLeay Mission (Raukkan) founded by the Aborigines Friends Association on Lake Alexandrina and run by the Congregationalist Minister George Taplin, Eylmann was well acquainted with their work and their impact on Aboriginal communities. His chapter gives quite a thorough and informative overview of missionary activity in South Australia and its Northern Territory in the nineteenth century. Yet it also begins with a critical observation, revealing some of Eylmann's own cultural prejudices:

> It appears that an unlucky star shone over the mission among the Aborigines of Australia from the beginning. Nowhere did the missionaries achieve the success they sought; on the contrary, in some regions they accelerated the death of the race. We need to seek the blame for these failures in a chain of causes of various kinds. Above all the Christian religion is not suited for a people of nature [*Naturvolk*], which stands on the lowest rung of culture. Can a human being such as the Australian, who has quite different conceptions of good and evil than we, and who every day must fight a tough battle to survive, devote himself lovingly to a God from whom he can expect no mercy, because in his weakness he cannot obey that God's commandments? Islam would certainly exert a greater appeal to the Aborigines ... But a good part of the blame for the fact that more or less all attempts at conversion have failed must be attributed not only in the doctrines of Christianity but also to their propagators, the missionaries.[9]

Oberes Bild: Zöglinge der Missionsstation Hermannsburg.

Unteres Bild: Schulkinder der Missionsstation Bethesda (Kilalpanina).

Photographs taken at the Lutheran mission stations at Hermannsburg (top, showing in back row the missionaries Johann M. Bogner and Carl Strehlow) and the Bethesda mission at Killalpaninna (below). (From Eylmann's *Die Eingeborenen der Kolonie Südaustralien*, Dietrich Reimer, Berlin, 1908, p. 177)

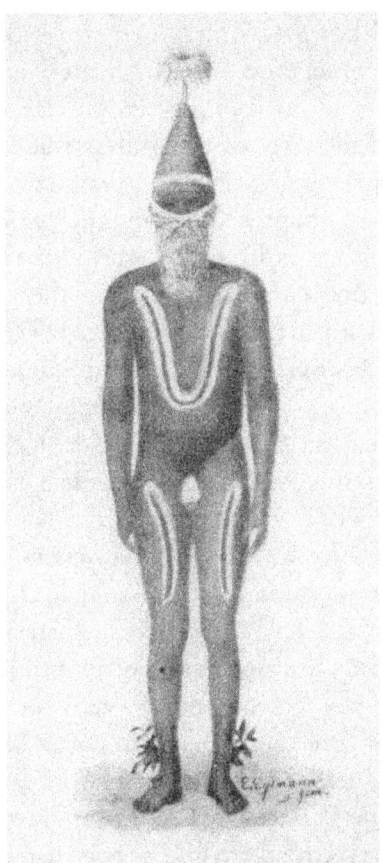

A west Aranda man decorated for Corroboree. (Based on a watercolour image by Eylmann in *Die Eingeborenen der Kolonie Südaustralien*, Dietrich Reimer, Berlin, 1908, title page)

Scholars in Europe reviewed Eylmann's work approvingly because he described many details that were hitherto unknown to them, thus making a major contribution to Europeans' knowledge of Australia and its peoples. An indication of the book's international importance was the appearance in 1961 of a facsimile edition by an American press.[10]

In both the original and the later facsimile edition an attractive feature is the inclusion of generous numbers of illustrations. Eylmann travelled with a camera and used it to good effect, but he was also a very gifted painter and draughtsman. Thus his descriptions of Aboriginal life and customs do not rely solely on the written word but are complemented by photographs, mostly of Aboriginal people, and also by watercolours and sketches. Most of these are contained in a series of appendices which record meticulously a broad range of cultural artefacts from various parts of South Australia and its Northern Territory.

Just as the last chapter of his major work was devoted to European missionaries, Eylmann's descriptive and analytical talents were applied to European Australians in the very last of his published works. It is an article published in 1922 under the slightly misleading title 'Das Bettelwesen in dem Staate Südaustralien und dem Nortterritorium vor dem Weltkriege' ('Begging in the State of South Australia and the Northern Territory before the World War').[11] As Eylmann concedes, in English there are a number of terms for the people he was studying: travellers, swagmen or swaggies, or, pejoratively, tramps, sundowners or loafers. Those he encountered were of numerous national backgrounds, including above all Irish, but also fellow Germans, Austrians, Italians, Swedes and Danes. During the depressed economic times of the 1890s he was struck by just how many of them there were throughout Australia. By the time of his visit in 1912–13 the numbers had declined, but he nonetheless found them worthy of study. They were people he had come to know well through his own extensive travels on Australian country roads; while he travelled in search of subjects for his ethnographic studies, they travelled long and far in search of work, relying on the generosity of those whose properties they came across. Eylmann by no means paints a rosy picture of the lives of the swagmen, many of whom he accompanied from great distances, giving him ample opportunity to enquire into their backgrounds and their hopes. As to a large extent he shared their lifestyle, it is not surprising that the objective tone of his report is not without a hint of empathy.

A sad fate
The First World War brought for Eylmann, as for many others, some dramatic changes. Until then he had lived using funds generated from his own property, which was invested in bonds; he paid for his expeditions and other scientific expenses from this money. Following the war, his capital was lost and he was suddenly

left without any income. He had to leave his flat in Hamburg and move to Rekum, a small settlement on the Weser. The reason for this choice was the presence of a big wool-combing enterprise in the vicinity, which meant for him a certain connection with Australia. However, Eylmann did not initially search out any contacts in his new home. The remaining money was sufficient to live in a very simple way. After some time, however, economic and other conditions deteriorated to the extent that the 60-year-old man had to take a job as a simple worker in the wool-combing factory. Each day he walked for an hour to the factory, where he spent his working hours, and at the end he walked home again. The combination of shift work, the unhealthy climate of the workshop and often insufficient food placed Eylmann in a very difficult situation.

In spite of this, he continued his scientific activity in his meagre free time. He had meticulously catalogued his ethnographic collection, and he subsequently devoted himself to his other collections, starting with the rock samples. His aim was to publish further results of his scientific expeditions in special publications, for example, his observations on begging in South Australia and the Northern Territory. At that time, however, there were few journals, and the possibilities for scientific exchange were also very limited for most researchers, including Eylmann. There were no jobs at museums, institutes and universities, and no money for Eylmann to purchase new scientific journals and books. He saved every penny from his wages, hoping to return to Australia once more; indeed he made detailed plans for a new expedition to this continent. In his loneliness, shared by many scientists of that time, he tried to occupy himself profitably, especially by cataloguing the geological part of his collection. He also attempted to flesh out his discussion of the medical aspects of his data, as in his great work he had only made preliminary statements about these issues.

The daily work, inadequate food and depressing circumstances wore down the otherwise energetic and vital Eylmann, a decline also aggravated by his bitterness over the lack of appreciation of his work. His connections to Australia were severed, too, because Germany had become the enemy during the war. He was quite isolated and was unable to follow the development of science or visit libraries, museums or institutes. The situation worsened from week to week, with the last years of his life characterised by famine and misery. The lonely scientist lost his strength, could not get up from his bed and had to be cared for by other inhabitants of the house. By the time he was hospitalised, it was too late, and he died soon after, primarily from hunger. He was buried on Christmas Eve in the year 1926. Nobody accompanied him on his last earthly journey. His death was as bitter and lonely as his last years.

Postscript

Some years ago, two of the most important Australian ethnographers were honoured in Adelaide, namely Baldwin Spencer and Francis J. Gillen. The latter had met Eylmann on his travels, both had benefited from Eylmann's fieldwork, and Gillen in a letter to Spencer wrote, 'I am sorry you did not meet him, he was a most interesting and really modest and unassuming man'.[12] In Adelaide however Eylmann's name was not even mentioned at this ceremony; his connection to them and their work has been overlooked. In the course of the history of science he was simply forgotten, as happens quite often. Nevertheless, ethnography in Australia lost in Eylmann one of its significant early participants. His book, as well as his other contributions, excel in both the scope and originality of his ideas. He anticipated areas of research that are still of considerable interest in the field of contemporary Aboriginal studies in Australia. As miserable as his life sometimes was, Eylmann has made himself an indispensable authority for his activities and publications. His name is being slowly rediscovered; it is inscribed in the annals of ethnography as a pioneer who will not be forgotten.

Notes

1 This essay is a revised and expanded version of a paper by the author published under the title, 'Erhard Eylmann: A pioneer of exploration and anthropology in Australia', *Anthropological Forum* 14, 1 (March 2004), pp. 43–51. Thanks to Peter Monteath and Chris Nobbs for assistance with the revised version.

2 His major work is *Die Eingeborenen der Kolonie Südaustralien* (D. Reimer, Berlin, 1908). Parts of Eylmann's publication have been translated into English. See Erhard Eylmann, *Selected chapters of Erhard Eylmann's 'Die Eingeborenen der Kolonie Südaustralien' in English*. Compiled by Robin Hodgson, translated by Renate Hubel (Robin Hodgson, Darwin, 1994);

Erhard Eylmann, *A further translation of selected chapters of Dr Erhard Eylmann's 'Die Eingeborenen der Kolonie Südaustralien' (The Aborigines of the colony of South Australia)*. Translated and transcribed by W.C. Gerritsen and Rupert Gerritsen (Intellectual Property Publications, Canberra, c. 2002). A shorter and earlier example of Eylmann's ethnographic work is his essay 'Das Feuermachen der Eingeborenen der Colonie Süd-Australien', *Zeitschrift für Ethnologie*, Vol. 34, 1902, pp. 89 ff.

3   See especially Wilfried Schröder, *Ich reiste wie ein Buschmann. Zum Leben und Wirken des Australienforschers Erhard Eylmann* (W.P. Druck Verlag, Darmstadt, 2002).

4   Eylmann, *Die Eingeborenen der Kolonie Südaustralien*, p. 6.

5   Baldwin Spencer and F.J. Gillen, *The Native Tribes of Central Australia*, Macmillan, London, 1899, p. 631).

6   Erhard Eylmann, Die Vogelwelt der Kolonie Südaustralien', *Journal für Ornithologie*, vol. 59, 1911, pp. 33–148 and 259–299; Erhard Eylmann, 'Die Vogelwelt des südöstlichen Teiles vom Staate Südaustralien', *Journal für Ornithologie*, vol. 62, 1914, pp. 1–35.

7   Eylmann, *Die Eingeborenen der Kolonie Südaustralien*, see fn. 2.

8   ibid., p. 5.

9   ibid., p. 464.

10 The reprinted edition is by Johnson Reprint Corporation, New York and London, 1966.

11 Erhard Eylmann, 'Das Bettelwesen in dem Staate Südaustralien und dem Nordterritorium vor dem Weltkriege', *Mitteilungen der Geographischen Gesellschaft in Hamburg*, vol. XXXIV, 1922, pp. 55–98.

12 Gillen to Spencer, 23 December 1898, in John Mulvaney, Howard Morphy and Alison Petch (eds.), *My Dear Spencer: The Letters of F.J. Gillen to Baldwin Spencer*, Hyland House, Melbourne, 1997, p. 248.

Colonial *Wissenschaft*
German naturalists and museums in nineteenth-century South Australia

Philip Jones

It is little known that the decision of the Prussian royal family to convert to Calvinism in 1613 ultimately benefited colonial science in Australia and in South Australia in particular. The movement towards national regeneration which followed Prussia's 1806 defeat by Napoleon's forces resulted in a reformed, superior system of education and produced several generations of outstanding German scholars. The defeat also hardened the theological resolve of Frederick William III. In 1817, marking the 300th anniversary of the Reformation, he decreed the unity of the Reformed and Lutheran churches, thus bridging the 'religious gulf which separated Reformed monarch and Lutheran subject'.[1]

The ensuing persecution of recalcitrant Old Lutherans resulted in the eventual decision of three influential pastors to choose exile over conformity to the Calvinist new order. One of those was August Kavel, who lost his pastorate at the Brandenburg village of Klemzig shortly after joining the Old Lutherans in 1835. He made his way to Hamburg immediately, seeking emigration agents who might provide a new future for his congregation. In South Australia's foundation year of 1836 Kavel found himself negotiating with agents of the South Australian Company, ultimately befriending George Fife Angas in London.[2] Despite his strict Baptist background, Angas regarded the Old Lutherans as fellow Dissenters. The resultant flow of German migrants to South Australia derived from this chain of events, even if their subsequent motives became primarily economic and political, rather than religious.

German immigrants featured prominently among ethnographers, natural scientists, artists, craftsmen and photographers in colonial

Australia. But South Australia's particular encouragement of German immigration from the first years of settlement meant that the scientific and cultural effect of this phenomenon was apparent in that colony before others, becoming so deep rooted that its effects may still be detected.[3] These scientific qualities had little to do with national identity per se; miners from the Harz mountains in the Kingdom of Hanover comprised 15 per cent of mid-nineteenth century German immigrants to South Australia, but few made a mark in the arts or sciences.[4] There were at least two determining factors: the quality of the immigrant's education and whether a framework existed for turning raw observation into 'science'. This process depended both on publishing verifiable records and on the preservation of specimens in museums – initially primarily in Germany or elsewhere in Europe, but progressively within the new colonial outposts of science.

The pioneer Australian science historian Roderick Home has shown how science became a distinctive 'German export' to Australia, fundamentally influencing colonial society.[5] The role of German scientists as 'the carriers of Western science' fits the three-stage model for the introduction of Western science into non-European countries, postulated by George Basalla.[6] In fact, they straddled the first two phases. In South Australia men such as Ferdinand von Mueller and William Blandowski played a small role as naturalist–explorers in a scientific project which was an extension of geographical exploration itself. These were minor forays however and it must be acknowledged that, in the absence of a Ludwig Leichhardt, most notable South Australian exploration was undertaken by British explorers and naturalists. German scientists made their greatest contribution to the second phase, in which colonial science emerged, drawing 'upon institutions and traditions of a nation with an established scientific culture'.[7] While these influences were largely British, German immigrants played key roles in strengthening incipient scientific institutions in South Australia, preparing the ground for Basalla's third phase, in which colonial science was to become largely self-sufficient.

This chapter explores the first and second phases of the German contribution to natural science in colonial South Australia, with special reference to museums. Significantly, the period spans the working life of that most influential German scientific immigrant,

Ferdinand von Mueller, whose encouragement and recommendations directly affected science in South Australia well beyond his brief residence in the colony from 1847 to 1852, and arguably persisted beyond his death in 1896.[8]

The notable German practitioners of colonial science were skilled, observant individuals, trained in those 'Humboldtian' *Gymnasia* and universities founded in Prussia following its 1806 defeat by France. While the *Gymnasium* system provided classical education for the elite, 90 per cent of German children also benefited from the eight years of broad education provided by the *Volksschule*. This equipped them for entry to the new technical universities founded in major German cities, including Hamburg, Munich and Frankfurt am Main. The comprehensive and effective system of education instituted by Wilhelm von Humboldt (older brother of the explorer and naturalist, Alexander von Humboldt) ensured that educated Germans reaching Australia in subsequent decades were sufficiently versed in the natural sciences to comprehend and make an effective record of their encounters.[9]

Wilhelm von Humboldt implemented his scheme well aware of the strong influence on German educationalists and teachers exerted by the progressive schools in Switzerland, established by Pestalozzi at Yverdon, by de Fellenberg at Hofwyl and by Froebel (originator of the kindergarten) at Keilhau and Frankenburg. All these schools paid equal attention to mental, moral and physical education and stressed the importance of 'object lessons' and nature study. One of de Fellenberg's pupils was Francis Dutton, author of *South Australia and its Mines* (1846) and a strong supporter of German immigration to the colony. He was a son of a former British official in Cuxhaven and had grown up in a bilingual household. He attributed his co-discovery of the Kapunda copper mine in 1842 to his 'habit of examining rocks and stones, whenever my attention was arrested by any curious appearance in them, a habit which I acquired at Hofwyl, Mr de Fellenberg's celebrated institute'.[10] Privileged students such as Dutton were not the only beneficiaries; von Humboldt's reforms affected all Prussian schools, so that by the time of the first German emigration to South Australia a wide cross-section of young men (and a narrower cross-section of women) was equipped to make such observations. Trained in botany, zoology and mineralogy, in addition to his profession as a doctor, the young doctor Hermann Beckler arrived in Australia determined to add to the scientific record. As he confided to his journal on reaching Moreton Bay in 1856:

> Australia is to be the place where I shall make comprehensive studies and assess them. Someone who resides for years in foreign lands without something new or valuable to report does not deserve the gift of life.[11]

This amounted to a Humboldtian principle. It was shared not only by those German scientists who have entered Australian history, such as Becker, Leichhardt, von Mueller, Krefft, Semon, Amalie Dietrich and Blandowski, but also by lesser-known Germans who left their mark on South Australian science, such as Marianne Kreusler, Johannes Odewahn, Herman Behr, Otto Tepper and Amandus Zietz. Many of these individuals made contributions in several fields, reflecting not only their broad scientific education but also their capacity to place their findings on record.

Beckler's confident assertion carried the assumption that his studies and assessment of new observations would be 'reported', received and evaluated by colleagues. Indeed, his observations could only become 'scientific' through that reception. In a small, recently founded colony it was hardly possible for this to occur until the establishment of collecting institutions such as a museum and botanic gardens, or until the formation of philosophical or natural history societies capable of discussing and publishing scientific records. The emergence of these South Australian institutions during the mid- and late-nineteenth century was a crucial step in crystallising scientific endeavour within the colony. Until then it was understandable that significant collections would be sent to museums and universities in Britain and Germany. Another avenue was through local publication. The early establishment of a printing press in Adelaide enabled the publication of Menge's *Mineral Kingdom of South Australia* and Teichelmann and Schürmann's *Outlines of a grammar, vocabulary, and phraseology of the aboriginal language of South Australia, spoken by the natives in and for some distance around Adelaide*, both in 1840.

German scientists did not play a direct role in establishing Adelaide's first cultural institutions, such as the small Natural

History Society founded in 1838, the Botanic Garden founded in 1855, the Mechanics Institute founded in 1839, or indeed, the South Australian Institute itself (precursor of the colony's Public Library, Museum and Art Gallery), founded in 1856.[12] It was a different matter in Gawler, the closest large town to the German settlements of the Barossa Valley, north of Adelaide. Gawler's Institute Museum opened in 1857, five years before Adelaide's Institute Museum. The first two directors were Germans – Richard Schomburgk from the nearby village of Buchsfelde, and Otto Wehrstedt, perhaps better known for his later role in founding the town's pioneering Shop Assistants Union during 1863. By 1881 Otto Wehrstedt had prepared a detailed catalogue of the Gawler Institute collection.[13] It was weighted towards natural history, particularly ornithology, conchology and mineralogy, but also contained more than 200 ethnographic objects, catalogued under the heading 'Fijian and other Curiosities', a telling indication of the influence of the 'exotic' on collecting priorities. Another Buchsfelde resident and keen naturalist, August bis Winkel, assisted in managing the museum.[14] Schomburgk's friend and future brother-in-law, Dr Carl Muecke, was another early supporter, and was later to supply the South Australian Institute Museum with fossils and geological specimens. A keen natural historian and a graduate of the Freiberg University of Mining and Technology, Muecke contributed 'four cases of mineral specimens, and one case of colonial and foreign insects' to the Gawler Institute's first anniversary exhibition of 1858. Of more than passing interest at that exhibition was 'a valuable collection of Mss and autographs, including one from the celebrated Baron Humboldt addressed to Mr Schomburgh [sic] of Gawler'.[15]

Several German naturalists maintained small museums in South Australia, including Carl Muecke, the geologist Johann Menge, entomologists Marianne Kreusler and Johannes Odewahn, and the Mount Gambier doctor, Eduard Wehl (brother-in-law of von Mueller). Of these, Menge's was certainly the most unconventional. Despite his broad education and an earlier apprenticeship to a Hanau mineralogist named Carl Cäsar von Leonhard, Menge was largely self-taught as a geologist. By the time of his arrival in South Australia in January 1837 he had come to spurn conventional taxonomic description, in favour of his own eccentric system based on 'types and analogies, links and connections, that would be ordinarily overlooked by others'.[16] Menge's approach is conveyed in this extract from a lecture given at the School of Arts in Adelaide during 1841:

> The formations of the magnesium rocks are very important in the Barossa Ranges, particularly the talc, the soapstone and the asbestos. The last occurs as a rock-wood, rock-silk, rock-flax, and rock-cork, and it enters, with its splendid fibres, into a great variety of silica minerals, imparting to them a chatoyant lustre, when polished into an oval shape, particularly to chalcedony, opal, opal-jaspar, cornelian, agate, hornstone, etc. Besides, it enters into bidderspar, white marble, and different sorts of limestone, so that we shall have a choice of precious stones peculiar to South Australia, which will excite particular attention to our colony when they become fashionable in other parts of the world.[17]

A peripatetic individual, Menge based himself for several years in a 'half cave, half hut' on a small island in Jacob's Creek, in the Barossa Valley. There he maintained an extensive collection, occasionally selling specimens to private collectors and museums. Today his Australian reputation rests rather uncertainly on his *Mineral Kingdom of South Australia*, an erratic compendium published during 1840, but Menge's authority as a mineralogist seemed undisputed during the late 1840s, when his services were sought by Queensland and Western Australia. The pioneer Australian historian James Bonwick encountered Menge shortly before his death at the Forest Creek gold diggings in Victoria in 1852. Bonwick regarded him as a mineralogist 'without a rival in Australia', who loved his adopted South Australia 'as a foster child'. He was:

> not only a *savan* [sic] of intellect, but a philosopher of the heart. The outward world was not the only subject of his investigations, nor did it claim his chief attention. He was still a dreamer from the lands of dreamers. He saw a beauty in the gem beyond its crystal charm, and heard music in our forests beyond the fall of waters, the voice of wind, or the melody of birds. For days and weeks the little old man would disappear from society, subsisting, like the natives, upon bulbs and fruits …[18]

Eight years after his death Menge's 'entire and complete collection of mineral specimens … comprising the most extensive and complete selection ever collected of South Australian specimens', was sold at auction in Adelaide.[19]

The German contribution to the study of insects (entomology) in South Australia was remarkable. On 6 August 1849, as a 38-year-old widow from the principality of Waldeck, Eugene Constance Josephine Marianne von Kreusler arrived in South Australia on the *Prinzessin Luise* with her three teenage children. In contrast to the first wave of German immigrants a decade earlier, passengers on the *Prinzessin Luise* were mostly bourgeois and highly educated. They were undoubtedly aware of the utopian vision of South Australia's own dissident founders. The passengers included the musician–composer Carl Linger, educationalist Martin Basedow and the artist Alexander Schramm. The ship had been chartered in Hamburg by the Berlin Migration Society, principally formed by three other passengers, the brothers Richard and Otto Schomburgk and Dr Carl Muecke, refugees from the revolutionary events of 1848. Although a Catholic, Marianne von Kreusler also seems also to have been a member of this society, which was partly sponsored by the Schomburgks' friend, Alexander von Humboldt himself, and by his colleague, the mercurial Prussian geologist and naturalist, Leopold von Buch. The land on the Gawler River's northern bank chosen for settlement by the small *Prinzessin Luise* group was named Buchsfelde in his honour, and we can assume that at least some of Kreusler's specimens, and those of other South Australian German naturalists, made their way to him.

Marianne Kreusler's husband Georg had died a few months earlier in South America, apparently of fever contracted during an attempt to form a German colony (perhaps in Brazil, where there were several such ventures). Marianne may have made plans to join him there, but was later convinced to join the South Australian venture. According to family tradition she severed links with her own noble family on leaving for Australia and dropped the 'von' in her name. Her life in South Australia would be one of genteel poverty, but her scientific expertise linked the young colony to world centres of science and collecting. She deserves recognition as South Australia's foremost female naturalist of the nineteenth century.[20]

Marianne Kreusler established a small but impressive house–museum on her three-acre property, adjacent to her friends, the

Entomologist and naturalist Marianne Kreusler (1811–1892), pictured in old age. (Philip Jones)

Schomburgk brothers. With its glass cases, mounted birds, minerals, shells, insects and animals, the Buchsfelde museum attracted many visitors and became a focus for German naturalists in the Barossa. Indeed, it is worth considering the possibility that Marianne arrived in South Australia with a small cabinet of specimens and an intention of making a living from natural history, just as her compatriot Amalie Dietrich was able to do in Queensland, supplying Hamburg's Godeffroy Museum.[21] In any event, on her arrival in South Australia Marianne Kreusler was clearly a knowledgeable and practised naturalist, able to skin and mount birds, and to differentiate species of tiny beetles, for example. She exchanged specimens with German museums and collectors, supplied the Gawler Institute Museum, and sold entomological specimens to the South Australian Museum.

The following quotation from an Adelaide newspaper illustrates Marianne Kreusler's location within an international web of science, despite her remote situation:

Her special line was entomology, particularly beetles. Many a day in the height of summer, in the quivering meridian heat, she has spent in the scrub in unremitting search after her beloved coleoptera. These, with the assistance of a favourite granddaughter, she skilfully mounted and treated with a secret preservative. The late Baron von Mueller was indebted to this indefatigable worker for many a collection of rare and almost unknown insects; and Professor French of Melbourne, and the curator of the Sydney Museum were also supplied from her store ... her correspondents were not confined to Australia. The famous Austrian naturalist, Dr. Franz Anton Nickerl, of Prague, was a particular friend ... she acquired the position of an authority on Australian entomology, and was elected an honorary member of the Linnaean Society. Through all this success she retained utmost kindness and refinement.[22]

Kreusler featured in the Australian and international entomological literature of the 1860s. Parramatta-based entomologist Rev. Robert Lethbridge King described her as his 'valued correspondent ... who has already done so much, especially in the detection of the more minute forms of the Entomology' of South Australia: 'I have dedicated this species to its talented discoverer'.[23] By 1882, when Kreusler's collection was offered to the South Australian Institute Museum for £500, it consisted of 70 small cedar cases containing Lepidoptera and Coleoptera specimens, about 350 bird skins, minerals (including 'copper ore, agates and other stones'), shells, corals, reptiles, animals, as well as some Aboriginal artefacts.[24] After visiting her museum during the late 1870s the South Australian biographer George Loyau noted that 'Mrs. Kreusler stated she intended parting with the collection, and that some gentlemen from the neighbouring colonies were in treaty for it'. The collection's ultimate fate is unclear, although it seems that the South Australian Museum purchased the bulk of her Lepidoptera specimens for £210.[25] It appears that few of these specimens have survived, so that Marianne Kreusler's best memorial lies in the various South Australian species of entomology and shells named after her.[26]

Kreusler was assisted in her collecting by her lodger, Johannes Odewahn, a German entomologist from Mecklenburg–Schwerin who had probably arrived in South Australia during 1848. He was also a skilled taxidermist, preparing his own bird skins as well as others sent to him by friends. Odewahn and Kreusler both sent insect specimens from the Gawler River region to the Rev. Robert Lethbridge King during the 1860s, and King reciprocated by naming several species in their honour.[27] Odewahn sent insects from the Hummocks (at the head of St Vincent's Gulf) to the Sydney naturalist and collector William Macleay, to George Masters at the Australian Museum (who visited Odewahn and Kreusler at Buchsfelde during the mid-1860s), to Godfrey Howitt in Melbourne, and to the English entomologists Joseph Baly and F.P. Pascoe, both of whom named species in his honour.[28] Odewahn sent live specimens of the wasp, *Paragioxenos brachypterus*, to the Czech entomologist Dr Otto Nickerl at the Prague Museum, for breeding purposes.[29] Odewahn also supplied the South Australian Institute Museum; its curator Frederick Waterhouse spoke of him in 1865 as 'a German friend' and 'our best entomologist'.[30]

But Odewahn had broader and riskier interests. According to a former Buchsfelde resident, Marianne Kreusler arranged her varied natural history collection in one of her cottage's two front rooms, leaving the other for Odewahn, who filled it with his own mounted birds, insects and other natural history specimens, together with a series of framed photographs – some from magazines and photographs, and others he had taken himself. These were presumably landscape views; none have been traced. In December 1876 Odewahn's career ended abruptly and tragically. Port Adelaide customs officers impounded a package of books he had imported from Germany, 'on account of obscene prints being found amongst them', citing his apparent intention 'to use some chemicals he had imported in multiplying copies of the prints'. A day later, on the eve of the trial, Odewahn took poison at Buchsfelde and died.[31]

The South Australian Institute Museum missed the first opportunity to acquire Odewahn's collection, prompting a scathing response from the President of the Royal Society of South Australia, Ralph Tate: 'The lack of patriotism among those who regulate the affairs of the Museum has been most deplorably shown in some instances that have come to my knowledge... why has not that choice collection of our native beetles formed by the late Mr Odewahn been secured for the country?'[32] It seems, though, that at least part of Odewahn's collection passed to Marianne Kreusler and was later acquired from her.[33]

The early curatorial reports of the South Australian Institute Museum provide an insight into the activities of several German naturalists. At least two of these had direct links to von Mueller. The chemist Moritz Heuzenroeder provided von Mueller with his first job in Adelaide at his Rundle Street pharmacy. A keen collector of plants and insects, he was among the first South Australian botanists to collect on Kangaroo Island.[34] Heuzenroeder's brother Heinrich (Henry) had accompanied von Mueller to Australia aboard the *Hermann von Beckerath*. He became a keen collector of coins and medals, sharing this interest with the Mount Gambier doctor and amateur naturalist Eduard Wehl, who married von Mueller's sister Clara in 1853.

As further evidence of the interlocking character of German natural history in the colony, Wehl had accompanied Wilhelm Blandowski to the Victorian gold diggings during 1852.[35] Von Mueller visited Wehl and his sisters Clara and Bertha at Mount Gambier en route to Melbourne a few months later. Clara maintained her own interest in botany following her marriage to Wehl during 1853, sending specimens of seaweed to her brother at the Melbourne Botanic Gardens in 1866, for example.[36] Undoubtedly assisted by Clara, Eduard Wehl kept a small private museum at Mount Gambier and sent various natural history specimens (including birds and small mammals) to the Adelaide and Melbourne museums, as well as to von Mueller.[37] He befriended the Penola-based geologist Julian Tenison Woods, and shared Friedrich Krichauff's scientific interest in growing resistant wheat strains; samples were included in South Australia's contribution to the 1862 London Exhibition.[38]

The impact of German science in South Australia can be measured in many ways, not least by noting the numbers of naturalists in the field at any one time. In late 1849, for example, at least 10 German botanists were in South Australia, 'busily making plant collections, and extending knowledge of the colony's flora'.[39] Undoubtedly, there were a great many more German men and women who were engaged in collecting plants as an absorbing interest or useful pursuit, and occasionally such names come to light.

Of the 1849 German botanists, Kraehenbuehl names Ferdinand von Mueller, Dr Herman Behr, William Hillebrand, William Blandowski and Ferdinand Osswald (who had arrived on the

Hermann von Beckerath with von Mueller in 1847). At least another six may join this list, including three Buchsfelde residents – Richard Schomburgk, Marianne Kreusler (who sent plant specimens to von Mueller in Melbourne and to Schomburgk in Adelaide) and the naturalist Friedrich Schultze. As well as Moritz Heuzenroeder and Eduard Wehl, one more botanical collector who sent specimens to von Mueller in Melbourne should be mentioned. This was Carl Wilhelmi, whose three-year collecting sojourn in South Australia began in March 1849, a week after his arrival in the colony, with a trip to the Macclesfield area, followed by expeditions to Wellington on the Murray, to Tanunda and Moorunde, to the Murray Mouth, and finally to the Port Lincoln area during the 1850–51 summer. Wilhelmi based himself there at the home of German missionary Clamor Schürmann (who also sent plants to von Mueller), resulting in a detailed ethnographic paper, which was one of the first to consider the Aboriginal classification of foods and seasons.[40] Wilhelmi's specimens were directed primarily to von Mueller in Melbourne, and he later joined his mentor there as a botanical assistant.[41]

Of the contributions made by this remarkable group of German botanists, perhaps that of the young physician Hans Hermann Behr (1818–1904) has been least appreciated. Kraehenbuehl's biographical sketch makes it clear that Behr matched von Mueller in his erudition, mastery of diverse scholarly fields and his appetite for fieldwork. His two visits to South Australia, during 1844–45 and 1848–49 (a trip arranged by his father in order to remove the radically inclined young man from the 1848 revolution), amounted to barely two years, but in that time he comprehended and described the flora and insect fauna from north of Adelaide, through the Barossa Valley to the 'Murray scrub'. He discovered at least 70 new plant species, and was among the first scientists to comment on the changes wrought on the South Australian landscape by introduced species of plants and animals. Significant remnants of Behr's collections are preserved today in Halle and Hamburg. The Buchsfelde naturalists had hardly established themselves by the time of his visit, but it is difficult to imagine Behr missing an opportunity to meet and converse with Richard Schomburgk, whose botanical observations of British Guiana, *Reisen in Britisch Guiana*, had recently been published in Leipzig.

Behr met von Mueller during his second visit to Adelaide, and the pair may have botanised together. Behr also met the German botanist William Hillebrand, who spent six months of 1849 in South Australia collecting plants at the Murray Mouth and Lake Alexandrina before travelling on to Honolulu, where he established its botanic gardens and became known as the founder of Hawaiian botany. Hillebrand later sent Hawaiian and Australian plant specimens to von Mueller at the Melbourne Herbarium, including two South Australian plants named for him: *Veronica hillebrandii* and *Phebalium hillebrandii*.[42] At one time Behr had as many as 27 Australian plants named in his honour, and it is interesting to speculate on what his scientific impact might have been, had he remained longer in Australia.[43] By September 1850 Behr had arrived in San Francisco, where he was to spend the rest of his life as the city's most celebrated botanist.

This passing parade of German naturalists through South Australia during 1849 preceded the establishment of the Gawler Institute Museum, the South Australian Institute Museum and even Marianne Kreusler's small museum at Buchsfelde, yet it is easy to imagine that their presence inspired several young German naturalists who later influenced those institutions. J.G.O. (Otto) Tepper arrived during 1847 as a six-year-old with his family, who were religious refugees from Prussia.[44] His eventual range of scientific and scholarly interests – encompassing entomology, botany, geology, anthropology and meteorology, as well as more esoteric subjects such as German *Lieder* and poetry – suggest that his father had benefited from a Humboldtian education. Tepper's family settled near Lyndoch, where the Gawler Institute had opened a branch, providing an early stimulus for Otto's scientific curiosity. In Lyndoch he also befriended Dr T.L. Richter, known in the district as naturalist and collector.[45] Otto's career as a schoolteacher began in 1867. During the next 15 years his postings allowed him to indulge his passion for collecting and classifying natural history specimens, particularly in botany and entomology, fields judged especially useful for an agriculture-based economy. He published a series of papers in German scientific periodicals such as the *Botanisches Centralblatt*, as well as in local papers. These dealt with the natural history of the Nuriootpa district in the Barossa Valley, Ardrossan

Johann Gottlieb Otto Tepper (1841–1923), entomologist and naturalist. (South Australian Museum)

on Yorke Peninsula, and Clarendon in the Adelaide Hills, where his teaching career took him.

In 1883 Tepper's efforts were repaid with his appointment as natural history collector at the South Australian Institute Museum, very likely on the recommendation of its outgoing German director, Wilhelm Haacke. Otto Tepper's working journals, spanning his time in the Barossa Valley and at the Museum in Adelaide, suggest his exposure to a constant ferment of discussion and ideas about natural science, emanating partly from the German community, and enabling him to form enduring bonds with other colonial naturalists and scientists. Like Schomburgk and von Mueller, who also published in Australia and Germany, Tepper's career epitomises that of the migrant–scientist, filled with curiosity about the new country, but drawing his primary references from the fatherland. His German publications are a reminder of that constant influence, and Tepper followed the lead of other German scientists in sending collections back to Germany. In 1868, for example, he sold a large collection, 'chiefly of Coleoptera [beetles]', to the Berlin Museum.[46]

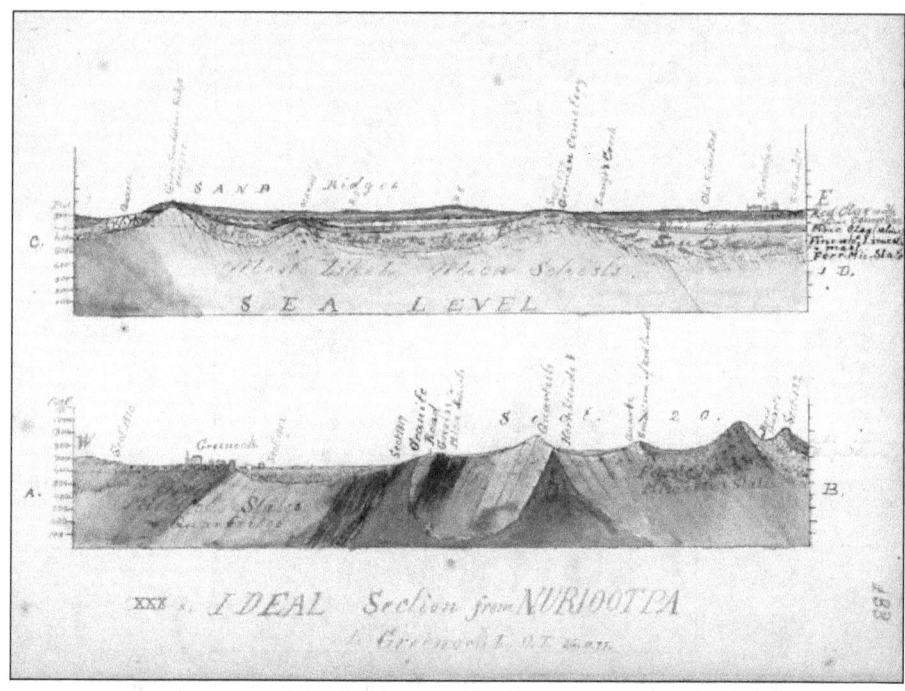

Tepper's 1877 sketch of a geological section from Nuriootpa to Greenock, Barossa Valley.
(South Australian Museum Archives)

While German scientists may not have directly influenced the birth of Adelaide's scientific and cultural institutions, they soon played an important role in their affairs. Both the Institute Museum and the Botanic Garden appointed German scientists to succeed the first, English directors of these small institutions. William Blandowski was appointed as the first director of the Melbourne Museum, and Gerard Krefft became the second curator at the Australian Museum in Sydney. Dr Wilhelm Haacke was appointed as the South Australian Institute Museum's second curator in 1880, but a German influence had already become apparent at this institution. During the mid-1860s curator Frederick Waterhouse had engaged Friedrich Schultze (another Buchsfelde resident) as a natural history collector. Schulze had previously contributed specimens, including mounted birds, to the Gawler Institute.[47] During 1865 he collected for Waterhouse at the North-West Bend of the Murray River (near present-day Morgan).[48] In that year Richard Schomburgk had succeeded Henry Francis as Director of the

Tepper's unpublished watercolour plate of 'new or rare'
South Australian moths, c. 1875.
(South Australian Museum Archives)

Adelaide Botanic Gardens and also engaged Schultze as a plant collector. By the time of the 1869 Goyder Northern Territory Survey Expedition, Schomburgk was able to recommend Schultze to Waterhouse as the expedition's botanist and naturalist.[49]

Appointed as Assistant Botanist on Goyder's Expedition, Schultze was accompanied to Port Darwin by his son Alfred.[50] The pair were assiduous collectors, consigning 12 boxes of dried plants and natural history specimens to the Adelaide Botanic Garden and the Museum within a month of the expedition's arrival at Port Darwin. They did so at some personal risk, as conflict with Larrakiah and Woolna (Djerimanga) people in the vicinity of the Port Darwin settlement had caused Goyder to erect a fence or stockade around it. The Schultzes needed to range more widely by necessity and on at least one occasion they returned to the stockade in fear of their lives.[51] Among the preserved bird skins, crustaceans, shells, insects, fish, reptiles, and corals were an Aboriginal weapon and some emu feathers 'used by the Natives as Ornament'.[52] More Aboriginal material followed in later months. 'Native weapons and manufactures', including 'spears, basket-work, amulets etc' were among their June consignment of natural history specimens. With another large consignment of 35 boxes of animals, birds, fish, reptiles, corals, insects and plants sent south by ship in January 1870, Schultze included examples of ceremonial Aboriginal headgear – the first recorded acquisitions of their type by the Museum.[53]

The Darwin region's distinctive flora and fauna attracted several German naturalists once settlement began in the wake of the Goyder Expedition's surveys. Before the Schultzes returned to Adelaide, Paul Heinrich Matthias Foelsche (1831–1914) arrived in Port Darwin as the first police inspector of South Australia's Northern Territory. He had reached South Australia from Hamburg in late 1854, and joined the South Australian mounted police after a trip to the Victorian goldfields. Foelsche is known today for his ethnographic work and his outstanding series of landscape and portrait photographs depicting the Aboriginal people and scenery of the Darwin region during the 1870s and 1880s.[54] But these interests were preceded by his enthusiasm for natural history. Soon after his arrival Foelsche began sending zoological specimens to Frederick Waterhouse at the South Australian Institute Museum. He sent plant specimens to Richard Schomburgk at the Botanic Garden, where they joined Schultze's specimens as part of the nucleus of the collection which would be stored and displayed in the Museum of Economic Botany when it opened in 1879.[55] Foelsche retained his interest in botany, and by the early 1880s was sending specimens to von Mueller himself and corresponding with him about his finds. Von Mueller named a particular broad-leaved eucalypt sent by Foelsche in his honour; it is known today as *Corymbia foelscheana*.[56]

Paul Heinrich Matthias Foelsche (1831–1914), police superintendent, ethnographer and naturalist, photographed aged 75 in his garden, Darwin, 1906.
(Philip Jones)

An 1874 letter from Paul Foelsche to South Australian Institute Museum Curator Frederick Waterhouse, noting the museum's proposed expansion and undertaking to send bird specimens.
(GRG 19, SRSA)

Foelsche made it clear that much of the collecting of small land animals was done by Aboriginal people, whom he paid in flour, an expensive commodity in the remote north. An 1871 letter to Waterhouse provides a remarkable insight into the methods and enthusiasm of this frontier collector, who used his contacts and ingenuity to further the Museum's interests:

> I could get many things such as bats, rats, mice etc from the natives but as I cannot get any damaged flour out of the store I have nothing to pay the natives with, and if one can get a tin of flour now and then, we have to pay 2s per lb for it; I shall write to Capt. van der Gevel by the next Timor mail and convey him your thanks, also will ascertain if arrangements can be made with the Batavia Museum to exchange specimens with the Adelaide one ... I have got some spirits from Dr

Millner also 20 lb of shot [for securing bird specimens] ... I should feel obliged if you would find me some few tin cans to put Reptiles in, for Rats etc I can not put in glass bottles, also some arsenical soap & one or two scalps [scalpels] for skinning & some cotton wool. I have got plenty of alum for skins of larger animals, should I be able to procure any. I am obliged to you for the insect pins. I have plenty now, but am sorry to say there are no insects of any description, the G.R. [Government Resident] has burnt the <u>whole</u> country for miles round the settlement & you may travel for miles & not see a single butterfly or other insect ... Mr Stapleton [telegraph station operator and naturalist] is here now & I gain a good deal of information from him. I enclose a cheque for £5 and should feel obliged if you would procure me a copy of Gould's Handbook on Australian Birds, by sending to England. I believe they are to be procured for about £3. Also send me a copy of Maunders Treasury of Natural History and a good work on shells with plates, if it is to be obtained and any other book you may think of any use to me as an Amateur Collector. I take a great interest in such matters and wish I knew a little more about it.[57]

Not surprisingly, as the new town of Palmerston expanded on the plateau overlooking Port Darwin itself, its small community of frontier naturalists and ethnographers began to form their own scientific circle, and to consider the idea of founding a local museum, just as had occurred in Adelaide. During October 1890 Paul Foelsche became one of three founding committee members of the proposed Museum of Mining, Products and Natural History, representing Natural History. The committee was chaired by John George Knight, who had played an active role in stimulating local collecting for the Northern Territory's contribution towards international exhibitions during the 1880s. The committee member representing 'Vegetable Products' was Maurice Wilhelm Holtze, who had arrived at Port Darwin in 1872 and who became the inaugural curator of the Palmerston Botanic Gardens in 1878. Holtze had benefited from a *Gymnasium* education in Hanover, had studied botany while working at the city's Royal Gardens, and had worked in St Petersburg's Imperial Gardens for two years. In the Northern Territory he successfully pioneered tropical agriculture and, despite cyclones and voracious pests, developed Palmerston's Gardens and the associated Experimental Plantation to a remarkable level of success. After Richard Schomburgk's death in early 1891 Holtze applied successfully for the Adelaide Botanic Garden directorship, with his application strongly recommended by Ferdinand von Mueller. He was to hold the position through austere times, managing to broaden the Botanic Garden's popular appeal while focusing more on horticulture and less on ornamental aspects.[58] Holtze's eldest son Nicholas had supported him in his botanical work and tropical agriculture research, and it was no surprise that he assumed the role of Curator of the Palmerston Botanical Gardens, aged 25 years, on his father's departure.

The tendency of South Australian German naturalists and scientists to be drawn to museums has been noted. The South Australian Institute Museum's second Director, Johann Wilhelm Haacke, graduated in zoology from the University of Jena in 1878 and was immediately appointed to the Canterbury Museum in New Zealand under the directorship of fellow German Julius Haast – himself the nucleus of a group of German scientists and naturalists in that colony. Haast undertook frequent exchanges of specimens with Frederick Waterhouse at the South Australian Museum, and probably recommended that Haacke apply for that curatorship on Waterhouse's retirement in 1882. Aged only 27, Haacke soon became a controversial director in Adelaide. He had firm and progressive ideas on raising the museum's professional standard, recommending the establishment of a scientific journal, discarding many useless specimens, and launching into a vigorous series of international exchanges. Frederick Waterhouse had also sent large quantities of natural history specimens and artefacts overseas, and it is easy to conclude that, being foreign, Haacke presented an easier target for criticism. Haacke also fell out spectacularly with his taxidermist, the eccentric George Beazley, and had him dismissed, but by 1884 Haacke himself had outlived his welcome and resigned.[59]

With his resignation Adelaide lost one of its most gifted scientists. One of Haacke's last achievements in South Australia had been to demonstrate the oviparous character of the echidna at a meeting of the Royal Society on 2 September 1884, thus establishing the connecting link between reptiles and mammals.[60] This discovery was announced four hours before the oviparous character of the platypus was revealed by Professor W.H. Caldwell in Sydney, although it

Wilhelm Haacke (1855–1912), zoologist, Curator and Director of the South Australian Institute Museum, 1882–1884. (South Australian Museum)

was Caldwell's announcement which was telegraphed first to London. Within months of his resignation, Haacke was appointed as chief scientist on the Australasian Geographical Society's expedition to New Guinea, apparently on the recommendation of Baron von Mueller.[61] This expedition was jointly funded by the governments of Queensland, Victoria and Sydney, but not by that of South Australia – even though, as one newspaper observed, 'its northern coast on the Gulf of Carpentaria approaches almost as near to New Guinea as that of Queensland'. The 'people of Adelaide' redeemed themselves by the decision 'to contribute an eminent naturalist, Dr Haacke, originally, we believe, of German birth'.[62] The expedition failed to live up to its promise in terms of new geographical discoveries, but Haacke made a rich haul of specimens and it did his reputation no harm. He became the Frankfurt zoo's scientific director from 1888 to 1893, and published a series of scientific papers and books.[63]

By the end of Haacke's brief tenure in Adelaide he had appointed four Germans to the museum staff, three on a full-time basis. All made durable contributions to South Australian science. The collector and entomologist Otto Tepper has already been mentioned. To replace the English taxidermist George Beazley, Haacke appointed the German museum preparator Otto Rau. His brother Johann and son Alan were to prepare most of the exhibits in the

Otto Rau, taxidermist and preparator, South Australian Museum, 1883–1928. (South Australian Museum)

museum for the next 90 years, from whale skeletons to tiny lizards. During November 1883 Haacke also engaged August Saupe, a German artisan–sculptor living in Adelaide, to make scientifically accurate hand-coloured plaster casts of freshly caught fish specimens, before their vivid colours faded in spirit jars. But Haacke's key appointment was that of marine scientist Amandus Zietz, recruited in 1883. Zietz reorganised the exhibits in the South Australian Museum, published a definitive account of South Australian fishes, and during 1893 undertook the gruelling but successful excavations for ancient Diprotodon skeletons on the shores of the salt Lake Callabonna.[64]

Zietz had gained early experience working for the Godeffroy Museum in Hamburg, both as a collector and an arranger of specimens, before gaining a position at the University of Kiel's natural history museum.[65] There he had formed a friendship with J.D.E. Schmeltz, who later rose to become head curator of the Godeffroy Museum in Hamburg, and subsequently the Curator and Director of the Leiden Ethnographic Museum. In an 1897 letter to his old friend Zietz, gave a revealing insight into what it was to be a German scientist in *fin-de-siècle* Adelaide. He noted that both Baron von Mueller and Richard Schomburgk had died in recent years, and that there were now few Germans in key scientific roles

Amandus Zietz (1840–1921), zoologist and assistant director, South Australian Museum.
(South Australian Museum)

Below:
Reconstituted skeleton of the large extinct herbivore, *Diprotodon australis*, excavated by Amandus Zietz at Lake Callabonna, SA, 1893.
(South Australian Museum Archives)

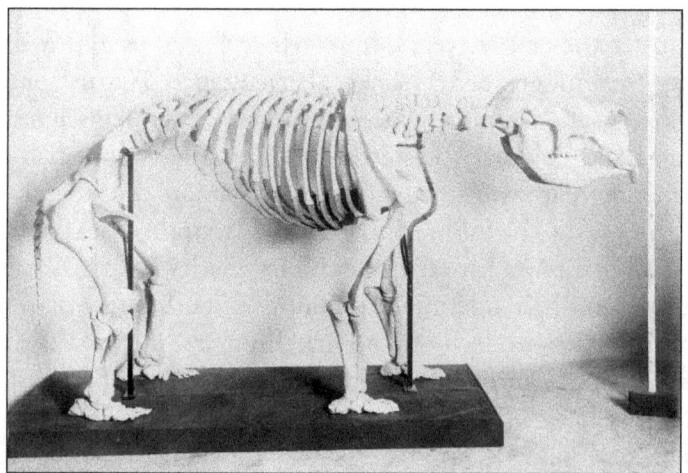

in Adelaide, apart from himself and the botanist Maurice Holtze. The ground had shifted. 'Being a German,' he wrote, 'is becoming a disadvantage here.'[66] Moreover, as Zietz wrote, there was now 'political friction between the land of our birth and England, to whom I have had to swear an oath of allegiance'. For this reason Zietz observed that he had 'good cause not to correspond too much with Germany ... if I was to be reproached that the Germans here are only striving for German interests, I am able to reply that I don't write to Germany much, apart from letters to my family'.[67]

It was a time of great financial stringency in South Australia. Zietz had written a few months earlier of the dismissal of a large number of public servants in Adelaide; for those remaining, there had been a 'fairly significant deduction in our wages, which we won't recoup'.[68] He had been obliged to shelve his plans 'to see the old homeland again' with his wife and son Robert, who was also employed at the South Australian Museum, as an ornithologist. If he decided to go to Europe 'under the circumstances currently prevailing', Zietz wrote, 'I would have to be fearful of losing my position, which is not what I currently want. We Germans here are being more and more restricted as Utlanders'.[69]

Amandus Zietz (left) and Joseph Verco, collecting marine specimens in Gulf St Vincent, South Australia, c. 1895.
(From B.C. Cotton (ed.), *Combing the southern seas*, Mail Newspapers, Adelaide, 1935)

Fifteen years earlier Zietz had arrived in Adelaide with great ambitions, no doubt encouraged by the example of other successful German scientists such as Haacke and von Mueller. Now his path was blocked, partly by the anatomy professor and zoologist Edward Stirling, who occupied the Director's position above him, but partly also, he felt, by a rising antipathy towards Germans and his own lack of a higher degree. As Haacke's own nominee, perhaps he had been stymied by Adelaide's English establishment, for Stirling had been appointed as Honorary Director shortly after Zietz's arrival in 1884, and in 1895 was confirmed as the museum's salaried Director.

Stirling was acknowledged as the senior author of the substantial monograph on the Lake Callabonna fossils, even though Zietz had been responsible for the excavations and had undertaken most of the scientific description. Zietz had worked hard at re-ordering the museum collections, organising the complex move from the cramped upper floor of the 1878 Jervois Wing to an entirely new museum building in 1895. He was committed to a museum organised on scientific principles, and probably considered that Stirling was reshaping the museum in a popular mode. These are familiar concerns, more than a century later. He wrote to Schmeltz:

> The understanding of scientific matters is very slight here, and a museum is here seen more as a Show, and anyway, the very expensive space is filled with huge mammals and big stuffed animals, so that there is only a small amount of space left over for extended Australian collections.[70]

Zietz faced the dilemma of the remote migrant scientist in a contracting milieu, reliant on local networks that had been established and maintained by local, largely exclusive elites. The institutional records of the South Australian Museum hardly hint at this dilemma; indeed, Zietz's Adelaide career appears to provide illustrious proof of yet another German exercise in successful 'colonial *Wissenschaft*', blending the best of Humboldtian education with the rich opportunities of untrodden fields of science. Zietz's private letters to Schmeltz tell a different story, though, reminding us that those opportunities were often constrained by colonial society and by a conservatism which, by the 1890s, had begun to reveal a racist bias.

Zietz turned to his own German networks. On the advice of an old colleague of Schmeltz, the Berlin craniologist Prof. R. Krause (whose two-month Adelaide research visit he had hosted in mid-1897), Zietz sent copies of his scientific papers to the Leipzig-based zoologist, Professor Rudolf Leuchart, seeking the ultimate prize, a German doctorate.[71] To this end he prepared donations of artefacts to send to Schmeltz as a potential referee. 'You would,' he wrote, 'have a chance to do a favour for a former school colleague and friend'. He supplemented the gift with a small set of ethnographic photographs of Aborigines of the Port Darwin area, taken several years earlier by Zietz's correspondent, Paul Foelsche.[72] Zietz also wrote long letters seeking references from his two former professors at the University of Kiel, Emil Kraepelin and Karl Möbius, undertaking to send Möbius 'several interesting objects for his museum to renew the connection with him again'.[73]

The responses by Zietz's mentors have not been traced, but he remained without a doctorate, serving out his years as Assistant Director under Stirling. In 1905 Zietz hosted another visiting German professor of physical anthropology, Hermann Klaatsch, who spent eight days in Adelaide. Writing to a colleague later, Klaatsch summed up Zietz as *'ein biederer Sachse'* ('an upright Saxon' or more colloquially perhaps, a 'solid citizen'). But while Zietz considered that German scientific influence had waned in Adelaide, Klaatsch was struck by its palpable presence:

> *Der deutsche Einfluss, der hier ganz besonders fühlbar ist, macht es begreiflich, dass ich in Adelaide mehr Verstaendnis für meine Absichten und mehr practische Hilfe fand, als an irgend einem anderen Punkte Australiens.*
> [The German influence, which is felt particularly strongly here, helps explain why in Adelaide I found more understanding for my intentions and more practical help than in any other part of Australia.][74]

Perhaps the two varying impressions are reconcilable if we consider that by the turn of the twentieth century South Australian German scientists had merged so effectively with their British counterparts that they were clearly visible only to outsiders such as Klaatsch, rather than to established, disenchanted residents such as Zietz. In any event, there is little doubt that their influence had imparted a particular, distinctive contour to South Australia's intellectual landscape, one which would remain apparent for decades.

Notes

1   D.A. Gerber, 'The Pathos of Exile: Old Lutheran refugees in the United States and South Australia', *Comparative Studies in Society and History*, vol. 26, no. 3, 1984, pp. 498–522.
2   D. Schubert, 'Kavel, August Ludwig Christian (1798–1860)', 2004, Evangelical History Association of Australia website, http://webjournals.alphacrucis.edu.au/journals/adeb/k/kavel-august-ludwig-christian-1798–1860/. Kavel spent two years in London, from 1836 to 1838, lodging for at least part of the time with the

Pennyfeather family, whose daughter, Anne Catherine Pennyfeather, journeyed to South Australia in 1840 to marry Kavel.

3   For a survey of Germans who contributed to natural science in colonial Queensland and New South Wales, see T.G. Vallance, 'Early German connexions [sic] with natural history, geology and mining in New South Wales and Queensland', in J.H. Voigt (ed.) *New Beginnings. The Germans in New South Wales and Queensland*, Institute for Foreign Cultural Relations, Stuttgart, 1983, pp. 269–78. Con Tanre's *The Mechanical Eye: A historical guide to Australian photography and photographers* (Macleay Museum, Sydney, 1977) documents a number of German photographers working in colonial Australia. The phenomenon was not confined to Australia; similar influences have been noted for North America, for example, S.G. Kohlstedt, 'German ideas and practice in American natural history museums', in H. Geitz, J. Heideking & J. Herbst, *German Influences on Education in the United States to 1917*, German Historical Institute, University of Cambridge, Cambridge, 1995, p. 106.

4   Renate Vollmer, 'Assisted Emigration from Northern Germany to South Australia in the Nineteenth Century', *The Australian Journal of Politics and History*, vol. 44, 1998, pp. 33–47.

5   Rod Home, 'Science as a German Export to Nineteenth Century Australia', *Working Papers in Australian Studies,* no. 104, Sir Robert Menzies Centre for Australian Studies, London, 1995.

6   G. Basalla, 'The Spread of Western Science', *Science*, 156 (no. 3775), 1967, pp. 611–22.

7   ibid., p. 613.

8   D. Morris, 'Mueller, Sir Ferdinand Jakob Heinrich von [Baron von Mueller] (1825–1896)', *Australian Dictionary of Biography*, vol. 5, Melbourne University Press, Melbourne, 1974, pp. 306–8.

9   Germany's ascendancy during the nineteenth century as a dominant intellectual and cultural force, 'more creative and influential than France, Britain, Italy, Holland, and the United States', has been charted most recently in Peter Watson's *The German Genius: Europe's third renaissance, the second scientific revolution, and the twentieth century* (New York, Harper Collins, 2010).

10 F. Dutton, *South Australia and Its Mines*, T. & W. Boone, London, 1846, p. 267.

11 H. Beckler, *A Journey to Cooper's Creek,* ed. S. Jeffries, Melbourne University Press, Melbourne, 1993, p. xx.

12 In 1839 the newly founded Mechanics Institute merged with the South Australian Literary and Scientific Association (which had been formed in London in 1834, prior to the colony's foundation) (*South Australian Gazette and Colonial Register*, 18 September 1839, p. 3). Opie refers to the 'Literary and Scientific Association and Mechanics' Institute as existing in 1840, with Charles Sturt as President, J. Brown, G. Stevenson and H. Watson as Vice-

Presidents, George Young as Secretary, and Charles Platts as Librarian (E.A.D. Opie, *South Australian Records Prior to 1841*, Hussey & Gillingham, Adelaide, [1917], p. 107). The Natural History Society of South Australia was founded in December 1838. It was to be modelled on the Linnaean and Geological Societies of London, 'for the cultivation of the various departments of Natural History and the formation of a Museum, especially of the indigenous productions of South Australia' (*South Australian Gazette and Colonial Register*, 11 November 1838, p. 2).

13 'Catalogue of the Gawler Institute, prepared by Otto Wehrstedt, March 1881', South Australian Museum Archives.

14 Derek van Abbe, 'The Germans in South Australia', *Australian Letters*, vol. 3, no. 2, 1960, pp. 26–34, p. 31.

15 Alexander von Humboldt had befriended Robert Schomburgk and admired the brothers' British Guiana endeavours, 'Anniversary of the Gawler Institute', *Advertiser*, Adelaide, 18 October 1858, p. 3. The historian R. Butler wrote of Carl Muecke that he 'was a shining example of the best of his native country's education system. Only in his mid-30s on arrival in South Australia in 1849, he had already taken degrees at the respected Bonn University, learned mining techniques in Freiburg [sic] (heart of Saxony's mineral districts), joined compulsory schooling committees and inspired Berlin workers with the rudiments of free education' (R. Butler, *A College in the Wattles: Hahndorf and its academy*, Lutheran Publishing House, Adelaide, 1989, p. 16).

16 W. Cawthorne, *Menge the Mineralogist: A sketch of the life of the late Johann Menge*, J.T. Shawyer, Adelaide, 1859, p. 18.

17 *Hobart Colonial Times*, 3 August 1841, p. 3.

18 *Argus*, Melbourne, 11 August 1858, p. 5.

19 *South Australian Advertiser*, 27 January 1860, p. 4b. Menge's collections are difficult to trace. For example, the collection sent to the Geology Museum of the University of Edinburgh (referred to by J. West, *The History of Tasmania*, vol. 1, Henry Dowling, Launceston, 1852, p. 152) is no longer held there.

20 Marianne Kreusler's life is barely known. According to a great-granddaughter, Marianne's mother was 'Lady Isobel Waterford', daughter of an Irish peer (Mrs Rowe, questionnaire response to University of Adelaide German Department, 1961, DG 20, MSS 994.2 G3888, Special Collections, Barr Smith Library, University of Adelaide; van Abbe 1960, p. 31), although this has not been established. Georg Kreusler's mother was Caroline Alberti, of a titled Catholic family in the Arolsen region (van Abbe 1960, p. 31; http://homepage.mac.com/graememoad/Family/PS108/PS108_405.HTM). Accordingly, Georg Kreusler had 'numerous servants, a coachman, footman, lady's maid … people curtseyed as they drove past'. Georg apparently journeyed to South America with Marianne's brother (possibly a 'Major Reuter', who was to marry Emma Eichhoff, a cousin to Bertha Eichhoff who

married the founder of Krupp's steelworks); 'Mrs Kreusler was to follow with their three children but word came of his death' (DG 20; ibid.).

21 B. Scheps, *The Sold Museum: The South Seas enterprises of the trading firm Jos. Ces. Godeffroy & Son, Hamburg, and the collections, 'Museum Godeffroy'*, Goecke & Evers, Keltern Keltern-Weiler, 2005.

22 *Observer*, Adelaide, 9 January 1924. See F.A. Nickerl, *Bohmens Tagfalter* ['Butterfly and Moth Lepidoptera'], Fürsterz-bischöfliche buchdruckerei Im Seminario, Prague, 1837.

23 R.L. King, 'Description of *Anapestus kreusleri*: A species of coleopterous insect inhabiting ants' nests in South Australia', *Transactions of the Entomological Society of New South Wales*, vol. 2, 1866, pp. 316–18.

24 Three boomerangs and a play-stick, presumably obtained from local Aboriginal people of the Barossa Valley, were eventually donated to the South Australian Museum by her grand-daughter, B.J. McNamara, in 1958. These objects are registered as A5058–61 in the South Australian Museum collection. Kreusler apparently obtained them from Aborigines of South Australia's mid-North as he passed through Gawler, probably during the 1860s or 1870s.

25 GRG 19/364/May 1882, p. 61, State Records Office, Adelaide.

26 These include the caterpillar *Ctenistes kreusleri*, the beetles *Omophaena kreusleri*, *Neocarenum kreusleri* and *Mecynotarsus kreusleri*, the borer *Atractocerus kreuslerae*, other coleoptera species including *Anthicus kreusleri*, *Anapestus kreusleri*, *Ctenisophus kreusleri*, *Carenidium kreuslerae*, *Liparetrus kreuslerae*, and *Earinis kreuslerae*, and shells, including *Notovoluta kreuslerae* (Kreusler's Volute) and *Alcithoe kreuslerae*.

27 For example, King wrote of the beetle, *Euplectus odewahnii*: 'This minute species is apparently not uncommon at Gawler. It was sent to me by my friends, Mrs Kreusler and Mr Odewahn, to the latter of whom I have dedicated the species' (R.L. King, 'On the Pselaphidae of Australia', no. IV. *Transactions of the Entomological Society of New South Wales*, vol. 1, 1866, pp. 299–315, p. 314.

28 These details have been gleaned from an examination of the entomological literature of the period. Species named for Odewahn by Pascoe and Baly include *Cossyphus odewahni*, *Cyphagogus odewahni*, *Eurynassa odewahni*, and *Leucispa odewahni* (from http://www2.nrm.se/en/col_o.html).

29 Published in one of the early *Bulletins* of the Entomology Section, Prague National Museum. Dr Otto Nickerl was the son of Prof. František Antonín Nickerl at the Prague Museum, with whom Marianne Kreusler corresponded.

30 A. Brown-May & T.W. May 'A Mingled Yarn: Henry Edwards, thespian and naturalist, in the Austral Land of Plenty, 1853–1866', *Historical Records of Australian Science*, vol. 11, no. 3, pp. 407–18; Frederick Waterhouse to the Curator, Australian Museum, 14 May 1865 (C:20.65.19,21, Australian

Museum Archives). Despite his suicide, Odewahn's grave lies in hallowed ground at Buchsfelde.

31 Marianne Kreusler's daughter Jane had heard Odewahn in the night, 'walking about his room, and went in to see if he was ill'. He had taken strychnine and died soon after (*Argus*, Melbourne, 18 December 1876, p. 5).

32 R. Tate,' Anniversary Address', *Transactions of the Royal Society of South Australia*, vol. 2, 1878, pp. 11–48, 45.

33 According to an historian of entomology writing in 1907, the South Australian Museum held the 'Kreusler and Odewahn Collection'. Formed 'between the years 1855 and 1875', it 'consists chiefly of Coleoptera collected about Gawler and Blanchetown, and the Murray River' (W. Froggatt, *Australian Insects*, William Brooks, Sydney, 1907, p. 414).

34 For Heuzenroeder's Kangaroo Island trip, see R. Tate, 'The botany of Kangaroo Island', *Transactions of the Royal Society of South Australia*, vol. 6, 1883, pp. 116–71. Carl Wilhelmi collected insects for Heuzenroeder near Port Lincoln during the summer of 1851–52 (R.W. Home et al. (eds), *Regardfully Yours: Selected correspondence of Ferdinand von Mueller*, Peter Lang, Bern, New York, 1998, vol. 1, p. 132). South Australian Institute Museum curatorial reports of the 1860s and 1870s contain several references to Heuzenroeder's coin-collecting.

35 Home et al. (eds) 1998, vol. 1, p. 135.

36 *Argus*, Melbourne, 29 September 1866, p. 4; Home et al. (eds), *Regardfully Yours: Selected correspondence of Ferdinand von Mueller*, Peter Lang, Bern, New York, vol. 2, 2002, p. 378.

37 During November 1866, for example, Wehl sent two small mammals in spirits to the South Australian Institute Museum, in exchange for two bird specimens (Curator's Report, November 1866, South Australian Museum Archives). Examples of Wehl's correspondence with his brother-in-law appear in Home et al. (eds) 1998–2006, vols 1–3.

38 *Advertiser*, Adelaide, 26 December 1861, p. 2. Five years later Wehl had sown 40 acres of 30 different species of imported grasses in an experimental farm, milling the grain in Mount Gambier's first flour mill, which he established in 1857 (*Advertiser*, Adelaide, 25 May 1866, p. 3, 26 February 1876, p. 16). Wehl made donations of natural history to von Mueller in Melbourne, such as a donation of 'two small hawks', recorded in the *Argus*, Melbourne, 14 January 1860, p. 4.

39 D.N. Kraehenbuehl, 'Dr H.H. Behr's two visits to South Australia in 1844–45 and 1848–49', *Journal of the Adelaide Botanic Gardens*, vol. 3, no. 1, 1981, pp. 101–21, p. 108.

40 See Wilhelmi's letter to von Mueller, quoted above. In that letter Wilhelmi mentions yet another German botanist, named Weber, whose foray into the Murray Mallee at the height of the 1851 summer had concerned von Mueller (R.W. Home et al. 1998, vol. 1, p. 132). See also T.A. Darragh, Translation

and introduction: 'My Journeys in South Australia 1848–1851: Lecture by Carl Wilhelmi, 14 September 1857', *Journal of the Friends of Lutheran Archives,* vol. 13, 2003, pp. 5–24; D.N. Kraehenbuehl, 'Karl [sic] Wilhelmi, the Seedsman from Dresden: His botanical endeavour in South Australia and Victoria', in P.S. Short (ed.), *History of Systematic Botany in Australasia,* Proceedings of a Symposium held at the University of Melbourne, 25–27 May 1988, Australian Systematic Botany Society, Melbourne, 1990, pp. 115–20; A. Heuzenroeder, 'European Food Meets Aboriginal Food: To what extent did Aboriginal food cultures influence early German-speaking settlers in South Australia?' *Limina,* vol. 12, 2006, pp. 30–9.

41 Wilhelmi's relationship with von Mueller was an uneven one, ending in the young man's dismissal. See R.W. Home et al. (eds) 2002, vol. 2, pp. 10–11.

42 See http://www.anbg.gov.au/biography/hillebrand-william.html

43 Kraehenbuehl 1981, p. 108.

44 D.N. Kraehenbuehl, 'Tepper, Johann Gottlieb Otto (1841–1923)', *Australian Dictionary of Biography,* Supplementary volume, Melbourne University Press, Melbourne, 2005, p. 379. See also D.N. Kraehenbuehl, 'Life and works of J.G.O. Tepper, F.L.S., and his association with the Field Naturalists' section of the Royal Society of South Australia', *South Australian Naturalist,* vol. 44, no. 2, 1969. pp. 23–42.

45 ibid. Richter was a medical graduate of Leipzig University. He died in February 1901, aged 74 (*Advertiser,* Adelaide, 21 February 1901, p. 6). He contributed several significant pieces to the South Australian Museum, including a carved shield obtained by him at Mannum on the Lower Murray during 1855.

46 Froggat 1907, p. 414. Tepper's papers are held jointly in the State Library of South Australia and the South Australian Museum Archives.

47 See for example, 'Anniversary of the Gawler Institute', *Advertiser,* Adelaide, 18 October 1858, p. 3.

48 Curator's Report, May 1867, South Australian Institute Museum, GRG 19/168, State Records Office, Adelaide.

49 For the Schultze genealogy see http://members.optusnet.com.au/~fredscott/fam00227.htm. It is likely that Schultzes' son was the eldest, Carl Wilhelm Friedrich, and was called 'Alfred' to differentiate him from his father. For Schomburgk's recommendation, see R.W. Home et al. (eds) 2002, vol. 2, p. 479.

50 Kerr 1971, p. 48.

51 P. Jones, *Ochre and Rust: Artefacts and encounters on Australian frontiers,* Wakefield Press, Adelaide, 2007, p. 160.

52 The weapon was described by Schultze as a 'kundillo', probably a wooden sword club. 'List of Specimens collected by Fr. Schultze, Naturalist [1869]' (GRG 19/399/15, State Records Office, Adelaide).

53 'Letter from Frederick Schultze (Naturalist and Botanist) concerning the extent of his collection. 1870' (GRG 19/399/22, State Records Office, Adelaide). None of this early material has survived in identifiable form in Adelaide, although specimens from these consignments were exchanged with a number of other museums.

54 P. Jones, *The Policeman's Eye: The frontier photography of Paul Foelsche*, South Australian Museum, Adelaide, 2005.

55 Having met Friedrich Schultze during his first months at Port Darwin, Foelsche had undertaken to send him duplicates of any specimens he collected. Foelsche heard no more from Schultze though, despite enquiring of Waterhouse, 'I suppose you never hear anything of Mr Schultze? I have not heard from him since he left here, strange man he must be.' (Paul Foelsche to Frederick Waterhouse, 19 September 1872, South Australian Museum Archives).

56 This correspondence and Foelsche's specimens are held in the Melbourne Herbarium. For an example of Foelsche's letters to von Mueller, see R.W. Home et al. (eds) 1998, vol. 1, pp. 284–87.

57 Paul Foelsche to Frederick Waterhouse, 30 August 1871, South Australian Museum Archives. In April 1872 Foelsche asked for a Latin dictionary, essential for a serious naturalist. An extract from the report on Port Darwin by Capt. van der Gevel, of the Dutch ship *Maria Elizabeth*, was published in *Perth Gazette*, 24 November 1871, p. 3. Foelsche consigned several collections of specimens to Batavia at this time (in the care of Captain van der Gevel, who regularly visited Port Darwin).

58 For a good summary of the Schomburgk and Holtze directorships, see R. Aitken, *Seeds of Change: An illustrated history of Adelaide Botanic Garden*, Botanic Gardens and State Herbarium, Adelaide, 2006. See also D.N. Kraehenbuel, 'Holtze, Maurice Willim (1840–1923), Botanist', in Bede Nairn and Geoffrey Serle (eds), *Australian Dictionary of Biography*, vol. 9, Melbourne University Press, Melbourne, 1983, pp. 353–4.

59 H. Hale, *The First Hundred Years of the South Australian Museum, 1856–1956*, South Australian Museum, Adelaide, 1956, pp. 38–48.

60 See for example, *Sydney Morning Herald*, 6 September 1884, p. 14; *Argus*, Melbourne, 8 October 1884, p. 5.

61 *Northern Territory Times and Gazette*, 18 July 1885, p. 3.

62 *Brisbane Courier*, 13 November 1885, p. 2.

63 For example, W. Haacke, *Bau und Leben des Tieres. Aus Natur und Geisteswelt*, 3. Bändchen, Teubner, Leipzig, 1899; W. Haacke & W. Kuhnert, *Das Thierleben Europas. 1. Das Thierleben Europas. 2. Das Thierleben Asiens, Amerikas u. Australiens. 3. Das Thierleben Afrikas. U. des Meeres*, Oldenbourg Verlag, Berlin, 1901; W. Haacke, *Die Menschenrassen*, Hermann Hillger Verlag, Berlin and Leipzig, 1904; W. Haacke, *Bau und Leben des Tieres. Aus Natur und Geisteswelt*, 3. Bändchen, Teubner, Leipzig, 1899.

64 See, for example, A.H.C. Zietz, *A synopsis of the fishes of South Australia*, 3 parts, Royal Society of South Australia, Adelaide, 1908–09; E.C. Stirling and A.H.C. Zietz, 'Part I. Description of the manus and pes of diprotodon Australis'; 'Part II. 1. *Genyornis newtoni*: A new genus and species of fossil struthious bird from Lake Callabonna, South Australia: Description of the bones of the leg and foot', *Transactions of the Royal Society of South Australia*, Adelaide, 1899–1901, pp. 191–211.

65 'Obituary: The late A.H.C. Zietz, R.A.O.U', *Emu*, vol. 2, 1922, p. 237.

66 A. Zietz to J. Schmeltz, 4 September 1897. Translation from original German by John Strehlow and Lois Zweck, 2009.

67 ibid.

68 A. Zietz to J. Schmeltz, 3 February 1897. Translation from original German by John Strehlow and Lois Zweck, 2009.

69 ibid.

70 ibid. Stirling's later careful and comprehensive exhibition of the Australian collections in the new 1914 East Wing would surely have earnt Zietz's admiration.

71 Schmeltz and Krause had published together in 1881: J.D.E. Schmeltz and R. Krause, *Die ethnographisch-anthropologische Abteilung des Museum Godeffroy in Hamburg. Ein Beitrag zur Kunde der Südsee-Völker*, L. Friedrichsen, Hamburg, 1881.

72 E. Venbrux & P.G. Jones 2002, ' "Prachtaufnahmen" of Aborigines from Northern Australia, 1879', in Linda Roodenburg (ed.), *Anceaux's Glasses: Anthropological photography since 1860*, Rijksmuseum voor Volkenkunde, Leiden, pp. 116–27.

73 A. Zietz to J. Schmeltz, 4 September 1897. Translation from original German by John Strehlow and Lois Zweck, 2009, University of Leiden Archives, Leiden.

74 Hermann Klaatsch to Otto Schoetensack, 26 September to 1 October 1905, aboard ship from Fremantle to Albany. Copy and translation provided by Corinna Erckenbrecht, May 2010. See also C. Erckenbrecht, *Auf der Suche nach den Ursprüngen: Die Australienreise des Anthropologen und Sammlers Hermann Klaatsch 1904–1907*, Rautenstrauch-Joest-Museum, Köln, 2010.

Wine, women and so on
Female labour in the Barossa

Julie Tolley

The Barossa Valley in South Australia has a long history of wine making, and women have played a significant part in its establishment and development. Photographs and archival documents record just how central their contribution was in colonial days. Moreover, interviews I have conducted with several women who currently participate in the wine industry show that female labour in and around the Barossa's vineyards cannot simply be consigned to the distant past – it is very much a feature of the present day.

In the past, women have been involved in a range of tasks and responsibilities in wine production, supplying casual labour as pickers and pruners, undertaking general work in the vineyard, and on occasions operating vehicles or machinery. They have a similar involvement in the wine industry today, but now are also employed full-time in areas such as wine making, laboratory work and viticulture.

The Barossa Valley is the oldest and best known of the wine-producing regions of South Australia. The first English settlers arrived in the late 1830s and German settlers began to settle in the Valley in the early 1840s. The area, which has a current population of about 10,000, has retained its strong German culture and heritage.

German settlers

Johannes Menge, a German geologist and friend of Pastor Kavel, arrived on 17 January 1837 at Kangaroo Island in South Australia, on the ship *Coromandel* at the age of 50 years. Menge was a solitary, rather eccentric man who made his home in a small cave not far from the Ann Jacob homestead at Morooroo, on Jacob's Creek, now the site of the Jacob's Creek Visitors Centre. In 1839 Menge explored the Barossa Valley extensively, and in a letter preserved in the Angas papers in the State Library of South Australia, he wrote enthusiastically about the valley to George Fife Angas, who was a leader of the South Australian Company: 'I am quite certain that we shall see ... flourishing vineyards and orchards'.[1]

In the late 1830s Augustus Kavel, the pastor of a group of Lutheran dissidents who were suffering religious persecution in Silesia wrote to George Fife Angas asking for financial assistance to bring immigrants to South Australia. Kavel had heard of the plans for the foundation of a model province in South Australia from him and knew that no convicts would be brought to the colony. He was aware of the enthusiasm of the Colonial Office in London to attract those who were willing to leave their own country and sail thousands of miles to begin a new life. He was also aware of Angas's sympathy for victims of religious persecution. However, legislation restricted assistance to British subjects, and Angas used his own money to enable the first German-speaking immigrants from Silesia to settle in South Australia. In February 1842, 28 families loaded up their wagons and reached the Barossa Valley, where the first village, Bethanien, now Bethany, was established. By 1851 7000 Germans had settled in the Colony of South Australia.

Unlike many of the English Protestants, who were opposed to the sale and use of alcohol, the German settlers, most of them Lutherans from Silesia –although the first (1837), Johann Gramp (Jacob's Creek), was from Bavaria – had a cultural tradition of making and drinking wine. Grape vines had been introduced to Silesia in the twelfth century and were cultivated mainly by religious orders and the aristocracy.[2] By the nineteenth century grape vines were commonly grown throughout the hills of Silesia, and it was part of the culture of the region to make wine for use in the home. When the immigrants arrived in the Barossa Valley they brought with them the experience and inclination to grow and harvest grapes, and the expertise to make wine.

The Barossa Valley, with many of its numerous vineyards now operated by descendants of German settlers, is one of the best-known winemaking regions in Australia. Among the nineteenth-century settlers who contributed to the wine industry in the Barossa Valley are several German women, including Johanne Fiedler, Sophia bis Winckel and Johanna Seppelt, who lived on small farms and took part, without pay, in all activities in the vineyard. Women such as these often assumed responsibility for the family winery on the death of their husbands.

Many women living in rural areas make essential contributions to farm labour daily, and there has always been a high proportion of women in the labour force of small and medium-sized vineyards. These include the family vineyards that dominated the Barossa Valley during the nineteenth century and are still numerous in other wine-growing regions, such as the small-scale vineyards in Clare and on Kangaroo Island. German settlers in the Barossa Valley carried on the tradition of all family members working on their property at the busy times of the year – shearing, ploughing, vintage, pruning and planting – with little distinction drawn between men's and women's work. In 1903 Ernest Whitington described a vintage time at Chateau Tanunda: 'A German woman arrived with her wagon of grapes and helped to unload them. In this district it is no

Gramp family and helpers, Barossa Valley 1898.
(Orlando Winery Archives)

uncommon thing to see the women pruning and working on the farms and in the vineyards like men.'[3]

Photographs and diaries that have survived among the records of family vineyards from the late nineteenth century onwards attest to the presence of women in teams of vineyard workers. For example, the photograph of the Gramp family and helpers at the 1898 vintage (page 239) shows a group of pickers in working clothes, mainly women, in a formal pose in front of a horse and cart filled with grapes.

While most German families had small plots of vines for their own use, the planting of the first commercial vineyard in the Barossa has been attributed to Johann Gramp. He arrived in the *Solway* at Port Adelaide on 16 October 1837 at the age of 18 years. He worked in Adelaide and on Kangaroo Island for several years in various jobs and then bought land at Jacob's Creek near Rowland Flat. Here, in 1847, he planted his first vines with cuttings imported from Germany, making his first wine in 1850. On his marriage to Lydia Koch in 1874, Johann's son Gustav was given a wedding present of 40 acres of land adjacent to the family vineyard. These holdings were gradually expanded to form the Orlando winery.[4]

A closer examination of the photograph suggests that the small group of four people on the right are probably Gramp family members. The older woman sitting on a chair may be Mrs Gramp, while her son and daughter-in-law stand beside her and their young daughter kneels in front of them. The other people in the photograph are positioned further apart and are unlikely to be family members. It is evident from the stains on their hands and clothing that the women and girls have been picking grapes. There is a young boy who kneels next to a metal bucket and whose job has been to carry buckets filled with grapes to the cart. This photograph records the details of the methods of transport, work practices and clothing of German wine workers in the Barossa Valley.

The photograph on page 241 (top) was taken around 1900 and shows grapes being harvested at Nuriootpa.

Two women, apparently unaware of the camera, are bending to pick, while a fourth stands gazing at the lens, secateurs in hand. In the background a man sits holding the horse's reins, ready to move the grape-laden cart. Another man, whose task no doubt is to

Vineyard, Nuriootpa c.1900. (Author's collection)

empty buckets of grapes, stands near the cart. In the foreground is a small boy, whose job is to take the full buckets from the pickers to the cart and return with an empty one. Helena, a woman I spoke to who once shared the ownership of a vineyard with her husband, described this very procedure: 'You'd sing out for a bucket ... the boy he'd come along and take the full one and give you the empty one, and you'd keep going.'

Hueppauff vineyard, Bethany 1911. (Author's collection)

In 1911, in the Hueppauff vineyard at Bethany, members of the family were photographed during vintage and we see a similar configuration of workers: the four women have been picking grapes from the trellised vines, with a boy supplying them with buckets.

Orlando vineyard, Rowland Flat c. 1920. (Author's collection)

One man sits on the cart holding the reins and another man, who has been loading grapes, stands nearby.

Again, the photograph above, taken around 1920 at Rowland Flat, shows four women picking grapes, a man carrying the buckets and another man loading grapes into the cart.

Primary sources such as diaries provide evidence of a long history of women working in family vineyards. Edward Salter's diary, written in the mid-nineteenth century, records work practices in his winery. Edward's father, Englishman William Salter, planted shiraz vines in 1859 on the outskirts of Angaston and called the property Mamre Brook. When he retired in 1870, his son Edward managed the winery. Edward's diaries reveal his thoughts about hiring pickers at vintage time.[5] 'Get all the married women pickers possible they are much steadier than yg women.' He lists the names of several women who were good strong workers, and notes that he intends to hire them for the next vintage.[6] Edward was willing to employ young women when necessary, but did not consider them to be worth the wage he paid married women. 'Arrange with pickers before beginning abt. Wages. Especially any under age. Tilley Weber wanted 3/- and her mother said she earned it. Gave it; but too much for a girl of her age.'[7]

Johanne Fiedler

When Johanne Fiedler took over the management of the family winery and distillery at Bethany on the property that had been acquired by her father-in-law, Johann Friedrich August Fiedler, she was one of the earliest women to take full responsibility for a vineyard. The Fiedlers arrived in South Australia in 1838 on the *Prince George* and first settled in Klemzig near Adelaide. In 1843 they moved to Bethany, and Johann is considered to be the first German recorded as owning a vineyard in the Barossa Valley. By the 1850s the Fiedler winery was well established and producing large quantities of excellent wine. By 1862, the vineyard was sufficiently large for Johann to qualify as a distiller of brandy. Legislation allowed anyone with a minimum of two acres of vineyard to apply for a licence to use a still.[8] Johann's son Alexander was also a winemaker. When Alexander died in 1875, when his father was nearly 80 years old, his wife, Johanne, took over the management of the winery and was granted a distiller's licence in her own name.[9] This new responsibility implies a long-standing involvement by Johanne in the family winery and suggests that she had acquired considerable skills and experience over the preceding years. The original vines are now incorporated in the Turkey Flat Vineyard on Bethany Road.

Sophia bis Winckel

Sophia bis Winckel was another women who took up the management of her family vineyard and winery when her husband died. The property, originally named Buchsfelde, had been established by Dr Richard Schomburgk when he purchased land on the Gawler River, west of Gawler. Before he immigrated, he had been employed as a gardener in Potsdam, was familiar with growing vines and had a keen interest in viticulture. By 1853 he had planted 93 different cultivars, using cuttings from the gardens of Potsdam, and gradually earned a good reputation for his wine. However, in 1865 he was appointed Director of the Adelaide Botanic Garden and could no longer maintain the property and so sold his five acres to his neighbour, Friedrich bis Winckel. George Loyau, editor of the local newspaper the *Gawler Bunyip,* visited the property in 1879. He was given 'some excellent wine … and would take first place at any exhibition where good wines are appreciated'.[10] After Friedrich died in 1879, his wife Sophia took over the property, which by this time included eight acres of vineyard containing 68 grape varieties, and a five-acre orchard of fruit trees. Maintaining and managing such a large property would certainly have meant extensive experience in the family enterprise.

Johanna Charlotte Seppelt

The women of the Seppelt family were probably unable to take as active a part in their family winemaking business as Sophia bis Winckel had in her family enterprise. Joseph Seppelt came from a middle-class background and was well educated and widely travelled. He emigrated from Silesia in 1850 with his wife, Johanna Charlotte, and their three children Benno, Hugo and Ottilie and settled on a large tract of land in the Barossa Valley. Joseph's background had been in cordial and liqueur making. He saw the potential of wine making in the area and purchased a substantial property in the colony. Charlotte was fully occupied with child-rearing and domestic responsibilities.

The first wine was made in the early 1850s in the dairy, which had been established soon after the Seppelt family settled on their land.[11] According to Len Evans, the building at Seppeltsfield used for milking and also for making wine was known as 'Frau Seppelt's dairy'. Operating a dairy was considered a woman's responsibility, and the Seppelt women continued the rural tradition of producing dairy products. They carried out milking, along with other farm activities, such as smoking bacon, rearing chickens and growing vegetables and fruit. In 1908 the author May Vivienne travelled throughout South Australia and visited Seppeltsfield, where, on a tour of the property, she saw the dairy. Sophie Seppelt, Benno's wife, also showed May '*her* bacon-curing and smoke-house ... *her* fowlyard and the beautiful garden, where all kinds of fruit, vegetables and flowers were growing' (my italics).[12] May accepted without demur that these responsibilities belonged specifically to Mrs Seppelt. It is interesting to note that the small-scale production of milk and milk products for the family was the responsibility of Mrs Seppelt, indicated by the term, 'Frau Seppelt's dairy', but once wine was made commercially, Johann Seppelt took control of the space and building.

Many other German families settled in the Barossa in the late nineteenth century, and while some had quite extensive vineyards, many others grew a few vines and made wine for use in their homes. However, the stories of these winemaking families are rarely mentioned in history books. For instance, Johanne and George Schmidt bought land at Vine Vale, Johanne and Johann Schrapel settled nearby at Bethany, as did Carolina and Samuel Stiller. Descendants of the Schmidt, Schrapel and Stiller families are still involved in the winemaking industry.[13]

Recollections

In the Barossa Valley, Helena – one of the women I interviewed – spent her working life in her family vineyard, purchased in the early 1950s. Although she has retired and her son now manages the family property, she still occasionally picks grapes and prunes the vines. Odette, another interviewee, who was the youngest child in a German family and unmarried, was brought up in the 1930s and 1940s on a farm near Bethany, where she lived and worked as an adult with one of her brothers, who had inherited the property. When Odette retired from active work and her brother died, the farm passed to her nephew. Amelia still works in the vineyard she co-owns with her husband near Nuriootpa.

Helena is representative of the women who not only work in family vineyards, but who also carry out their domestic duties and responsibilities. She described working with her husband in their vineyard situated out from a small town in the Barossa Valley. When they married in the 1930s, they bought a house in the town and 70 acres a few miles away containing 40 rows of old untrellised shiraz bush vines, as well as orchard and scrub. In her interview Helena recalled pushing her small children in a pram from the house to the vineyard, and then picking or pruning with her husband. They worked among the old vines and, as the scrub was cleared, extended the vineyard by planting new vine cuttings. Helena remembered that, during the early years of her marriage, she took her six-year-old daughter and three younger boys into the vineyard while she worked there: 'Well, I used to go out with the children when they were young. They had to sit and play in the vineyard and I used to go out. A lot of the times most probably when they were little I couldn't go, but once they were school age then I used to go out nearly every day with my husband.' Explaining what the children did while she worked, she said:

> They would play around with the sticks. They had little sticks and tractors and they would go in and out like dad would do – like we'd do with the vines. They would make out they were pruning, they had all these little sticks and they would go up the row and cultivate ...

Helena recalled that her tasks also included driving the tractor to enable her husband to operate an implement known as a dodge to hoe the weeds and grass. After working in the vineyard all day, Helena would walk home again, pushing the pram. She described grape picking as dirty arduous work and this is shown in the Gramp family photograph. Nevertheless, at the age of 80 years, she still occasionally helps out picking and pruning in her sons' vineyards.

Odette pointed out that working with young vines was difficult, because the stems, called 'rods', were so fragile: 'One would break off and that meant less bunches of grapes, didn't it!' She learnt by observation and experience how to carry out the work in different weather conditions and decided 'never to go out on a frosty morning because the rods are very crisp. Go out in the rain and you'd hardly ever snap them.' Tying-on – attaching the rods to the supporting trellis – is usually allocated to women, because it is an exacting task and one that requires dexterity rather than physical effort.

Odette said that she continued to carry out both her duties in the household and her work outside. 'I was still out there in the vineyard and ... I helped with the milking in general.' A machine-milking system had been installed and a new dairy built about three years before Odette's mother died. The size of the herd was increased, and milk and cream were sold. At this point Odette's brother took over the milking, with Odette 'helping' him. There was a tendency for males to take control of the production process when it became mechanised and when the product developed into a marketable commodity, as Mrs Seppelt's experience also illustrates.

Odette began using farm machinery as a young girl:

> I would have been about fourteen. That was a big monster of a tractor; my feet wouldn't reach down to the clutch. And you couldn't adjust

that seat in those days. But I liked outside work and I liked driving, oh yes ... And then harvest time I'd be driving the tractor again cutting hay and stooking, putting up sheaves in all nice shaped stooks.

She spoke modestly of her own efforts:

I wouldn't drive that tractor straight and when the seed germinated and you could see the crop coming through in crooked rows and then the corners were not well done and I used to get told off. I just felt I'd like to pull that crop out and go and do it again!

She said that she did not feel out of place doing what was generally considered men's work. 'I think I might have been an odd one there. There were a few other scattered ones that used to help out on the farm like that.' Odette admitted that she sometimes felt self-conscious about working with the large farm machines: 'I did somehow because I thought, how many other women are doing this? If they'd seen me they must think I'm a real tomboy.' She went on to tell a self-deprecating story:

There was one very funny experience I had. After it had been seeded we always had to go along with the harrows afterwards and there I was out in the paddock by myself, my big brother, he was looking after his customers serving fodder and that and I was going around merrily around this big forty-acre paddock, and from up that rise up there he saw the harrows had come unhitched, and were left on the other side of the paddock.

Odette saw her life as inextricably involved both with routine work in the farm and with the maintenance of the household; she was also expected to participate in additional seasonal work in the property.

When Martha and her husband were establishing their vineyard in the Barossa Valley, she was employed in a nearby town, earning an income away from the farm, while managing the house and working part-time in the vineyard. 'When I first got married I went out and worked in an office, but then after I had my children I never went back.' Instead, she began to work intensively in the vineyard, where she was able to arrange her hours to fit in with her child-rearing and housework.

Martha said in her interview that, even when working long hours in the vineyard, her domestic responsibilities continued: 'You fit them in between. We pick five days of the week during vintage ... if my husband has to shift vehicles at night for machine picking you do a bit of that. You come home and cook some tea then if you have to go out, shift a few more trucks. Like I said, it only goes for six to eight weeks so it's not too hard, you just adjust and do the best you can with everything else.' Looking after the children and cooking meals, for instance, are two responsibilities that could not be neglected, even at the busiest seasons in the vineyard: 'We usually have a cooked meal at night. I've got to pick my son up from school at three-fifteen and then you come home. So you've got a bit more time to do stuff during the winter months than what you have during picking, where you pick until four and then you shoot home to get tea for your husband, so you can go out and start picking at six-thirty, seven o'clock at night.'

In Martha's family vineyard, for instance, the division of labour is quite distinct. She identified particular tasks in her family vineyard that are assigned to men or to women:

> The men won't tie-on; the men won't train the young vines. They're busy pruning, and you need strong hands for that. Tying-on is probably a job that they just wouldn't want to do. I don't know, I guess they've never done it ... there's probably ladies that prune as well as tie-on and there may be men that tie-on too, but in our family they don't do it.

Martha explained that 'tying-on' is done after pruning, and requires care and a delicate touch. Every vine is cut back to leave four to six long rods, and these are tied onto the wires in the expectation that they will shoot, grow longer and bear fruit.

Women needed to be well endowed with patience, not to say stoicism. Martha said that a positive attitude is essential for a women working in a vineyard: 'I think if they're going to come home and work on the land they've got to be prepared to put up with what weather you get. You've got to go out when it's hot and you've got to go out when it's raining. I really couldn't imagine myself going out and doing another job because I've probably done it for so long and like I said I really enjoy training young vines.' Martha, who married into a third-generation German family in the Barossa Valley, works every day in the family vineyard. 'It's just probably tradition,' she said. 'My mother-in-law did it so I am probably in a way expected to do it as well.' Clearly family custom partly dictated the tasks that should be performed by women.

Martha implied in her interview that, in her family vineyard, the management of the vineyard is more in keeping with tradition, and most of the day-to-day practical decisions are in her husband's hands. The men also carry out particular tasks such as ploughing and watering:

> Once the picking is finished by the women, that's when the guys get in and they work the vineyard and put in the cover crop. So once that's done then we start the pruning side of it. After the planting's finished, the men go through and put in the posts and the dripper wires, where they water from, and then they put the wire on the top as well. The men look after the watering. We do a lot of machine picking, because we've got our own machine, and there we employ another three guys to help us with that.

Martha said that in the Barossa Valley there had always been women working in family vineyards, 'like I do, otherwise we'd have to employ people to do it'. She also declared that increasing numbers of women are working on other people's properties for wages, and suggested that this may reflect women's efforts to achieve gender equality. Martha noted that the wine companies, however, have provided increasing employment opportunities for women, speculating that the entry of women to winemaking careers was a result of broader social changes: 'When you think about twenty years ago, the wife stayed at home and the husband went out and worked, so whether it's from that and because society's changing so much that more women are getting into it.'

Conclusion

Although viticulture has always been considered a male occupation, scattered information suggests that many women settlers were involved in all aspects of wine production. In the early days of settlement in the Barossa Valley, most German women were encouraged by their cultural background to participate in grape growing, and the Lutheran religion did not preclude them from making or drinking wine. Women continue to be attracted to employment as winemakers and in other professional occupations. Leonie Lange is a winemaker at Peter Lehmann wines in Tanunda, Prue Henschke is the viticulturist at Henschke cellars and Tania Schrapel is employed at Bethany wines as marketing manager. All of them continue the long-standing German tradition of being involved in wine production.

Notes

1 George Fife Angas Papers, State Library of South Australia (hereafter SLSA), PRG 174.
2 Annely Aeuckens et al., *Vineyard of the Empire: Early Barossa vignerons 1842–1939*, Australian Industrial Publishers, Adelaide, 1988, p. 7.
3 Ernest Whitington, *The South Australian Vintage*, Adelaide, Register, 1903, p. 32.
4 Aeuckens et al. 1988, p. 125.
5 Edward Salter Papers SLSA BRG 1/A/20/8, 10, 19.
6 ibid., BRG 1/A/15–21.
7 ibid., BRG 1/A/20/10.
8 Reginald Munchenberg et al., *The Barossa: A vision realised, the nineteenth century story*, Barossa Valley Archives and Historical Trust Inc., Tanunda, 1992, p. 55.
9 *South Australian Government Gazette*, 7 September 1875, p. 1684.
10 George Loyau, *The Gawler Handbook: A record of the rise and progress of that important town*, Goodfellow and Hele, Adelaide, 1880, p. 96.
11 Aueckens et al. 1988, pp. 46, 250.
12 May Vivienne, *Sunny South Australia: Its city, towns, seaports, beauty-spots: From 1837–1908*, Hussey and Gillingham, Adelaide, 1908, p. 221.
13 Aueckens et al. 1988, p. 228.

A region, its recipes and their meaning
The birth of The Barossa Cookery Book

Angela Heuzenroeder

Introduction

Thinking of Australia as a collection of regions has generated research and discussion in the past few years. Whether in connection with decentralised government, or with variants in language, or with promoting cultural tourism, the concept of region is viewed as a recent construct. Regional food must surely occupy the most public space in this discussion, with chefs travelling around Australia to present local dishes regularly appearing on our television screens. Australian regionalism is not new, however. Because of its size, Australia has always been occupied and settled in separate isolated spaces and people in those spaces had their own tribal loyalties long before they thought of themselves as Australian. When local council districts were created, they provided a framework for people's ideas of 'home'. Some districts had natural geographic boundaries like a river valley or a distinct boundary between hills and plains, and when people living in these areas developed a particular way of life, the district began to have a regional culture.

One such region was – and is – the Barossa Valley in South Australia. The shallow river valley in the range of hills north-east of Adelaide has fertile soil that supports farms of wheat and barley, fruit and vegetables and increasing numbers of vineyards. The formal naming of the geographic region came relatively late. The concept of a Barossa region was first applied to the Barossa District Council at the southern end of the valley in 1888, to the Barossa and Light Cricket Association from 1888, and to the Barossa and Light Lawn Tennis Association in 1894.[1] The district newspaper, founded in 1908, called itself the *Barossa News,* publishing a series of articles promoting the Barossa as a cooperating region under such headings as 'Booming Barossa' and 'Boosting Barossa'.[2] People were seeing the Barossa as a particular entity to which they belonged.

What set the region apart was the large group of European settlers who had migrated from Silesia, Brandenburg and Posen from 1842 onwards. Their Lutheran faith and their Germanic language, dress, buildings and food had a strong influence on the region's material culture. When Germans and English began to intermarry in increasing numbers towards the end of the nineteenth century, cultural mingling of the two separate groups might have proceeded unselfconsciously but for the abrupt challenge to the region's identity brought about by the First World War. It was partly in response to this identity crisis that members of the community published the first *Barossa Cookery Book* in 1917.

Like other forms of material culture, cookery books can reveal much about a society. The recipes, wording, ingredients and the amendments in subsequent editions can all make the book a social, economic and even political document, and in this way a recipe book can reflect the society that produced it. *The Barossa Cookery Book* in its two major editions of 1917 and 1932 is a good example, for it shows a South Australian country community at two critical moments in its history: when a hybrid population of German and English people were coping with the external pressures of the First World War and, later, the economically depressed period of the 1930s. Both editions were making a self-conscious statement about the region and its food to the wider Australian public.

Does this intent make *The Barossa Cookery Book* one of Australia's earliest regional cookbooks? If the recipes are contributed by the local community and draw on the produce and culture of the region in order to present the region's cooking to the rest of the world, then it may well do so. As a social document and as a possible early example of a regional cookbook, the publication offers much of interest. This chapter will examine the history of *The Barossa Cookery Book* and give some insights into the context of its publication. It will also describe the way editions of the book conveyed a sense of region to both the local people and to the outside world, and examine the extent to which the 1932 edition represented the region's original cuisine.

How *The Barossa Cookery Book* came into being

The Barossa Cookery Book first appeared at a town gala event in September 1917 to raise money for the South Australian Soldiers' Fund.[3] Such events, called Australia Days, were held annually in South Australian districts, as in other parts of Australia, from 1915 throughout the First World War and beyond. Towns in the Barossa held processions, queen competitions, gala stalls and twilight concerts, and their plans were published in the *Barossa News* in the months before the events. In 1917 Tanunda's planning began on 4 July, largely at the instigation of Dr F. Jüttner, who had presided over the earlier Australia Day committees. Among the sub-committees was a women's committee, and among ideas tentatively put forward at the general meeting was the compiling of a cookery book.[4] On 17 August an advertisement in the *Barossa News* announced that a 'cookery book containing 400 tried recipes' and priced 6d (but valued at £1) would be on sale on the appointed day.

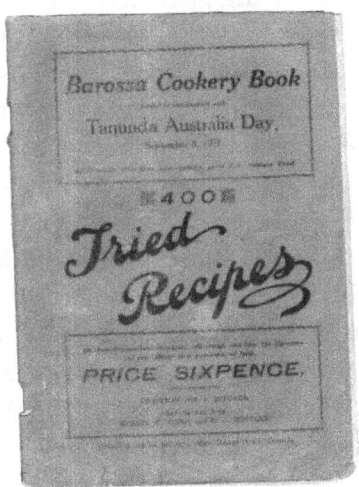

The first *Barossa Cookery Book*, published in 1917.

Beginning in July, the entire process – canvassing for recipes, compiling and editing the contributions, preparing the book for printing and then folding and collating the pages – cannot have been more than eight weeks.[5] As no request for contributions had appeared in the local press, the committee, probably assisted by the 'ladies' group in charge of the stalls', must have acquired the recipes by approaching people personally.[6] In fewer than five weeks they had managed to gather 400 recipes from 216 donors. Most were from the local district, and 124 of these had German surnames. Some were from further afield, and 32 of the donors were from Adelaide.

The newspaper report in the week following Tanunda's Australia Day said that the event organisers were pleased with the sales of the book at 6d per copy and hoped to make £50 for the soldiers from its publication.[7] Sales of the book continued long after the war was over. Hundreds of copies sold each year from reprints and a slightly revised edition, and the profits went to the maintenance of the Tanunda Institute hall, which was later dedicated as a memorial to the soldiers. The institute building was an important place of entertainment in the town, providing a library and a venue to hold concerts, balls, children's frolics and, most important of all, moving pictures.

In 1930, however, cookery book sales fell dramatically, just at a time when the institute funds needed a boost. In the depressed financial climate of 1931 the state government withdrew its funds for institutes at the time when the committee needed to buy equipment for showing the new sound movies from England and Hollywood. It was essential that the institute continue to attract patronage and income since they still had to pay off their overdraft. They planned some concentrated fund-raising, and on 2 May 1932 they resolved to revise and enlarge the recipe book.[8] This time the process involved public consultation, for all ladies were invited by an advertisement in the local paper to attend a meeting on 16 May 'to discuss and arrange for the revision of the very popular *Barossa Cookery Book*.'[9]

The public appeal brought a widespread response, and two weeks later nearly 600 more recipes had reached the committee. On 1 September 1932 the Institute Committee announced that copies of the new edition of *The Barossa Cookery Book* had arrived from the printers with a 'very attractive ... new cover design ... of considerable artistic merit'. That same artistic design is still on the cover today, and, even after 32 reissues, the basic contents, illustrations and layout remain the same as they were in 1932.

The cookery book as political barometer

The contents of the first edition of *The Barossa Cookery Book* make clear the kind of Barossa image Dr Jüttner and the rest of the committee wanted to communicate to the outside world. That first edition was an exercise in patriotism. In a time of war the Barossa region and other German-speaking settlements across Australia, accused of disloyalty, were suffering discrimination. In 1917 a xenophobic state government announced that the Lutheran schools would close, and a year earlier unknown people had tried to burn down the Lutheran church in Angaston.[10] Understandably, the book contained very few recipes taken from the Germanic heritage of many local people.

Essentially it was a book of English recipes, such as drop scones, meat roll and ginger nuts. They included a wholesome recipe for scalloped fish from Sister Ronaque (a nurse at the Keswick army barracks) and a recipe purportedly sent from the trenches by Private Offe for porridge made from soaked army biscuits, reminding readers of the discomfort suffered by local lads in the war. Many recipes had flag-waving names like Prince of Wales cake, Victoria pudding and Exeter stew. All of this, prominently supported by the names of Adelaide's contributing society ladies, was saying, 'Look at us! We are all loyal citizens, too, and we even eat the same foods as you do!' In part they were correct, as recipes in informal hand-written women's notebooks dating from the first decades of the twentieth century show.

But in culinary matters they were only partly correct, for a certain amount of concealment was taking place. For some of the Tanunda ladies in the book these English recipes were merely a supplement to an accustomed fare that included sauerkraut and fermented pickled cucumbers. They knew that German food was a sensitive subject. 'Better not to talk about these things in public', the daughter of one explained later in her autobiography.[11] Indeed, about five traditional recipes did slip into the published book, printed under innocuous names. One was a traditional German recipe for Christmas biscuits commonly called *Weihnachtskuchen* or 'ammonia biscuits' because of their unusual ingredient. Margie Homburg of Tanunda called them 'Kilbourne biscuits', and 70 years later people in the district still knew that to make their ammonia biscuits they could look in *The*

Barossa Cookery Book and find the Kilbourne biscuit recipe of Margie Homburg. The book's publication involved a certain pragmatic complicity in creating an image for the outside world.

Other political undercurrents eddied around the production of *The Barossa Cookery Book*. One concerned the teacher at the Tanunda Lutheran School, J.F.W. Schulz, who had worked energetically for the South Australian Soldiers' Fund since the beginning of the war. Not only had he been on the committee and organised the procession in the two previous years, but he had also spoken on behalf of the local repatriation committee at public meetings of farmers and their families in outlying areas, encouraging people to donate money for returned soldiers.[12] In June 1917, following a Bill passed in state parliament six months earlier, the Lutheran schools in South Australia closed, and Schulz lost his employment.[13] When the 1917 list of committee members for the Australia Day fundraising appeared in the *Barossa News* a few weeks later, J.F.W. Schulz's name was conspicuously absent. Whether any hurt and resentment he might have been feeling were assuaged by the letters of thanks for his hard work sent by C.A. Pollitt on behalf of the patriotic committees remains unrecorded.[14] His case however shows that people in the local area faced a hostile broader world.

For other reasons, the situation was just as sensitive for Florence, the wife of Dr Jüttner, and her sister Gertrude, wife of the local solicitor W.E. Heuzenroeder.[15] As daughters of the Church of England chaplain of St Peter's College for boys in Adelaide, one of the oldest educational institutions in the state, these two women must have felt keenly their situation in this country community that outsiders were viewing with suspicion. They needed to show both the loyalty of their local community and their loyalty to the English establishment. Not surprisingly, they contributed between them 19 recipes for the first edition, and it is likely that many of the 32 Adelaide contributors were recruited by Florence and Gertrude. Their contacts lived at Rose Park, Robe Terrace (Medindie), St Peters, North Adelaide and Unley, all salubrious addresses for the Adelaide society matrons and their daughters who came to the help of their country friends racing against time to assemble a collection of suitable recipes.

The enlarged 1932 edition of *The Barossa Cookery Book* was, like the first edition, a political barometer. By the time of its appearance, pressure from the First World War had long since subsided. Women in households that had maintained their traditional family food were still cooking German dishes and were no longer careful to conceal the fact. Now they felt inclined to contribute some of these when the organising committee asked publicly for recipes. The new wave of contributions included about 50 German recipes, a few with overtly German names like *Armer Ritte* and *Blitzkuchen*. Some were very old recipes handed down through centuries. They included the instructions for making sour salted cucumbers fermented in vine leaves, the sausage called mettwurst and the yeast cake that by then was known in the region as 'German cake'. It is made in a large slab and has a crumbled topping of flour, sugar, butter and spices called *Streusel*.

All these recipes required an understanding of fermentation and had the characteristic yeasty flavours of fermented food. The mettwurst, moreover, required smoking (although directions for this procedure did not appear in the recipe). Another ancient recipe contributed by many cooks was for spiced Christmas honey biscuits (related to gingerbread and dating back to the sixteenth century). Occasionally a German word replaced the English. For example, in her recipe for fowl soup Miss Eichele instructed cooks to add 'spaghetti, commonly called nudeln'.[16] These German insertions gave the revised *Barossa Cookery Book,* which appeared on 1 September 1932, a distinct local character. Announcing the reissue of the book in the *Barossa News* and in the minutes of the institute meetings, the sub-committee expressed great pride in the recipes, thanking the local printing firm, Auricht's, for the hard work of its editor and compositor, J.F.W. Schulz.[17]

The production of this revised cookery book was merely one of a growing number of overt expressions of people's German ancestry. The worsening world economic situation might have contributed to this renewed emphasis of cultural identity; anthropologist Jonathan Friedman has observed that people's cultural and religious associations become important to them in periods of economic decline.[18] Many Australians of German descent throughout the country were renewing contact with extended family members

The revised edition of *The Barossa Cookery Book*, 1932.

in Germany. Occasionally, Barossa people hosted visitors from Germany who happened to be passengers on ships berthed at Outer Harbor.[19]

How other people read these developments depended on their own backgrounds. Journalist Duncan Holmes, who was a boy living in Angaston at the time, claims that people of English descent began to feel unnerved because more people were speaking German and they could not understand them. Holmes's perception was that even food was used as a political statement, and that English people in Angaston supported butcher Turner, who sold innocent lamb chops, distinguishing themselves from the so-called Germans, who went to butcher Schulz to buy the garlic-filled wursts hanging in his window.[20]

Whether in the years before the Second World War large numbers of locals were aware of this sentiment or not, the truth is that many people of German descent were also eating lamb or mutton chops, some via recipes in *The Barossa Cookery Book*, and that they simply regarded themselves as Australian, even if their names happened to be Schiller or Obst. For many like the Tanunda land agent and community leader Friedrich (Fritz) Homburg (half-brother of the state's Attorney General at the time) German songs, music and food simply belonged to a mixed range of normal activities. Homburg would spend the afternoon playing cricket or bowls and go out to conduct the local *Liedertafel* men's choir in the evening, having polished off a typical meal of cold meat, potato salad and sour cucumbers.[21] This was not a declaration of German sympathies; it was just the way life was.

In his capacity as chairman of the Institute Committee, Fritz Homburg presided over the production of the 1932 edition of *The Barossa Cookery Book*.[22] The fact that the book included German family recipes may partly be due to Fritz Homburg's influence. Certainly, the committee members seem to have obtained some recipes by personal request, for the local newspaper of 30 June 1932 said that they were still looking to certain well-known cooks to deliver their recipes, suggesting some sort of deliberate editorial direction.[23] Deliberate or not, the book introduced German recipes at a time when the whole country regarded Germany with positive interest. In 1933 the *Advertiser* newspaper in Adelaide averred that Hitler was good for Germany.[24] As late as 1938 Australia's Prime Minister Robert Menzies said about Germany in federal parliament: 'There is a good deal of really spiritual quality in the willingness of young Germans to devote themselves to the service and well-being of the state.'[25]

The recipes in the 1932 edition of *The Barossa Cookery Book* indicated the climate of the times. They were a barometer but not a political statement, neither on the part of the organisers nor on the part of the contributors, who were likely to contribute a recipe for mettwurst and follow it up with another for good old English steak and kidney pudding.[26] They reflected a society where two strong cultures lived together. At the subsequent outbreak of war other segments of South Australian society could not see this integration. It is unfortunate that, as a result, two prominent community members who contributed much to local community life found themselves interned for un-Australian activities; they were Fritz Homburg and J.F.W. Schulz. Their internment was not, of course, the result of their connection with *The Barossa Cookery Book*. In truth, their diligent work on this community fundraiser and the book's combination of German recipes in a principally English collection are a good indication of where their values lay.[27]

Australia's first regional recipe book?

The 1917 *Barossa Cookery Book* may have had a more political message than the 1932 edition, but in another way both editions had a single purpose. They aimed to promote the Barossa as a region of note within the district and to the world at large. The verso of the front cover in 1917 addressed the reading audience of cooks beyond the boundaries of the Barossa region. The editors invited people to send the *Barossa News* a postcard if they wanted information about local industries. They called the Barossa 'The Canaan of Australia', and gave a brief summary of the income brought to the region from its wine, apples, cereal crops, marble and other minerals. Advertisements and photographs scattered through the pages offered mail-order facilities and gave names and views of local hotels and their dining rooms. This was an active promotion for potential visitors and investors. The Barossa was on display as a region in its first published collection of recipes.

The producers of the 1932 book, like the 1917 committee, aimed to extend the Barossa's reputation much further than the boundaries of the region. Advance publicity in the local newspaper had expansive ideas about the book's future:

> If this appeal by the committee meets with the response it deserves, there is no doubt that the new issue of the cookery book will be regarded throughout Australia as the one cookery book of outstanding excellence, *bring added fame to the district*, distinction to those who contribute to its contents and pleasure to thousands around the dinner tables of the commonwealth.
>
> As in the past, every recipe printed will carry beneath it the name of the person by whom it was donated, thus carrying the names of our most capable cooks to every corner of the Commonwealth, from Queensland to Western Australia. The new edition will, as past editions have done, find its way into every district [emphasis added].[28]

These bombastic claims proved to have some substance, for the Institute Committee has continued to receive orders for *The Barossa Cookery Book* from other states for many years, helping them to pay for the maintenance of the institute hall. The promises of Australia-wide distribution appealed to cooks in the area in 1932. The extra 600 contributions came in from 190 people. Most put their name and home town on their recipes, and, by offering these along with their recipes, the donors, including five men, were also identifying themselves with the Barossa as a region. The overwhelming response to a single advertisement in the local newspaper in such a short time does seem to indicate increasing social cohesion and enthusiasm for a project representing the whole of the Barossa.

Because of the widespread use of its successful offerings for at least three generations, *The Barossa Cookery Book* subsequently became an essential tool in a great many local households, on farms and in towns, where cooks affectionately called it *The Barossa*. An informal survey that I conducted among local Barossa cooks in 2005 showed that they still referred to the book in this way. Its recipes had their own identity because they were signed. Barossa people loved to share food at social events, and when someone asked for the recipe it was easy to identify it by the contributor's name. They might say: 'That's Mrs Nettelbeck's recipe for Henley cake. It's in *The Barossa*.'[29] *The Barossa Cookery Book* thus reinforced already existing networks in the region, networks created by linked church congregations, sporting and cultural liaisons and marriage patterns across the community.[30] Numerous, too, were the recipes making use of local produce, including apples, dried fruits, native currants, oranges, plums, nuts, tomatoes, potatoes and other vegetables, local game (pigeons and hares), poultry, butter, cream and eggs. People would not find it difficult to obtain these ingredients in the region.

To the extent that the publication claimed to represent the cooks of a region, it was a regional cookery book. To the extent that it circulated signed recipes, it created psychological links and articulated regional practices. The use of local produce in large numbers of dishes made the recipes representative of the region and accessible to most local cooks. Those factors, together with the title created in 1917 and the deliberate promotion of the Barossa to the rest of the world, made it a regional cookbook, one of the first in Australia.

A comprehensive account of the region's cuisine?
A regional cookbook would surely be the first place to look for a general profile of the culinary practices of a region. In this regard, the 1932 edition of *The Barossa Cookery Book* presumably gave a

more reliable account than the 1917 edition, because the recipes in 1932 came initially from a public request. A close examination of this edition shows that, whereas in 1917 the number of local women with German names contributing recipes was twice the number of English, in 1932 it was approximately six times the number. The local women with German names among the additional contributors numbered 146 compared with 23 English. This preponderance of local German cooks in 1932, however, delivered only 47 recipes from their German ancestry, with 490 recipes identified as English.

The numerical evidence shows an overwhelming adoption by these cooks of dishes that appeared in English recipe books, including scones, tomato sauce, and steamed puddings, all contributed by women with German names. The picture does not include those in debt-ridden families who were so poor, for example, that they were thankful to receive the life-saving gift of a bowl of dripping from their neighbours, and who had to sell any produce of their own like eggs and butter to meet the family's financial commitments, but it does show what many people were eating in the Barossa. Their food habits were accommodating new dishes and were relying less on food practices from the past.[31]

The 50 German recipes in the third edition of *The Barossa Cookery Book* of 1932 gave the book a character that prompted people in later years to regard its combination of German and English recipes as an accurate account of the food culture of the Barossa. But the assumption that this cookbook faithfully recorded a regional cuisine requires further examination. To have a regional cuisine, writes Barbara Santich, a geographic area needs cultural cohesion and a distinguishing regional identity. Regional cuisine is usually epitomised, according to Santich, by 'a collection of recognised dishes that depend on certain locally available ingredients and illustrate certain flavour combinations and cooking preparation methods characteristic of, if not particular to, the region'.[32]

The Barossa region and its food had those elements. Cultural cohesion existed when the cookery book was published and later revised – as far as any community can remain cohesive and still have contact with the changing world. The characteristic flavour combinations and cooking preparation methods of the traditional dishes constituted a definite cuisine with cultural and, at times, local regional foundations. How completely the 1932 version of *The Barossa Cookery Book* represented this cultural and local regional cuisine now requires some consideration.

In the first place, the book's coverage of the local cooking practice was not comprehensive because cooks derived their recipes from other sources as well. My informal survey showed that, when it came to the really old recipes, many people preferred to use their mother's notebooks, although they still looked to the published book for a good many cakes, biscuits and puddings and particularly for jams, sauces and relishes that would use up home-grown produce. Some households also used the *Green and Gold Cookery Book* as a supplementary source.[33]

Secondly, all people interviewed said that they adapted recipes from *The Barossa Cookery Book* to suit their own tastes. Referring to their tattered, greasy copies, they read out notes that had been made in the margin not only by themselves but by their mothers and even grandmothers: 'not so much pepper; use less salt; add an extra egg'. Cooking of this kind was for many a creative process not bound by prescriptive recipes, and the comments formed a link between generations in a family, producing family characteristics in food rather than regional ones. Family versions developed beyond *The Barossa Cookery Book* (which however sometimes captured these nuances when several versions appeared for the same recipe, for example, honey biscuits).

Most significantly, some important recipes made by a great many people across the district did not reach the pages of the 1932 edition. Familiar farm recipes for small-goods (fermented, cooked or smoked) from pig-killing day, such as blood sausage and liver sausage, were excluded, perhaps because they were unlikely to attract town cooks. Missing, too, was the traditional dish of smoked meat, stewed pie melon and dumplings, commonly called *Pompenbrei*, made from the meat smoked at the pig-killing.[34] This, like the sweet poppyseed pudding *Mohnklöße* served on Christmas Eve, was the fare of Lutheran families whose Silesian German traditions were deeply entrenched, families for whom nevertheless *The Barossa Cookery Book* might be a common reference for cooking.[35]

Local cheeses like quark (a fresh curd) and *Kochkäse* (an aged curd denatured by gentle heating) did not appear, and yet even townspeople made these. Fermented sauerkraut escaped the list, although its preparation is similar to that of sour cucumbers, which appeared in the book. The name sauerkraut possibly still grated on the sensitive ears of people who had heard Germans called 'Krauts' during the war. More surprising was the omission of the liquid yeast preparation necessary to make German cake. Two recipes in the book required it and expected that cooks would know the procedure.[36] And most remarkable was the absence of a recipe for the salad of finely sliced cucumbers with cream and vinegar that has always accompanied Christmas dinner in nearly every Barossa household.

These recipes were all unsophisticated German fare, part of the repertoire of country women coming to Australia from eastern central Europe. Their absence from the book was regrettable. Even more regrettable in terms of the collection of a regional Barossa cuisine was the omission of unique dishes that had been adapted to the environment and resources in Australia. For example, the book completely ignored several delicious and well-loved variations of German yeast cake. It gave no instructions for the version that had layers of fresh sultana grapes under the streusel. The version with grapes is unknown in Germany. It appears to have developed in the Barossa, and although widely made for several generations did not appear in a printed cookbook until 1994.[37]

When people began to adopt chemical raising agents instead of fermented yeast for leavening, two other versions of German cake topped with streusel circulated in the community. They had beer or cooked mashed potatoes mixed into the dough, to create the yeasty flavours and springy texture of baked yeast dough without losing the convenience of chemical technology. Beer cake and potato cake became popular local cakes.[38] Topped with streusel, they were significantly different from the *Bierkuchen* and *Kartoffelkuchen* in German recipe books, and yet they received no mention in *The Barossa Cookery Book*. Such an oversight excluded unique recipes that should join the Barossa's contribution to South Australian regional cuisine.

Most surprising of all was the omission of a very simple recipe commonly made by anyone with access to wine grapes, *Rote Grütze*. This is a simple dessert of fresh sweet juice from black grapes thickened with sago, commonly served with fresh cream. With abundant fruit to use from the Barossa's flourishing wine industry, local nineteenth-century cooks adapted the northern European way of serving berries from the woods and made a unique regional dish by substituting grapes.[39] It may be that the simplicity of *Rote Grütze* caused it to be overlooked. And yet this and the yeast cake variations were important Barossa dishes. They are the local cuisine's founding elements. A self-proclaimed regional production *The Barossa Cookery Book* may have been but, like numbers of regional cookbooks published in Germany and other places from the middle of the nineteenth century onwards, it was not a complete representation of local regional cuisine and it did not record dishes that were original local adaptations.[40]

Conclusion

The anthropologist Mary Douglas maintains that food and the way it is served can be a code, expressing messages about social hierarchy, inclusion and exclusion.[41] Searching for Douglas's code in the two major editions of *The Barossa Cookery Book* reveals some hidden communications about the political, economic and social exclusions of the day. At times the messages are furtive, particularly in the 1917 edition, where the omission of German recipes, the printing of others under innocent-sounding names, and the rallied support of society matrons and their daughters from Adelaide all worked together to promote the image of a loyal community to the outside world. Knowing some of the events behind these messages strengthens their voice as they evoke a society in the Barossa at the time of the First World War.

The codes in the 1932 edition of *The Barossa Cookery Book* convey the voices of a much broader range of Barossa people who responded to the public appeal for recipes. For them, political pressures were not as strong as they had been 15 years earlier. The pages of their donated recipes disclose two distinct messages about community identity. One is the growing confidence of women to share the German recipes that had long been part of their family life, but which did not appear in the 1917 edition. Including a relatively small number of these in the 1932 edition gave a more balanced portrait of Barossa food customs of the day.

At the same time, however, a parallel message in the overwhelming number of English recipes donated by cooks with German names demonstrates how extensively Barossa cooks had embraced the culinary patterns offered to them by English cooking and food customs. This message about people and their food in the Barossa represents of course only those women with the literacy, culinary skills and time to respond to the call for recipes. Those excluded from a cookbook representing their own region often lived on food bearing no resemblance to the middle-class recipes from the Barossa, whether English or German. Their omission is typical of many publications purporting to be regional cookbooks.

Nevertheless, the recipe book is a partial history of its times, of people's fortunes as well as of their food. It is justifiably a regional cookbook, showing a self-conscious pride in the district on the part of the contributors and on the part of the editorial committees promoting the book and the region to the outside world under the name Barossa. Because the book did not record some significant foods that were very familiar to local people at the time of its publication and because it completely overlooked adaptations of some dishes that were the small beginnings of an original local regional cuisine, *The Barossa Cookery Book* did not entirely represent regional food as it had developed after the arrival of the first immigrants. Nevertheless, local people regarded the book as a familiar resource. Although the reasons for publishing the two editions have long been forgotten, the book remains an important institution in the local community to this day.[42]

Notes

1. Donald Ross & Reginald Munchenberg 'The everyday way of life', in Reginald Munchenberg, Heinrich Proeve, Donald Ross, Anne Hausler and Geoffrey Saegenschnitter (eds), *The Barossa: A vision realised,* Barossa Valley Archives and Historical Trust, Tanunda, 1992, p. 140.
2. *Barossa News,* 6 March, 2 April 1914.
3. F. Jüttner, W. Tuohy & W.A. Bentley (eds), *Barossa Cookery Book,* Australia Day Committee, Tanunda, 1917.
4. *Barossa News,* 6 July 1917.
5. A note of appreciation on one of the pages of the 1917 edition thanked the ladies of the Cheer-Up Society for folding and collating. This article refers to 'ladies' because it was the contemporary local term for women.

6   *Barossa News*, 4 August 1917.
7   ibid., 24 August 1917.
8   Minutes of the Tanunda Institute, Tanunda, 2 May 1932.
9   *Barossa News*, 12 May 1932.
10 ibid., 15 June 1917, 4 August 1916.
11 Vera Bockmann's mother was Mrs Chris Hoffmann, a well-known winery owner, who contributed a recipe for Harrison Cake (Vera Bockmann, *Full Circle*, Wakefield Press, Adelaide, 1987, p. 10).
12 *Barossa News*, 13 July 1915, 30 June 1916, 13 October 1916.
13 Elizabeth M. Schulz, 'Guilty Till Proven Innocent', BA Hons thesis, University of South Australia, Adelaide, 1987, p. 26.
14 ibid.
15 John M. Bishop, *Birrell: Three brothers Birrell*, The Author, Uraidla, 2003, pp. 22–3.
16 *The Barossa Cookery Book: 1000 selected recipes*, Tanunda Institute Committee Tanunda, 1932, p. 5.
17 *Barossa News*, 1 February 1934; Minutes of the Tanunda Institute, 2 May 1933.
18 Jonathan Friedman, *Cultural Identity & Global Process*, Sage, London, 1994, p. 39.
19 Schulz 1987, p. 40.
20 Duncan Holmes, 'This is War', manuscript of unpublished article, Toronto, 1996.
21 Robert Homburg, son of Fritz Homburg, Tanunda, interview May 2005.
22 Minutes of the Tanunda Institute, 2 May 1932.
23 *Barossa News*, 30 June 1932.
24 Ian Harmstorf, 'South Australia's Germans in World War II', South Australian German Association website, Adelaide, 1987, viewed May, December 2005, http://www.sagermanassociation.asn.au/images/WW11.doc.
25 ibid. (The parliamentary reference is Australia, House of Representatives, *Debates*, 1 September 1938.)
26 Mrs G. Stelzer, recipes for mettwurst and beef steak and kidney pudding in *The Barossa Cookery Book* (Tanunda, 1932), pp. 14, 21.
27 Fritz Homburg's internment lasted only six weeks.
28 *Barossa News*, 16 June 1932.
29 Di (Koch) Litterini, Tanunda; Jenny Kolovs, Tanunda; Yvonne Burgemeister, Nuriootpa; Dianne Sonntag, Tanunda; Olga Lehmann, Gomersal; Linda Kroschel, Angaston; Esma Hein, Tanunda; Melva Schmidt, Nuriootpa; Gloria Rosenzweig, Moculta; Malcolm Seppelt, Seppeltsfield; Colin Gramp, Tanunda; Leonie Tscharke, Bethany, inter-

views, 2005. Countless conversations with local people over five decades reinforce this statement.
30 Di (Koch) Litterini, Tanunda; Jenny Kolovs, Tanunda, interviews, 2005.
31 Ivy Zwar, Nuriootpa, interview 1997; Olga Lehmann, Tanunda, interview 2005; Beverly Pech, Vine Vale, interview 1994. These people all described their struggles at times of extreme poverty.
32 Barbara Santich, *Looking for Flavour*, Wakefield Press, Adelaide, 1996. pp. 130–1.
33 Annie L. Sharman (ed.), *Green and Gold Cookery Book*, Congregational and Baptist Churches of South Australia, Adelaide, 1923.
34 Although it did contain a similar recipe with pickled pork, dumplings and quinces, without naming the dish.
35 Wally Stiller, Tanunda, interview 2005.
36 *The Barossa Cookery Book* 1932, pp. 101, 112.
37 Renate Schach von Wüttenau, German food writer, Hanover, interview 1996; *Riches from the Vine*, Soroptimist International Barossa Valley, Nuriootpa, 1994, pp. 73–4.
38 Angela Heuzenroeder, *Barossa Food*, Wakefield Press, Adelaide, 1999, pp. 98–9.
39 Renate Schach von Wüttenau, 1996.
40 Kirsten Schlegel-Matthies, 'Regionale Speisen in deutschen Kochbüchern des 19. und 20. Jahrhuderts', in Hans-Jürgen Teuteberg, Gerhard Neumann & Alois Wierlacher (eds), *Essen und kulturelle Identität: Europäische Perspektiven*, Akademie Verlag, Berlin, 1997, p. 215.
41 Mary Douglas, 'Deciphering a Meal', in Carole Counihan & Penny van Esterik (eds), *Food and Culture: A reader*, Routledge, New York, 1997, pp. 36–54.
42 With thanks from the author to Dr A. Lynn Martin and Dr Robert Dare for their assistance and advice.

National Socialism in South Australia

Barbara Poniewierski

Of all the years of a German presence in South Australia, the most controversial are those of the Nazi dictatorship in Germany, 1933–45. In some quarters there has been an understandable but unfortunate silence, an unwillingness to broach a topic of great sensitivity, so that many aspects of that time have remained shrouded in mystery. Where attempts have been made to break that silence, typically by people of German origin drawing on oral history sources and subjective experiences, the perils of distortion or retrospective self-justification have not always been avoided. Attacks on the Australian police and military, for example, are legion, yet they are often demonstrably misinformed about the facts. Comparing Australian Security organs to the Gestapo is not only offensive, it is also ridiculous. How many internees in Australia were interrogated under torture? How many were hanged, shot, beheaded, beaten or starved to death? That Australian authorities made mistakes is undeniable, but their observations were usually well founded, even if interpretations were sometimes astray. It is only fair that their side of the story should also be told in order to construct a more complete and nuanced picture of how Nazis and their sympathisers behaved in South Australia in the Nazi era, and why the Australian authorities responded in the ways they did.

Nazism in the Antipodes
After the First World War ended in 1918, Barossa Germans might have settled back into relative normality, despite simmering resentment about the closing of Lutheran schools and the changing of German place names in 1917. It was convenient to blame the

demise of the Lutheran day schools on a State Government decree, but in reality the German Consul-General Richard Kiliani had reported as early as in April 1913 that German schools in South Australia were already on the point of collapse.[1] This observation showed that a process of assimilation was already taking place. Although that process might have resumed in the years after the war, as memories of hostilities faded and some German place names were restored, further resentment was fostered with the advent of Nazism in Germany, and, from 1932, the founding of branches of the Nazi Party in Australia and in South Australia.

A key figure in the spread of Nazism in Australia was Dr J. Heinrich Becker. Born in 1898 in Thuringia, Becker arrived in Adelaide in September 1927 aboard *Main*. After serving in the First World War as a frontline sapper and being wounded several times, he had studied medicine at Marburg and Munich and made at least one trip to Australia as doctor aboard *Crefeld*. He claimed later that he had joined the Nazi Party while a student, but the earliest evidence of membership shows that he was accepted on 1 March 1932, his number being 952,550.[2]

In 1931, Dr Hans Nieland, a Hamburg member of the *Reichstag*, contacted Nazi sympathisers abroad asking them to found local Nazi Party branches. His contacts in Australia were Dr Becker in Tanunda and a certain Johannes Frerck in Sydney.[3] Owing to political infighting in Germany and doubts about admitting overseas members, the Australian branch started shakily. The first South Australian applications date from 1932, some early recruits being men who had emigrated by a ship on which Becker was the medical officer or a fellow passenger. One such recruit was Becker's friend Franz Drake, who joined the Party as a consequence of his association with Becker.[4] (He was member number 1,562,392.) To a number of fellow passengers Becker had given free medical attention or had lent money. By the time he left for Germany in October 1933 to visit his mother, there were at least 14 confirmed members in South Australia and two applicants.[5]

Becker was back in Adelaide in March 1934, having probably done a training course for Nazi Party leaders. He later denied this, but so did most men about whom it could be proven that they had taken part in such a course.[6] Seeing the benefits of bringing expatriates under control, the Party now encouraged overseas recruiting, despite membership rolls in Germany having closed temporarily from 1 May 1933.[7] Even abroad, only German nationals were eligible for membership; that is, 'Aryans' who had been born in Germany and who had not become naturalised elsewhere, or females who had married Germans and were racially acceptable. The German Consul-General Dr Rudolf Asmis reported to the Foreign Office in July 1935 that there were branches in Brisbane, Sydney, Melbourne and Tanunda,[8] while Consul Dr Walter Hellenthal reported in August that branches at Tanunda and Adelaide had about 12 members each.[9] There was considerable ambiguity about the political stance of consular representatives. Asmis, who arrived in Sydney on 6 October 1932 aboard *Mooltan* – not in June, as is sometimes claimed – was a dedicated Pan-German nationalist but was somewhat ambivalent about Nazism; he had applied to join the Party in August 1933, then withdrew his application in October 1935 and did not apply again until April 1938, when membership became, in theory, compulsory for diplomatic and consular personnel.[10]

Despite claims that he was concerned only with German citizens, Becker was not content to leave ethnic Germans (*Volksdeutsche*, that is, people of German heritage but other nationality, in this case Australian, as opposed to *Reichsdeutsche*, who were citizens of the *Reich*) entirely in peace. One of his targets was Adelaide's German Club. On 6 June 1934 the German Club (*Süd-Australischer Allgemeiner Deutscher Verein*, or SAADV) moved that no one be admitted as a member if he belonged to 'a non-Australian, or international political party'.[11] Working through Heinrich Krawinkel, the former Honorary Consul in Adelaide, Becker ensured that this ban was lifted and that Nazi nominees gained control of the club. Within a short time, *Stützpunktleiter* (Local Branch Leader) Ernst Starke became president, while Party member Theodor Bay was secretary. To gain Krawinkel's backing, Becker had promised to support his bid to regain the post of Honorary Consul, a promise he could not fulfil.[12]

In theory, consuls handled relationships between Germany and Australians, but in matters concerning German nationals, even the Consul-General was obliged to consult Becker as the senior Nazi

Group portrait of some of the original members of the National Socialist German Workers Party, Adelaide Branch, standing beside a tree wrapped in a swastika flag on the Gomersal Road near Tanunda. It is understood that the members of the group are, from left to right, Carl Christoph Fienemann, a storekeeper from Pinnaroo; Ernst Emil Starke, a Nazi Party member from 1 March 1934, for a time Ortsgruppenleiter and President of the SAADV, interned 4 September 1939 to 24 November 1947, deported; Karl (or sometimes Carl) Johann Rohde, a member of the Brisbane Stützpunkt (stronghold) visiting South Australia in 1934, interned 25 November 1942 to 12 December 1942; Heinrich Wallenstein, allegedly a stonemason, left Australia probably about 1936; Wilhelm Friedrich Abel, NSDAP member from 1 November 1932, interned 4 September 1939 to 12 February 1946; Walter Ernst Bartsch, NSDAP member from 1 November 1932, interned 4 September 1939 to 19 December 1944; Harry Hahn, NSDAP member, believed to have left for Germany about 1937; Oluf Bohlens, NSDAP member from 1 November 1932, interned 4 September 1939 to 4 March 1946. The photo was taken by J. Heinrich Becker and passed to security services early in the war.
(Australian War Memorial P01738.003)

official in Australia. This led to an anomalous situation, whereby consulates issued passports, but the *Landeskreisleiter* (National Branch Leader) had to approve their issue, or to report to Germany if he thought one should not be issued. Power went to Becker's head. Among other things, he controlled the Gestapo in Australia, which operated through the harmless-sounding *Hafendienst* or Harbour Service. Its function, as its name suggests, was to provide assistance to and entertainment for crews of German ships while they were in Australian harbours, but it also reported on their conduct. On 2 August 1934 Becker appointed the first and senior *Hafendienst* cum Gestapo agent, Wilhelm Heiler, the *Stützpunktleiter* in Melbourne. Formalising the appointment, Becker told Heiler that he belonged to the staff of the *Landeskreis* (National Branch): 'All onboard cells and *Stützpunkte* on German ships will be subordinate to you; you are responsible to me.'[13] He enlarged on this on 4 December 1934, writing that 'you belong to *my* staff and are not subject to the *Stützpunktleiter*, except at meetings'.[14] (At that time, F.W. Kersten was *Stützpunktleiter* in Melbourne.) Heiler collated information from sub-agents in other states. Becker then reported to the *Auslands-Organisation* (the AO or Foreign Organisation, a Nazi Party body responsible for all Party activities outside Germany), which forwarded the reports to the Gestapo. This is by no means to suggest that Becker should be considered a 'Gestapo officer'. Regular Gestapo officials were professionally trained police; Becker was merely an amateur informant who did not have the power of arrest; rather, he provided information upon which the Gestapo acted.

The nature of this work is indicated in a letter of 28 November 1935, when Becker asked Heiler for information regarding an emigrant returning to Germany. Without a favourable report from Becker he would not receive work.[15] There is also a recorded case where a German seaman was imprisoned in Germany for a disparaging remark he made in a Tanunda hotel.[16] Becker threatened men visiting their families in Germany that they would be detained there if they did not join the Party before they left Australia. It was noted later that some men joined the Party a few weeks before leaving on holiday to Germany, but never paid another subscription and became naturalised soon after returning to Australia, which meant that their membership automatically lapsed.[17]

To ensure that they were not given German agencies or contracts, Becker reported on firms that were owned or managed by 'Jews', or even merely employed 'non-Aryans'. This occurred on a bigger scale in Sydney and Melbourne, but German goods sold in South Australia included cars, tractors and musical instruments. Party members were instructed to ensure that other Party members obtained these agencies as far as possible. Thus Centenary Motors inevitably secured distribution rights for DKW (*Dampf-Kraft-Wagen*, a well-known German car and motorcycle manufacturer) and Auto-Union products, for no other firm could match their Nazi credentials. Three of the four principals (Starke, Schlenk and Bay) were Party members.[18]

Becker's tactics and 'style' antagonised many people. He overstepped the mark when he heaped vulgar abuse on Asmis, calling him a liar and 'a common rascal', and writing to the German Club in similar terms. Henry William Borchers, former President of the German Club, wrote to Asmis while the latter was on leave in Germany: 'The people can't respect him, as he earns no respect ... And then he is surprised that one does not want to work with him. I can't and won't do it ... the man can't differentiate between truth and lies, that is, in the way that a colour blind person can't say a colour is red or green or yellow. Perhaps something is not quite right in his head.'[19] Borchers's suspicions might have had solid foundations. One of Becker's war wounds had been to the head. It is possible that, as well as the psychological trauma of trench warfare, Becker had indeed incurred some physical brain damage, for time and again he recklessly told untruths that were bound to be found out.

Many complaints were sent to the Party and the Foreign Office in Germany about Becker's bullying, and the bickering in Australia between Becker and both Asmis and the ethnic Germans was notorious. As it was Party policy to settle disputes in private, it was intolerable that the Party leader should use such language in referring to Germany's senior diplomatic representative and allow it to become public. His career as Party leader was as good as over when he fell out with Admiral Menche, who controlled the AO's *Amt VIII* (Office VIII), which monitored Australia. When Asmis was on leave in Germany in 1935–36, he consulted with Menche and had a personal interview with Hitler.[20] To depose Becker openly would have exposed the split in the Party and tarnished its image. In October 1936, Gotthart Ammerlahn, a senior Hitler Youth leader, spent some time in Tanunda while visiting Australia in the course of a world tour; it was probably as a result of his observations that the local groups in Adelaide, Tanunda and Brisbane were dissolved in December of that year.[21] A month later, Asmis wrote to Ammerlahn, reporting with evident satisfaction that 'the [*Landeskreis*] of the Party has been dissolved and Germanism delivered from the unholy workings of Dr. Becker'.[22]

When the *Landeskreis* reopened in 1937, leadership was

transferred to Walter Ladendorff in Sydney, but it was difficult to find a new leader for South Australia, as Adelaide's German citizens were mostly labourers and tradesmen; there were few well-educated, wealthy German nationals who could be considered potential leaders. The branch reopened in March 1938 under the leadership of Vice-Consul Paul Beckmann, a career consul who had served in the London Embassy while Joachim von Ribbentrop was German Ambassador to Britain. The centre of activities shifted to Adelaide, one meeting a month being held in Tanunda.[23] The former leader, Ernst Starke, became Deputy Leader, while Emil Kuhri remained *Hafendienst* agent. Consular secretary Johanna Jung and Ludwig Heinle ran the *Winterhilfswerk* (Winter Relief). Pastor Lorenz Methsieder, a former New Guinea missionary and then a librarian at the Lutheran book store, became secretly the head of the *Volkswohlfahrt* (National Welfare) and mediator for the Party Court of Honour.[24] Power was centralised in Beckmann's hands, as he was for a time also Vice-President of the German Club. He became close to Hermann Homburg's family through Homburg's daughter, Marsi. It may not have been a serious romance, but they were still writing affectionately to each other in late 1940 when Beckmann was in Japan.[25]

When the *Deutsche Arbeitsfront* (German Labour Front, DAF) was founded in March 1935, it too was administered Australia-wide from Tanunda, by Kurt Schubert.[26] Later, the national leadership was transferred to a Captain Koehler in Sydney, and it was administered in South Australia by Richard Bernhard Schlenk of Centenary Motors, who had arrived in Adelaide in 1930. However, men were unwilling to pay dues to an association from which they gained little benefit, and it remained small. The Adelaide DAF branch was disbanded on 1 December 1937, the remaining members being transferred to the Sydney branch.[27] The *Frauenschaft* (Women's Group), however, flourished, despite confusion over eligibility for membership.[28] Australian women married to Germans automatically acquired German citizenship and were eligible. German women who had married Australians technically were not, while Australians citizens of German descent could be admitted only with approval from Germany. The Adelaide group was run for a time by Johanna Jung, then by Ernst Starke's

The Australian National Group (*Landesgruppe*) pictured next to the *Landesgruppe China* at an international NSDAP gathering in Germany. The date of the photo is unknown, but it had to be before the end of 1935, as the name was changed to *Landeskreis* about that time. (National Archives of Australia D1915: SA19447: Auslandsorganisation of the NSDAP Part 1)

mother, Pauline. It was stressed that membership of the *Frauenschaft* was not equivalent to Party membership, but each group leader had to be a Party member.

Australian citizens and the attractions of Nazism

The material given above refers mainly to the so-called *Reichsdeutsche* or German nationals, but ethnic Germans (*Volksdeutsche*) who were Australian citizens by birth or naturalisation were also exposed to massive propaganda extolling the merits of Nazism. Indeed, some were more enthusiastic about Nazism than the *Reichsdeutsche*, but regulations barred them from Party membership. To cater for them, and with permission from Germany, Becker founded a group called the *Freunde der Hitler-Bewegung* (Friends of the Hitler Movement). At the insistence of Asmis, who thought this too provocative, he changed the name to the *Fortbildungsverein* (Club for Further Education).[29] This sounded harmless, but in Nazi parlance 'education' meant propaganda. Among its leading members were Pastor Richard Held in Tanunda and Pastor Julius Meier in Loxton, who associated with it openly as sponsors for film shows and lectures. Fritz Homburg, then Chairman of the District Council of Tanunda, also allegedly attended meetings.[30]

The Vice-Consul Paul Beckmann and the Adelaide Consul, Dr Oskar Eugen Seger, tried to bridge the gap between German Australians who enjoyed social standing in the city and the widely scattered farming community, and also that between *Reichsdeutsche* and *Volksdeutsche*. The German Club had deteriorated to an extent that horrified Seger and Beckmann. Although refurbished not many years earlier, it was run down and shabby, and the moral tone was such that respectable women were reluctant to attend dances or let their daughters attend. Older members left in disgust, which hastened the deterioration.[31] In Adelaide, however, the German Club catered for only a fraction of ethnic German residents; most lived too far away or had no use for clubs. Both the consulate and the Party worked on exposing these people to as much propaganda as possible. They asked for details of people to whom propaganda could be sent, and these were inundated with material. The German Club received regular shipments, and most Lutheran pastors were on the lists. A system was set up, whereby individuals in Germany of impeccable Nazi background extolled the wonders of the New Germany in letters exchanged with Australian Germans.[32]

The 1936 centenary of European settlement in South Australia provided an opportunity for Germans to organise again. The German Centenary Committee espoused several projects. One was the restoration of German place names, which had been changed during the war. Another was the refurbishment of the Klemzig pioneer cemetery, with the erection of a suitable monument, and a third was a memorial to Carl Linger, who had written the music to *Song of Australia*, popular in South Australia.[33] Only three place names were restored: Ambleside, Gaza and Tweedvale resumed their old names of Hahndorf, Klemzig and Lobethal. Although Asmis wrote in March 1933 that he did not hope for much owing to the expense involved in changing such things as maps and signposts, he had greater ambitions by 1936 and was not entirely satisfied with a symbolic victory.[34] Talk of a Linger memorial inspired H.W. Häusler, an Australian-born farmer at Lyndoch, to write German words to *Song of Australia*. Published by Karl Reber in the *Queensländer Herald*, they replaced the 'Australia, Australia, Australia' in the chorus with a threefold 'Heil Hitler, Heil'.[35]

In order to maintain enthusiasm, the committee was converted

The German Club (SAADV), Adelaide, decorated for Hitler's fiftieth birthday, 20 April 1939. The decorations were organised by Ilma Bohlmann.
(National Library of Australia PIC/8152 LOC Drawer A51)

in 1937 into the South Australian German Historical Society, with the aim of fostering recognition of the role of early German settlers. Hermann Homburg pushed Heinrich Krawinkel, his son-in-law, into taking over leadership of the Centenary Committee and the Historical Society. In April 1937, Asmis urged Krawinkel to affiliate the Historical Society with the *Bund des Deutschtums* (which can be roughly translated as 'League of German Culture', an association of German cultural organisations in Australia assembled by Asmis), 'whose objects after all differ in no way from yours'.[36] Six months later, Seger told Krawinkel that he had no right to term it 'German' unless he did affiliate.[37] Krawinkel kept clear of the *Bund*, but he was in the awkward position of being considered by authorities as a threat to national security, while Ilma Bohlmann (more on her below) denounced him to Germany as hostile to the Third Reich.[38]

The Homburgs and Bohlmanns

Hermann Homburg had long been a 'person of interest' to authorities. In January 1915 he had felt obliged to resign from his position as the South Australian State Attorney-General and not to stand for re-election in March. His brother Robert also resigned from parliament. However, they were not interned, and the most telling denunciation of them was not made until 1916, by their brother-in-law, Reginald Fraser. The latter wrote to (Sir) George Pearce, Minister for Defence, that John Homburg was loyal, but the other brothers were not. Robert was the 'arch-traitor'; Hermann however was shrewder. When heavy Australian casualty lists came through, Hermann said 'that it would be a good thing for a few thousand Australians to be shot off as they were mostly loafers', and another brother, Fritz, had agreed with him. Fritz expressed regret that he could not fight for Germany and claimed that, if conscription came, he would do something to get himself interned rather than fight for Australia. Concerning Hermann, Fraser wrote that he had not believed what was said until he heard it himself, because he could not imagine that 'any man Australian born ... could be such a bastard'.[39] Strangely, despite having called Robert an 'arch-traitor', Fraser made no specific charges against him, and between the wars, probably under the influence of his Anglo-Australian wife, Robert seems to have distanced himself from Hermann's views and activities.

Between the wars Military Intelligence continued to watch the Homburg family. Not surprisingly, attention sharpened with the outbreak of another world war. The first to be interned was not one of the Homburgs but Krawinkel, arrested by authorities on 30 May 1940. In September, a woman close to the family reported that Hermann Homburg had threatened to 'get even with [Philip] McBride' because he was presumed responsible for Krawinkel's internment.[40] It took five months for Krawinkel to get an appeal against his internment heard before an advisory committee. Claims that appeals were heard by a military tribunal are untrue: the advisory committees were headed by someone who was, or had been, or was eligible to be, a Justice of the Supreme Court, and most other members were senior legal men.[41] His appeal heard, Krawinkel was released on 14 November under a 'restriction order', after Hermann Homburg put up a bond of £500.

In the meantime a case had long been building against Fritz Homburg, who was finally arrested on 29 October 1940. There was much background material on his association with Becker and the editorial policy of the *Barossa News*. He had allegedly said that the war would not have happened if England had not intervened when Germany invaded Poland. (He seems not to have considered that it might not have happened if Germany had not invaded Poland.) Within days, his appeal was heard before the committee that had reviewed Krawinkel's case. He claimed that he had never heard Becker make disloyal statements, despite being very friendly with him. Although he had belonged to the *Fortbildungsverein*, he also contended that he knew of no Nazism in the whole Tanunda district. Although parts of his evidence were highly improbable, he was released unconditionally on 14 November.[42]

Two weeks later, Hermann Homburg was interned. There have been claims that he was found 'not guilty' at his appeal, as evidence against him was false, which some clearly was. It was untrue that parties the family held in March and September (1938 and 1939) were in celebration of Hitler's victories; Military Intelligence discovered that by an unfortunate coincidence there were family birthdays around these dates. However, there was a solid case against him from evidence by family members and fellow parliamentarians. It was reported that from 1933 he failed to attend the Governor's address at the opening of parliament, or the address in reply. It was known that he had insisted that Asmis keep secret the financial support he had given the *Bund* and its paper (*Die Brücke*) and the plan to establish a German secondary school in Melbourne. The behaviour of his daughter Marsi when she and her mother visited Germany reflected badly on Hermann. In an interview published in a Stuttgart newspaper Marsi had said that they were going to the Party congress in Nuremberg to see the *Führer* and expressed admiration and respect for all Hitler had done.[43] Moreover, Hermann abused his sister-in-law, Maud Prisk, when her son Gordon enlisted in the Australian armed forces.[44] Maud said that Hermann had always been a traitor to the country of his birth, and Gordon said that he refrained from striking his uncle only because he was an old man. Not all Maud's allegations were accurate in details, but they were true to the spirit of their contact.[45]

In the judgments of the advisory committee considering appeals against internment, the terms 'guilty' and 'not guilty' did not apply. Rather, the committee decided whether it was 'necessary' or 'advisable' to keep the appellant interned. Of the three members considering Homburg's appeal, two thought he should remain interned, and one thought it would be advisable, though not necessary in view of Homburg's age. (By this time he was 66.) They agreed that 'it would be unsafe to accept his sworn testimony': put more bluntly, it was known that he had committed perjury. His release on Christmas Eve was a political decision, overriding the recommendation, and the army complained that this had given rise to a view that Homburg was above the law.[46] Military Intelligence reported that it caused a decrease in the cooperation they received from the public.

Homburg was restricted to Ballarat, and Marsi accompanied him, but the Americans complained that they were pressing servicemen from a nearby base for secret information while drinking with them. In December 1942 he was allowed to return to Adelaide. Once there, he repeatedly broke his restriction order by receiving visitors. This was an awkward issue to handle, as visitors included parliamentarians, Archie Cameron (United Australia Party) and Arthur Calwell (Labor Party), which might help to explain Homburg's release.[47] He also failed to carry an identity card, claiming that he was so well known that he should not be expected to do so. His son, Renolf, also neglected to carry an identity card, and he failed to register with the Manpower Office.[48]

The Bohlmann family was another example of Australian-born Germans whose loyalty belonged to Germany. Ilma Bohlmann, née Menzel, boasted that she had sent secret information to Germany during the 'Great War' via the captain of a Dutch merchant ship. The energetic moving spirit in the *Frauenschaft*, despite not being a German citizen, she had supervised decorations in the German Club for Hitler's fiftieth birthday celebrations in 1939. She carried out consular requests to write letters to papers in defence of National Socialist Germany. She visited German ships to smuggle propaganda ashore, and was so self-important that some captains dreaded her arrival.[49] At Beckmann's request, she acted as hostess for the Vienna Boys' Choir and claimed she sent secret information to Germany coded into a concert program. In 1938 Stanley Bohlmann, wharfinger at Port Adelaide, was caught gaining illegal access to data on oil supplies. Other members of the Bohlmann and Menzel families, horrified at this behaviour, broke off all contact with him.[50]

The Bohlmanns' son Angas (aged 24 in 1939) enquired about obtaining a certificate proving Aryan ancestry, doing Labour Service (*Arbeitsdienst*) in Germany and joining the Luftwaffe;[51] their daughter Joan had already arranged to perform Labour Service and her passage to Germany was booked for November 1939.[52] Through Seger, Ilma was arranging to exchange their Woodville home for the house of a Berlin Jew who wanted to emigrate. When, at the outbreak of war, Stan was dismissed from his position on the wharves, he blamed not their own conduct but 'the Jews'.[53]

The foregoing are individual extreme cases, but there were clusters of people in the Barossa, particularly in Tanunda, who not only expressed the hope that Germany would win the war, but who also espoused Nazi ideology and were devoted to Hitler. In such circles there was an eagerness to accept uncritically Nazi Germany's depiction of itself. President-General Stolz of the United Evangelical Lutheran Church in Australia (UELCA) wrote to Pastor Theile in Brisbane that Nazis in New Guinea knew only the 'ideal side' presented by propaganda, and would judge things differently if they saw the reality.[54] Stolz's remarks applied equally to Australian Germans. Few had seen Germany under the Nazis, their opinions being shaped by propaganda, printed or radio. They were unpleasantly shocked when the 'Nazi women from New Guinea' arrived early in 1942 and scolded them for not being good Nazis.[55]

German Australians complained of being harassed, persecuted and interned unjustly. They protested that all they had done was to listen to enemy radio broadcasts and proclaim that only these told the truth; smuggle letters to an enemy country through neutral countries; possess ammunition and unlicensed firearms; tell neighbours that Nazism was the best system in the world; and proclaim that Germany deserved to win and would win. It is true that in Australia it was not forbidden to listen to foreign radio broadcasts, but declaring them the only source of truth was regarded unfavourably.

The Lutherans
There were two places where Military Intelligence assessed the national security situation in South Australia as particularly bad:

Loxton and Tanunda. For this the local pastors were largely responsible. Undercover agents reported on the pastors considered to be the greatest threat. These reports appear to have been well founded, for they named the very same pastors whose devotion to Germany had been praised by Asmis and Hellenthal in reports to the Foreign Office in the 1930s, and by Dr Carl Schneider in his book *Bei den Deutschen Lutheranern in Australien* (*Among the German Lutherans in Australia* [1929]): Julius Meier in Loxton and Richard Held in Tanunda. Hellenthal wrote that Held and Meier 'have always openly adhered to the New Germany and the ideas of our Fuhrer'.[56] Other pastors were included less consistently, and their attitude was partly a matter of opinion: Johannes Julius Stolz (the Adelaide-based President-General of UELCA), Theodor Hebart (Tanunda), Johannes Riedel (Sedan), Johannes Paul Loehe (Immanuel) and Werner Riedel (Immanuel). In trying to placate everybody, Stolz satisfied nobody; his correspondence was intercepted and recorded for most of the war.[57] Loehe was discreet, but something caused Party member Pastor Methsieder to write to the *Auslands-Organisation* that Loehe belonged to 'the "silent admirers" and "followers" of our Führer and his great work'.[58]

Although Stolz through the *Lutheran Herald* urged Australian Germans to do their duty to Australia, some pastors urged parishioners to do the opposite and not to turn against 'their blood'. In September 1916, a doctor at Nuriootpa had submitted a statutory declaration that Held had said that he had been appointed by the German Government to send secret reports to Germany and had been promised a good position if he returned to Germany after the war.[59] In 1917 Held's church was closed down.[60] His attitude did not improve in the ensuing 20 years. He made enemies among the section of his congregation that was loyal to Australia; he was reported frequently, and he lost parishioners to Pastor Obst, of the other UELCA parish in Tanunda, to the Evangelical Lutheran Synod of Australia (ELSA, another branch of the church), and to non-Lutheran churches. Some children refused to attend confirmation classes because of the Nazi propaganda he introduced.[61] Held said that he trusted that God would see that Germany was rewarded for the injustices she had suffered at the hands of international Jewry and English capitalists, and he would never change his mind with regard to his Fatherland. Fearing repercussions and the loss of the services of their pastor if he was interned, the worried elders of the parish begged him to be more discreet in expressing his opinions.[62]

Owing to poor health, Held was not interned, only subjected to restrictions which he accepted with his sworn word. These included receiving no visitors but his family, a condition that he and Hebart broke frequently. Hebart made little secret of this, telling one parishioner that he was 'God's servant' and he had 'every right to discuss Church matters with Held'.[63] He had told his flock that 'the Almighty had sent Hitler to put the people on the right track', and said less publicly that he wanted to see Germany win the war.[64] Hebart, too, was not interned, nor has a copy of a restriction order for him been found.

All those discussed above were UELCA pastors. Officially, ELSA opposed close contact with Germany, but there was ambiguity about the attitude of President-General William Janzow; he too succeeded in pleasing few. Thus Military Intelligence viewed him warily, while on the other hand Ilma Bohlmann denounced him to Germany as a 'disloyal German'.[65]

The security situation in Loxton revolved around the Meier and Hoffmann families. In mid-1936, Dr Erich Meier, recently returned from studying agriculture at the University of Leipzig, wrote a series of pro-Nazi articles for the *Murray Pioneer*; apart from the sections relating to his personal experiences, these were largely adaptations of official Nazi propaganda circulating in Australia. By May 1937, he was teaching at Renmark High School. Having earlier joined Oswald Mosley's British Union of Fascists and National Socialists, Meier tried to form an Australian branch, but he told Becker they would not use the word 'fascist', as it aroused antagonism.[66] The Douglas Social Credit Party would be the sheepskin to cloak the fascist wolf. The secretary of the Loxton branch of this party was Carl Wilhelm Hoffmann. A Sudetenlander, he had served in the Austrian Air Force and arrived in Adelaide with his family in 1923 on a Czech passport. After a run of bad luck he was introduced about 1927 to Social Credit, which seemed the answer to his woes.[67] He attempted to found a 'gliding club', but attracted few members apart from the Meier and Thiele families, and they did no gliding.[68] His wife and sons returned to Germany in 1939; he was to follow after winding up their affairs, but the war intervened.

Since Hoffmann was newly arrived, it was reasonable that he should still have pro-German sentiments. That could hardly be said of the family of (Richard) Edwin Thiele, whose ancestors migrated in 1838. Illogical, obnoxious and dangerous though their attitude was, it was in their favour that they stood by their convictions honestly and courageously, but they were an embarrassment to other members of the extensive Thiele family. At least four denunciations came from family members, yet their own statements made informants superfluous. More than any other example, they provide a convincing refutation of any assumption that everyone who was born in Australia and had never left the country would be loyal. Unlike many Germans, their disloyalty extended to support for the Japanese. Three of Edwin's children were interned in March 1942. Manda told an interviewing officer that if Britain won the war she would rather be dead.[69] Her brothers, Reg and Murray, continued to cause trouble, giving the Hitler salute and carving swastikas on camp property, while constantly quoting the Bible, 'which they said definitely proved the right of Nazism and Hitler'.[70] This led to a comment entered on a detention warrant from March 1942, that they displayed 'a degree of disloyalty which has shocked and disgusted us ...'[71]

There was also overwhelming evidence against Pastor Meier. After he was interned, his wife Minnie wrote bitter letters to politicians labelling the actions of parishioners who denounced him for disloyalty as 'a Judas act', and she did no good for her cause by the constant use of 'we Germans'.[72] Military Intelligence was gratified that there were some loyal citizens in Loxton. Meier was replaced by Carl Julius Pfitzner, later President of the South Australian branch of the UELCA. Pfitzner was young, and he was both born and trained in Australia. He was also appalled by the situation he encountered in Loxton. In September 1943 he told a military officer that some parishioners should have been excommunicated for failing to follow the church's teachings of loyalty to temporal authorities.[73]

Held's commitment to Nazism caused most of the trouble in Tanunda, but even Hebart, less openly indiscreet, said that this 'unjust war' would never have begun if Churchill had not been head of state (*sic*), and he had obtained his position only because 'the Jews' had chosen him and bribed him 'to act for their devilish enterprises'.[74] It was mainly the older German-born UELCA pastors who held this view, but one newly ordained Australian-born ELSA pastor, notorious for vacating his pulpit and leaving the church when the National Anthem was sung, also maintained that the Lutheran tenet of loyalty to temporal powers did not apply here, for it was not a just war, but 'the biggest swindle ever devised by man and its chief object was to ruin Germany physically and spiritually for the sake of profits only'. As this conflicted with ELSA policy, some parishioners objected.[75]

Reactions varied with the changing fortunes of the belligerents. There was satisfaction as Hitler overran Poland and when Norway was occupied quickly. After France fell in June 1940, the manager of the local Savings Bank in Tanunda (Leo Pyne) reported a run on the bank, because local ethnic Germans expected their accounts to be frozen,[76] while Ernst Schrapel, owner of one of the major stores in town, advised people to withdraw their money and buy goods, as money would become worthless.[77]

The Victoria Hotel became the setting for alcohol-fuelled discussions of Germany's virtues and successes, based on what people heard from German short-wave stations. In February 1942 one informant reported that most rumours circulating through Tanunda originated from the hotel. He asked that his name not be revealed, as 'any such disclosure would endanger my livelihood and perhaps my personal safety'.[78] This nervousness was not unfounded; in the First World War, there had been two semi-serious attempts to kill Constable Lenthall in Loxton, and threats had been made against Sergeant Kavanagh.[79] Once again threats were made against those who spoke against Germany, especially if they were of German ancestry; although no informant was killed, as far as is known, some suspects had their businesses ruined, and pro-Nazi farmers made plans to confiscate the farms of anti-Nazis when Hitler won.[80] One told an undercover agent: 'They've got it coming to them ... Bill Dempster is the first. I know the boys are trailing him day and night and one night we'll get him.'[81]

The war exacerbated spiritual divisions between generations, especially concerning military service. Many of the younger men realised their obligations to their country, and braved parental opposition to volunteer for service. Six sons of Pastor Johannes Riedel enlisted, the older ones as soon as they did not need consent, and the younger ones, when militia service became compulsory, within a few days of turning 18 years old.[82] Riedel refused to attend the embarkation party that the Sedan district gave his son Leo in October 1940, saying that he had to work on a sermon, but he had told his son privately: '[If] you are going to fight for England against Germany, I will not recognise you as a son any more'.[83] Other pastors tried to deter their parishioners' sons from enlisting.[84]

When told that his sons intended enlisting, one Australian-born Mount Torrens farmer said: 'I'll bloody well shoot them first'. Three of them enlisted, but he also refused to attend a district farewell party.[85] In other cases the sons were glad to take advantage of their father's ability to buy them enough land for them to claim exemptions.[86] This was their legal right, and it was not only fathers of German descent who did this. It was reported that Tanunda solicitor Berthold Teusner used his 'excellent connections' to obtain for young German Australians exemption from military service, for which he charged 'very high fees'.[87] One Schrapel employee, who had two sons in the army, was told that he would be dismissed if he tried to influence other young men to enlist.[88]

The role of Military Intelligence

Even in times of peace, there were small, understaffed organisations collecting information on activities that might threaten the security of the Commonwealth. In the 1920s, they were concerned mainly with communist activities, possible Japanese espionage, and the links between revolutionary socialists and Sinn Fein. Then they began to monitor the Italian Fascists. It was not until about 1934, when *Die Brücke* began to mention Nazi Party meetings, that much notice was taken of the small groups of National Socialists.

Military Intelligence contacted former servicemen, mostly officers, to watch their local areas for subversive activities. The Special Branch of the various state police forces compiled dossiers, as did the Commonwealth Investigation Branch. Naval Intelligence watched activities around harbours. During the war, their staffs and activities expanded and their powers were increased. In 1941, the Commonwealth Security Service was formed, in theory to coordinate the work of other departments. At times all overseas airmail was opened, as well as – secretly – some domestic mail. Telephones could be tapped, and details of bank accounts obtained. It was stressed that information obtained by these means could not be used in criminal proceedings; the purpose was to ensure Australia's freedom and survival.

Some people had long been reporting on pan-German activities in the Barossa district, and later on specifically Nazi activities. This was part of police duty. One Tanunda constable reported in June 1940 that Germans with unregistered firearms were oiling these, putting them in boxes and burying them in the scrub or throwing them down wells.[89] Although Pastor Meier and his son would have been interned in any case, the immediate trigger was a report that Erich, who did not have a licence for a weapon, had tried to buy high-powered ammunition, and a search discovered five firearms.[90] In some places there were also Military Reporting Officers, often former army officers. Others were themselves of German descent, outraged by the disloyalty of some of their neighbours.

During the war Military Intelligence inserted professional undercover agents, a difficult task in a community that kept outsiders at a distance. The first one known was Otto Bieri, well known in New Guinea and hence to pastors connected with the missions. People thought he was German, but he was actually Swiss, and when he had reported on Nazi activities in New Guinea, his life had been threatened.[91] Stationed first at Tanunda by early 1943, he had been indiscreet about his activities and was shifted to Lobethal.

In October 1943 Bieri submitted a long general report. He wrote that the Barossa people acted shrewdly and cautiously from self-interest, and only in unguarded moments did they betray themselves. They would take no drastic action that would jeopardise their security or freedom. Most were sentimentally pro-German, but they were farmers concerned mainly with their own welfare. Nevertheless, they could be a great danger to national security. '[They] will engage in any kind of subversive activity provided it is not dangerous and is hard to prove ... They can and do destroy morale ... Everything eventually leads back to Tanunda, where the nucleus of all existing or possible subversive activity exists.'[92] He wrote that people seemed unaware that what they were saying or doing was disloyal.

A second agent, introduced in mid-1943, was known as A4; he gave details of the attitude of individuals. He stayed in Tanunda for two years, playing the part of a Nazi sympathiser, although it was hard when local Nazis taught his son to 'Heil Hitler' and draw swastikas.[93] He wrote in 1943 that he had been unprepared to find such widespread and shameless disloyalty, and repeated in January 1945 that he had thought he would have to investigate only a few cases. When it was revealed to him how all but a small section behaved he was shocked.[94] He did not understand, he wrote, 'how a decent, normal and loyal British subject could live at ease for any length of time in such a place'.[95] Only a brief overview of his reports can be given. Anyone doubting the general conclusions should read them in full.

Some attention should be paid to these much-maligned casual informants and regular undercover agents. Owing partly to Australia's convict history, there is a deep-seated antipathy to 'dobbers', or 'whistle blowers', but at times these people have done great service to society. To stigmatise them without substantiation as having base motives, as Gary Gumpl and Richard Kleinig do in a recent book, to call them servile, sycophantic, slippery, double-dealing and obsequious,[96] is somewhat akin to the attitude of those who called serving soldiers 'six-bob-a-day murderers' and abused pensioner veterans as 'holding out their hands for their blood money every fortnight'.[97] Much of their vilification of 'informers' falls apart because they jumped to a basic erroneous conclusion: 'Offe rejoiced in the code designation A4 ...'[98] This assumption is maintained throughout their book, yet A4 was not Victor Rudolph Offe: he was Luis Alfred Tepper.

The Offe family was settled in Tanunda by 1850, and Victor was born there in 1894. He had given information concerning disloyalty early in the First World War, and, obedient to Lutheran teachings on loyalty to temporal authorities, he had enlisted in July 1915. He served at the front in France, until he was invalided home in 1917 suffering from 'trench fever'. His younger brother, William Oliver, also enlisted, but was sent home ill without frontline service. Victor was reporting on Nazi activities in Tanunda by 1934, but while

Gumpl and Kleinig vilify him as a 'paid informer',[99] he was in fact paid by the Commonwealth Investigation Branch – at the rate of £3 per week – only from 24 February to 16 March 1938, a total of £9.[100] One unfortunate result of Offe's activities was that the term 'the Hitler Club' entered into the vocabulary of the security services; the meaning was not quite clear either to them or to Offe, since some of the meetings he recorded, to judge by their procedure, were clearly based on Nazi Party meetings, while others, judging by the number of people attending, must have been meetings of the Friends of the Hitler Movement. Understating his age by one year, Offe enlisted again in September 1940, and was discharged in October 1945 as a sergeant at an Air Observer School, having served Australia loyally.

Tepper's history was very different. He was eight years old in 1918 and did no reporting during the First World War. He came from a family that had trekked to the Wimmera from South Australia, and which had a worthy record of service in peace and war. When Offe was reporting in 1934, Tepper was at Concordia College in Adelaide, and in 1938 he was attending to his parish at Rockhampton, in Queensland, for he was by then an ELSA pastor. He resigned from the ministry at a date and for a reason unknown, and enlisted in the army in December 1941. Assigned to intelligence work, he was sent to Tanunda in 1943 as being the best available prospect for penetrating to the heart of the conspiracies existing in Tanunda. In one of his first reports, he said that he had never set foot in the town previously, and obviously he had nothing to do with the internment of Fritz Homburg or of 'Monsy' Schulz.[101] Tepper's only Tanunda contact was an ELSA parson with whom he had studied at Concordia. To his chagrin, he found that this contact was one of the people on whom he was obliged to report.

During 1942 there were grounds for believing that victory for Germany and Japan was possible; some Australian Germans looked forward to this. Their view in 1943 that the German retreat in Russia was part of Hitler's 'grand strategic plan' to shorten his lines for a summer campaign came from German short-wave broadcasts.[102] By 1944, Tepper was firmly established in Tanunda, and people were becoming more bitterly outspoken as the war turned against Germany. In April 1944, Hitler's birthday was celebrated at the Tanunda Club. At least three private parties were also held, one being hosted by Kurt Hörisch, a Nazi Party member who had been released from internment owing to ill health.[103] People said, of course, that this 'proved' that he had done nothing wrong, or else that the authorities were afraid to keep him interned. Throughout May people maintained that England would never dare invade Europe, and that invasion talk was 'all bluff'. The aforementioned ELSA pastor said that he would refuse to conduct a prayer for an invasion, and if Hitler went down it would be 'another Biblical instance of the unrighteous nation overcoming the righteous'. Tepper commented that this pastor was a menace to his congregation.[104]

Those who listened to the German broadcasts parroted Berlin propaganda again when the Allies landed in France on 6 June. First, they followed the line that the Allies would never get a foothold in France, but would be thrown back into the sea, then that Hitler was letting them land so that he could wipe them out; the French would not help them because they were well off under German rule. They chose to believe that Germany's military strength was being saved to stop the Americans at the Rhine, and that German forces had ample reserves to defeat them at Germany's borders. They rejoiced that 'flying bombs' and rockets would soon smash England. Hitler's escape from an assassination attempt in July 1944 was viewed as 'an act of God'. Germany would recuperate over the winter and drive the Allies out of Europe in a summer offensive. When a captured newsreel showing the *Wehrmacht* on the Western Front was screened, there was spontaneous clapping, which faded into embarrassed silence.[105] Pyne, the bank manager, said that the change that came over people when things went well for Germany was 'just bloody disgusting'.[106] Finally people asserted that, even if Germany were defeated militarily, National Socialism would never be exterminated; the Führer's legacy would live on.[107] In this belief, at least, they were partially correct.

Pastor Hebart said that the invasion of Normandy was satanic, and 'everything the devil had to spare was now inspiring the Allied Army to carry out their job of murdering innocent victims of International Jewry'.[108] His abuse of Churchill as a tool of the Jews was typical of what was being said by many in Tanunda, who railed that England was 'nothing but a hide-out for the Jews who manufacture all the wars', and that democracy was 'a rotten system suitable only for the Jew', and that Hitler was 'the appointed scourge to punish the Jew'. Roosevelt too was a 'butcher' under the influence of his wife, who was also a 'full Jew'.[109] Such anti-Semitic diatribes marked true Nazis, not simply persons with a sentimental attachment to their ancestral homeland. One labelled the English and the Bank of England as warmongers, along with 'the Jews' whom England harboured 'like so many rats'.[110]

Tepper was not surprised when UELCA pastors expressed aggressively pro-German sentiments, but it hurt him when his ELSA colleagues did. He was shocked to hear them from William Janzow, recently retired as head of ELSA, who greeted him with: 'I think the poor old Germans are done for'. He said that England could easily have avoided the war, and Roosevelt had been 'dragged into the war by the warmongers of England'. Later he added it was only because 'the Jews' bankrupted Germany that the Great War had been lost. One of Janzow's sons said that England would play 'their old game' of making others fight for them; if they reconquered France, they would push French troops ahead to 'do their dirty work', and he hoped that the sea around English ports would be filled with so much blood that it would be a lesson to them. Janzow's married daughter had said earlier that all the heads of England ought to be shot; 'I hope Hitler catches up with every one of them.'[111] At Gawler, another ELSA pastor said that if ever there was 'a cesspool of evil' it was 'the Jew' and his fellow workers in Wall Street, from whom Churchill and Roosevelt took their orders.[112]

Tepper learned that a Nazi movement run by Hörisch continued operating underground, but he could never get an invitation to a meeting. It appeared to be a continuation of the Friends of the Hitler Movement, to which only those who were members before the war were admitted. One man told him that they held meetings of a 'secret society' to which he belonged, although he was Australian-born.[113] Others gave glimpses of what was discussed, and mentioned an Argentinean connection.[114] Another said that a secret meeting had to be postponed for the funeral of the local member of state parliament.[115] Before Bieri or Tepper arrived in Tanunda, there were reports of secret meetings at Renmark, and of night meetings in a café at Inman Valley, where they hung up a swastika flag and heiled Hitler.[116]

Even in April 1945 seven parties were held to celebrate Hitler's birthday, at which guests toasted and heiled Hitler as in the past. There was little hope now of a German victory, but some said that divine retribution would overtake England; 'if not, there is no God'.[117] As the war ended, some people planned vengeance. Hörisch said that the German Consuls would demand the names of informants and those responsible for internment. Then, he said, 'we will get our own back'.[118] However, internment policy was implemented more leniently in the Barossa than elsewhere in Australia. South Australia was not strategically critical, and it was considered that Barossa farmers were too selfish to risk anything unless a German victory was assured.[119] Consul-General Kiliani remarked on this selfishness in 1913, when he wrote to the *Reichskanzler* (Imperial Chancellor) that South Australian Germans would make no sacrifice for the old homeland.[120] In addition, disloyal sentiments were so rife in Tanunda that expressing them did not cause undue unrest. As plans for post-war reconstruction were made, Fritz Homburg said that he might attend meetings, but he would be the last man to assist the government in any way. 'I am finished,' he said, 'with this glorious thing they call the British Empire'.[121]

The consequences
As claims of massive unjust persecution of the ethnic Germans who had done so much to develop South Australia are frequently made, it may come as a surprise to learn that, of an estimated 20,000 ethnic Germans in the state, only 21 native-born South Australians were interned, one of whom, Manda Thiele, was interned from Victoria.[122] It is a very small number from which to generate so much resentment and self-pity. Among these there were two Homburgs, three Bohlmanns and three Thieles. That left a total of 13 others, of whom three were pastors. The vast majority of internees had arrived in Australia after 1923, and of these about a quarter were Party members; many of the rest were ex-soldiers still in Reserve I, or young men notionally in Reserve II of the German armed forces.

Australia was surprisingly generous in allowing people with notably unfavourable political records to remain in the country – including even Party local branch leaders and several known

Photograph of J. Heinrich Becker taken during his internment.
(National Archives of Australia D1915 SA5163, Dr Johannes Heinrich Becker)

Gestapo informants. Otto Woelke, the Brisbane leader, and his family were even allowed to *return* to Queensland after the war, during which he had served in the German navy. Very few were deported against their will; these were mainly men who had made a public display of their Nazism, such as Becker in Tanunda, Frerck in Sydney, and Dr Neumann at the University of Sydney. There were also a few with serious criminal records. Gumpl and Kleinig complain that Justice Simpson was the one to decide who should be deported (p. 305),[123] which was unjust, because he had been responsible for the internments and knew the contents of their dossiers. Would it have been fairer if the task had been allotted to somebody totally ignorant of the situation? In addition, Simpson was not responsible for most of the internments. The Commonwealth Security Service did not exist until March 1941, and Simpson did not join it, as Director-General, until September 1942. By then, most decisions had been made by others.

In putting a case to be allowed to stay in Australia, Becker claimed that he had left the Party in 1936, or had been expelled in 1941. In fact, it was only the leadership that he had lost in 1936, not his membership. In late 1941, a Party Court of Honour found him guilty of writing a letter falsely defaming Dr Franz Joseph Haslinger, a senior Party member, and of lying to cover up his transgression. It was for this reason, and not for lack of enthusiasm for Nazism, that his expulsion was recommended on 22 November, although there is no evidence in Party archives in Berlin that this was implemented.[124]

Demobilised in August 1945 as a corporal, Tepper had probably left Tanunda when the Adelaide *News* of 11 September 1945 ran an article about Nazis in Tanunda, claiming that they had held large quantities of ammunition and engaged in subversive activities. There were outraged protests, but it was a year before the paper was obliged to publish, on 4 September 1946, a report of a meeting called by Teusner, now a member of parliament, as well as chairman of the Tanunda District Council. He read out correspondence and a report clearing the district of such allegations, which he denounced as 'unwarranted and pernicious'.[125] Of course many farmers had kept ammunition, but 'large quantities' is a subjective term. If undermining morale and hindering recruiting is subversive, some had done this too. One worker was known to have boasted that he and some friends were sabotaging the war effort by sub-standard work and go-slow tactics in factories.[126]

In 1945, Melbourne University Press published *German Settlers in South Australia*, a booklet written by Charles A. Price and based on his Master of Arts thesis. Gumpl and Kleinig call the book 'craven', complaining that Price 'unquestioningly accepted the accusations of Intelligence and Security sectors'.[127] He had good reason to accept them, for he had conducted many of the investigations personally. However, he could not use this evidence, and he built up his case largely from material published in local newspapers by the local Germans themselves. Price, born in 1920, enlisted in the militia in October 1938 while a university student. Found unfit for general service, he was seconded to the Security Service Intelligence Corps, and was discharged in March 1945 as a lieutenant of the South Australian Lines of Communication Area Intelligence Corps to resume his university work.

Gumpl and Kleinig write that the booklet 'justifiably angered [Hermann] Homburg, whose own writing was a clear-sighted analysis of the misuse of the legal system', while they refer to Homburg's work, *South Australian Lutherans and Wartime Rumours* as 'a valuable monograph'.[128] Some of Homburg's criticisms of the advisory committee that heard his appeal against internment are not without foundation, but overall it was a wilfully misleading, self-serving, self-pitying auto-hagiography, aimed at concealing the truth about his activities behind legal jargon. It appeals to emotions and produces little in the way of refutation of charges against him. At the time of its publication, in 1947, Price was studying at Oxford. The confidentiality of security investigations, which was to protect the internees and suspects rather than the investigators, would have made it difficult for him to respond.

Both Bieri and Tepper had reported that the Germans would blame 'Jews' and 'traitors' for their defeat, as in 1918, and that Barossa Germans had adopted a two-faced principle, saying that they were 'sitting pretty', whoever won the war. They would 'crawl and cringe to the world pleading their innocence and saying they never harboured any sentiments of disloyalty'.[129] Tepper wrote that this should arouse fury, but they would get away with the 'whole rotten show'.[130] More than 60 years after the end of the war, complaints of injustice are still almost a cottage industry in the Barossa. No presentation of facts will alter these ingrained feelings, which have been reinforced by poorly researched publications, but any serious historian should be wary of repeating subjective complaints without reading official reports, especially those by Tepper, a former Lutheran pastor who understood the obligations of loyalty to temporal authority.

Those so-called 'German Australians' who had failed to honour their national responsibilities as Australians, as well as their religious responsibilities as Lutherans, brought no credit to themselves by hiding behind the sacrifices of the many Australians of German descent who during both wars had worked, fought, suffered and died for the their love of and loyalty to Australia. Those who supported Germany while she was winning did a disservice to their descendants by denying this and leaving a legacy of resentment and paranoia. It would have been more dignified to have admitted their sentiments. They were entitled to their instinctive feelings; they were not entitled to deny them hypocritically, lie to their children, vilify investigators and blame authorities for the atmosphere that had prevailed during the war.

Notes

1 Australian Joint Copying Project (hereafter known as AJCP): M274: Auswärtiges Amt VIA. Akten betreffend Deutsche Kirchen[wesen?] in Australien, L938/L266637. Band I. Evangelische Angelegenheiten. Mai 1875–Mai 1936. M274 is the reference allotted by the National Library of Australia, Canberra; the Mitchell Library has this material but under different numbers.
2 Party card on microfilm (3200/B004) in Bundesarchiv, Berlin-Lichterfelde. Gary Gumpl & Richard Kleinig (*The Hitler Club: The rise and fall of Australia's number 1 Nazi*, Brolga, Melbourne, 2007, p. 98) give Becker's number as 9,525,500, and wonder why he had such a high number when he joined relatively early.
3 Hans Adolf Jacobsen, *Nationalsozialistische Aussenpolitik, 1933–1938*, Metzner, Frankfurt, 1968, pp. 91–2; Donald McKale, *The Swastika outside Germany*, Kent State University, Kent, OH, 1977, p. 19.
4 Drake's membership was revoked when he was naturalised on 30 December 1938.
5 The claim by Gumpl and Kleinig (2007, p. 81) that most of the men whom Becker 'collected' originally were already Party members is untrue. As far as can be ascertained, none was.
6 See, for example, B741: V/18386S: Suchting, Hans Johannes. To authorities he denied having taken such a course, even though he had given a lecture on it to the Tivoli Club late in 1936.
7 Officially this closure was called *Mitgliedersperre*; colloquially it was known as *Torschluss*. This was modified from 1 May 1937, but applicants within Germany had to have a record of Party service in some other organisation, such as the Hitler Youth or the Labour Front.
8 AJCP: M274: Deutschtumspolitik in Australien, L938/L266781 (Asmis to *Ausw. Amt*, 22 July 1935).
9 AJCP: M274: Deutschtumspolitik in Australien, L938/L266403 (Hellenthal to *Ausw. Amt*, 20 August 1935).
10 SP 1714/1: N39039: Walter Ladendorff (Letter, 4 August 1938: Asmis to Menche). See also *Ausw. Amt* memo in C414: 6: Nazi activities (Security Service reports) concerning suspension of an admission fee to the Party for diplomatic personnel. Asmis applied for membership of a proposed 'Special Party Group of the Foreign Office' in August 1933, but this was not formed until 1938 (ST1233/1: N25012: Heinrich Eugen Ernst Ringwald: Letter, 30 March 1934, Asmis to 'a friend'). In October 1935, Asmis was on leave in Germany.

11　D1915: SA18121: German Club.

12　A367: C68820: Heinrich Krawinkel (Letters, 24 January 1935, Becker to Krawinkel; 25 January 1935, Krawinkel to Becker); D1915: SA18121: German Club (SAADV Minutes, 5 December 1934); *Die Brücke* (1935: 4 May, p. 26; 11 May, p. 26; 1 June, p. 27). Hellenthal reported that in July 1935 the SAADV had 179 members, of whom 35 were German nationals (AJCP: M274: L937/L266403).

13　*Stützpunkt* = small local group; *Landeskreis* = 'Country' (or National) Circle; *Leiter* = leader.

14　D1915: SA22205: NSDAP Party (Harbour Service Section, p. 36. Letters, Becker to Heiler, 2 August and 4 December 1934). At one time, Heiler was both *Stützpunktleiter* and *Hafendienstleiter*. The *Hafendienstleiter* was the head of the Gestapo reporting system in a country; in Australia Becker appointed him and handled all reports, so Becker was de facto Gestapo chief in Australia.

15　D1915: SA22205: NSDAP Party.

16　D1919: SS827: Schulz, Johann Friedrich Wilhelm (statement by Minnie Offe, 12 February 1941. The man was the brother of Peter Mayr, an employee at Seppelts.); see also D1915: SA20419 1: NSDAP (National Sozialistische Deutsche Arbeiter Partei, National Socialist German Workers Party).

17　For example, Ernest (Ernst) Jacob Pohl (D1915: SA5023), or R.R.R. von Broock-Rhien (A659: 1943/1/199). This Gestapo function of the *Hafendienst* lapsed when the *Inspektionsamt* of the AO was formed on 1 February 1937 (A9108: ROLL 7/13: Nazi activities [material received by the wartime Security Service on the organisation of the Nazi Party overseas]: Royal Canadian Mounted Police Report, 15 February 1938). Details of the Gestapo organisation in Australia are then lost until May 1939, when Henschel took over, although reports on Germans disloyal to the 'New Germany' still reached the Gestapo through Consuls.

18　D1915: SA20419 1: NSDAP.

19　D1915: SA2049: Borchers (Letter, 11 November 1935, Borchers to Asmis). Gumpl and Kleinig write (2007, p. 141) that Borchers obviously told Asmis what he wanted to hear. This is an unjustified slur on Borchers, a former president of the SAADV; what he told Asmis was the truth.

20　*Die Brücke*, 25 January 1936, p. 16.

21　D1915: SA19907: German Consulate Records. Letter, 18 December 1936: Blaesing (Melbourne) to Hellenthal (Wellington).

22　SP1714/1: N39039: Walter Ladendorff.

23　*Die Brücke*, 26 March 1938, p. 16; D1915: SA16752: Dr O.E. Seger (Letter, 19 March 1938, Ladendorff to Seger).

24 A9108: Roll 8/5: Nazi activity in South Australia. He did not want the church to discover the full extent of his Party activities.
25 A367: C73684: Disposal of personal effects of Mr P.F.W. Beckmann and Dr O.E. Seger.
26 *Die Brücke*, 30 March 1935, p. 2. At first it was called the *Deutsche Berufsgruppe*; the date of the name change is unclear.
27 D1915: SA20419 Part 1: NSDAP (Letter, Captain Koehler to Schlenk, 12 November 1937).
28 Its proper title outside Germany was the *Arbeitsgemeinschaft der deutschen Frau im Ausland*, but it was generally called the *Frauenschaft*.
29 A9108: Roll 8/4: Nazi activity in South Australia.
30 Dossiers in Series D1915: Fritz Homburg (SA2813), Held (SA1068), Meier (SA19922).
31 D1915: SA16752: Dr O.E. Seger (German Consulate documents); Seger to Menche, 4 October 1937.
32 The writers in Germany were called *Lesepaten* (literally 'reading godparents'). Letters were sent out to people recommended by others as being receptive to propaganda; if they replied, the correspondence continued.
33 Later, but really only in South Australia, it was a contender for the role of Australia's new national anthem.
34 AJCP: Reel M272: pp. L266125–46. Letter, Asmis to Ausw. Amt, 17 March 1933. Programme for *Deutschtumspolitik*; A367/1: C68820: Krawinkel (Letter, Asmis to Hennings, 23 July 1936).
35 *Queensländer Herald*, 8 May 1935. Cutting and translation in A9108: Roll 8/10: German Newspapers in Australia. Häusler, a member of the 'Friends of the Hitler Movement', was not interned until March 1941.
36 *Bund des Deutschtums in Australien und Neuseeland:* League of 'Germanism' in Australia and New Zealand. It was the association sponsored by Asmis to influence Germans of Australian citizenship.
37 A367: C68820: Krawinkel (Letter, Asmis to Krawinkel, 16 April 1937); Seger's comment: D1915: SA19132 PART 2: Heinrich Krawinkel; D1915: SA16752: Seger.
38 A9108/3: Roll 8/5: Nazi activity.
39 A367: C65376: Homburg, Hermann and Marsi (daughter) – Internment. This letter is sometimes erroneously considered to refer to the situation in the Second World War. See Gumpl and Kleinig (2007, p. 189).
40 D1915: SA19132 PART 2: Krawinkel. Philip McBride was Minister for the Army, although not until August 1940.
41 A1608: V20/1/1: War – 1939 Internees. National Security (Aliens Control) Regulations; and A472: W2121 Part 1: Aliens Tribunals – Regulations and appointment of personnel.
42 D1915: SA2813: Homburg, Fritz. His internment lasted 16 days.

43 A9108: Roll 8/7: Nazi activity in South Australia. The publication was dated 5 August 1937.

44 Having served in the Middle East in the 2/3 Machine Gun Battalion Staff Sergeant Dudley Gordon Prisk was shipped to Batavia in February 1942, captured by the Japanese and forced to work on the Thai-Burma railway, leading to his death, caused by beri beri, in August 1943.

45 A367: C65376: Hermann Homburg; D1915: SA19132 PART 1: Heinrich Krawinkel.

46 A367: C65376: Homburg (Report from Keswick Barracks, 10 March 1941).

47 D1915: SA19132 PART 2: Krawinkel.

48 MP742/1: H/5/563: Homburg, Renolf Mr – Failure to enrol for service (Letters, 1 July 1943; 16 July 1943).

49 A367: C74718: Bohlmann, S.G. (Report, 20 September 1938, District Naval Officer to Secretary of Naval Board).

50 Material in this and the following paragraph is mainly from D1915: SA5734: Ilma Carola Bohlmann; Stanley George Bohlmann.

51 D1915: SA15592: A.S.M. Bohlmann.

52 B741: V/24713: Homburg, Hermann and Marsi. Gumpl and Kleinig (2007, p. 104) seem to regard the Labour Service as some sort of penal camp.

53 A9108: Roll 9/1: National Socialist Party of Australia.

54 A9108: Roll 8/6: Nazi activity in South Australia (Pan-Germanism in South Australia. 1838–1944. Part 'B'. Letter, 14 October 1939).

55 These were mainly wives of missionaries; many were Party members.

56 Asmis: AJCP, M273: Die Förderung des Deutschtums in Australien, 1927–36: L397/266125–186: Official trips to Victoria, Queensland and South Australia, reported 17 March 1933, esp. L266138. Hellenthal: D1915: SA1068: Held, Johann Adolph Richard (26 February 1936); Carl Schneider, *Bei den Lutheranern in Australien*, Centralvorstand des Evangelischen Vereins der Gustav Adolf-Stiftung, Leipzig, 1929.

57 D1919: SS999: Censorship – special scrutinies, instructions etc. [XRD censorship]. Other pastors named by Asmis as 'good Germans' – Basedow, Siegle and Zwar – were no longer active by 1939. ELSA = Evangelical Lutheran Synod of Australia (ELCA from 1944).

58 A8911: 15: Pan-Germanism in South Australia [1838–1944] (Letter, 15 July 1939).

59 D1915: SA1068: Held.

60 D1915: SA2813: Homburg, Fritz.

61 D1915: SA20418 Part 2: Lutheran Church and local organisations.

62 A9108: Roll 8/6: Nazi activity (A4 report, 29 July 1944).

63 A9108: Roll 8/6: Nazi activity (A4 Report, 17 June 1944).

64 D1915: SA2813: Homburg, Fritz (Annexure H, p. 17); A8911: 15: Pan-Germanism [1838–1944] Part B (Annexure D, p. 21).
65 D1915: SA5734: Ilma Carola Bohlmann; Stanley George Bohlmann. However, she invited him to her Silver Wedding Anniversary party. Born in the USA and probably naturalised in Australia, Janzow owed no loyalty to Germany under either civil or church law.
66 D1915: SA19070: British Union of Fascists. Letter, 7 November 1936, Meier to Becker.
67 A367: C81878: Carl Wilhelm Hoffman (sic).
68 A367: C81878: Hoffman. The Minutes of the club are in D1915: SA19922: Meier family, Folder on Hugo Ernst Meier.
69 D1915: SA18976: C.M. Thiele.
70 D1915: SA18976: Thiele (Statement, 2 September 1943, by internee Heinrich Pahnke). Manda Thiele was interned from Victoria (VF2179).
71 D1915: SA18976: Thiele.
72 MP508/1: 255/741/261: Carl Wilhelm Julius Meier (Letter, 23 July 1941, to Fadden); MP508/1: 52/703/4: Department of Army [Censorship of Mail] [Family's wish to write to son in Germany – Meier, Mrs J.] (Letter, 4 November 1939, to Minister for Defence, G.A. Street).
73 D1915: SA18976: C.M. Thiele (Report by Lt W.A. Langford, 7 September 1943 on interview, 2 September). Also in D1915: SA20418 Part 2: Lutheran Church and local organisations.
74 A9108: Roll 8/6: Nazi activity (A4 report, 17 June 1944). It was Chamberlain, not Churchill, who had been head of state when war was declared. Many weird statements by Tanunda Germans show a bizarre ignorance of history.
75 D1915: SA1068: Held, Johann Adolph Richard; A9108: Roll 8/5: Nazi activity (A4 Reports, 14 April 1945, 9 September 1944).
76 MP729/6: 65/401/82: Enemy Aliens 4 MD (Report, 28 July 1940, Lt-Gen. J.S. Whitelaw).
77 D1915: SA19561: Schrapel, Walker (sic) Schrapel, Ernst Erdmann Schrapel, Aubrey. (He sold the goods he was advising people to buy.)
78 D1915: SA155: Schmidt, Carl Wilhelm.
79 D1915: SA22156: Loxton Royal Commission Germanism.
80 D1915: SA20419 1: NSDAP (p. 71).
81 D1915: SA177: Reidel [Riedel] Max Otto (A4 Report, 24.02.44–6.04.44). Dempster was a police officer. It was not Riedel who made this threat.
82 World War 2 Nominal Roll, http://www.ww2roll.gov.au/.
83 D1915: SA18854: W. Riedel. Leo and Konrad reached the rank of captain, and Leo stayed in the permanent army until 1967.
84 A9108: Roll 8/6: Nazi activity (A4 report, 15 July 1944).
85 A8911: 15: Pan-Germanism in South Australia, 1838–1944.

86   A9108: Roll 8/6: Nazi activity (Bieri Report, 18 October 1943).
87   D1915: SA2813: Homburg, Fritz.
88   D1915: SA19561: Schrapel. One of these sons was killed in December 1942.
89   D1915: SA20419 Part 1: NSDAP (Report by Constable E.J. Boylan, 14 June 1940).
90   D1915: SA19922: (Meier family).
91   D1919: SS1031: Espionage. German Intelligence Service Methods (Report, 9 April 1943, Sergeant Otto Bieri).
92   A9108 Roll 8/6: Nazi activity (Bieri Report, 18 October 1943).
93   A9108: Roll 8/5: Nazi activity (A4 report, 25 April 1945).
94   A9108: Roll 8/6: Nazi activity (Undated summary, about October 1943); A9108: Roll 8/5: Nazi activity (A4 report, 27 January 1945).
95   A9108: Roll 8/5: Nazi activity (A 4 report, 17 June 1944).
96   Gary Gumpl & Richard Kleinig, *The Hitler Club: The rise and fall of Australia's number 1 Nazi*, Brolga, Melbourne, 2007.
97   Personal family experiences.
98   Gumpl & Kleinig (2007, p. 138).
99   ibid., p. 137.
100 D1915: SA20419 Part 1: NSDAP
101 Despite the claims of Gumpl & Kleinig (2007, pp. 185, 189), Arnold E. Schulze was the pastor on whom A4 reported.
102 A9108: Roll 8/6: Nazi activity (Summary of reports by A4 and Bieri, 14 July 1943 to 22 October 1943).
103 A9108: Roll 8/6: Nazi activity (A4 report, 6 May 1944). Hörisch, Otto Goern's stepson, arrived in Australia with his mother in 1930; Goern and Hörisch joined the NSDAP together in 1934.
104 A9108: Roll 8/6: Nazi activity (A4 report, 3 June 1944). A4 was a member of this congregation.
105 A9108: Roll 8/5: Nazi activity (A4 summary, 25 April 1945).
106 A9108: Roll 8/6: Nazi activity (A4 report, 13 January 1945).
107 A9108: Roll 8/5 and Roll 8/6: Nazi activity (Various reports, 17 June 1944–25 April 1945).
108 A9105: 8/6: Nazi activity (A4 report, 17 June 1944).
109 A9108: Roll 8/6: Nazi activity (summary, October 1943, of A4 reports, 14 July to 22 October, 'Tanunda and the Surrounding Districts'. Bieri's general report of 18 October 1943, in the same file, is also of great interest).
110 A9108: Roll 8/6: Nazi activity (A4 report, 3 June 1944). The Nazi propaganda film. *Der ewige Jude*, portrayed Jews as plague-carrying rats swarming out of drains.
111 A9108: Roll 8/6: Nazi activity (A4 reports, 1944: 13 August, 17 June, 3 June).
112 A9108: Roll 8/6: Nazi activity (A4 report, 29 July 1944).

113 A8911: 15: Pan-Germanism in South Australia, 1838–1944 (Part B: p. 88).
114 A9108: Roll 8/5: Nazi activity (A4 report, 14th April, 1945). The comment about Argentina came from Fritz Homburg.
115 A9108: Roll 8/6: Nazi activity (A4 report, 6 May 1944).
116 D1915: SA20419 1: NSDAP (Report, 23 January 1940). This was unlikely to be the same group; neither Renmark nor Inman Valley is in the Barossa.
117 A9108/ Roll 8/5: Nazi activity (A4 report, 25 April 1945).
118 A9108: Roll 8/5: Nazi activity (A4 report, 27 January 1945). Similar sentiments were expressed by others. Hörisch was naturalised in September 1946.
119 D1919: SS1031: Espionage (Bieri report, 9 April 1943); A9108: Roll 8/5: Nazi Activity (A4 report, 27th January, 1945).
120 AJCP: M274: L938/L266649.
121 A9108: Roll 8/5: Nazi activity (A4 report, 14 April 1945).
122 S3076 H. Homburg; S3077 J.F.W. Schulz; S3079 Pastor E. Materne (UELCA); S3080 H. Häusler; S3087 E.A. Schwerdt; S3102 W.E. Meier; S3110 A.S. Bohlmann; S3116 A.C.v.d. Borch; S3117 H.E. Rothe; S3119 H.T. Eime; S3120 Pastor C.W. Stolz (UELCA); S3121 Pastor T.W. Lutze (ELSA); S3123: W.A. Herold; S3125 S.G. Bohlmann; SF3126 I.C.A. Bohlmann; S3127 F. Homburg; S3128 B.O. Schubert; S3134 C.M. Thiele; S3135 R.H. Thiele; S3142 W.F. Hebart; VF2179, M. Thiele. Although born in Sydney, Hans Meinck was not an Australian citizen, as his father had been a member of the Consular Corps. Until 1938, Australian-born women who married German missionaries had lost their citizenship. Wives of New Guinea missionaries are not included in this count, as they had lost their citizenship by marriage.
123 Gumpl & Kleinig (2007, p. 305).
124 A367: C70614: Franz Joseph Haslinger (Report, 16 September 1944); A367: C68926: Heinrich (Hermann) Scherhag. As Haslinger, mediator of the Party court, was the person defamed, he stood down while Becker's case was considered.
125 D1915: SA20419 1: NSDAP; A373: 11756: Press allegations regarding disloyalty of residents, Tanunda district.
126 A9108: Roll 8/6: Nazi activity (A4 report, 16 December 1944).
127 Gumpl & Kleinig (2007, pp. 401–2).
128 ibid. Homburg's book was self-published in Adelaide in 1947.
129 A9108: Roll 8/6: Nazi activity (Bieri report: 18 October 1943); A9108: Roll 8/5: Nazi activity (A4 report, 25 April 1945).
130 A9108: Roll 8/5: Nazi activity (A4 report, 31 March 1945).

South Australia's Lutheran churches and refugees from Hitler's Germany

Peter Monteath

The German immigrants who arrived in South Australia in 1838 had been enticed by the prospect of pursuing their beliefs in a colony which made much of its commitment to religious freedom. They were Lutherans, but in their native Prussia they had been subjected to the state's vigorous efforts to impose a union of the Lutheran Church and the Calvinist Reformed Churches. The single church, placed under the administration of a state ministry, became more repressive as the years went by, reaching a peak in the mid-1830s. With its promise of religious freedom, South Australia became an attractive option for those persecuted for their beliefs. As it happens, one of the earliest proponents of the religious freedom for which the new colony was renowned, and from which so many Christians benefited, was a Jew. Jacob Montefiore, after whom Montefiore Hill is named, was one of the most active of the South Australian Commissioners entrusted with organising its settlement. In 1844 he wrote with palpable pride: 'The principles of civil and religious liberties are intertwined with the foundations of South Australia and the members of the different denominations enjoy in Adelaide the opportunity of worshipping God according to the dictates of their consciences'.[1] Although published in South Australia, Montefiore's words were penned in England, where Jews were still not politically emancipated.

The promise of freedom brought many more Lutherans than Jews to the colony. In the early years the Jewish population was not only small but predominantly English; the Adelaide community has been aptly described as a 'snug nest of Anglo-Jewish respectability.'[2] That changed little in the nineteenth century; although Germans could be found in many parts of urban and rural South Australia, few were Jews. Indeed, census figures for 1933 suggest that the overall number of Jews in South Australia in that year was 528, of whom few would have been of German extraction.[3]

In 1938, a century after persecuted German Lutherans arrived in South Australia, that changed, as the antipodean fates of Jews and Lutherans intersected again in a most unusual and unexpected manner. The trigger was a story which was first broken in an Adelaide newspaper, the *News*, in its 17 November edition under the heading 'Local Germans to Assist Nazi Victims',[4] but it spread to the other side of the globe with the aid of a small report in the London *Times*. The story run there on 18 November 1938 announced that the General President of the Evangelical Lutheran Synod of Australia, a certain Dr William Janzow, would assist refugee Jews from Europe should they wish to migrate to Australia. The timing of the offer was crucial. Just over a week earlier, in the night of 9–10 November, German Jews had been subjected to a horrific pogrom, often known as *Kristallnacht*, or the Night of Broken Glass. In explaining what seemed to be a most extraordinary offer, Dr Janzow pointed quite explicitly to South Australia's tradition of religious tolerance. 'Australian Lutherans,' he was quoted, 'would never forget how the British aided them at a time of their own distress. The Australian and British Governments had given them religious and civil freedom, which was denied them in their own land.'[5] For Janzow and his supporters it was time to return the favour done to their forebears a century earlier. Now held in the Lutheran Archives in Adelaide, the letters document an extraordinary episode in which German and South Australian history collided.

The response to the report in *The Times* was greater than Dr Janzow could have anticipated. Over the following weeks he received 73 letters, most of them from European Jews or their spouses who were desperate to leave their home countries. Those who had held hopes that Nazi anti-Semitism was a mere aberration, that order and decency would be returned to their lives, had been so shocked by the events of *Kristallnacht* as to turn their thoughts to seeking refuge, even if it meant making their way to the Antipodes. Most of Janzow's correspondents were from Germany, but there were

AUSTRALIAN GERMANS AND THE JEWS

IMMIGRATION SCHEME

FROM OUR CORRESPONDENT

ADELAIDE, Nov. 17

The General President of the Australian Evangelical Lutheran Synod, Dr. Jarzow, has announced that this organization and the United Evangelical Lutheran Church are combining in a plan to bring refugee Jews to Australia.

Already a number of Jewish workers rendered homeless by the earlier Nazi drive have found homes and employment through the efforts of Lutheran organizations. The Lutheran Churches are raising money to make loans to the latest victims, enabling them to land in Australia. They are also trying to arrange for employment.

Dr. Janzow described the recent pogrom as pagan, and said he could not understand how a civilized nation could perpetrate such horrors. Australian Lutherans would never forget how the British aided them at the time of their own distress. The Australian and British Governments had given them religious and civil freedom, which was denied them in their own land.

Women graduate refugees from Austria and Germany who are prepared to do domestic work are being brought to Adelaide by the University Women Graduates' Association. The first group is arriving early in the New Year. The association is working with the International Federation of University Women, whose headquarters are in London.

Text of the article in the London *Times*, 18 November 1938.

others from Austria – since March of that year forcibly annexed to Germany – or from Czechoslovakia. Their circumstances varied, but what all had in common was the sense of desperation painfully evident in the letters they sent to a complete stranger on the other side of the world.

Vienna III.,
Hegergasse Nr.4/Tür 21.
December th 1938.

Dear Sir,

The sad circumstances here force me to appeal to foreigners for compassion and human help. From all sides I hear that many noble men take a warm interest in the Jewish fate, so I took courage, too, to beg for an immigration. It is known to me that only household positions in your country are open to women. I would seize such a chance with joy as domestic work corresponds to my abilities and inclination. About my person I beg to submit the following dates: I am of a good family, born in Vienna (on May 6 th 1891), 47, unmarried, of normal height and figure, healthy and good-looking, and able to work. When I finished my schools I got matriculated. Afterwards I studied piano, singing, accompanied singers on the piano. At the same time I attended a sewing school, am school of design and applied arts. Later on I had a post with children during several years. Finally I had a small flat of my own and gave piano lessons to children in my free hours. In my own household I got well versed in domestic work, cooking, learned making necessary repairs as to the preservation and care of a flat. I also know how to manage children because I am fond of them and have patience with them. I would like to add that I possess a good knowledge of English both in speaking and writing.

I entreat you to answer me by return of post as there is the danger that the situation might become still worse and then there would be no way out for us Jews.

Thanking you in advance for your kindness,
I remain,
Dear Sir,
yours faithfully
Nelly Löwy
Miss Nelly Löwy

ENCLO.
PHOTOGRAPH

The letter sent by Nelly Löwy to Dr Janzow in December 1938.
(Lutheran Archives Adelaide)

One of the letters was from Nelly Löwy of Vienna, who entreated Dr Janzow: 'The sad circumstances here force me to appeal to foreigners for compassion and human help. From all sides I hear that many noble men take a warm interest in the Jewish fate, so I took courage, too, to beg for an immigration.' She went on to explain that she was a music teacher, but would happily take on household work in Australia. Moreover, she already possessed a good knowledge of both written and spoken English. She closed her letter with a prophetic appeal to Dr Janzow 'to answer me by return of post as there is the danger that the situation might become still worse and then there would be no way out for us Jews.'

Another correspondent was Robert Elsasser. His situation was quite unusual in that, although German, he was writing not from Germany but Geneva. He was married to a woman who had been born in Switzerland and, accompanied by her husband and their two daughters, was visiting her sick mother. But as his wife had been forced to give up her Swiss citizenship, the family was required to return to Germany by the beginning of February 1939, clearly at some risk, given that they were Jewish. Elsasser informed Dr Janzow that he had already made a request to the Department of External Affairs in Canberra, but he had learned that such requests were more likely to meet with success if an acquaintance or some other representative might support the application. Elsasser hoped that Dr Janzow or another member of his church might be that representative.

Curt Bejach of Berlin was a quite unusual case, since he did not even think of himself as Jewish. He had been christened as a child, he had married a woman who had no Jewish ancestry at all, he was the father of three daughters, all of whom had been brought up as Christians, and he had taught at a school run by the Protestant Church in Berlin. His dilemma, however, was that, according to the Nuremberg Laws introduced in 1935, he was regarded as Jewish. For German authorities in the Third Reich, Jewishness was not a religious but a racial feature; conversion to Christianity made no difference to Bejach's identity as far as the Nazis were concerned. His predicament was especially precarious because he was a widower and thus could not benefit from whatever protection marriage to an 'Aryan' might afford. The position of his three daughters was similarly perilous. According to German law, they were now classified as so-called *Mischlinge*, that is, they were part-Jewish and part-Aryan, and thus subjected to discrimination. What made things even worse for Bejach and his offspring was that they inhabited a strange, in-between space, not regarded as 'Aryans' – and thus not always welcome among their Protestant co-religionists – and not able to call on the assistance of the Jewish community, to which, despite their ascribed racial identity, they did not belong. Not surprisingly, then, Bejach's anxiety was palpable in his letter to Dr Janzow: 'As you can imagine I am in a desperate mood, only the idea, that I trust in the eternal justice of the Almighty and the help of Christian brotherhood, keeps me upright and makes me write to you this letter for help. That you can help me if you give me the possibility of entering your country or showing me a way how I can leave Germany. That is my principal aim.'

Alfred Schick was not even living in German-occupied Europe, and yet he feared the worst. He was an inhabitant of Brno in Czechoslovakia. For 37 years, as he explained to Dr Janzow, he and his family had lived in harmony with the Czechs until the dramatic change of the preceding months: 'One would never believe, how fast things can turn. Like an avalanche, the large wave of German anti-Semitism overflowed our country. Everyone thinks to save himself by attacking the Jews. "Out with the Jews" is heard everywhere. My colleagues of yesterday – some with tears – say to me: "We know, it is wrong and unjust, but we cannot help you." The possibilities of employment are gone.' Like many of the correspondents, Schick closed his letter plaintively: 'I hope you will forgive my impudence. In such times of horror, pursued people may be allowed to knock at the door of men.'

Australia and the refugees

For most European Jews in the 1930s, Australia must have seemed a most unlikely place to seek refuge. The overall Jewish population was small and tended to be concentrated in Melbourne and Sydney. Moreover, community sentiment in Australia by no means favoured immigration on a significant scale. The so-called White Australia Policy enjoyed broad support, and, although it targeted primarily Asians, suspicions extended to all who did not derive from the preferred 'British stock'. Reservations concerning non-British migration were by no means the preserve of the political Right in Australia. On the Left, as the Australian economy emerged at best torpidly from the Great Depression, concerns were voiced that immigrants would take the jobs of Australian workers. Even among Australian Jewry there were fears that growing numbers of Jewish immigrants from continental Europe would trigger anti-Semitism, an outcome that the Anglo-centric Jewish communities were eager to avoid.

By and large, government policy reflected community opinion and ensured that the arrival of European immigrants – officially identified as 'white aliens' – was kept to a minimum. That was achieved above all by imposing a very heavy fee on new arrivals. 'Landing money' to the exorbitant tune of £500, a small fortune for most at that time, was extracted. In recognition that the demand was excessive, Cabinet in 1936 reduced the requirement to £200; it also administered a system whereby non-British migrants nominated by persons or associations prepared to act as guarantors needed to pay merely £50. In addition, the landing money requirement was removed altogether for dependent relatives of aliens already resident in Australia.[6]

With this revised policy the volume of Jewish immigration could increase, but it could by no means keep pace with the growing demand. In 1938 there was a dramatic jump in the number of applications received from Europe. The Nazi annexation of Austria in March 1938 increased the Jewish population of the 'Greater German Reich' literally overnight. These Jews of Austria and their German co-religionists were being delivered the very clear message that it was in their own interests to emigrate. The Department of the Interior in Canberra, a section of which was devoted to immigration issues, was bombarded with applications at a rate reflecting the growing desperation of Europe's Jews. By May 1938, the Minister of the Interior, John McEwen, decided that there was no alternative but to impose a quota which, on his suggestion, Cabinet agreed to set at 5100 per year.[7] It was a figure quite inadequate when measured against the scale of the deepening crisis, and yet Cabinet considered that it represented such a level of generosity that it was wise not to release it to the public.

When President Roosevelt called an international conference at Evian in France in July 1938 to discuss the growing refugee crisis, Australia decided to send a delegation of its own. Its leader was Lieutenant-Colonel Thomas Walter White, the Minister for Trade and Customs, who, as fortune would have it, was in Europe at that time. To any Jew contemplating refuge in Australia, White's contribution at the conference was less than encouraging. He told his fellow delegates:

> Under the circumstances, Australia cannot do more, for it will be appreciated that in a young country man power from the source from which most of its citizens have come is preferred, while undue privileges cannot be given to one particular class of non-British subject without injustice to others. It will no doubt be appreciated that, as we have no real racial problems, we are not desirous of importing one by encouraging any scheme of large-scale foreign migration.[8]

The attitudes voiced by White were sadly typical of Evian; of all the participating states, only the tiny Dominican Republic agreed to increase its quota.

The failings of Evian were soon compounded by developments in Germany. Until November 1938 many German Jews clung to the hope that Nazi anti-Semitism was an aberration; in time things would return to normal. *Kristallnacht*, bringing with it murder, incarceration, the burning of synagogues and the destruction of Jewish property, changed all that. Even the most sanguine were persuaded that emigration was the only option, yet for many – as Evian had shown – not a viable one. With quotas imposed and rigidly enforced in most parts of the world, possibilities were limited.

Australians were by no means insensitive to the Jews' dilemma. Voices pressing for an expanded immigration program grew more voluble, while applications continued to flood in. One of those who argued for an increased quota was former Prime Minister Stanley Melbourne Bruce, now serving as Australia's High Commissioner in London, and as such the recipient of countless desperate requests from Europe. Bruce pressed the Australian Government for an expanded quota of 30,000 over three years. Prime Minister Joseph Lyons and his Cabinet responded with what appeared a significant concession. On 1 December 1938 Interior Minister McEwen announced before Parliament that Australia would allow 15,000 refugees into the country over three years. In this way, he claimed, 'it is felt that it will be possible for Australia to play its part amongst the nations of the world, in absorbing its reasonable quota of these people, while at the same time selecting those who will become valuable citizens of Australia and, we trust, patriots of their new home, without this action disturbing industrial conditions in Australia'.[9] In reality, the announced quota was no larger than that already being tacitly applied.

The Synagogue on Synagogue Place in 1938. It accommodated the South Australian Branch of the Australian Jewish Welfare Society. (State Library of South Australia. SLSA: B 7691)

The Jews of Europe could know little of the debates and policy developments on the other side of the world, and in any case they could do little more than send in their applications. As Australia had no diplomatic representatives in continental Europe, the process operated via British embassies. They would advise hopeful emigrants to Australia, ensure that the appropriate forms were submitted, and then send the forms all the way to Canberra for consideration by the Department of the Interior. That stage of the procedure alone could take considerable time, especially during the period of greatest demand in 1938 and 1939. Months could elapse before an answer was received in Europe, and then most commonly in the negative.

Such was the size of the task at hand that the Australian authorities drew on assistance from non-government organisations. The most important of them was the Australian Jewish Welfare Society, or AJWS, whose major activities were in Sydney and Melbourne, but which had branches in other states, including South Australia. Its role was not only to assist the government to meet its quota of refugee Jews but also to provide support for Jews when they arrived in Australia. In South Australia the contact person for the society was the secretary of the synagogue, while the Rabbi (at that time Reverend L. Rubin-Zacks) and the treasurer of the congregation were the welfare workers, providing loans and assistance to refugees where required. Running their activities from a modest space inside the synagogue in Synagogue Place, just off Adelaide's Rundle Street, they probably helped bring more than 100 Jews from continental Europe to the state.[10] One of the more curious arrivals at the time was not a person but a Torah scroll, sent out to Adelaide in the wake of the synagogue vandalism perpetrated by the Nazis during the November pogrom. A consecration service was held by the Adelaide Hebrew Congregation on 3 September 1939, just as the Second World War was beginning.[11]

Not all potential refugees were Jewish. To assist in bringing Catholic refugees to Australia the government worked hand-in-glove with the so-called Continental Catholic Migrants Welfare Committee. Then there were those who regarded themselves as Christians, and who had indeed been christened, but whom the Nazis persecuted on the basis of their ascribed racial identity as Jews or as *Mischlinge*, that is, as 'half-Jews' or even 'quarter-Jews'. These did not qualify for the services of Jewish organisations, whether in Germany or in Australia, so the government worked with another body which championed their interests. This was a group of Quakers which went under the name German Emergency Fellowship Committee (GEFC) and was led by the redoubtable

Camilla Wedgwood, the principal of Sydney University Women's College, who worked tirelessly to promote the interests and save the lives of so-called 'Non-Aryan Christians'.

Lutherans and Jews

Thus there was a place for non-government organisations to lend assistance to refugees, and therefore an opportunity for Dr Janzow and the Lutheran churches. They could work closely with such organisations as the Australian Jewish Welfare Society, the German Emergency Fellowship Committee or the Continental Catholic Migrants Welfare Committee. Alternatively, they could step into the role of guarantor, providing needy potential immigrants with landing money and an assurance that they would look after their material needs after their arrival in Australia.

Yet just as Australia must have seemed an unlikely destination for European refugees, the Lutherans must have appeared improbable providers of a helping hand, especially to Jews. Anti-Semitism had a long tradition in the Lutheran Church; it can be traced back to Luther himself. In the twentieth century it was still firmly present, with many Lutherans assuming the traditional form of religious chauvinism and intolerance. They clung doggedly to the doctrine of 'supersessionism', that is, the view that Christians had supplanted Jews as God's chosen people; salvation was attainable by Jews only if they chose to reject their religion and convert to Christianity.

Moreover, the Australian Lutherans who appeared to be reaching out their hands to help were overwhelmingly of German origin themselves, and in Australia's Lutheran communities in the 1930s there was a good deal of sympathy for Germany and for the national revival which appeared to be occurring under Adolf Hitler's leadership. Degrees of support for Nazism varied immensely. At one extreme was unreserved support, including in some cases Nazi Party membership and a firm belief that Hitler was indeed Germany's saviour; he would haul Germany from the ignominy of its defeat in the Great War and its humiliation in the postwar settlement. A photograph taken in the German Club in Adelaide on Hitler's birthday in 1939 (see page 278 in Barbara Poniewierski's chapter) records this adulation in some circles. At the other extreme there was a clear rejection of Nazism and a contempt for its crudeness and propensity for violence.

The Lutheran churches in Australia in the 1930s were divided into two main groups. Dr Janzow, as *The Times* article had indicated, was General President of the Evangelical Lutheran Synod of Australia (ELSA). The other – and in many regards rival – Lutheran church was the United Evangelical Lutheran Church in Australia (UELCA, although known sometimes also by its German acronym VELKA). These two organisations had gone their separate ways as a consequence of a doctrinal schism reaching back many years. In the 1930s relations were as icy as they had ever been, although it is noteworthy that the article in *The Times* implied that on the refugee issue the churches would be working in collaboration. In reality, much of the initiative on refugee matters appears to have been taken by United Evangelical Lutheran Church in Australia.

At that time UELCA's President-General was a South Australian, Johannes Julius Stolz. He was the son of Johannes Martin Stolz, the first pastor to come to Australia from the Neuendettelsau Mission Society. The younger Stolz was born in Point Pass in South Australia, but like his father before him he had received training in Germany, both at Neuendettelsau and at the University of Erlangen. This contact with Germany was by no means unusual for UELCA, which, more than Dr Janzow's ELSA, worked hard to maintain its links with Germany. Janzow himself was in fact American-born, and ELSA's links with the United States were cultivated carefully. UELCA also invested greater effort than ELSA in maintaining German language and culture in Australia, a task which had received a huge setback during the First World War. In 1938 it founded at its Immanuel College in North Adelaide a seminary for the training of teachers of German in its schools, and it re-opened church primary schools of the kind which had existed before the war, offering bilingual education. Apart from encouraging its Australian-born pastors to receive an education in Germany, it was by no means averse to recruiting Germans for its Australian work.

By the 1930s, and in the wake of Hitler's rise to power, there were many who were not just willing but eager to come. Some had very good reason to reject the Nazis' anti-Semitism, although they must have been painfully aware that many of their fellow Lutherans embraced it. As we have seen, the Nazi version of anti-Semitism insisted that Jewishness was a matter of race, not of religion. A Jew who converted to Christianity would still be a Jew. But this kind of thinking was rejected by Pastor Stolz, to the extent that he was prepared to tell Hitler so. Upset also by Hitler's (ultimately unsuccessful) attempts to create a unified Reich church, Stolz wrote to Hitler in October 1934.[12] Although he couched it in conciliatory terms, Stolz nonetheless made his rejection of Hitler's attempts to impose unity on the German churches plain, indeed he could cite the foundation of Lutheranism in Australia as stemming from an earlier state-sponsored attempt to impose unity. But he also informed Hitler that he abhorred the incursion of the Nazis' racial thinking into church matters. Hitler himself did not deign to reply, but an underling lectured Stolz in a reply sent early in the following year:

> National Socialism's racial hygiene is first and foremost a matter of demographic policy in this world, which has been alarmingly neglected for generations. The fact that there are various races is certainly also anchored in God's vision of creation. Or are you of the opinion that the racial laws of the United States (for example hindering the immigration of members of the slavic and romanic nations) are similarly irreconcilable with the Christian spirit? In the Middle Ages the Catholic Church demanded pure-bloodedness and evidence of ancestry over several generations from large sections of the clergy.[13]

That Stolz differed from Hitler in this matter is illustrated in deed as well as in word. It was largely through his efforts that Karl Mützelfeldt from Hermansburg in Germany was able to make his way to Adelaide in 1934. Mützelfeldt himself was not Jewish, but his wife was half-Jewish, a so-called *Mischling* First Degree, and the children were classified as *Mischlinge* Second Degree. Uncertainty over their futures persuaded the family to emigrate, a step which proved of lasting benefit to the Lutheran community of Adelaide. Mützelfeldt soon took up an appointment to the Lutheran Seminary; he also became the driving force behind the Lutheran Immigration Aid Society (LIAS), keenly interested in assisting people in situations perilously similar to that of his own family.

Not surprisingly, Mützelfeldt and LIAS were aware of the work of Camilla Wedgwood's German Emergency Fellowship Committee, with its concern for 'Non-Aryan Christians'. The cooperation between the two groups led to at least one very tangible and positive outcome, namely, the rescue of a young man by the name of Horst Salomon. On both his father's and mother's side the Berlin-born Salomon was of Jewish descent, but he was raised a Christian. Due to the precariousness of the situation in Germany, he was sent as a teenager to Denmark to attend an agricultural school. Eventually his Danish visa expired, forcing him to seek other options. He wrote to the Society of Friends in London on behalf of himself and his brothers Ernst and Gerd. The society forwarded the request to Camilla Wedgwood, who through an arrangement with the Lutherans of South Australia had Horst placed under the care of Karl Mützelfeldt. The latter used contacts with the Lutheran farming community on the Yorke Peninsula to place Salomon on a farm outside Kadina. His brother Ernst followed some months later to another farm. Horst many years later recalled the harshness of his life on the farm, persuading him to turn to his mentor Mützelfeldt:

> And I wrote to Mützelfeldt and he said, 'How are you getting on?' I said, 'Bloody awful'. He said, 'My boy', he said, 'I know it's hard, but you are a pioneer. You must stay in your position the same as I used to stand in the field in 1914.' He said, 'But if you fail, then none of the other boys who are faced with concentration camp will be able to come out. You have to show that you are a success', and so there I was.[14]

Mützelfeldt and the Lutheran Immigration Aid Society were indeed able to help others. The society reported on its work in the pages of the *Lutheran Herald* through 1938 and 1939. In the issue dated 7 November 1938, for example, it informed its readers, 'We are continuously receiving new applications from overseas', and at the beginning of the following year claimed it was dealing with over 50 cases. It also cautioned, however: 'More assistance is urgently needed, as in a number of cases liberation from concentration camps is depending upon the possibility to emigrate. It is written (Matthew 25: 36): "I was in prison and ye came unto me".'[15]

The doggedness with which the Lutherans were prepared to

help refugees, and also the stumbling blocks placed in their path, are abundantly clear in the most unusual case of Pastor Alfred Freund-Zinnbauer. He was not German but Austrian, and like so many others in whom the Lutherans showed interest, he was a *Mischling* and 'Non-Aryan Christian', the christened son of a Bohemian Jewish father and an Austrian Catholic mother. Indeed, he was brought up a Catholic, but in 1928, at the age of 18, he converted to Lutheranism. In 1936 he was ordained as a pastor, but it was becoming apparent that his Jewish background was going to hinder any church career he might pursue in Austria, even well before the *Anschluss* of 1938. Dismissed from his parish in rural Austria, he returned to his home city of Vienna, where he investigated the possibility of emigration. He came to hear of Pastor Stolz in South Australia and wrote to him in the middle of 1938, expressing his eagerness to pursue his career in the Antipodes. Stolz's reply was cautiously optimistic, setting in motion a chain of events which were to change Freund-Zinnbauer's life. A representative of the Martin Luther League assessed the Austrian's suitability, reaching the conclusion: 'As far as his outward appearance is concerned you would hardly expect that he is Jewish'.[16] Thereupon Stolz encouraged Freund-Zinnbauer to submit an application to immigrate to the Department of the Interior, which Stolz would support. While that was being considered, he encouraged Freund-Zinnbauer to learn English so that he would be able to take up his expected pastoral role on arrival.

Unfortunately, Freund-Zinnbauer and his wife Helga had more time to learn English than they might have hoped. By May they had at least managed to make it to England, where they awaited further news from Australia. They received a landing visa to enter Australia as visitors, but not as permanent residents. Without the appropriate visa no shipping company would sell them berths. Finally in mid-August the Department of the Interior in Canberra informed them that an entry permit would not be required, and with that news the Freund-Zinnbauers were set to sail on September 6. However, the outbreak of war intervened; berths were put at the disposal of Australians returning home. Moreover, the Freund-Zinnbauers' status changed – they were now regarded as 'enemy aliens', and as such they would need not only exit visas to leave England but also permission from Australian military authorities to enter Australia.

As their despair grew, Pastor Stolz doubled his efforts. Through the Commandant of the 4th Military District of the Commonwealth at Keswick he secured permission for entry into South Australia. The Freund-Zinnbauers for their part sought exit visas, but they were told they needed new landing permits for Australia, permits which could be issued only in Canberra. In January 1940 Australia House in London finally received word from Canberra that the permits had been granted, so that after seven fretful months in England the Freund-Zinnbauers departed for Adelaide aboard the *Orontes*. On 22 February Pastor Stolz himself greeted them at Outer Harbor and took them to his residence at Hill Street in North Adelaide.

Fates

The case of Alfred and Helga Freund-Zinnbauer highlights how difficult it was for European refugees to reach Australia before it was all too late. From the time of their initial contact with Pastor Stolz, through to stepping foot on South Australian soil in February 1940, some 20 months had elapsed. The outbreak of war meant that, tragically, even the quotas were no matter. For the period 1933 to 1940 altogether only some 7000–8000 European Jews made it to Australia.[17] After 1940 all lawful emigration from Germany ceased.

Those who wrote to Dr Janzow at the end of 1938 had even less time at their disposal than the Freund-Zinnbauers. For many that proved crucial. Nelly Löwy's fate was sadly typical. From her native Vienna she was eventually deported to the East on 27 May 1942, where she perished at Maly Trostinets, a concentration camp near Minsk, just five days later.[18] Alfred Schick was taken from his home town of Brno in Czechoslovakia to the concentration camp at Theresienstadt – in Czech Terezin – at the end of March 1942. But two-and-a-half years later, on 28 October 1944, he was transported further to Auschwitz, the most notorious of the Nazi death camps, where he almost certainly was gassed upon arrival.[19]

As for Curt Bejach, not only the failure to secure passage to Australia but the death of his wife brought about his demise. In most cases Jews who were married to 'Aryans', as Bejach had been, survived the Holocaust. But Bejach's wife had already died, as he had explained to Dr Janzow, exposing him to the full savagery of the Nazi racial mania. Neither his own conversion to Christianity nor his role as father to three Christian daughters could save him. On 10 January 1944 he was deported on an old persons' transport to Theresienstadt. Like Alfred Schick he was transported further to Auschwitz later that year, and, like Mr Schick, he was murdered there some time soon after his arrival.[20]

Robert Elsasser was luckier, in large part because he was not in Germany when he wrote to Dr Janzow but in Switzerland. Moreover, as he had explained to Dr Janzow, he had already lodged an application to emigrate with the authorities in Canberra. The application was successful, so that on 26 August 1939 he, his wife Marcelle, and his two daughters Charlotte and Gretel, arrived in Australia, just days before the outbreak of war.[21] The family soon changed their name to Ellis, and in other ways too demonstrated their loyalty to their adopted homeland. Like many refugees, Robert, who had earned the Iron Cross, both First and Second Class, serving in the German army in the First World War, joined the Australian armed forces and served in an employment battalion. The two daughters attended school in Mittagong in New South Wales, but at the end of the war the whole family moved to Adelaide, where Robert for many years taught German at Prince Alfred College, while Marcelle tutored in French at the University of Adelaide. 'Doc Ellis', as he was called, is still remembered fondly by many of his former students. As for Marcelle and Robert's younger daughter Gretel, she was to marry a dashing young Adelaide lawyer by the name of Don Dunstan, destined to become Premier of South Australia.

There was one other of Dr Janzow's correspondents who finally made it to Australia. Hellmut Lindenstaedt, a young Berlin Jew raised as a Christian, arrived in Sydney a couple of weeks after the outbreak of war. Like Robert Elsasser he changed his name – to Helmut Linden – and, like Robert Elsasser, he volunteered to serve in an employment battalion.[22] In his case there is no evidence that the refugees received any concrete assistance from Dr Janzow, whose good intentions may not have come to much in practice. Indeed, in a letter written early in 1939, Dr Janzow conceded, 'As a matter of fact I have not been able to do much about those refugees from Germany etc. as considerable guarantees are required'.²³ Well meaning though he undoubtedly was, harsh realities, especially limited time and resources during a troubled period for South Australia's Lutherans, rendered the task a Herculean one.

For those to whom Pastor Stolz and UELCA's Lutheran Immigration Aid Society were able to extend the long arm of help, blessings were sometimes mixed. Karl Mützelfeldt and his family remained in Adelaide, Mützelfeldt continuing his career at the Lutheran Seminary in North Adelaide. His son Bruno, a teenager when he left Nazi Germany as a *Mischling* Second Degree' in 1933, followed his father's interest in refugee matters. He began working for the Lutheran World Federation in 1950, when the service to refugees established a field office at the Bonegilla Migrant Centre near Albury. Later he moved to the Geneva secretariat as Secretary for Resettlement and Material Relief with the Department of World Service, serving as department director from 1961 to his retirement in 1980.²⁴

Horst Salomon was eager to fight for his adoptive homeland, but for 'enemy aliens' like him this was no easy matter. He attempted unsuccessfully to sign up with the army in Adelaide after the outbreak of war, then tried his luck with the airforce in Melbourne – with a similar result. He returned to Adelaide, where he was employed in the munitions industry. One day, however, and quite unexpectedly, he was arrested and escorted to Adelaide Gaol, where he remained for three days. From there he was taken to the District Army Headquarters at Keswick, and thereafter to the Tatura internment camp in Victoria. On appeal he was eventually released and returned to Adelaide. Along with his brother Ernst he later joined an employment unit stationed in Melbourne, but he returned to Adelaide after the war to pursue a successful business career.

Alfred Freund-Zinnbauer and his family suffered a similar fate. For a few months after their arrival things went well enough. Their host Pastor Stolz introduced them to the Lutheran communities of Adelaide and the Barossa Valley, and Alfred found work among the congregation of North Adelaide. But in June 1940 two policemen appeared on his doorstep with a warrant for his arrest. The warrant declared that it was the opinion of the Commandant of the 4th Military District that for public safety and the defence of the Commonwealth Alfred Freund-Zinnbauer, being an 'enemy alien', should be detained for the duration of the war. Information had been received suggesting that the Freund-Zinnbauers possessed an overly positive view of their European homeland. Moreover, a businessman who had driven Helga from Freeling to Adelaide had been perturbed by her offer to pay her way. Such behaviour, he reasoned, was suspiciously inconsistent with her claims to being an impecunious refugee. Nonetheless, it was only Alfred who was incarcerated, at first in the city watchhouse, then at Keswick, before transfer to Tatura, where he found himself in the company of other 'enemy aliens', many of them genuinely sympathetic to Nazi Germany.

His mentor, Pastor Stolz, was understandably outraged, and was driven to write the following words directly to Prime Minister Menzies:

> His internment is a severe blow to him as he deeply feels that he, being of partly Jewish descent and not a Nazi, has to spend time amongst German nationals to whom men of this type are so very objectionable ... Is it really the policy of the Government to treat a man who is not a Nazi who was anxious to leave Germany, for whose good behaviour an honourable body, in this case a Church, has pledged itself, who is absolutely out of place in an internment camp for German nationals and who is thereby hindered from doing the work which he so ardently wishes to do in the service of his heavenly Master and of the country of adoption, to treat him in the same way as other enemy subjects?[25]

By this time the authorities were not at all convinced that the United Evangelical Lutheran Church in Australia was 'an honourable body', and, as the war went on, Stolz himself was falling increasingly under suspicion. Repeated appeals on Freund-Zinnbauer's behalf were rejected, although in January of 1942 he was at least transferred to the Loveday camp near Barmera in South Australia. Meanwhile, Stolz was able to ease Alfred's concerns for the wellbeing of his wife by providing her with secretarial work. Happily, she was then able to find employment in the Barr Smith Library at the University of Adelaide.

A photograph of Pastor Freund-Zinnbauer after the war. The motorbike is a Czech-manufactured Jawa Trivan, bought by Pastor Zinnbauer in 1951. He used the bike with its special tray to collect for his mission work, adopting the slogan, 'Your junk is my delight.' (Lutheran Archives Adelaide)

It was not until February 1944 that Alfred was finally released from internment. Just as the war in Europe concluded, he was appointed to UELCA's City Mission in Adelaide. His role entailed performing a wide range of tasks, including a tireless commitment to the wellbeing of immigrants, whom he would greet on the wharves and railway platforms of Adelaide before escorting them to accommodation. From 1951 his duties included the management of the Marlborough Street Lutheran Hostel, a kind of halfway house for immigrants and travellers. In 1963 he initiated the Johannes Stolz Prize, of which he was also benefactor, as a tribute to his mentor. The prize was to be awarded to a high-achieving immigrant. In congratulating its first recipient, Freund-Zinnbauer wrote, 'Dr Stolz was interested in migrants. When people fled from Hitler's Germany, he helped many to escape to Australia.' Pastor Freund-Zinnbauer died in 1978, his wife Helga, two years later.

As for Dr Janzow, he gave up the office of President of the Evangelical Lutheran Synod of Australia in 1941 but continued as pastor at the Bethlehem Church in Flinders Street until his retirement in 1945. He died in 1949 and is buried in the

West Terrace Cemetery. Pastor Stolz himself narrowly escaped internment; he remained active in United Evangelical Lutheran Church in Australia during the war and beyond. He died in 1962.

Notes

1. *Register*, 30 October 1844 (cited in J.S. Levi & G.F.L. Berman, *Australian Genesis: Jewish convicts and settlers 1788–1850*, Rigby, Adelaide 1974, p. 291).
2. Levi & Bergman 1974, p. 286.
3. Cited in C.R. Rayner, 'The Response of the South Australian Jewish Community to International Events 1933–1948', Honours thesis, University of Adelaide, 1978, p. 5.
4. *News*, 17 November 1938, p. 21.
5. 'Australian Germans and the Jews', *The Times*, 18 November 1938, p. 15.
6. For a more detailed discussion of Australian immigration policy in the 1930s see especially Suzanne Rutland, *Edge of the Diaspora: Two centuries of Jewish settlement in Australia*, rev. edn, Brandl and Schlesinger, Sydney, 1997, pp. 174–201, and Michael Blakeney, *Australia and the Jewish Refugees 1933–1945*, Croom Helm Australia, Sydney, 1985, pp. 121–56.
7. The figure derives from a quota of 300 per month for non-guaranteed immigrants, 500 per annum sponsored by the Australian Jewish Welfare Society, and 1000 per annum to be guaranteed by friends and relatives.
8. National Archives of Australia A434, file 50/2/41837, 'Refugees from Austria: Special Committee Proposed by U.S.A., Evian', Speech by Lieut.-Colonel the Honourable T.W. White, Delegate for Australia at Evian-les-Bains Conference on 7 July 1938', cited in Paul Bartrop, *Australia and the Holocaust 1933–1945*, Australian Scholarly Publishing, Melbourne, 1994, p. 71.
9. Australia, House of Representatives, *Commonwealth Parliamentary Debates*, vol. 158, 1 December 1938, p. 2536 (cited in Bartrop 1994, p. 116).
10. Rayner gives the figure of 63 male Jewish arrivals for the period 1931–1940, which would extrapolate to an overall figure over 100 (Rayner 1978, p. 5).
11. ibid., p. 35.
12. J.J. Stolz, letter to Adolf Hitler, 10 November 1934, Lutheran Archives Adelaide.
13. Letter from Hermann von Detten of the Abteilung für den kulturellen Frieden, Nationalsozialistische Deutsche Arbeiterpartei. Reichsleitung, 9 January 1935, Lutheran Archives Adelaide.
14. Transcript of an interview with Horst Salomon conducted by Anthony Kaukas, October 1983, J.D. Somerville Oral History Collection, State Library of South Australia, OH347/2, p. 15.

15 *Lutheran Herald*, 7 November 1938, p. 366; *Lutheran Herald*, 16 January 1939, p. 29.
16 Margaret Rilett, *And You Took Me In: Alfred and Helga Freund-Zinnbauer: A biography*, Lutheran Publishing House, Adelaide, 1992, p. 23.
17 Hilary L. Rubinstein, *The Jews in Australia: A thematic history: Volume One, 1788–1945*, William Heinemann, Melbourne, 1991, pp. 177–8.
18 Namentliche Erfassung der österreichischen Holocaustopfer, Dokumentationsarchiv des oesterreichischen Widerstandes, Vienna.
19 Information on Alfred Schick provided by Michal Frankl of the Terezin Initiative Institute.
20 Terezinska Pametni Kniha/Theresienstaedter Gedenkbuch, Terezinska Iniciativa, vol. I–II Melantrich, Praha, 1995, vol. III, Academia Verlag, Prague, 2000.
21 Information provided by Lionel Sharpe, Australian Jewish Genealogical Society.
22 National Archives of Australia b884 V377781; A435 1945/4/1515.
23 Dr Janzow, letter to a Mr Grossmann of Horsham dated Adelaide, 23 May 1939, in Janzow Correspondence, Lutheran Archives Adelaide.
24 http://www.lutheranworld.org/News/LWI/EN/1004.EN.html, viewed 6 April 2007.
25 Cited in Rilett 1992.

Penguins that flew
Paul Pfeiffer and Modernism in war and peace

John Miles

It had been easy fighting in some Plain
Where Victory might hang in equal choice
(Metaphysical poet Andrew Marvell, 1621–78)

The country of the three plains was a far one from that of an Angry Penguin rebel band. Australia, Rocky, and Geranium Plains all lie in the South Australian Hundreds of English, Bright and Bundey, hard marginal land eastward of Point Pass that straddles Goyder's telling rainfall line. On one, on 5 December 1916, Paul Gotthilf Pfeiffer was born and on another he grew up and went to school. Academic promise showed early, but family loss was at first to threaten any chance of further education. At age 15 years, however, Pfeiffer was able to reach out for higher learning, in doing so leaving the close rural world into which he had been born for the Adelaide he held in awe. There, lost time was made up for in geometric progression, against a poetry backdrop that at its height would create headlines around the world.

A fifth-generation shy child from the German stock that had been instrumental to the survival of the South Australia colony in its first crucial years, Paul's life was coloured by both coincidence and paradox. Linguist and translator, university student and honours tutor and acclaimed poet were endeavours enough to crowd a long lifetime, let alone Pfeiffer's 28 short years. To be added, however, were the roles of airman in the RAAF's legendary 461 Squadron, and mentor for the band of idealistic and vocal young undergraduates at Adelaide University who were determined to compose their new kind of poetry and right the world.

Born on his grandparents' Geranium Plain Hundred of Bundey farm, Paul was the youngest of nine children of Gottlieb August

Pfeiffer and Marie Augusta Mathilde, née Schutz. 'If you were from Bundey, you really were considered a country boy,' former pupil of Paul's at Immanuel College, retired pastor Dr Erich Renner recalled.[1] 'My father took some of the church services out at Geranium during World War I, when their regular pastor was interned. He used to say some members of the cloth of his time found it hard to pray for those living beyond Goyder's Line, in they were tempting God too much in the first place!'

Acquired on their marriage in 1899, August and Mathilde's own Geranium Plain property was to prove a land not of milk and honey for these great-grandchildren of religious émigrés from the villages of Rakau and Janny. Rakau lay in the Prussian province of Brandenburg, about five kilometres north-west of Klemzig, from where Pastor August Kavel set out with the first group of Old Lutheran émigrés for South Australia. Janny, some 15 kilometres south of Klemzig, was across the River Oder in the province of Lower Silesia. From these two locales came the bloodlines of Paul Pfeiffer, his great-great grandparents Johan Georg Pfeiffer and wife Christiane, née Schliefke, from Rakau, while his mother Mathilde's Schutz line was from Janny. Johan Georg and his family were among the 188 hopefuls to arrive in South Australia in 1838 aboard Captain Dirk Hahn's *Zebra*.

Drought and poor harvests, interspersed with some barely average years, saw August and Mathilde move in 1918 for a short time to the kinder clime of Lobethal in the Adelaide Hills, until, despite its harshness, the pull of home brought a return to the plains. At first it was for an equally short stay at Rocky Plain, still on the wrong side of Goyder's magical divide. Then a third move in 1920 saw the family settle on property at Australia Plain, critically to the other side of Goyder's Line. Across that farm ran a creek line that came down from the western higher ground of Julia Hundred, where a family called Thiele had their own holding.

The Pfeiffer property, to be called Mirtlefield after a grevillea-like shrub that grew along its humble watercourse, was to give, in most years, a basic livelihood right down to the generation of August and Mathilde's grandchildren. It was at Mirtlefield Paul Pfeiffer would spend his childhood of memory, and he would return there at vacation times during his Adelaide secondary and university years.

Paul Pfeiffer on the steps of Mirtlefield Farm, Australia Plain via Point Pass.
(Una Pitt and Des Pfeiffer)

To Mirtlefield too would come his wartime letters, over a period of nearly four years, from places as far flung and varied as savannah and desert Africa, Scotland and the North Atlantic.

Australia Plain had its classic one-room, one-teacher primary school of the day. Paul would ride the four miles each day on the children's farm horse, Tabby, taking his lessons from one Charles Brooks, a teacher remembered after his time for his dedication and insight. Brooks was to prove the first watershed of Paul's life. Nephew Des Pfeiffer and niece Una Pitt recalled the family saying that near the end of Paul's primary schooling Brooks advised: 'the boy is too good *just* for the farm, he must continue with education.'

'A household of books; unusual at the time,' said Dulcie Held née Gehling, a young contemporary of Paul's. 'Already a respect for knowledge in that family.'

Confirmation of the family's regard for learning lay in August Pfeiffer's once active role on the Australia Plain school committee. He and his wife would certainly have wished to follow Brooks's advice. Standing in the way of things, however, was August's state of health due to serious injuries received in a horse-yarding accident some time earlier, from which he would never fully recover. Dying in the spring of 1931, he left behind his wife, the seven of their children who had survived infancy, and the education dilemma surrounding one of them.

That Paul was the youngest determined things in the end. Two robust brothers, Jack and Otto, and four equally active daughters, Lydia, Elsa, Hulda and Martha, were available to carry on with farm and family life. A decision was reached that sent Paul off to Adelaide to continue his education at the start of the next year. Sister Lydia would accompany him, although not as a fellow student. As a kitchen hand at the destined Immanuel College and Seminary, she would put a presence to the family and the financial commitment being made.

Founded in 1895 as a humble extension to the Point Pass church and manse, Immanuel became a victim of its own success. By the time of its quarter-century it had outgrown its premises and rural setting, to the extent that a bold expansion and relocation were planned. In 1923, along with the Barossa Valley's fledgling Tanunda seminary, Immanuel was relocated to the former Whinham College at North Adelaide, there to find, in the words of its house journal, the *Echo*: 'the turmoil of city life, Library, Art Gallery, Museum, University, all at our door'. Nine years on, this was the setting that a 15-year-old Paul Pfeiffer found himself in, far from the Plains, and where young men would go from poetry rebellion to a quite different kind of war.

For Paul, as both a student and boarder at the new Immanuel, a world of challenge would begin, one that would only peak at the nearby university and its even closer wing of St Mark's. A devout and rural close-knit upbringing where 'Barossa Deutsch' was still spoken in the home and church came into contact with the urban and urbane and the rigour of academic questioning and debate. The very notions of a German and Lutheran heritage would be put to the test, in that South Australia's First World War hysteria over all things German had never gone away; nor would they in all the years between one war and the next. 'Very reluctantly does the historian go ... to the horrible years ...' wrote Pastor Theodor Hebart in his 1938 historical work on the Lutheran Church in Australia.[2] 'The Lutheran people were made to feel ... not as Australians but as hostile Germans ... all former recognition of the loyalty and the great pioneering work of the Prussian Lutherans, forgotten.' In 1932, Paul Pfeiffer's commencement year at Immanuel, the *Echo* itself pleaded the case: 'A country's future lies in the hands of its youth. The scholars of Immanuel are to be fitted to become useful citizens, not of a Little Germany, nor a Little England, but of Australia.'

Pfeiffer's reactions were mixed. He largely thrived in Immanuel and Adelaide life. Core curricula were enhanced by enthusiastic involvement in the school orchestra and in the dramatic and other clubs. Prizes in music and scripture, particularly scripture, throughout his time at Immanuel, came his way, as did the writings of one Lancelot Andrewes, prominent cleric, and contemporary of the Metaphysical poet John Donne. Theirs had been the time of an England in turmoil – the anti-Catholicism and persecution of the Counter Reformation and Jacobite wars – when Donne and other Metaphysical poets would attempt to write a 'new' poetry for the expression of a society in upheaval. Donne, would agonise throughout his lifetime over his faith, journeying to the extent that he would go from Catholic-born and raised, to being an ordained Anglican priest. In a small volume of Andrewes's writings, inscribed in Paul's tiny and careful hand, are a number of quotes from Donne's *Divine Poems*. The collection, said to be a timeless expression of the conflict of faith in society, contains famously the 'Death, Be Not Proud' sonnet. More or less forgotten for more than 200 years, the Metaphysical poets were 'rediscovered' early in the twentieth century by those seeking an example for their own new-formed expression in yet another overturned age. They became the Modernists.

Paul Pfeiffer's exposure to the movement would be signalled in a letter he wrote to his close friend Siegfried Held while home on the farm for harvest after his 1934 Matriculation exams. Firstly in the letter came a whimsical moving back and forth from English to German with seeming ease, showing that a young man's life was not all on the grim side of reality. Paul wrote: 'Sieg ol' boy, how are you getting on? Have been doing quite a bit of work since I'm home. Have sewn about 300 bags. *An welchen Tagen war es etwa ganz unangenehm warm – ähbend! und da habe ich nur im Sports Singlet gearbeitet und habe meine Armens und Schultern alles verbrannt!* It gave me beans in bed a couple of nights and it's not quite healed off yet!'

Over that harvest the prospect of university life for Paul was discussed. Tipping the balance academically and financially in favour of university was the news of real importance to be imparted to Sieg. Should he go on to become an undergraduate, Paul wrote, the College Director Pastor Loehe ('Harry Napper' to the students) had informed him he could look forward to a continued association with the college as a part-time teacher: 'Awfully sorry wasn't able to say good-bye that morning I left. When finished with Director, you were in for breakfast! What Harry suggested and advised, took me quite by surprise! Teaching staff had considered my position and decided to give me the opportunity with the Primary Class (Year 8) next year! He said he thinks I would be quite capable.'

Going up to university in 1935 saw Paul still boarding at Immanuel, as a 'student attending university classes' like others, including Colin Thiele. In 1936 he took private lodgings, staying first with a North Adelaide family near Immanuel. They were the recently widowed Mrs Marjorie Kerr and her four children, the eldest of whom was D.B., Donald Beviss Kerr, to become known to all as Sam. On campus in 1935, meanwhile, the launch of a new and eager literary journal called *Phoenix* took place. In its first editorial it proclaimed: 'No need for apologies, it is time to change!' Seen as arising from the ashes of its staid predecessor, the *Adelaide University Magazine*, *Phoenix* 'clamoured for food' of a most modern kind. The choice of name, it was also made clear, was due to the importance of that mythical bird to the Metaphysicals, and now to the Modernists.

'Break the pentameter,' Ezra Pound had said in relation to liberating poetry in America, while in England T.S. Eliot wrote the groundbreaking *The Waste Land*. Away with tradition was the call, by example from the past. Liberate rhythm and rhyme, reshape meter and verse, to reflect soul-searching in a new age of religious uncertainty and war.

Arriving in Australia, Modernism was to find ready ground at the University of Adelaide of the 1930s. On a world scale it was a small institution in a small and seemingly provincial city, but it boasted a faculty of quite disproportionate excellence. Stanton Hicks, Kerr Grant, John McKellar Stewart and Douglas Mawson ranged across the disciplines of pathology, physics, philosophy and geology. In history and geography were G.V. Portus and A.G. Price, the latter also to be Master at the university's residential and tutorial wing of St Mark's College. In English, Emeritus Professor C.R. Jury would prove of particular importance to poetic Modernism's cause. Colin Thiele, in his book *With Dew on My Boots*, recalled his time at university concurrent with Paul. 'The amazing possibility for undergraduates, to sit at a refectory meal table, side by side with such staff; whilst they talked and argued, it was an incredible experience just to listen to their conversation.'

For five years from 1935 and after its rebirth from 1940, *Phoenix* took the kind of food it said it clamoured for. To shock and delight were its reasons for being. The poetry of the Jindyworobaks edited by Rex Ingamells was published, along with that of the enquiring and young Colin Thiele and Geoffrey Dutton. A further contrast was provided in the work of Max Harris, at first a Jindyworobak, then otherwise. In 1936, still a matriculation student, D.B. Kerr made his first appearance, encouraged by his family's boarder, then in his second year on campus. Pfeiffer's poems in *Phoenix* were often included in other publications. For the long and angry poem *Spain*, a response to the destruction during the Spanish Civil War of the Basque town of Guernica by the German Condor Legion, Paul was awarded the University's Bundey Prize for English Verse.[3] The publication of a number of poems in Immanuel's *Echo*[4] anonymously was understandable, given the full extent of his involvement at the college.

Taking up the offer of a part-time teaching role at his old school, Pfeiffer, although still reserved at times, became a favourite with students at all levels.[5] Appetites beyond poetry and a Charles Brooks eagerness saw him tutor in Greek as well as English, at the time when Erich Renner, Leslie Grope and Lorenz Gehling were Immanuel students. Language skill naturally extended to German, to the extent that he was engaged as one of the translators

Paul Pfeiffer in university days. (Una Pitt and Des Pfeiffer)

of Theodor Hebart's centenary work on Australian Lutheranism published by the United Evangelical Lutheran Church of Australia.

Poetry, however, was his particular love. Two thick workbooks of Paul's from his time as a teacher at Immanuel have survived.[6] They contain, in his tiny and careful hand again, the drafts of lectures for his charges. Colin Thiele, boarding at Immanuel while attending university, suggested some of the notes were for more than regular classes, such as the evening meetings of the Senior School Arts Club. 'It met on Friday night, after the evening meal,' said Thiele. 'Apart from debates and discussions the programme often centred on a guest speaker, especially in areas such as literature, history and religion. I attended a number of those meetings, both as speaker, and a member of the audience. Paul would have been an ideal guest on a subject like modern poetry.'

In those notes, Paul, in his own words and those of John Donne and William Wordsworth, reflected on poetry and Modernism:

Every great age decides for itself, what is to be the essential material for its poetry. A new age, developing its own distinctive genius, will be in reaction against its predecessor, and all that it implied and took for granted. The genius of the new spirit in the heat of creation is likely to dispense with all the established conventions, and to work out a medium, a technique that is wholly its own.

Poetry is the first and last of all knowledge. The new philosophy calls all in doubt, the element of fire is quite put out. What the lover of literature relishes in a poet of the past is exactly the same essential qualities as he loves, enjoys in the poet of his own day: life and passion and art.

But around us today among some modern poets we find a reaction against style. We might call this atmosphere as the heresy of stylelessness. But perhaps it is not quite fair to call it the heresy of stylelessness: it would be more accurate to describe it as the heresy of style without labour. It springs of course from the idea that great poetry is all a matter of first fine careless rapture. It is a strange reasoning that assigns to the musician or painter, technique or craftsmanship, and denies it to the poet.

As *Phoenix* from 1935, then newly titled from 1940 as *Angry Penguins*, the university's literary journal took a central role in Australia's Modernist story.

'And there were the Angry Penguins, so named by Charles Jury, consisting of myself, D.B. Kerr, Paul Pfeiffer and later Geoffrey Dutton',[7] said Max Harris of that time when *Phoenix* would cease, in name at least. Stop publication, the magazine's opponents said, these believing licence in poetry led to the same in life, and that there were enough of these – despite the overall open-mindedness of the university – was confirmed when monies from the Student Union, which funded the printing of the magazine, were cut. Argument over *Phoenix* came to a head late in 1939. It was sufficiently heated to bring the University's Vice-Chancellor into the fray. His ruling would be final, all parties agreed, but an opinion on the poetry's quality was required and so the services of one C.J. Jury were requested.

Charles Rischbieth Jury, dramatist and poet in his own right, was a leading Adelaide cultural figure over a number of decades who was to become paradoxically central to the Modernist story. Emeritus Professor of English and a confessed classicist ('I had fallen in passionate calf-love with Greece'), he nevertheless encouraged the avant-garde among his students. 'Boundaries of form and style should be crossed,' he espoused. 'The nearer the manner of poetry to the contemporary, the better the poetry is likely to be.'

When a young D.B. Kerr turned up literally on his doorstep with the proposed typescript of *Phoenix* under his arm, Jury had to decide its fate. To the young man before him, nothing was more important that year. Rising through the university's activist ranks, Kerr had become a member of the Arts Association, after first helping edit the perennial *On Dit*. From *On Dit* he moved to editorship of *Phoenix* for what was to be its embattled year. The surviving transcript of a 1950s radio talk that Jury gave speaks of the doorstep encounter:

> One morning my door bell rang and I found outside a young man, who had he lived, could have established himself as one of the great masters of English verse. He was D.B. Kerr, Sammy, and he came on a curious errand. The Vice-Chancellor had questioned 'Phoenix' that year and had said that if I approved of the literary quality, it might be printed. What part my literary conservatism, which was known, played in inducing that imposition on me I do not know. Sammy left with me the typescript of 'Phoenix'.
>
> I thought, and still think, it was the best literary document produced by students I have seen, a vitality so astonishingly alive. It contained among others an early Max Harris, two of Donald Kerr's poems, and three of Paul Pfeiffer's including 'At the Window'. One of the best reasons I have to be proud of myself, is that I was responsible for the latter's first printing. In my experience of short poems the sublimity, the restraint, the sharpness, and the tragic intensity of that poem are equalled only by Simonides writing in Greek.

The year 1939 saw Paul Pfeiffer triumph in linguistics and poetry but 1939 was to prove *Phoenix*'s nemesis year. In December, funding was cut after all, and it was believed that was the end of the matter. Then early in the first semester of 1940, through the Arts Association, which held its own budget, steps were taken to see at least one *Phoenix* arise from its ashes.

'That is what you young iconoclasts are, angry penguins', tradition has Jury saying at a particular tutorial, following the reading of a poem employing that phrase.

'The poets, a description that fitted almost everyone at the time, met in Paul Pfeiffer's rooms at St Mark's', said Colin Thiele of 1940. Pfeiffer had graduated with a Bachelor of Arts with Honours at the end of 1939 and progressed from part-time teaching at Immanuel to an appointment as a resident tutor at St Mark's. In his foreword to *Lost Angry Penguins*, Thiele described those gatherings:

> They were volatile meetings, yeasty with poetry and intense with argument about literature, art and politics. Claret of doubtful vintage tended to illuminate the debates early in the evening, but blurred them after midnight. As clarity of thought and speech diminished, vehemency intensified, until some of the more passionate were in danger of being thrown out. In the surge and zest of ideas in 1940 I came close to agreeing with Wordsworth that to be young was very heaven. By 1945 I had a more sober vision of the world. To be young meant death for Sam and Paul and thousands of others, death that robbed us of the riches they would have given us if they had been allowed to live.

The minutes of the Arts Association for its April 1940 meeting, with Kerr as Secretary, record the passing of the motion 'that in view of the abolition of *Phoenix* the Association undertake the production of a literary magazine, with D. Kerr & M. Harris as editors, P. Pfeiffer & G. Dutton as sub-editors, Mr C.R. Jury as the magazine's patron'. At the next month's meeting, with Kerr now the Arts Association's President, the motion was put and passed again. For patron Jury, *Angry Penguins* was chosen as the title for a *Phoenix* rebirth. For the use of the phrase from his poem, Harris was made Kerr's co-editor and Pfeiffer and Dutton their subs.

Angry Penguins carried on from where *Phoenix* left off. National reviews praised or damned it, although all acknowledged it as Modernism's voice. Later the Ern Malley affair guaranteed international headlines, becoming Australia's greatest and one of the world's great literary hoaxes. Kerr, Dutton and Pfeiffer, however, were by this time penguins that flew, having enlisted, like Colin Thiele and many others from the university and St Mark's in the RAAF for war service.

> Height: five feet eight inches; weight: 144 pounds; chest: thirty-four inches; complexion: medium; eyes: blue; hair: fair; wounds-scars-marks: nil, said Pfeiffer's enlistment papers. Next-of-kin: Mother; Home: Mirtlefield Farm via Point Pass; Occupation: tutor; Special qualifications: speaks foreign languages, French, fluent German, some Greek … Religion: Anglican, they concluded.

Giving his religion as Anglican may have been one way by which the committed scripture student merely assumed that he would continue his church attendance in any non-Lutheran sphere of the war, such as Britain. We could also speculate that Donne-like dilemmas might also have been behind the declaration.

John Donne, in a lifetime's journey from Catholicism to Anglican priesthood, had also faced war and religious intolerance. Paul Pfeiffer, studious reader of Donne and Bishop Andrewes, faced similar times. A fifth-generation South Australian, Pfeiffer was nevertheless confronted by his German and Lutheran heritage. Ill feeling among the general South Australian population regarding people of such backgrounds had stretched from one world war to another. Lutheran school closures, internments and the removal of honoured German settler names from the map all flew in the face of what Immanuel's *Echo* and Pastor Hebart had both tried to say on behalf of their community: that they were pioneering and loyal Australians, neither English nor German.

But as the second of the German-centred wars burst upon the world, young South Australian men, suddenly regardless of background, were expected to flock once again to enlistment offices. They did, and in the heady *Angry Penguins* inaugural year of 1940, they came from the university in virtual procession, as well as from factory and farm. University courses were revised or cancelled and when it lost so many students and young staff, St Mark's itself would close, to be turned over to the RAAF for use as a billet.

We can only conjecture whether Paul Pfeiffer agonised over going to war against his ancestral homeland. Many young men of his background did, but Pastor Hebart's and the *Echo's* words invariably held true. Loyalty was for the land of birth, as a matter of conscience. Martin Luther himself had said: '*Ich kann nicht anders*', when placed in a similarly difficult position. Asked to recant and

Paul Pfeiffer on the eve of departure for war service with the RAAF.
(Una Pitt and Des Pfeiffer)

therefore ignore the dictates of his conscience, the rebel monk explained that conscience was not the individual's to oppose, as it belonged to God.

'Speaks fluent German', was one thing to have on the enlistment papers: a common-sense military, could after all, put that to advantage. Religion, however, might be nobody else's business, the concern only of conscience bearer and conscience owner.

Two confirmation certificates exist for Paul Pfeiffer. The Lutheran certificate is dated November 1931, around the time when the decision that Paul would leave the farm and continue his education in Adelaide was made. Then there is the Anglican one, for a ceremony performed in St Peter's Cathedral next door to St Mark's on Michaelmas Day 1940, but this has not been signed by Pfeiffer.

Paul commenced navigational training in March 1941 at the RAAF base at Somers on Victoria's Western Port Bay. There in early autumn heat, he penned the lyric 'Somers Off Duty', already yearning for home. He did see his family once more, back on Australia Plain as autumn turned to winter and final farewells were made. He travelled via troopship from Sydney, disembarking in Durban, South Africa, in July to undergo specialised training and base operations duty in the Transvaal and Rhodesia. 'Let us hope that the end of this war is not in the too far distant future', he wrote in one of the first of many letters to Mirtlefield. 'The Lord is King but the people never so unquiet.'

The war was not to be over in any near future. Departing from southern Africa, Paul arrived in beleaguered Britain in its spring of 1942, commencing full operational flying attached to the RAF. Flying in Blenheims and Wellingtons as both navigator and bomb aimer, he ranged from the Irish Sea to Gibraltar, and North Africa, where the vital Western Desert Campaign was being waged. In early 1943, assigned to the RAAF's 461 Squadron attached to British Coastal Command, he began life in the Sunderland flying boat, a craft to become as legendary as the Spitfire or the Junkers. With two interior decks, crews of up to a dozen, armed front, rear, above, below and both sides with Vickers and Browning machine guns, this lumbering seaplane became 'the flying porcupine' to its German opponents, a craft that could give as good as it got and more in dogfights with what became its aerial foe, the Luftwaffe's Junkers. But the Sunderland's principal role was as hunter–killer, and, also armed with depth charges, its prey were the U-boats wreaking havoc on Britain's shipping lifeline.

'The weather out there that winter had to be seen to be believed', said Ivan Southall, who was to become, like Colin Thiele, an acclaimed children's author. 'The cloud was very low, the air rough, the sea raging. The wind was at gale force and the rain all but continuous. And the water was freezing. The turret gunners and pilots looked for U-boats, but it was a gesture only, merely to square themselves with conscience. The only virtue of that weather was its freedom from the Junkers 88.'

Southall was speaking in *They Shall Not Pass Unseen*, his official Second World War history of 461 Squadron, for which he took the Squadron's motto as a title. For months he and Pfeiffer flew together as pilot and navigator in such North Atlantic weather, escorting Allied convoys and searching out their predators. Both airmen came to know the other's writing ambitions. Southall had published his first short stories in Melbourne, while in Adelaide the manuscript of *Hymeneal to a Star*, the poetry collection that Paul had finished at Somers, was coming off the press at Hassell, the default publisher for the University of Adelaide's work. Back in their barracks at 461's

Bristol Channel base of Pembroke Dock, the two shared a billet as they did a Sunderland, a spartan room with a chair and bed each and each side of a low double-sided bookcase–partition. There the aspiring author and the poet would exchange writing ideas and books to read. 'Sometimes; not too often, sadly I now say', Southall later told me. 'Most of the time we were too tired, worried or just plain scared.'[8]

As detailed in Southall's book, on patrol one particular day, 28 January 1944, Southall and Pfeiffer's craft was part of a formation of three. Suddenly from nowhere a U-boat was spotted on the surface. It was the U-571, and the Sunderlands were deployed, one peeling off in response to a convoy report of a further U-boat. The second Sunderland, making its pass on the U-571 in the face of machine gun and light cannon fire, straddled the submarine in copybook style, dropping depth charges. Breached on both sides of its hull, the submarine began to sink almost immediately, as the surviving crew abandoned ship. With no lifeboats or rafts available, the 30 or so remaining submariners had no choice but to jump straight into the icy waters. 'It was intensely cold, in the wind chill and water itself. They were dead men already', said Southall. Nevertheless, the third Sunderland, Southall and Pfeiffer's craft, then passed over the survivors and released its own survival dingy, to see it hit the water and successfully inflate. But none of the U-571 crew reached it, even from the short distance involved. 'They couldn't get into it. They didn't even try. I don't think they could', concluded Southall.

Back at base the mission was written up and an official enquiry convened over the dropping of the life craft. A censure was issued to the Sunderland crew, stating such equipment was for saving their lives and not those of the enemy.

During 1944 Pfeiffer and Southall continued to fly in a Sunderland, with the call sign of Z-Zebra, echoing the name of Captain Hahn's ship, the ship that had brought Paul's ancestors to South Australia. By the end of the year Paul's logged operational flying time tallied well over 1000 hours. He was then transferred to a tutoring role again, but of Sunderlands rather than language and poetry. Paul had also found romance and was about to become engaged to a woman named Ethel Philip, two years Paul's senior

The crew of Sunderland Z-Zebra, Paul Pfeiffer seated far right, Ivan Southall, pilot, seated centre. (Ivan Southall)

and the daughter of a Scottish GP. The couple had met in the south of England and done most of their courting at leave times in London or the Essex town of Leigh-on-Sea. Ethel's original home, where her father still had the family farm, was the Scottish highland town of Inverness.

In his role of instructor Paul was transferred to northern Scotland, to Cromarty Firth in Ross-Shire. From the RAF's Alness base near Invergordon, Sunderlands were patrolling the North Sea and waters out to the Arctic Circle and Greenland. Sunderland advanced flight training was also being carried out at Alness. By Christmas 1944 Pfeiffer was there, 50 miles south of the windswept town of Melvich, from whence the great-grandparents of fellow Penguin Sam Kerr had come to settle in South Australia near Point Pass. A bare 20 miles west, was Inverness.

The letters home continued. 'Dear brother', said one. 'Would give anything to swap with you. A bit of wattle for me and yours the flakes of snow. Surely it won't be too long now.'

On the morning of 3 January 1945, when a return to Australia was indeed not far away, a Sunderland took off from Alness on a photographic and reconnaissance training flight. On board were

Flying Officer Paul Pfeiffer and Flight Sergeant John Eshelby, also from Z-Zebra. With them were another veteran instructor and four trainees, which was thought a good enough ratio for safety. The cause of the crash of the Sunderland was left open. There was the possibility of novice error, certainly in the face of the sudden and violent turbulence that swept into the mouth of Cromarty Firth, just as the craft turned and ran towards open water. As the engines strained, the wing floats and then the fuselage broke free from their planing surface, so that the craft became airborne, but only for a moment. Almost immediately out of control when free of the water, the Sunderland veered sharply to landward away from the open sea and storm front. The starboard wingtip clipped water, and with plumes of spray, the giant seaplane cartwheeled, until finally coming to rest. Two trainees of the total complement of seven crew members were pulled alive from the sinking craft. So was Pfeiffer, who was taken unconscious and critically injured to the small Invergordon infirmary. There he died the same afternoon without regaining consciousness.

A sea chest of Paul's reading material did return home: poetry books, the works of the Greek philosophers, English, German and Australian tales. For 60 years they sat at Mirtlefield and other farmhouses, until musty trunk and all, they found their place in Immanuel College's historical collection. The only exceptions were two books of the poetry of John Keats, which in the year 2000 it was my pleasure to take to Healesville in Victoria to return to Ivan Southall, whose name was inscribed in them. After a long and difficult moment on their handing over, we took a pleasant enough lunch, Ivan and my wife and I. From that trip, however, came something the other way, confirmation, by means of Ivan's flying log and Paul's, of my mother's memory and her diary.

'We would have passed right over your head', Ivan said, when I told of my time as a 20-month-old evacuee, playing daily on the pebbly North Devon beach of Ifracombe, chattering and waving at the giant seaplanes that passed just a few hundred feet over my and my mother's heads, 50 years before I had heard of the Angry Penguins and of Paul Pfeiffer, and decided to write a book about them. 'That was one takeoff path across the Bristol. We would have passed right over.'

In Paul Pfeiffer's will was a bequest — along with others — to Charles Jury, in memory of much enthusiasm and encouragement in the days of young poetry rebels. On hearing of it, Jury immediately signed the bequest over to Pfeiffer's mother.

Dutton, Thiele and Southall did return and went on to have successful and rich writing and teaching careers. Kerr was shot down in the skies over New Guinea, three days into his RAAF service there. His volume of poetry, *Death, Be Not Proud*, the title taken to reflect his favourite poem, was also published by Hassell, but posthumously. Biographical notes there and in other sources over the next three years, acknowledged Kerr as the founder of *Angry Penguins*, and Pfeiffer as a further original force in the creation of the journal.[9]

Modernism died, or perhaps just evolved, as all such brave and supposedly new ideas do and that is considered to have happened in the 1960s. A decade in which to be young, as both Thiele and Wordsworth would have said, was indeed very heaven. Not that my generation were interested in poetry movements then, not exclusively. In that decade there was too much else, so much overall to attract our passion and hope in a time of a New Camelot, thanks to a legacy left by others, who would not know of its freedom.

Notes

1. Unless otherwise noted, quotations and extracts, with sources, are from John Miles, *Lost Angry Penguins D.B. Kerr & P.G. Pfeiffer: A path to the wind*, Crawford House, Adelaide, 2000.
2. *Die Vereinigte Evangelische Lutherische Kirche in Australien: The United Evangelical Lutheran Church in Australia*, English version ed. J.J. Stolz, translators P.G. Pfeiffer & others, LBD, Adelaide, 1938.
3. Coincidental to Bundey Hundred. Prominent early family that gave their name to various locales and bequeaths.
4. Identified with assistance of Dulcie Held, Eric Renner and Colin Thiele. Thiele especially pointed to their 'off-beat and oblique' Modernist style.
5. Seminary and five years of secondary schooling.
6. Immanuel Historical Collection. Saved by Eric Renner from discarded material in 1942 when the college was relocating to Walkerville. Renner had seen the unmistakable hand of a teacher he remembered well.
7. 'Forty Years On', in *The Poems of Ern Malley*, M. Harris & J. Murray-Smith, Allen & Unwin, Sydney, 1988.

8   This and following quotes from correspondence May 2000 between the author and Ivan Southall for the syndicated series *U-571, The True Australian Story*.
9   D.B. Kerr, *Death, Be Not Proud*, Hassell Press, Adelaide, 1943; M. Harris and J. Reed (eds), *Angry Penguins*, issues 4–7, Reed & Harris, Melbourne, 1943–46; *Voices: A Quarterly of Poetry*, E.L. Vinal, New York, 1944.

No man's land
A tale of love and longing during wartime

Christine Winter

In early December 1942, in the Barossa Valley town of Tanunda, a small group of 16 German women, wives of Lutheran missionaries from New Guinea, lined up in front of the local police officer W.T. White, Lieutenant W.A. Langford from Military Intelligence, and an interpreter, Miss H.J. Samuel. The women gave the Hitler salute, then declared that they hoped Germany would win the war and that they held the same beliefs as their husbands. The party of three officials then moved on to Nuriootpa and Light Pass, where they interviewed another four women, asking them whether they were Nazi sympathisers, admired Hitler, loved Germany, hoped that Germany would win the war and desired to return there after the war. Officer Langford compiled a report on the incident and recommended the women and their children be interned. The spokeswoman of the group, he wrote, had stated 'that it was the best Christmas present that they ever had' and that they were looking forward 'with keen anticipation and pleasure to their internment'.[1] Shortly before Christmas 1942, 20 women and 45 children arrived at internment camp Tatura 3, a cluster of barracks among wheat fields in country Victoria, about 20 kilometres south-east of Shepparton. Another group of 10 women and 14 children were brought to Tatura 3 in February 1943.

For the Lutheran community in the Barossa the internment of the women, members of the Lutheran Mission Finschhafen, was in some way an embarrassment. The United Evangelical Lutheran Church of Australia (UELCA) had put itself out accommodating the families, who were evacuated from the Australian administered Mandated Territory of New Guinea after the fall of Rabaul. The removal of the German women from the Barossa, however, also ended a difficult time for the families who had sheltered them, and those around them.

In this chapter I examine the motivations of the German Lutheran women's declaration of support for the Third Reich and consider some implications and wider meanings of their actions so as to map out a contextualised understanding of the Barossa communities during the Second World War and the complex issues of identity which confronted them.

Looking today in the National Archives at the women's security files with the attached intelligence report, it is easy to misunderstand their actions as fanaticism during wartime or blind devotion to National Socialism, when actually it was also an act of desperation in exile on their part, and most probably an act of kindness or exasperation on the part of the respective officers.

Until that day in December 1942, when the women lined up declaring their allegiance to Hitler, all decisions had been made for them by others. In December 1941, in anticipation of an imminent Japanese attack on Papua and New Guinea, white and Chinese women and children and their domestic help had been evacuated to mainland Australia. After a dramatic journey in boats, large and small, and private and government planes, the trip to safety continued via train from Townsville to South Australia. The president of the United Evangelical Lutheran Church of Australia had negotiated with government officials that his church would look after its fellow Lutherans. A few women and children went to Queensland, while the majority were taken in by Lutheran families in South Australia. The Commonwealth Government was happy. All but a handful of the male missionaries had already been interned as enemy aliens, but the German women evacuated from New Guinea could not be interned without provoking serious repercussions. From the beginning of the war, when Australia released seven German women from internment to placate Germany, which had threatened to retaliate by incarcerating all British women living in the Reich, a policy had been put in place that meant that no German woman would be interned by Australian authorities, unless regarded as absolutely unavoidable for the security of the nation. The government thus was grateful that the problem of the female evacuee enemy aliens had been resolved elegantly. Or so they thought. The women, however, were desperately unhappy. They were (enemy) aliens in an alien land. In New Guinea, being away from their homeland and separated from their husbands over long stretches of time was part of their life as missionaries. The older children were sent to school in Germany. Separation and sacrifice had a purpose. Deprived of this purpose, the women were no longer willing to make such sacrifices. Language and schooling facilities were, in the end, the issues which made the women take action.

An officer from the Commonwealth Investigation Branch who had accompanied the 31 women and 55 children to Adelaide commented that 'the women generally were a frozy [sic] type and few could speak English. The children spoke German and knew little English.'[2] Appropriate schooling for these children proved difficult to arrange.

The issue of schooling in the language of the enemy revived resentments which, fewer than 30 years earlier, during the First World War, had led to a shift away from German culture amongst Lutherans in Australia. By the early 1930s two of the UELCA districts, Victoria and New South Wales, had switched to English as their official language, Queensland had decided on bilingualism, and only the South Australian district had kept German. The trend, however, amongst the younger members of the church was to move away from German language and culture, and not only because of political, social and economic pressures. A fellow Lutheran visiting South Australia in 1931 reported back to his German mission motherhouse in Neuendettelsau that the education in schools was 'consciously nationalistic-Australian'; moreover 'the young people from German families want to be regarded not as Germans, but as Australians'.[3]

A representative of the newly established German Protestant Church Federation, Carl Schneider, who came to Australia in mid-1928 to invite UELCA to become a member, had similar experiences. He reported back to Germany that, while the older generation had been educated in Germany and spoke German fluently, the younger generation of UELCA had little interest in Germany. He quoted one of the sons of the church president,

Tatura, 7 March 1945. Family groups of German internees at No. 3 Camp, Tatura Internment Camp.
(Photo by Ronald Leslie Stewart, Australian War Memorial 030243/15)

Johannes Julius Stolz, as identifying the Great War as the origin of an Australian Lutheran identity: 'The younger [clergy] see the war as the hour giving birth to an English–Australian church and worked towards this. He [Stolz] told me: "The war has helped our church".'[4]

These somewhat defiant assertions of being English–Australian masked tensions within the Lutheran communities about heritage, traditions and belonging. At the beginning of the National Socialist reign in Germany, there were a number of strong supporters for a new, strong Germany amongst leading members of UELCA. Church President Stolz sent a note to the new chancellor, Adolf Hitler, congratulating him on his election in March 1933. In April that same year a German navy cruiser, *Köln*, which had left the Weimar Republic of Germany in late 1932, arrived in Australia. The journal *Kirchenblatt* published a lengthy article entitled 'Thoughts on the Visit of a Warship'. The arrival of *Köln* and the admiration it received were an opportunity for the journal to bathe in the reflection of the glory the ship exhibited as part of Germany and German culture, and to reassert a pride in heritage. The *Kirchenblatt* declared: 'We also don't want to conceal that we felt proud when we inspected the wonderful engineering of the ship and realised how, in this regard as well, our ancestral people march at the forefront of all peoples'.[5]

For some Australian Lutherans in Adelaide the reception of *Köln* by the wider public became a counterpoint to their wartime and post-war humiliation, as well as a long-awaited symbol and demonstration of rehabilitation. Relationships between Australia and Germany, home of 'our ancestral people' were slowly normalising, and with it relations between Anglo-Australians and Australians of German descent.

In 1993 at the Archives of the Lutheran Church in Adelaide I was welcomed – after some initial reservations – with great warmth, and invited each afternoon into the back room for a cup of tea. There, as I sat at the table next to a photocopier, a sink and a small fridge, I spoke of my research topic, provoking anecdotes about the Second World War, such as the story of how maverick pastor Ludwig Doehler had outsmarted the Security Services.[6] Soon the talk turned to the First World War and to stories of house raids, public hostility, destruction of church buildings, arrest and the internment of Australian Lutherans. The Lutheran ordeal during the First World War extends the story of religious persecution in Prussia during the mid-nineteenth century, and is, like one of the most important founding stories of the Australian nation, Gallipoli, a deeply traumatic series of events, still alive in family and community memory today; it is also a story through which later events are interpreted.

At the heart of this story of persecution is the struggle for the preservation of Lutheran religious and cultural identity. In response to the events of the First World War, the Australian churches and synods, which in 1921 formed the United Evangelical Church of Australia,[7] had to redefine and renegotiate their place in the Australian nation, as well as their links to Germany. To secure a safe space within the nation, UELCA opened its own seminary for training clergy and gradually shifted from bilingualism to the exclusive use of English. Yet, for Lutherans, whose religious and cultural centre was the cradle of the Reformation – Germany – this shift disrupted long-standing links with German religious and educational organisations.

Initially, in the early nineteenth century, most Lutheran lay people and clergy had come from Prussia. However, the influence of the mission society in Franconian Neuendettelsau, a small village about 40 kilometres south-west of Nuremberg, on UELCA during the late nineteenth century and until the First World War was considerable. Of all the pastors who had received their training before the end of the war, and who were still in active service in 1938, about 40 per cent had been to the seminary in Neuendettelsau.[8]

During the interwar period of transition the Neuendettelsau Lutheran mission in New Guinea played an important role. The mission became the catalyst for the formation of the UELCA and provided continuity of connection. The Australian Lutherans had supported the New Guinea mission from its foundation in the last decades of the nineteenth century, had looked after the 'orphaned' organisation from 1914, and had continued to send lay workers to New Guinea. A number of German missionaries had also married into local families. When the Barossa Lutherans took in the female missionaries from New Guinea, it was done on the basis of long-standing connections with this mission on a practical and emotional level.

While internal Lutheran debates focused on the problem of how to maintain a Lutheran identity in Australia, government officials, journalists and historians have tended to discuss the role of Australian Lutherans during both world wars in relation to the concept of 'loyalty'. The debate whether Lutherans were pro-German during the First World War or patriotic and loyal Australians became more complex in the context of the Second World War.[9] The central location moved from mainland Australia to the margins of the nation, New Guinea, and the problem of Lutheran loyalty was merged with a separate, but related, debate about the loyalty of Australia's colonial subjects.

One day in the Lutheran Archives in Adelaide I was taken to a bookshelf, and shown the first and second editions of George Johnston's book *New Guinea Diary*. In January 1942 Johnston, known today primarily for his semi-autobiographical novel *My Brother Jack* went to New Guinea as a war correspondent for the *Sydney Morning Herald*, the *Age*, and the London *Daily Telegraph*. In 1943 Angus and Robertson published his experiences and observations of war in New Guinea as the *New Guinea Diary*. In it Johnston writes: 'The most interesting feature of this advance [up the Markham Valley from Lae] is that certain Lutheran missionaries – of Australian, British or American nationality – have been acting as guides for the Japs, and our guerrillas over the other side are very anxious to meet some of the white traitors.'[10]

Mixing elements of truth with rumour and fantasy, Johnston went on to claim that Lutherans were the leaders of 'a little network of Nazi espionage and fifth-column activities', engaged in printing swastika flags and armbands, keeping airstrips ready in case of an Axis invasion, and sending information to the Japanese in the Carolines via a secret transmitter. Johnston added to the theme of 'white Lutheran traitor' that of the 'native traitor': 'There are stories of native children in the area round Finschhafen being taught the Nazi salute and the Horst Wessel song. Some of these natives, no doubt, are now acting as guides for the Japs.'[11]

Immediately after the publication of the first edition of Johnston's book, the United Evangelical Lutheran Church of Australia decided to take legal action and this was successful. The second edition of Johnston's *New Guinea Diary* was printed without the passage on Lutheran traitors guiding the Japanese. Despite this, rumours have persisted and found their way into numerous publications. In 1984 the National Library of Australia published Johnston's original diary, including the section on Lutherans, treason and National Socialism, without any further explanation or critical footnote.[12]

One of the central concerns implicit in the debate about what 'European' Lutherans did or did not do in New Guinea is, of course, that these men were missionaries. Part of the concerns voiced by Australians about the missionaries' loyalty during the war was their and their colleagues' behaviour before the war. Had German Lutheran missionaries, or, for that matter, as Johnston implied, Australian or American Lutherans, indoctrinated New Guineans, so that they were predisposed to collaborate with the Japanese? While the term 'loyalty' and the anxiety about (German) Lutheran traitors are most dominant during the period of the Second World War, they accompany the period of Australian administration like a *leitmotiv* from the beginning, when Australia took over the German colony.

Tatura, 10 March 1945. School classes II/A and II/B and teachers
Miss Liselotte Wagner and Mrs Else Zischler, all German internees at No. 3 Camp,
Tatura Internment Camp.
(Photo by Ronald Leslie Stewart (original damaged), Australian War Memorial, 030246/03)

The presence of German mission women in the Barossa brought the issues about Lutherans traitors from New Guinea to Australia and highlighted the problem of loyalty not only in regard to the women, but also in regard to the South Australians who had taken them in. The women's campaign for German schooling for their children re-opened debates about loyalties or the potential disloyalty of communities of German descent in the Barossa.

In March 1942 the Premier of South Australia sought approval for the establishment of a small bilingual school in Tanunda for approximately 20 German children from six to 10 years of age.[13] The Department of the Army, however, advised, that having more German spoken 'freely' in a district suspected of harbouring strong German sentiment was not advisable 'for security reasons'.[14] The Prime Minister's Department was, in principle, sympathetic to a temporary bilingual facility 'as a means towards education in English'. It speculated that the idea of segregating German children into a permanent special school was motivated either by sympathy for them or hostility against them: 'It would seem that in the case of Tanunda the case has been raised either by some persons or bodies, antagonistic to the children, who do not wish them to mix with Australian children or by some persons or bodies who are sympathetic to these German evacuees and who realise that their lot at a State school would not be a happy one'.[5]

The department conceded that there might be some antagonism towards German children in local schools. A special school in Tanunda, however, would necessitate more children in the district, particularly in Nuriootpa and South Kilkerran, where 29 German children resided. And what would be done to accommodate four German children in Laura, three in Taplan and one in Torrensville? Thus attempts to establish a German school came to nothing.

With the question of education unresolved, 21 of the German women who were housed in the Barossa wrote to the Prime Minister's Department in May 1942, volunteering for internment. There was a family camp in country Victoria, they argued, where they could have their children properly educated in the camp's German school, cease being a burden to their hosts, and be reunited with their husbands.[16] Their proposed solution did not match government policy. They were informed that their request could not be granted. Adults were to be interned only for security reasons, and children were not to be interned at all, unless both parents were.[17]

The women continued to lobby government and church officials. Church president Stolz, who had negotiated their billeting with Lutheran families, and his colleague Friedrich Otto Theile, a Lutheran clergyman and Queensland-based Australian representative of the Lutheran Mission Finschhafen, were becoming exasperated. They had initially hoped that the women's 'readiness to go to a family camp' would cease once they had 'settled down to [a] regular life'.[18] Instead the interned Lutheran male missionaries began to flood the two church leaders with demands to arrange German schooling for the children and to assist the families' transfer to internment camp Tatura 3. Theile, who like Stolz had been trained in Neuendettelsau, complained about the missionaries' lack of understanding for the situation of UELCA:

> I am afraid the brethren do not realize how difficult these abnormal times are for us, for us in our country. And they do not realize how little right they, the enemy aliens, can have in our country. The internees may have some claims in accordance with international arrangements and rulings, but I am afraid that the women and children we have in

view have little claim except to charity. I can see no other course for them but to accommodate themselves to the present conditions.'[19]

Three of the German women billeted in Queensland, Theile continued, were sending their children to local schools and had been very happy with the progress they were making.

Stolz and Theile feared that the missionaries' lobbying would have adverse effects on UELCA. As in the First World War, UELCA was under close surveillance, and at every turning point of the Second World War, when authorities stepped up surveillance and other measures against people and organisations suspected of being a potential security risk, members of the Lutheran church had been affected. In 1940, when Italy joined the war, several house searches had been conducted, and a number of Lutheran clergy had been interned, amongst them one of Stolz's sons. Stolz had sent a protest note to Prime Minister Menzies, asserting the loyalty of UELCA, which had been in Australia 'for over a hundred years'. 'How many more generations must spring up in Australia', Stolz wrote, 'before Lutherans of German decent are regarded as Australians of good standing.'[20] The still existing entanglements of UELCA with German culture and German organisations, however, were increasingly black marks against leading men of UELCA. The existence of a NSDAP (Nationalsozialistische Deutsche Arbeiter Partei – Nazi Party) stronghold amongst the Lutheran Mission Finschhafen had, amongst other matters, led to Theile's internment, and it was mainly because of his declining health that he was released in late January 1942. The threat of internment was hanging also over Stolz, whose house had been searched by Military Intelligence in April. Theile admonished the interned missionaries: 'Don't you agree that it is better for you and your families that he [Stolz] and I care for you within the limits of your possibilities, as we see and understand them, rather then joining you [in the internment camp]?'[21] The leaders of UELCA decided that they would not take on the issue of German schooling or the transfer of the women to Tatura 3. Theile wrote to Stolz: '[W]e cannot accede to the requests of the ladies and their husbands. They will have to bear their cross and we have to bear ours. And part of my cross is made up of the work and care they cause.'[22]

In the end it was one of the local pastors in the Barossa who was no longer prepared to carry his cross. Pastor R.B. Reuther of Light Pass requested to be interviewed by Military Intelligence, for he had important and confidential information. On 25 August he was visited at the Lutheran Manse at Light Pass by Major W.D. Sharland and Lieutenant W.A. Langford from the Intelligence Corps of the 4th Military District. Reuther welcomed the officers warmly: 'Gentlemen, I am very pleased to see you, as I have been deeply concerned because of the situation which has arisen due to the presence of the German women refugees from the mission in New Guinea, who are billeted with my parishioners in this district'.[23] He then proceeded to paint a bleak picture. The women were ardent Nazis, gave the Nazi salute, and publicly sang the German National Anthem. They refused to attend church when services were held in English and did not send their children to school, as they would have to salute the Union Jack and sing 'God save the King'. Reuther was disgusted, and many of his parishioners were concerned. After showing the officers a copy of a petition the German women had given him, which they had also sent to the Prime Minister and in which they begged for their internment, Reuther stated 'on behalf of the Lutheran residents' that 'any action to have these people interned would be welcomed'. The local police officer supported Reuther's claims that he, too, had 'experienced considerable trouble with the refugee women.'

For the authorities all boxes were ticked to move to further action. Here was publicly expressed support for the enemy and burgeoning local resentment towards this support – against a backdrop of existing political frictions within the Barossa. After all necessary approvals had been obtained, Lieutenant Langford returned, together with an interpreter, and travelled in the company of the local police officer from Tanunda through the district to interview the women and arrange for their internment.

Reuther's intervention had been successful. In the process he also voiced his dissatisfaction with his church president: 'I have protested at this state of affairs to Pastor J.J. Stolz on several occasions, but I have received a most unsympathetic hearing. I cannot understand the attitude of Pastor Stolz and I consider that he has a queer concept of loyalty, and makes things very hard for us younger pastors who wish to conduct our religious activities in accordance with our ideas of loyalty to the British Empire.'[24] Reuther was part of the push after the First World War to create a new English–Australian church, and he had no hesitation in acting against the old leadership when it came to finding a solution in regard to the German evacuees. The story he told Military Intelligence had a clear purpose; it was convincing and unambiguous. The women were Nazis, hostile to Australia and the British Empire. The story he told Military Intelligence was not a fabrication but rather an embellishment. In his tale the women refused to attend English church services because of their political convictions. From earlier letters by and reports about the women, however, it is clear – and Reuther must have known this, too – that hardly any of them spoke or understood English.

Whether his actions where motivated by compassion for the women or a desire to rid the district of them or both is difficult to assess. It is also difficult to know whether it was Reuther or the women who worked out that the only way to get interned was to be seen as a security risk. From the archival record, it seems that by the beginning of winter 1942 the women had increased public displays of support for the Führer and the Fatherland. Was this genuine support of National Socialism? After all, a number of the women were members of the NSDAP stronghold Finschhafen. Or was it a concerted effort to get themselves interned after their petition for compassion to the Prime Minister had been rejected, a German school was not forthcoming, and winter made life that extra bit difficult?

Letters from some of the German women accommodated outside the Barossa who were unaware of the solution of presenting themselves as a security risk put the importance of politics into perspective. After the internment of the women from the Barossa, pleading letters started to arrive from others: 'I very much desire to be reunited with my husband', 'Being the mother of three little children aged 3, 4 and 5 years old I find it extremely difficult to manage under the present circumstances',[25] 'I personally feel the strain of the forced stay in the country amongst Australians, as I am not conversant with the English language … [this] is a condition akin to solitary confinement', 'in order that the boy, who is of an extremely shy disposition, should not suffer lifelong harm', 'my husband hardly knows the children',[26] 'I cannot understand why our children are forced to go to the English school',[27] and, 'Why are we treated so brutally', asked Clara Hofmann in the name of herself and her friend Hedwig Hertle, 'we are not putting up with such injustice'. Clara stated that there was no sense in her children attending an Australian school, when they would as soon as possible 'leave this country to continue their education in Germany'. Clara begged, pleaded, described how her health, her nerves had begun to suffer.[28] When I read Clara Hofmann's letters in the archives I cried. I brought the subject up with some of the women who lived in retirement in Neuendettelsau. Was Clara, I asked carefully, a bit nervous, a bit frail or prone to depression? 'Of course not', they laughed. 'Clara, she was a clever one!'

Looking at these letters and petitions today is somewhat perplexing: here are women who prefer being placed behind barbed wire to staying with families and communities who had volunteered to take them in. After over a decade of living in Australia, I am reading the women's letters to the government; they are tactful and circumspect, trying to find the right tone, but unable to contain the heat of patriotism inflamed by war, and the longing for home, language and familiarity, stirred up by exile. I read the passionate refusals to send the children anywhere but to a German language school, and I know that after the war, when the German missionaries rejoined a changed and reorganised Lutheran mission in New Guinea, many of these children went on to be schooled at St Peters in Brisbane. So what did the women object to? Did they react to a loss of purpose and an absence of choice?

At the time I spoke to some of these women in the early 1990s I understood them. I had just fallen in love and relocated to Australia, leaving behind in Germany a fledgling university career and a short marriage. Despite having learned English at school, I had difficulties following conversations. Reading the newspaper took a great deal of time, as my eye could not run down the pages. I could not skip but had to read each line. So there I was, prepared to go into the unknown for reasons of love, sitting in German living rooms adorned with billums, wood carvings and shells from New Guinea, listening to the women's stories. One of them told me of four years of separation from her husband, living behind a curtain in a church hall, having to keep the children quiet during church meetings, which they were not welcome to join. Occasionally, short letters arrived, riddled with holes where the censor had cut the text. Would I be able to find excerpts in the archives to fill in the gaps? I wondered how I would have coped, and at the same time I was unsure how I would cope. 'My dear, as long as you try not to long for German forests, you will be fine.'

The children in Tatura 3, the family camp, grew up without walks through these forests, the jaybird's call warning the other animals of human intrusion, the smell of wet leaves rotting on the forest floor and the rays of sunlight cascading down into a clearing. Instead they and their families went for Sunday walks along the barbed wire fence. The internees called the fenced-in stretch of land which separated the internal compounds from each other and the camp from the outside 'no man's land'. In this chapter I am using the term slightly differently, by naming the entirety of the internment – the place, actions and emotions – as no man's land. I started thinking of it as this during a visit to the former site of the camp. There is an exhibition at the local museum in Tatura, and an official internment graveyard. Of the camp itself – the huts, barracks, sports grounds, and watch towers – nothing remains but a few scattered remnants of concrete foundations amidst the wheat fields. At the time of my visit I myself had felt somewhat in mid-air, in my own no man's land of disconnection and inabilities: my English seemed not to be progressing, while my abilities in German were slipping from me. I felt deaf and mute. No man's land is the space in between, neither here nor there.

Some time ago Lois Foster and Anne Seitz argued that a few internees decided to remain in Australia after the war, because they had already been there for a number of years and had become attached to it.[29] The heat of summer, the cold during winter, the dust and dryness of country Victoria were, apart from some exchanges with the guards, all that the interned Germans and Italians were able to experience of Australia. Helga Griffin, who had been interned in Tatura 3 as a child, reflects: 'Amongst its interned community, Camp 3 at Tatura was usually referred to as *Das Lager*. The description has an old lineage. It is essentially a nomadic term.

In English it means a camp, a resting or staging place. Tatura camp, however, was just a prison without any particular purpose except to keep us locked up out of harm's way, and out of the reach of Australians.'[30] Only a minority had lived in Australia prior to their incarceration. The majority came from overseas, from Palestine, Singapore or Persia.

No man's land, however, I came to understand later, is also defined by its boundaries and borders, by ongoing connections. I have argued elsewhere in a transnational analysis of the politics of Tatura 3 and Tatura 1, the single men's camp, that although isolated from the surroundings, the camp was connected in other ways to a multitude of agencies, which enabled National Socialists inside to take control. The barbed wire was open to pressure from German authorities, who desired to establish one Aryan camp in each country. Building on work by Konrad Kwiet and Paul Bartrop, I have argued that the Australian Army tolerated the political activities inside, and used Tatura 1 and 3 as holding camps for radical internees to keep the pressure off other camps. In the three Nazi compounds within the family camp – the fourth was reserved for Jewish refugees – there was little space for dissent. Interning those whom Australia regarded as potentially subversive paradoxically brought them under the immediate control and surveillance of the Third Reich. Threat, pressure and fear sat side by side with a renewed sense of belonging.[31]

In a poetic and reflexive memoire, Helga Griffin, who was brought to Tatura 3 from Persia as a young girl along with her family, devotes three chapters to the camp. In her chapter 'The imaginary homeland', she continues the long dialogue we have been having and contextualises politics inside the family camp within a wider yearning for home and belonging:

> Both our schooling and our social life turned our minds to a *Heimat* (homeland) which most of us had scarcely visited and were perhaps never to see. Perhaps the exaggerated nostalgia of the people in the camp can be explained by the need to preserve an identity at odds with a foreign land, especially as we had no idea what lay beyond our prison ... In the camp my *Heimweh* (longing for home) was directed at Germany, a place I had only visited for the briefest few weeks. I knew

it was a green and pleasant land. My mother's stories of home were reinforced by the rhetoric of our teachers. An imaginary Germany pushed my vivid experience of Iran into the background.[32]

The same was true for the German Lutherans from New Guinea, the women and children who had come via the Barossa, and the male missionaries, who were transferred from the single men's camp to Tatura 3 to join their families. The people in the camp did not hold on to their life prior to internment, be it in Persia, Palestine or New Guinea. They skipped over the lived lives, rhythms and cultures of their diaspora communities and sought to strengthen pre-existing diasporic attempts at staying connected to their origins.

In 1944 many Italians accepted the offer of release from internment on the condition that they enlisted in civilian alien labour corps, mending fences, helping with the harvest, and other such tasks. The Germans in Tatura 1 and 3 collectively refused a similar offer. Instead they reiterated, as they had done before, that they wanted to be repatriated to Germany on the first occasion available. (Only a very small number did not sign this.) The exiled in Tatura 3 established a community with a new purpose, a new dream and destination: the imaginary homeland identified with Germany.

After the capitulation of Germany, however, the unified front fragmented. Most of the Templars from Palestine, a religious German Diaspora group who had settled there in the nineteenth century, sought to remain in Australia. Palestine was unreachable, and Germany was in ruins. The German missionaries from New Guinea, apart from a few who insisted on returning to Germany, changed their minds as well. New Guinea was where they longed to go, to continue their missionary work. The first were allowed back in 1947. Others however, with adverse security service reports on their file, had to wait until 1951, working as farm hands in rural Australia, mending fences and helping with the harvest.

When I first went to the Barossa in 1993 the bus went along winding roads past vineyards stretching over hills, scattered old fruit trees and clustered villages. In Tanunda I was greeted by an elderly couple, German missionaries who had retired to the Barossa. Before taking me to their place, they walked me over the local graveyard as an introduction to the community and a sign of respect. I had walked through a number of graveyards in Australia, but this one – its layout, the gravestones, the care given to the graves – was reminiscent of home. On Sunday I was taken to church and greeted in German by a number of Australians, including one woman who was the daughter of an Australian Lutheran missionary killed in New Guinea during the war while serving as a coast watcher.

For the German evacuees from New Guinea, life in the Barossa during the war was an alienating experience. On one hand, their defiant action of intertwined patriotism and nationalism was a response to their loss of purpose and choice. Keeping the children 'German' became the symbol of a great need for belonging. Hand in hand went a yearning for their men, from whom they were no longer prepared to be separated without the rationale of mission work. It was also genuine support, at least by some, of both National Socialism and the fatherland. On the other hand, when they lined up in front of the Australian officials in December 1942, they also removed themselves from a divided, fragmented community under surveillance. Potentially they were a danger to their hosts, a constant catalyst to an internal debate about heritage, traditions and loyalty which had not ceased since the experiences of the First World War and which had again become passionate and unforgiving during the Second World War. Stolz, who had placed them with Lutheran families, had not understood the sacrifice he demanded of everybody involved. What initially looked like a simple act of care and consideration to fellow Lutherans was, in Reuther's analysis, based on a 'queer concept of loyalty'. Stolz and Theile were naïve and lacked the vision and courage to find a solution. Instead they attempted to sacrifice individuals to the greater good of the church, yearning for cultural and religious continuity at a time when both German and English–Australian identities were intrinsically and inescapably linked to mutually exclusive political identities.

Notes

1   Report 25/8/1942 Lieut. WA. Langford, National Archives of Australia (hereafter NAA) Adelaide, D1915, SA 19706.
2   16/1/1942 W.H. Barnwell, Inquiry Officer, to The Inspector, Commonwealth Investigation Branch, Sydney, NAA Canberra, A518, ED 16/2/1.

3   A. Schuster (NG) 1929; Im fremden Land und doch daheim. Reiseeindrücke während eines 6 wöchigen Aufenthalts in Australien, ALC NG LMF 56/51.
4   7.7.1928 Carl Schneider to D. Rendtorff, Evangelisches Zentralarchiv in Berlin, 5/2871.
5   *Kirchenblatt*, 3 April 1933, vol. 9, no. 7, p. 98.
6   Several versions of this story are in circulation. This one was told to me in the Archives, and I repeat it from memory: Interned during the Second World War, Ludwig Doehler had to leave his frail wife and sick daughter behind where they faced the difficult task of preparing the garden for potato planting. Answering his wife's question whether he knew anybody who could help them, Doehler, in a letter from the internment camp, replied that the garden best be left alone, as he had hidden important documents there. The next day, after a thorough search by security personnel, who had dug up the garden and of course found nothing, Mrs Doehler went and planted the potatoes. For another version see Philip W. Holzknecht, 'A Priesthood of Priests? The German Lutherans in Queensland', Manfred Jurgensen & Alan Corkhill (eds), *The German Presence in Queensland over the Last 150 Years*, Department of German, University of Queensland, St Lucia, 1988, pp. 168ff.
7   The church had two names, United Evangelical Church of Australia (UELCA), and Vereinigte Evangelisch Lutherische Kirche Australiens (VELKA). Correspondence and meetings were partly in German and partly in English. German and English church journals existed.
8   The statistical data have been compiled using details given by T. Hebert, *The United Evangelical Lutheran Church in Australia*, Book Depot, Adelaide, 1938, pp. 303–30.
9   See, for example, Gerhard Fischer, *Enemy Aliens: Internment and the homefront experience in Australia, 1914–1920,* University of Queensland Press, St Lucia, Queensland, 1989; John F. Williams, *German ANZACS and the First World War*, UNSW Press, Sydney, 2003.
10 George Johnston, *New Guinea Diary*, Angus and Robertson, Sydney & London, 1943, p. 55.
11 ibid., p. 56.
12 George Johnston, *War Diary 1942*, Sydney, Collins, 1984, p. 35. For a debate about the public hysteria and an exoneration of the missionaries remaining in New Guinea during the Japanese occupation see Hank Nelson, 'Loyalties at Sword-Point: The Lutheran missionaries in wartime New Guinea, 1939–1945', in *Australian Journal of Politics and History,* vol. 24, no. 2, August 1978, pp. 199–217.
13 11/3/1942 T. Playford, Premier of South Australia to Prime Minister J. Curtin, NAA A518, ED16/2/1.

14 8/5/1942 F.R. Sinclair, Secretary, Department of the Army to the Secretary, Prime Minister's Department, NAA A518, ED16/2/1.
15 25/5/1942 Memorandum Prime Minister's Department 'German evacuee children in South Australia', NAA A518, ED16/2/1.
16 23/5/1942 Imma Zimmermann to The Secretary, Prime Minister's Department, NAA Canberra, A518, ED 16/2/1.
17 6/8/1942 Memorandum for the Secretary, Department of External Territories, NAA Canberra, A518, ED 16/2/1.
18 8/1/1945 F.O. Theile to J.J. Stolz, Lutheran Archives Adelaide, UELCA Correspondence Theile–Stolz.
19 5/8/1942 F.O. Theile to J.J. Stolz, Lutheran Archives Adelaide, UELCA Correspondence Theile–Stolz.
20 2/11/1940 J.J. Stolz to Menzies, Lutheran Archives Adelaide, UELCA Gen. Pres. Office 940.
21 7/8/1942 F.O. Theile to W. Flierl, Internment Camp No. 1A, Tatura, Lutheran Archives Adelaide, UELCA Correspondence Theile–Stolz.
22 22/3/1944 F.O. Theile to J.J. Stolz, Lutheran Archives Adelaide, UELCA Correspondence Theile–Stolz.
23 25/8/1925 Lieutenant W.A. Langford, Dossier 'Enemy alien German female refugees from New Guinea', NAA, SA 19706.
24 ibid.
25 15/2/1943 Clara Hofmann to Halligan, Department of External Territories, NAA Canberra, A518, ED 16/2/1.
26 12/2/1943 Frida Horrolt to the Prime Minister, John Curtin, NAA Canberra, A518, ED 16/2/1.
27 28/6/1943 Else Alt to Brack, NAA Canberra, A518, ED 16/2/1.
28 19/7/1943 Clara Hofmann to Halligan, NAA Canberra, A518, ED 16/2/1.
29 A. Seitz & L. Foster, 'German Nationals in Australia 1939–1947: Internment, forced migration and/or social control', *Journal of Intercultural Studies*, 1989, vol. 10, no. 1, pp. 13–31.
30 H. Griffin, *Sing me that lovely song again*, Canberra, Pandanus Books, 2006, p. 102.
31 See C. Winter, 'The Long Arm of the Third Reich: Internment of New Guinea Germans in Tatura', *The Journal of Pacific History*, vol. 38, no. 1, 2003, p. 85–108.
32 Griffin 2006, p. 127.

The educator
Karl Mützelfeldt

Volker Stolle

Karl Mützelfeldt arrived in Adelaide with his family on 5 August 1934. There he was received with great acclaim: 'We regard Reverend Mützelfeldt as a real gift of God to our Church and are sure that our expectations will not lack fulfilment', proclaimed Dr Johannes Stolz (1878–1962), the General President of the United Evangelical Lutheran Church in Australia (UELCA), into whose service the pastor now entered.[1] With his help – and as Mützelfeldt himself hoped – the German language and tradition within this church was to be given new strength.

Mützelfeldt had felt forced to leave Germany because his understanding of *Deutschtum* ('Germanness', but perhaps best translated as 'German culture and identity') was at odds with the ideology of National Socialism. He hoped that in overseas German Lutheran communities he would be able to continue to observe his beliefs and pass them on to his children.

It was because he considered himself to be German that he chose the path of emigration. He was at odds with the new National Socialist or Nazi state as a result of the passing of new laws in two ways. First of all, in his view the future of his children was compromised, because, on the basis of having a Jewish maternal grandfather, they were now regarded as partly 'non-Aryan'. And, secondly, Mützelfeldt felt he could not meet the requirement imposed on him as a school principal that he 'support the national state without reservation and at all times'. How had it come to this?

Life and work in Germany
Karl Mützelfeldt came from a Lutheran pastor's family. When

he was born on 30 April 1881 in Hermannsburg, his father was inspector at the missionary seminary there, and he was actively involved in the training of missionaries.

After his school education Mützelfeldt studied theology and philosophy. Having passed his first theology exam in 1907, he did not enter the preparatory service for a career in the church, choosing instead the path of teaching. He became a teacher at the Evangelisches Pädagogium in Bad Godesberg, a private school for boys with a clear *reformist* approach. He subsequently continued his studies and, after successfully completing the exams for a state diploma in education (in the subjects religion, philosophy and Hebrew), he was appointed to the position of Senior Teacher of Religion at the school where he already worked.

What distinguished this time in Bad Godesberg was Mützelfeldt's work in the *Keplerbund* (Kepler League), a body which had been formed in 1907 that held the conviction 'that the truth bears within itself the harmony of scientific facts alongside philosophical awareness and religious experience'. Through his authorship of a pamphlet titled 'Allerlei Missbrauch der Naturwissenschaft'[2] ('Various Abuses of the Natural Sciences'), he signalled his opposition to the rise of a materialistic world view. As early as in this work he expressed convictions that were to lead him later to reject the Nazi doctrine of race.

In the autumn of 1913 he transferred to the Städtisches Oberlyzeum in Düsseldorf, a school for girls with an attached college for the training of women teachers for high schools. His work here was interrupted by the First World War and on the fourth day of the war he was deployed to the Western front. He was awarded the Iron Cross First Class and Second Class and before his discharge had entered the officer ranks. A sermon he delivered during the war gives an indication of his patriotism: in a situation in which his homeland on earth appears far away and perhaps beyond reach, he stresses the certainty of heaven as one's final destination, but he also keeps in view the temporal perspective of Germany's calling in this world. After the war, too, Mützelfeldt continued to be guided decisively by his sense of national identity, even if he had been greatly disappointed by the outcome of the war and its consequences.

From the beginning of October 1923 he was appointed Director of the Secondary Lyceum at the Institute for Deaconesses in Kaiserswerth, a position for which he felt ideally suited. The education system in Kaiserswerth was in a state of acute crisis when he took up his position, with its financial foundations having been eaten away by inflation. Furthermore, the education system, directed as it was toward preparing female students for jobs considered appropriate for women, experienced massive turmoil in the conditions which prevailed in the Weimar Republic, when identical standards of education for girls and boys were demanded. Previously the higher education of women had been the domain of the social work of churches. And, compounding this, Kaiserswerth was located in the area which was occupied by allied troops whose role it was to ensure that Germany made its reparations payments. Mützelfeldt quite consciously formed a link with the Kaiserswerth tradition as articulated in the motto: 'You have just one Lord: Christ'. He devoted himself with great energy to renewal in both the curriculum and administration. With clear goals in mind he successfully built up the institution in a new style as a Protestant denominational school. At the same time he was responsible for the overall administration of Kaiserswerth's extensive school system.

The convictions which guided him through this period are articulated in his programmatic publication of the 1925 work *Evangelisches Führertum und höhere Schule: Ein Weckruf an die deutsche evangelische Christenheit*[3] (*Protestant Leadership and Secondary Education: An alarm call to German Protestant Christendom*). He recognised in the new conditions of the Republic a weakness of Protestant Christendom, evinced by its apparent shortage of 'personalities who in our spiritual and cultural life can somehow really play a leading role'. He proclaimed: 'Our Protestant Church thus has a pressing need, indeed it is a matter of its continuing influence on the German people, *to develop a leadership with firm roots in the gospel*. For this reason we need Protestant personalities in education, we need distinctively Protestant high schools.' In this belief he was being guided not by a desire to strengthen a particular denominationalism, but rather by a general interest in the German people. 'We hope that the keenly desired solid community of the people (*Volksgemeinschaft*) might be able gradually to bring us closer to a spiritual unity. We believe that such an essentially German community of the people can grow only on the foundations of a national rebirth determined by Christian values. The school should help us toward this goal!'

In order to broaden the impact of his ideas, Mützelfeldt dedicated himself intensively to constructing and implementing the administrative framework for the school system. He became the President both of the *Vereinigung positiver evangelischer Religionslehrer an höheren Schulen* (Association of Positive Protestant Teachers of Religion in High Schools) and of the *Vereinigung privater evangelischer Mädchenschulen* (Association of Private Protestant Girls' Schools, which from 1926 was the *Bund evangelischer Mädchenschulen* or Federation of Protestant Girls' Schools). In addition, he played a leading role in the umbrella organisation *Evangelische Schulvereinigung* (Protestant School Association). At this time girls' schools were placed on the same footing as that of boys' schools, a move which brought with it a greater state influence on this type of school – previously within the domain of the church. Consequently, much depended on the energetic representation of the interests of private Protestant schools. With the assistance of others Mützelfeldt also founded the specialist journal *Schule und Evangelium* (*School and Gospel*) and edited the *Evangelische Religionsbuch für höhere Schule* (*Book of the Protestant Religion for High Schools*). Moreover, he took a lively interest in discussions concerning state curricula.

As for politics, Mützelfeldt became active in the *Deutschnationale Volkspartei* (German National People's Party or DNVP). The policies of this national conservative party largely corresponded with Mützelfeldt's Christian-influenced nationalism. Nevertheless, in its political practice the DNVP was susceptible to anti-Semitic and National Socialist ideas. From the very beginning, however, Mützelfeldt developed, on the basis of his resolutely Christian attitudes, strong reservations about National Socialism, whose totalitarian claims left little space for a committed Christian upbringing.

On 28 August 1909 Mützelfeldt married Gertrud Herzfeld, who had been born in Stuttgart on 14 May 1886. She too had grown up in a self-consciously German and Christian family. However, her father, Bruno Herzfeld (1855–1930) was a Jew who, after marrying a Christian, fully embraced the Protestant faith.

In the year Hitler came to power, 1933, the children born into the Mützelfeldt family, namely, Hanna, Elfriede, Bruno and Dorothea were 21, 18, 15 and three years of age respectively. The 'First Decree for the Implementation of the Law for the Restoration of the Civil Service (7 April 1933)', which came into effect on 11 April 1933, stated: 'Those who are descended from non-Aryan, in particular from Jewish, parents or grandparents, are to be regarded as non-Aryan. It suffices if just one parent or grandparent is non-Aryan.' For the Mützelfeldt children this meant that a career in the public service was closed to them, but subsequently their chances of studying or receiving higher education were severely compromised with the passing of the 'Law Against the Overfilling of German Schools and Universities' on 25 April 1933.

Emigration
After the end of Nazi rule Mützelfeldt recalled: 'I can still remember clearly the moment when I read about the establishment of the Gestapo. At that moment I felt almost instinctively that in a state of such arbitrariness there would be little room to operate.' The principle which he followed from the beginning he later articulated in the following way: 'Principiis obsta! Resist from the very beginning! Unconditional loyalty towards a country, a government, or a person, as it for example was demanded for Hitler in an oath of allegiance from public servants, can only end in idolatry.' From very early on in their regime the new rulers had him in their sights. He was spied upon and persecuted.

After the introduction of the 'Aryan Paragraph', contained within the 'Law for the Restoration of the Civil Service', and after his most intensive efforts, Mützelfeldt also recognised that his children were unlikely to be granted exceptional status. 'My wife on many occasions confronted the danger of a complete psychological breakdown, and I do not need to tell you how things were under the surface for my adult children,' he reported in the summer of 1933 to a friend from his student days. He saw no alternative but to emigrate with his family. As his destination Mützelfeldt envisaged one of the overseas German Lutheran communities of the kind that existed in

North America, South America, South Africa and Australia, where Lutheran Churches with a German character had been established by immigrants.

Friedrich Ulmer (1877–1946), Professor of Practical Theology in Erlangen and at the same time President of the Martin Luther Federation, an aid agency for minority Lutheran churches in a non-Protestant environment, interceded on his behalf and wrote a letter of recommendation to President Stolz of the United Evangelical Lutheran Church of Australia. For its part UELCA saw in Mützelfeldt's enquiry 'clearly a gift from God to our Church'. For some time the organisation had been looking for a man of Mützelfeldt's qualifications to build up its church education system. At the time the church was in the process of introducing a two-year preliminary course at the seminary and engaged Mützelfeldt primarily as a lecturer for this course. This was despite the costs that would be incurred, which they justified in the tight financial situation only with the 'courage of faith' and in the hope that by expanding their offerings they would gain more students.

In a letter which reached Mützelfeldt on 11 December 1933, General President Stolz, while accepting Mützelfeldt's application for the position, described frankly the straitened circumstances in Adelaide: 'If after receiving the description of our smallness and modesty it still appeals to you to come then we would welcome your coming with great joy and regard you as a gift to our Church by God ... who made this gift to us in such a special way through the great political events.'

Mützelfeldt was happy 'that [he had] received the call to Australia, not only as a Lutheran but expressly as a German, of whom it is expected that [he] will maintain, cultivate and expand the German cultural heritage'. He accepted the appointment immediately.

Mützelfeldt submitted his resignation, his position formally ending on 31 March 1934, and began to prepare for emigration. Bearing in mind that in Australia he was to be employed in the education of pastors, he then completed his own theological training, which he had interrupted in 1907 after his first theological exam. He passed his second theological exam and was ordained on 13 May. After 'thoroughly tedious negotiations with the authorities'

Karl Mützelfeldt and his family soon after their arrival in Australia.
(Lutheran Archives Adelaide)

concerning emigration, the Mützelfeldt family was able to board the Norddeutscher-Lloyd freighter *Witram* in Bremen on 11 June, bound for Australia via the Cape of Good Hope.

On the day of his departure he recorded in his sister's guest book the question, 'Will it [that is, Australia] become a new homeland for us after our old, much-loved fatherland can no longer offer us an honourable place to live?' He provided an answer to that question 12 years later when he wrote in a letter to his sister on 2 July 1946: 'God has allowed me to find in a land of freedom not just refuge but a new homeland'.

Mützelfeldt saw the path he trod as already decided for all those people who, like his family, were affected by the racial laws. From the outset Mützelfeldt's efforts to seek a future overseas for his own family were, for that reason, closely linked to his dogged commitment to establishing an aid office for other German Protestants affected by racial policy, so that emigration would be made easier.

As early as in summer of 1933 he demanded: 'The Protestant Churches *must* in some way support these poor, innocent Protestant "Non-Aryans" who in countless cases have fallen into spiritual and in some cases the most acute material need. That is the most pressing social task!'

He attempted to win broader church support for his endeavours. He expanded contact with the German branch of the Moravian Church, an organisation called the *Deutsche Brüder-Unität* which was prepared to assist through the establishment of special homes. On 11 November 1933, in a meeting held in the Reich Church Office, Mützelfeldt presented his suggestion that the *Deutsche Evangelische Kirche* (DEK, the German Evangelical Church) set up a specialist agency with the task of solving problems caused by the situation confronting Christians of Jewish descent. He nominated three practical fields of activity for the proposed Church agency:

1. Special boarding schools, for example in cooperation with the Moravian Church, for Protestant children of non-Aryan Descent,

2. A limited employment service for those non-Aryan whose commitment to a Protestant world-view was beyond question,

3. Arrangement of settlement possibilities, for example in South America.

At the end of 1933 he learned of a similar initiative by the Berlin gynaecologist Dr Karl August Fiessler, in whom he found a partner with whom he could work. In April of 1934 he reported to the Church Office of the DEK that plans would soon be approved by the Reich Interior Ministry. He expected that the State of Prussia would make space available for settler schools. The intention was to form a working group titled *Christliches Jugendwerk für deutsche Auslandssiedlung* (Christian Youth Service for German Overseas Settlement) after permission had been gained from the state.

When Mützelfeldt left Germany in June 1934 he was assuming with confidence that the initiative being pursued would soon be realised. In reality, things by no means developed as favourably as Mützelfeldt had expected. Because so many different interests had to be accommodated, negotiations went on and on, with the project ultimately relying on the favourable convergence of foreign policy, interior policy and educational and financial concerns. Realisation was continually delayed until, at the beginning of 1936, it was abandoned altogether.

Impact in Australia

Mützelfeldt emphasised 'that in our decision to leave Germany the thought of our children's future was paramount'. Yet the educational and career prospects for the children in Australia were not particularly favourable, although ultimately all the children made their way. Even before the war the family made an application for naturalisation, which was suspended after the outbreak of war. Gertrud Mützelfeldt died, at the age of just 57, on 2 November 1943.

Although hard of hearing as a result of an injury incurred in the First World War, Karl Mützelfeldt was able to make a substantial impact in Australia, as he had in Germany. His first task was to establish the two-year preliminary seminary program conducted at Immanuel Seminary. In the UELCA education system this course was positioned between college and the main seminary at North Adelaide, and its function was to impart the basic knowledge required for theological training at the seminary but also, and above all, to teach a detailed knowledge of German history and literature – in German. At the seminary itself most of the teaching was done in German. In the following year Mützelfeldt participated in the teaching program at Immanuel Seminary. He took over Biblical history, Old Testament exegesis, philosophy and, in particular, the teaching of the catechism. Despite his hearing difficulties, he managed the adjustment to teaching in English in 1943 in response to student demands. He retired in 1953. Although he did not come to Australia until the advanced age of 53, his work at Immanuel Seminary in Adelaide spanned a longer period (19 years) than his employment at Kaiserswerth (just over 10 years). Mützelfeldt died on 30 November 1955.

Mützelfeldt's particular task – and at the same time that closest to his heart – was the maintenance and cultivation of German culture, which to a significant degree had long been suppressed by the dominance of English language. He devoted himself to this task with great commitment, although he was immediately aware of the difficulties, to which he gave considerable thought. The language problem, he reported back to Germany, was 'a very fundamental aspect of the basically very baffling lives of Germans in foreign countries.' The youth converted 'with a rather rapid tempo to the English language', with German could only being maintained in a bilingual context. The practice of speaking German was largely confined to church life since immigrants had not brought with them the written language of New High German but rather various dialects. Moreover, the German typescript made language learning more difficult (since in those times German was in most cases not yet written with Latin letters).

> Now I am attempting through my whole approach to teaching to awaken joy in the German language and German culture, and where possible also a little pride in the German cultural heritage, at least a serious sense of responsibility for the preservation and rejuvenation of the heritage passed on by the German forefathers who immigrated. And it appears that I have found receptive hearts and minds. To provide this service for the Australian Lutheran Church and at the same time for the fatherland is a great joy for me and my family, because all of us have this goal, everyone in his own way.

This commitment seemed important to him, because it was his firm belief that there was a close connection between Lutheranism and German culture. He was of the view that the future of the Lutheran Church in Australia depended on the preservation of the German language. In the 1930s he further consolidated his views with the argument that a world war was inevitable, and that in the aftermath of it many German Lutherans would flee to Australia; consequently, the Lutheran Church would have to be equipped to integrate these immigrants into their congregations.

The issue of preserving the German language within the Australian Lutheran Church was analysed in detail by Mützelfeldt in an essay he wrote for a *Festschrift* dedicated to Professor Ulmer on his sixtieth birthday in 1936. On the basis of the historical background of church statistics on the proportional usage of German and English in church work and of his own experiences and observations, he paints a detailed picture of the 'unavoidable process of anglicisation' and indicates what conscious efforts, adapted to the great variety of circumstances, were necessary to preserve a place for the German language.

In this regard he considered it essential to clarify the exact nature of the relationship between German culture and the Lutheran Church. The Lutheran Church could not be perceived to be limited to any one nation; rather, the 'awakening of a feeling of solidarity in world Lutheranism' had to be embraced with determination in order to counter the danger of 'a certain Australian particularism'. Mützelfeldt drew attention to the fact that, in 1935, the United Evangelical Lutheran Church of Australia joined not only the Lutheran World Convention (LWC), the forerunner of the Lutheran World Federation (LWF), but also the Martin Luther Federation, the goal being to serve the multilingual community of the Lutheran churches – as had been done in Australia among the Estonian community in Sydney and the missions to the Aborigines of central Australia. Equally important was retaining an association 'with the wealthy spiritual and intellectual stream flowing from the Lutheran Mother Church in Germany'.

Moreover, it was absolutely necessary, Mützelfeldt argued, 'to clarify the difference between allegiance to a state and ethnic identity in all respects, including theological aspects'. Apart from the linguistic dimension of German culture, he also dealt, at least in passing, with issues of customs. He was motivated by the idea of 'creating for Lutherans in the southern hemisphere Church practices which are appropriate to the climatic and other features of the country, which at the same time would have to reflect the depth and intensity of the German temperament'.

The extent to which he devoted himself to this issue is evident. His concern with the actual circumstances in which overseas Germans lived in Australia led Mützelfeldt to reflect more deeply on his own ideas and convictions. To some extent this process of intellectual deliberation was overtaken by the tumultuous political developments, which ran contrary to any consolidation of German culture in Australia, especially as after the outbreak of the war any open efforts in this direction could raise suspicions of collaboration with the enemy, and so became impossible.

Although Mützelfeldt's children had grown up entirely with the German language, Mützelfeldt became aware just how strongly the new environment influenced even them. 'How infinitely difficult it is to maintain the German tongue with the children, who otherwise speak only English. One can appreciate this only if one has experienced it with one's own children. Every day new efforts are required, along with dogged consistency and conscious teaching.'

In the Mützelfeldt family the children often spoke German with their parents, especially with their father in his last years, but among themselves they spoke English.

Moreover, there was little Mützelfeldt could do to separate his efforts for German language and culture from its political connotations, as the following episode illustrates. In 1935 he received an official request from the German Consul General in Sydney to consult with him regarding the plan to establish a German–Australian college. Mützelfeldt was delighted that a representative of the German Reich wanted to accept his help in this matter, so he travelled to Sydney and thereafter submitted a memorandum, not realising that by doing so he had supported the policies of Hitler's Germany, promoting its ideas and goals overseas. However, it must be said that the Nazi Party, for its part, had not even been requested his assistance. When the party's Foreign Organisation, the AO, examined the initiative, he was categorised as an 'enemy of the state of the highest order', and the project failed.

By emigrating to Australia, Mützelfeldt had by no means left his confrontation with National Socialism behind. As it happened, the attention of Hitler himself had been drawn to Mützelfeldt's fate, as the German–American Marie Gallison-Reuter, herself an alumna of Kaiserswerth, reports in her recollections of a conversation she had with Hitler.[4] Immediately upon Mützelfeldt's arrival in Adelaide someone let him know – in German – that he was still under surveillance by the Nazi Party. Refusing to be intimidated, he received a group of musicians called the Comedy Harmonists in his house, a group that had been formed by the Jewish members of the Comedian Harmonists, who under pressure from the Reich Music Chamber were expelled from Germany and forced into emigration. In 1937 and 1939 the new version of the group made successful tours of Australia.

Apart from his teaching activity, Mützelfeldt also undertook a full travelling program of teaching and lecturing. In doing so he participated assiduously and willingly in the church life of the United Evangelical Lutheran Church of Australia. One important aspect of this was his promotion of a reinvigorated parish school system.

A law had forced the closure of all its parish schools in 1917, but in 1924 the UELCA regained the right to maintain private church schools, and from 1929 became entitled to teach the German language to a small extent, although initially for not more than one hour per day. Parish schools such as these could not expect to receive any kind of state subsidy; the financial burden had to be carried entirely by private interests, while the state school system of course imposed no fees. At the time Mützelfeldt arrived in Australia, not even one new parish school had been established. Mützelfeldt now set about translating the recently achieved rights into practical reality.

From the beginning an important element of his thinking was the idea that, in the areas where the Lutheran parishes were in close proximity to each other (in the Barossa Valley and further to the north), 'German could be maintained or revived as the everyday language'. At the same time he conceded that: 'The maintenance of German culture is not the reason for Church schools – the reason is to be found solely in the realm of religion', but it was certainly valid 'to preserve the heritage of the fathers and if possible to bring it to bear once more'. He developed a program based on his educational convictions and which was designed to accommodate Australian conditions.

In a 1936 synod lecture, 'Why Christian Day Schools?', he offered an explanation for his belief in the necessity for Christian schools, which assumes that a deficient sense of humanity is inherent to the secular school. For that reason a Christian school was necessary. 'The Word of God must really rule in the school, and Jesus Christ must really be her Lord in all things, so that not only all the teaching, but also the expression of the school-life, down to the last detail, must be permeated by a Christian spirit.' He reminded his audience of their duty to educate, a duty that God had given parents, and the possibility available through the parish for acting communally. It is noteworthy that there is now no longer a role for German as the language of instruction or as a subject for parish schools, and the idea of national solidarity with the German people is not even touched upon.

In 1935 the Light Pass parish opened the first UELCA parish school; Tanunda–Langmeil and Appila followed. Further schools were constructed, although by the time of Mützelfeldt's retirement, the total number of students had only reached just 260. Greater support was not achieved until later.

In 1938 Mützelfeldt was also able to introduce special training for parish school teachers, even if the numbers were small; in that year, just one student, in 1941, four, with 10 in 1947, of whom four participated by correspondence.

Mützelfeldt was a member of the Intersynodical Committee, which in 1941 commenced a lengthy process of discussion of several doctrinal positions that until that time had divided the two Lutheran churches in Australia, namely, the United Evangelical Lutheran Church and the Evangelical Lutheran Church of Australia (ELSA). These negotiations prepared the way for the amalgamation of the two churches, one characterised by close connections with German Lutheranism and one with American Lutheranism. During the time of this process ELSA changed its name in 1944 to the Evangelical Lutheran Church of Australia (ELCA). These negotiations, which experienced a decisive breakthrough in 1949, are manifested in the comprehensive *Theses of Agreement* document finally published in 1956. Another German played a significant role on this path to mutual understanding, namely, Professor Dr Hermann Sasse (1895–1976),[5] who came to Australia in 1949 and who taught at the same seminary as Mützelfeldt. In 1966 the unification of what is today the Lutheran Church of Australia was completed. Mützelfeldt's initiative in founding all-day schools had contributed to the amalgamation of the two churches, as had his suggestion to commence the training of deaconesses, which was agreed in 1947, the first course for which began in 1961. In both these areas ELSA/ELCA had been more advanced, but by the time of unification UELCA had also made considerable progress.

In February 1938 Mützelfeldt reported to the pastors' conference held in South Australia on the plight of the 'non-Aryans' in Germany, on queries he himself had received and on an aid society which had already been founded. A month later Stolz informed the equivalent committee in New South Wales about the 'German Emergency Fellowship Committee' (GEFC) and encouraged collaboration in a sub-committee which had been formed in South Australia. The Fellowship Committee had been founded in December 1937 in Sydney at the instigation of the anthropologist Camilla Wedgwood (1901–55) and had links to a Quaker-organised central agency in London called the 'German Emergency Committee of the Society of Friends', an organisation devoted specifically to helping 'non-Aryan' Christians. The 'Lutheran Immigration Aid Society' (LIAS) was then established as a branch of it. Apart from Mützelfeldt, the General President of UELCA, Stolz, and two teachers at Immanuel College were committee members – G.A. Keller, who was the chair, with Mr Doecke the treasurer. A partnership developed between LIAS, the Berlin aid office run by Laura Livingstone and the 'Pastor Grüber Office', also in Berlin. At the beginning of November the Lutheran Immigration Aid Society gratefully acknowledged the cooperation of the Council of Churches, at the time Mützelfeldt also seeking to gain support in England and from ELSA. This contact was the source of the press release by the General President of ELSA, Dr William Janzow, of 17 November 1938, which led to the arrival of 73 letters pleading for assistance.

The process was extremely protracted. When a request from overseas was received by LIAS, the first step was to attempt to find employment in Australia for the applicant. If that were achieved, the applicant had to be informed and, at the same time, an application for an immigration permit sent to the Australian Government in Canberra. In most cases the required landing money (£200) also had to be found. Once the landing permit was finally issued by the government authorities, it had to be sent to the applicant. All of this consumed a great deal of time. However, beginning the journey to Australia immediately was still impossible, because in many cases a passage by ship had to be booked months in advance. Consequently, not only the refugee but also his prospective new employer was subjected to a test of patience with an uncertain outcome.

The Lutheran Immigration Aid Society reported continuously on the steps required, the progress made, its mode of operation, the requests received, offers of employment, immigration permits, arrivals in Australia and letters of gratitude in both the English-language magazine of UELCA, the *Lutheran Herald*, and in the German language *Kirchen-Blatt*. The reports in both publications were largely identical, but as no names were mentioned, it is not possible to know personal fates. Even the numbers cited do not allow firm conclusions, because the periods referred to are not known. For example, in a report from 16 January 1939 it is stated: 'The LIAS is dealing at present with over fifty cases. Of these there are several family cases ... Three young persons are expected to leave during this month; five are on their way.'

These reports were always accompanied by fresh appeals for collaboration and support in the form of offers of employment, donations and loans and became ever more urgent as the situation in Germany for those hoping to leave the country deteriorated steadily. At the end of September 1938 it was reported: 'Father Bodelschwingh once said, "Hurry up, brethren, otherwise they will die" ... This applies here.' In November 1938 the request was underlined with the well-known words of Jesus, 'Inasmuch as ye have done it unto one of the least of these my brethren, ye have done it unto me (Matthew 25: 40)'. In early 1939, by citing the words of Jesus, 'I was a prisoner and ye came unto me' (Matthew 25: 36), attention was drawn to a string of cases in which the prospect of emigration would mean liberation from a concentration camp.

It is possible to retrace in some detail the fate of Horst Salomon, who died in 1994. From a Berlin Jewish family, he was brought up as a Christian and sent as a schoolboy initially to Denmark. When he was not able to remain there, he managed, with the assistance of GEFC and LIAS, to come to Australia, where he lived in Adelaide under the care of Mützelfeldt, until the latter arranged for him to be sent to a farm in the vicinity of Kadina on the Yorke Peninsula. After a few months his brother Ernst followed. The rather miserable conditions on the farm persuaded Horst Salomon to turn to Mützelfeldt, who encouraged him to persevere so as not to jeopardise assistance for others who might still be rescued from concentration camps. After the outbreak of war the young man applied in vain to join the army; he was subsequently employed in the armaments industry. For a time he was held by the authorities and interned until, finally, with his brother Ernst, he was allocated to a non-combatant logistics unit. They were accused of disloyalty because they were Germans. After the war Horst Salomon became a successful businessman.[6]

The work structures adopted by LIAS were very informal. Horst Salomon later recalled that Mützelfeldt had said to him: 'The

Lutheran Immigration Society is me'. This low level of organisation did however allow, in cooperation with the larger and more professional networks, an effective system of aid for 'non-Aryan' Lutherans in the period 1938–39, acting subsequently as a catalyst for a wide-ranging program of assistance for Jews. Nonetheless, a revival after the war along the lines suggested by Alfred Freund-Zinnbauer – in this instance no longer applied to immigrants of Jewish ancestry – did not take place.[7]

By organising aid packages for Germany after the war, Mützelfeldt helped to reduce privation among his family and his former colleagues. The deaconess Luise Fliedner, who lived through this period and who had succeeded Mützelfeldt as a director of the Theodor Fliedner School in Kaiserswerth, recalled: 'The postal services had only just recommenced when a stream of packages of gifts arrived here; they came from the Mützelfeldt household and from the most varied sources from within the Lutheran World Federation and were addressed to his friends at the school, to former colleagues, students, to those who had cared for his family in times of sickness, and they were a welcome relief in times of scarcity and need.'

People and faith

Mützelfeldt came to Australia with quite specific expectations. He wanted above all to continue the life's work he had begun in Germany, but under changed circumstances. As an educator, he pursued the goal of working 'to affirm community and promote the people's wellbeing'. He approved a 'national state', in which 'the development of the individual's personality is limited only by the needs and wellbeing of the people as a whole' and which by renouncing 'internationalism and pacifism' gains living space for its people, by force if necessary. However, at the same time he rejected biologically based racial thinking.

Mützelfeldt had an unbounded admiration for the German people, shaped as they were by Christianity, and in particular by Lutheranism. He understood Catholicism as a competitor, if not a rival. Because he understood German culture and Protestant Christianity to be so tightly interwoven, he recognised that National Socialism's racial thinking was based on a materialistic world view.

Because of his philosophical approach, Mützelfeldt saw Judaism and German culture as clearly separate cultural and religious entities. In Mützelfeldt's view a Jew who followed the Christian faith had abandoned Judaism and become a member of a different community of people. It seemed to him that, by accepting the Christian faith, the previous Jewish identity was extinguished. Consequently, through his commitment to 'Christian non-Aryans' Mützelfeldt wanted to help a particular group of *Germans*. It cannot be regarded as a commitment to Jews.

He consistently made it his goal to preserve German culture among the 'non-Aryan' or not entirely 'Aryan' Christians in Germany by seeking to integrate them into the community of overseas Germans, in particular by strengthening and maintaining the German roots of the Protestant Church overseas. He himself provided a model in this regard. He did not question the fundamental value of the German character and spoke of 'my Germany beloved above all else, to which in all circumstances I shall remain forever true'.

However, his battle to maintain in an interconnected relationship the values of both – that is, the Lutheran faith and German language and culture – led him in reality to relativise German culture. He confessed: 'For me and my thinking on the Church it has become a matter of crucial significance that through God's wonderful leadership I am genuinely able to experience the ecumenical character of the Lutheran Church'. He does not appear to have followed further any paths towards a critical reconsideration of this. Nevertheless, the negative attitude towards everything English which grew out of his own national consciousness lost significance in the face of the practical circumstances with which he was confronted. And in his lecture 'Church and State', which he gave in 1946, he dealt with this topic without in any way enlarging on the notion of a community of the people encompassing all cultural, religious and social life. Rather, the starting point is an open society; the national idea no longer has a role.

Mützelfeldt's son Bruno (1918–2002) followed in his father's footsteps, going some distance further. Having married Helene Maria, the daughter of President Stolz, in 1947 he became pastor at the government migrant centre at Bonegilla, where by the following year there were more than a thousand Lutherans. Later – from 1961 to 1980 – he was director of the Lutheran World Service in Geneva, a department of the Lutheran World Federation.

The German sensibility which had meant so much to Karl Mützelfeldt did not prevent him from devoting himself fully and absolutely to the life of the church and to tackling actual everyday needs pragmatically. Thus he performed an enduring service for the Lutheran Church in Australia by helping it to integrate more strongly and to develop its Lutheran identity independently from its German and American roots. In this regard he proved himself to be a gifted teacher and educator who promoted his students' development not by imposing his own convictions upon them but rather by encouraging them to think independently. Through the lively manner of his teaching, by which he encouraged his students' enthusiasm for their subject, he made a lasting impression on the next generation. On the fiftieth anniversary of his death a group of former students gathered in his memory.

Translated by Peter Monteath

Notes

1 This chapter draws primarily from material held in private, church and state archives. A detailed presentation of these sources may be found in my book, *'Den christlichen Nichariern nimmt man alles': Der evangelische Pädagoge Karl Mützelfeldt angesichts der NS-Rassenpolitik*, LIT Verlag, Berlin, 2007.
2 Karl Mützelfeldt, 'Allerlei Missbrauch der Naturwissenschaft', *Schriften des Keplerbundes* 4, Naturwissenschaftlicher Verlag, Godesberg, 1909.
3 Karl Mützelfeldt, *Evangelisches Führertum und höhere Schule: Ein Weckruf an die deutsche evangelische Christenheit*, Wichern Verlag, Berlin, 1925.
4 Marie Gallison-Reuter, *Mein Leben in zwei Welten*, Eugen Salzer Verlag, Heilbronn, 1950, pp. 273–5. Hitler's response, as the author notes in her memoirs, was that he became 'more and more agitated', so she changed the topic.
5 See Ronald Raymond Feuerhahn, *Hermann Sasse as an Ecumenical Churchman*, rev. edn, Cambridge, Mass., 1994.
6 Salomon's reminiscences on his immigrant experiences are recorded in an interview given to Anthony Kaukas in 1983 ('Horst Salomon, 1920–1994, Immigrant's experiences: Extract from oral history', State Library of South Australia, OH 347/2/).

7   The Austrian pastor Alfred Freund-Zinnbauer, himself regarded in Germany as 'non-Aryan' because of his Jewish family, and his wife Helga came to Australia with the aid of Pastor Stolz and UELCA. They did not arrive until February 1940, after the outbreak of war. Interned some months later for most of the war, Freund-Zinnbauer devoted much of his energy after the war to helping migrants in Adelaide. See the contribution by Peter Monteath in this volume, also Erna Mayer-Lange, *Niemand hat grössere Liebe: Pastor Alfred Freund-Zinnbauer: Eine biographische Zusammenstellung aus persönlich Erlebtem, Dokumenten und Berichten von Zeitgenossen*, Lutheran Publishing House, Adelaide, 1989; Margaret Rilett, *And You Took Me In: Alfred and Helga Freund-Zinnbauer*, Lutheran Publishing House, Adelaide, 1992.

Hermann Sasse's way
Scholar, churchman, immigrant

Maurice Schild

Lutheran theologian and church historian Hermann Sasse worked in Germany for the larger part of his life. Then, in 1949, with his wife and two sons, he migrated to Adelaide, teaching theology here for a full 20 years. Motives for this transfer from Erlangen University were primarily religious and theological. It is intriguing in this context, and particularly from a South Australian angle, to note that in some ways the Sasse story fits neatly into the pattern set by the earliest Lutheran migrant groups from Germany to the state a century earlier. They initiated or entered a free-church scene here, having left behind the state-church landscape of the Prussian Union (in which Sasse also grew up). Like them he took on the long diagonal journey across the world, moved by conviction and understanding.

Hermann Sasse was born in 1895 at Sonnewalde, a town south-east of Berlin, in the province of Lusatia. His father was a pharmacist. During the course of Hermann's secondary education the family moved to the capital. At university he studied philology and theology. Adolf von Harnack, a figure of Goethean stature and appreciated as such by Sasse,[1] was perhaps the most famous of all his teachers, but, along with Ernst Troeltsch, Reinhold Seeberg, Julius Kaftan, and Ulrich von Wilamowitz-Moellendorff, his star-studded Berlin university scene included the initiator of the 'Luther renaissance', Karl Holl, whom Sasse regarded as perhaps the greatest of all church historians.[2] He wrote his licentiate/doctoral dissertation for Adolf Deissmann, a well-connected and ecumenically active New Testament scholar, archaeologist, and author of the internationally regarded biblical work, *Light from the East*. By that time, however, the First World War had interrupted his studies.

Passchendaele to Bethel Confession

'And then we went up to Passchendaele', he was to write later.[3] It was the school of war, he said, that taught him 'practical theology' (otherwise often a somewhat tame church-domestic discipline in faculty curricula of the time).[4] At Passchendaele colonials and Germans met in horrific combat and slaughter. Les Carlyon records the Canadian official historian writing: 'It is not too much to compare the Canadian troops struggling forward, the pangs of hell wracking their bodies, up the Ridge, their dying eyes set upon the summit, with a Man who once crept another hill, with agony in soul and body, to redeem the world and give Passchendaele its glorious name'. After later battles there, an Australian, a Lieutenant Lawrence, wrote to his mother that 'the Germans had recently made thirteen attacks on the front', and that on this occasion Australian machine gunners 'piled them up and piled them up'.[5] Many lessons for life were learned by those who escaped death in the field there. In what was to be perhaps the last essay of his life, 'Ten Years after the Council', Sasse described the wisdom of Pope John XXIII with obvious empathy: 'It was the practical wisdom of a man who has shared the life of the simple soldiers in the barracks, where you learn to know men, and on the battlefields, where you see the crude realities of this world'.[6] Sasse was one of the six men of his company of 150 to survive the carnage.

Hermann Sasse's lectures in church history frequently evinced an almost uncanny grasp of the significance of events going well beyond their mere factuality. The young candidate for the ministry would have perceived how a new period began with that war, one that was 'incredibly unlike anything that had gone before, an era of vast and growing uncertainties, of change on every side of life escalating with every decade, of the conquest of society by technology, of the diminution of Europe, of the political expansion of Marxism'.[7]

Upon ordination in 1920, the young pastor worked in Templin and the Oranienburg parish at Berlin, becoming, in addition, social

Photo of Hermann Sasse. (The author)

pastor (*Sozialpfarrer*) for the city. Daily exposure to harsh and worsening economic and societal realities, culminating in the Great Depression (1929–34), became an integral part of his life experience. It undoubtedly conditioned his understanding of working-class people and of unionism and Marxism. Yet even in those years Berlin meant more than misery. As Rudolf Alexander Schroeder was to point out after the Second World War, one of that city's endearing characteristics was the ease with which it 'owned' you and made you feel at home – as if that were a self-understood thing. 'Nowhere, it seems, did I work so easily, quickly, productively as in those years [spent there]', Schroeder wrote.[8] Sasse would have endorsed these sentiments of the Bremen poet and hymn writer.

In 1923 the busy city *Seelsorger* took his doctoral degree, and three years later his STM (Masters) at Hartford, in the United States. The year spent there resulted in a notable report, 'American Christianity and the Church'. He became 'a conscious Lutheran', and later wrote: 'What Lutheranism is, I learned in America in 1926'.[9] In 1924, during a period of high inflation, he had married Charlotte Naumann at St Nicolai's, Oranienburg. Later in Australia he wrote: 'When we were married we had one week in September at one of the beautiful lakes in the Mark Brandenburg. We were very rich at that time, having a salary of 40,000,000,000 Marks (equivalent to $10 a month), but we were very happy.'[10]

The stressful period of the 1920s saw the young churchman rapidly finding his feet. As it happened, these were also the years in which the ecumenical movement began to assume an organisational profile, developing as it did from the background of missionary experience first shared globally and trans-denominationally at the Edinburgh world mission conference in 1910. In 1925 the organisation known as 'Life and Work' ('Practical Christianity' as it was known on the Continent) held its first world conference at Stockholm. Sasse's teacher, Adolf Deissmann, was present there as a guest of Archbishop Nathan Soederblom.

Two years later Deissmann and Sasse both attended a further landmark event in the history of the ecumenical movement, the first world conference of the organisation, Faith and Order, held at Lausanne. There Sasse acted as a German–English interpreter, and then compiled and edited the official German conference report (including all speeches and papers) – a stately 600-page volume which contained a substantial 80-page introductory history of the Faith and Order movement from his own pen. It was 'the first comprehensive historiography of this area of the modern ecumenical movement'.[11]

Sasse was appointed to the conference continuation committee, and his international connections, especially with England and Scandinavia, began to grow apace; for example, with the bishops of Chichester (George Bell) and of Stockholm (Soederblom). Sasse's writing started to appear in international publications, for example, his study, 'Jesus Christ the Lord', in a 1930 British volume titled *Mysterium Christi*.[12]

The receptiveness of the young scholar and churchman to formative influences from his teachers is clear from his many later critical and laudatory references. This is especially true of Deissmann. Along with the scholarly and ecclesial aspects of this man's fine legacy to his students came an added emphasis, one that would be severely tested in the time of troubles ahead: the issue of Christian ethical responsibility in the world beyond churchly confines. Deissmann feared its almost complete privatisation in the face of the popular excuse that politics and the world would (and were meant to!) operate in their own self-regulatory ways (the fateful *Eigengesetzlichkeit* that would bother the churches throughout and beyond the years of tyranny).[13] Adolf Deissmann lived just long enough to witness far worse than he had warned of. He died in 1937, and Sasse was one who took up the cause after the master departed. The effects would mark his life.

Hermann Sasse certainly acknowledged far-reaching ethical imperatives. In 1932 he wrote a sizeable essay on the significance of the state. Although he was heard to say much later (on an ABC television interview in the 1970s, and then perhaps with a cutting irony) that Germans do not go in for revolutions, that early essay was extremely close to the mark. In principle, he maintained, a regime which undermines basic orders of justice, and of marriage and family, *forfeits its authority as a government*. History is replete with examples, Sasse considering the then current situation in Russia as one such. There may be no choice but submission to overwhelming might, but 'any obligatory duty to obey such a power no longer exists', and a church that would acknowledge a regime of this kind as government (*Obrigkeit*) would make itself 'guilty of a great sin'. An uprising (*Empörung*) against such a power would no longer constitute revolution but rather a war of defence on a par with actions undertaken in emergency situations.[14]

But Hermann Sasse was already a marked man with the Nazis, having publicly and in print crossed swords just prior to their seizing power. In 1932 he sharply criticised their platform, article 24, in the *Church Yearbook* (*Kirchliches Jahrbuch*), of which he had recently become the editor. Article 24 affirms 'a positive Christianity'. But, almost as a quid pro quo, it required churches not to 'offend the German race's sense of decency and morality'. To which Sasse responded:

> One can perhaps forgive National Socialism all its theological sins, but this article 24 excludes any possibility of a dialogue with the church, whether Protestant or Catholic. Rosenberg's *Myth of the 20th Century*,[15] for all its blasphemies and its extravagant nonsense about the history of religions and of the world, is a harmless and venial lapse compared with this article; the same can be said of the whole theology of the swastika and the messianic cult of the Fuehrer. Evangelical theology can enter into dialogue with the National Socialists on all the points

of the Party programme, even about the Jewish question and its understanding of race, it may perhaps be able to take seriously the whole of the rest of the programme. About this article, however, no discussion at all is possible ... For the Protestant church would have to begin such a discussion with a frank admission that its doctrine constitutes a deliberate, permanent insult to the 'German race's sense of decency and morality', and hence that she can have no expectation of tolerance in the Third Reich ...

According to the Protestant doctrine of original sin, the newborn infant of the noblest Germanic descent, endowed in body and mind with the optimal racial characteristics, is as much subject to eternal damnation as the genetically gravely compromised half-caste from two decadent races. And we must go on to confess that the doctrine of the justification of the sinner *sola gratia, sola fide,* is the end of Germanic morality ... We are not much interested in whether the Party gives its support to Christianity, but we would like to know whether the church is to be permitted to preach the Gospel in the Third Reich without let or hindrance, whether, that is, we will be able to continue undisturbed with our insults to the Germanic or Germanistic moral sense, as with God's help we intend to do ...[16]

From this tough position Sasse was not to resile. His early post-war analysis of the precarious situation of Lutheranism in Germany, written in July 1945, laments the role of widespread anomalous theology in the rise of the Third Reich. Among other things, it had helped breed a curious type of *Staatsverehrung* and subservience to authority among educated groups and in wide sections of the bourgeoisie – a sort of 'secret religion', having much to do with the thought of philosophers like Fichte and Hegel. 'As for the average German, the state took the place of the church.' This result was also tied up with the misuse of Luther! The Reformer certainly taught Christian people to pray for good government, and accordingly, to thank God for its normal life-preserving reality. But why was it forgotten that Luther regarded sensible rulers as 'rare birds', that he stood up to and told kings, princes and electors, as well as powerful bishops, unpalatable, hard truths, and, along with the *Augsburg Confession* of Phillip Melanchthon, reminded people of divine limits on their otherwise due obedience to lawful earthly authority? As for the Nazi catastrophe, now, right after the war, Sasse called for repentance – by 'all of us', our whole church. For, he says, although the church continues to be divided, and is even apparently disintegrating into single congregations, separate groupings and different directions, 'before the Lord and before her people she [the church] remains one in her guilt!'[17]

The church, a community of guilt. This surprising turn affords a glimpse into the depth of Sasse's ecumenical commitment. He was not quite alone. Indeed, his view of the way forward for the 'one holy catholic and apostolic church' after 1945 here preluded the historically important Stuttgart 'Declaration of Guilt' of October that year – a statement of grief and regret over the feebleness of Christian witness, prayer and action during the Nazi years, presented by Germany's Protestant leaders at a meeting with ecumenical churchmen at Stuttgart. Sasse's words, as above, were on a wavelength similar to the much larger and more harrowing statement of Dietrich Bonhoeffer written during the war as part of his seminal book, *Ethics*.[18] As Melbourne pastor Johannes Achilles was to write of the Stuttgart confession much later: 'Such courage opened the ecumenical doors for the churches in Germany'.[19]

The 1932 Yearbook statement provided a measure of the man. Rosenberg responded, but was not taken too seriously even by leading Nazis of the time, most of whom were, as Richard Steigmann-Gall has shown in his *The Holy Reich* (2003), at least nominal Christians. Sadly, the majority of the Protestant population were content to line up with nondescript and quiescent national forms of theology offering little or no resistance to Hitler. They called themselves the German Christians (*Deutsche Christen* – DCs). It certainly remains astonishing in the circumstances that Sasse was able in that fateful following year (1933) to take up his appointment as professor of church history and symbolics in the theology faculty of Erlangen state university; and even more so, that he could continue in that post throughout the dark '1000 year reign' and beyond its deadly ending. Part of the explanation was the stance of Werner Elert, the faculty dean and a renowned Lutheran theologian. Elert, who first met Sasse in Lausanne, was able to keep his faculty intact and was determined to provide a buffer of protection for individuals like Sasse. And Sasse, a popular lecturer, did his part by drawing students to Erlangen and filling lecture halls.[20]

With the Nazis now in power no one could make statements with words similar to those Sasse published in the previous year. Yet, walking the tightrope, and knowingly so, he told students in an Advent sermon that year how essential to the church's *existence* it was that she dare to speak the commandments of God to the mighty of this world. A fortnight later he dared to assert that 'what one today calls the myth of the 20th century grows out of the destruction of the church's dogma'.[21]

In 1933 the Confessing Church movement was taking shape around Berlin pastors like Martin Niemöller and Gerhard Jacobi. It grew out of clergy and congregational resistance to Nazi-inspired governance within German Protestantism. Although a minority, the movement gained legitimacy as the true Evangelical (Protestant) church in 1934. By then 6000 pastors (roughly a third of the Protestant pastorate) had signed a statement rejecting Nazi 'Aryan' restrictions in the church (the banning of non-Aryan clergy!). Sasse and his younger Berlin associate, Dietrich Bonhoeffer, had been nominated to work out a doctrinal statement, a confession for the movement. They collaborated on the original draft at Bethel (the *Bethel Bekenntnis*) in August. It included clear pro-Jewish affirmations. Thus: 'With the Jews [God] wants to complete the salvation of the world, which he began with the call to Israel', and: 'It can never be the duty of a people to avenge the death on Golgotha upon the Jews'. Moreover, 'Christians coming from the heathen world rather have to lay themselves open to persecution than ever in one single aspect give up, whether freely or under coercion, the churchly brotherhood with the Jewish Christian established by Word and sacrament'. Nowhere else in 1933 was the demand for the non-expendable communion of all Christians put so clearly and uncompromisingly,[22] writes Klaus Scholder in 1977. 'The original version of the Bethel confession,' he states, 'remains a brilliant, sharp and impressive witness to what theological effort was still capable of achieving in the summer of 1933 – indeed specifically because of the great German Christian (*Deutsche Christen*) upsurge in German theology at this time. Ponderous though it was and loaded with numerous passages from the Bible, from Luther, and above all from confessional texts, this confession was nevertheless theologically and politically clearer and more exact in some passages than the famous Barmen declaration of May 1934.'[23] Lowell Green is even more forthright in his assessment. His book *Lutherans against Hitler* contains detailed analyses of both the Bethel confession and the Barmen statement of the following year. Green argues that the former was a much stronger statement; the Lutheran original draft at Bethel 'remains the best reply written against Nazi ideology'. However, the influential Reformed theologian Karl Barth regarded it as 'too Lutheran', with the result that, as Green argues, it was sentenced to a quiet death and to the forgetfulness of history.[24]

Events moved quickly, other voices grew stronger, the original Bethel draft was muffled, changed, delayed. It was finally printed in watered-down form by Martin Niemöller in 1934. That year the Confessing Church movement raised its voice more audibly in adopting a different document altogether, the famous 'Declaration' at Barmen. With its chief formulator Karl Barth present, Dietrich Bonhoeffer absent, working as a pastor in London, and Hermann Sasse leaving the crucial meeting at Barmen before the Declaration was unanimously adopted, Barmen's laudable opposition to the rising political idolatry was, however, not matched by any statement on the concomitant worsening plight of the Jews. Barth later expressed his deep regret at this omission. What motivated Sasse's early withdrawal from the Synod was his view that the Confessing Movement was de facto acting as a church, as if the previously divisive differences between Reformed, Lutheran and Union territorial churches, from which its members came, did not exist. These churches were not united. Therefore their members could, albeit for immensely urgent purposes, only act as a group of Christians, and not on behalf of a (new) united church body. However, Sasse's quarrel was not primarily with what Barmen stated, and he continued as a member of the Confessing Church movement through its brief and fragmenting duration.

In 1935 Sasse's passport was cancelled and his attendance at international and ecumenical meetings ceased. Meanwhile the 'German Christians' (DCs) were wreaking havoc in territorial churches, most of which were pressed and pressured to join one Protestant church (*Deutsche Evangelische Kirche, DEK*), a body causing Hitler little or no trouble. Opposition to the corrupting DCs, and so to the Führer's policies, came from the Confessing Church movement, which, in the dire circumstances, Bonhoeffer controversially espoused as the one and only legitimate Church! Bonhoeffer also took an independent path in his understanding of the 'councils' (conferences such as Stockholm or Lausanne), crediting them with great authority as the voice of the Church.[25] Here Sasse's ways clearly diverged from those of his younger partner.

Sasse's 'ambition never to be cut off from the surrounding world', noted by Tom Hardt,[26] remained strong – and communicable. Even in that harsh and claustrophobic year of 1938, Sasse, student pastor as well as faculty professor, reminded his listeners of wider horizons. On Easter Day of that year he told them that the small Lutheran Church in Australia was celebrating its centenary, then drawing on the global dimensions of the message still sounding out as a greeting between Russia's faithful in that country's political and spiritual darkness. In another sermon of 1938 he recalled the historical figures of John Wesley and Luther and connected them with the ecumenical present: in 1738 Wesley heard Luther's famous Bible 'Preface' to Romans read aloud and with that understood salvation (Wesley's 'conversion'), an event which that very week English Christendom was celebrating – *'ein hohes Jubiläum'* (a high-jubilee anniversary).[27] Sasse continued to scan the wider, indeed divine horizons as late as 1944, when gloom, defeat and disaster were looming larger by the day: 'Even in this time of dire judgement, there is no moratorium on grace', he proclaimed.[28]

In the terrible aftermath of war, the many territorial churches of Germany and the remnants of the 'Confessing Church' struggled to establish a Protestant federation (in which was to be included a union of Confessional Lutheran churches), an umbrella organisation, which nevertheless insisted on calling itself 'The Evangelical Church in Germany' (EKD). To Sasse this body appeared far too much like its predecessor the 'German Evangelical Church', which had been coerced and cobbled together with unseemly haste mainly for the convenience of Hitler. This was union on a shaky basis, lacking real doctrinal agreement (later referred to in Australian debates as 'sinful unionism'). Sasse was thus unable to support the 1948 arrangements, and he noted what appeared to him to be a distinct whiff of intolerance when Bavarian Lutherans and their pastors were required by their bishop, Hans Meiser, to accept EKD membership. On an international level, in 1948 the World Council of Churches (to which Lausanne had led) was finally established at Amsterdam. It too offered Sasse little comfort. He saw the Council, together with the Lutheran World Federation established a year earlier at Lund, as tending to *dismiss* differences as unimportant, rather than identifying and clarifying them and then suggesting ways by which the *churches* might approach their resolution. For in this way, in Sasse's view, confessional loyalty and true ecumenicity have to be held together.[29]

Erlangen to North Adelaide

That year Sasse joined the small Lutheran free church in Germany and toyed with thoughts of leaving Europe. Then in 1949 he accepted a call to teach theology in an Adelaide Lutheran seminary. In a fascinating and brief comparison of Bonhoeffer, Sasse and Edmund Schlink, Eugene Skibbe states: 'He [Sasse] left everything as an act of witness for the Lutheran church'.[30]

There were undoubtedly church political disappointments of a high order behind this move when he made it. But there was more — as there always is.[31] De-nazification had begun, and the American military authorities wanted assurance that Nazis were not teaching at Erlangen, perhaps even in the theological faculty! The Americans knew (or knew of) Sasse, and made him a pro-rector of the university. He agreed to supply a report on the faculty. It was brief, forthright, not unfair, and no jobs were lost because of it. However, he was naïve if he believed that the matter would not become public, or that if it did, his colleagues would take no notice.[32] The ensuing atmosphere and his decision to leave his professorship and fatherland were in all likelihood linked.

In February 1949 the President of the United Evangelical Lutheran Church of Australia, Rev J.J. Stolz, appealed for special contributions to bring the Sasse family to Australia. Stolz wrote:

> Articles from his pen, and particularly his book, *Here We Stand*, translated from the original German into English, has [*sic*] made him known and loved by many of our pastors. His ability to use the English

language freely, acquired years ago as an exchange student in U.S.A. and as a frequent visitor to England ... is beyond doubt. A further recommendation is that he is highly esteemed in the Missouri Synod, U.S.A., as a conservative Lutheran, so much so that his recent trip to U.S.A. was largely sponsored by that Synod. He will therefore be an asset in our union negotiations with the E.L.C.A. Further, he is well acquainted with the Ecumenical Movement, and recognised as a leading theologian by British and other scholars. The reason which led him to think of going overseas was that developments in the Lutheran territorial Churches in Germany, due in part to the State still having a decisive voice in the filling of positions in theological faculties, led to a situation in which his conscience did not permit him to remain. Like the founders of the Lutheran Church in Australia, he wants to emigrate 'for conscience' sake.[33]

Sasse quickly began to appreciate his new country, while remaining in close touch with the fatherland and with his friends there and around the world. Thus he claimed: 'I chose freedom',[34] and yet he stayed well 'in the loop' overseas, making several visits to Germany and sending students to university theological faculties there for postgraduate training and research. He also began to establish a network of informative, theological and pastoral correspondence with colleagues and soul mates around the globe. The flow of reviews and journal articles (as well as some larger publications) from his pen reveals that his intellectual horizons did not narrow, despite difficulties of access to new work and to older literature. His achievements in this country earned him notice in the *Australian Dictionary of Biography*. In 1972 he was appointed to the Order of Merit by the Federal Republic of Germany; and in 1976 Robert Banks in *Colloquium*, the Australian and New Zealand Theological review, hailed him 'Australia's most distinguished acquisition from the Continental theological scene'.

Sasse taught historical theology at Immanuel – later Luther – Seminary, North Adelaide, between 1949 and 1969, and almost immediately began to make a contribution to synods and pastoral conferences. His work on church committees quickly gained recognition. Stolz was right: with his life and ecumenical experience, Sasse's influence would be considerable. And indeed, after in-depth doctrinal discussions that were greatly assisted and stimulated by him, the long historic schism of the two Lutheran churches in Australia was healed (1966) – a 'happy crown to his ecumenical ideals'.[35] Here the 'Lausanne principles', to which he often appealed and 'which he judged had been jettisoned during the "movement" of events',[36] such as Amsterdam and the formation of EKD, had been successfully applied.

Australian doctrinal discussions provided a local stimulus for him to go on developing his leading interests, particularly in three interrelated areas of Christian theology and history. These may be listed as: the status and character of the Bible; Reformation research; and ecclesiology and the interconnections between confessional identity and genuine ecumenicity.

The first of these topics involved continuous historical and systematic expertise. Sasse kept up with 'the historical Jesus' debate and the issues raised by Rudolf Bultmann, both in Europe and as they impinged on the English-speaking world. But he was equally able to deal with the historical record of the ways of scriptural exposition in the church, and especially by the Reformers. Sasse understood modern difficulties with the authority and inspiration of the canon, whether in Protestantism or in the Roman Church. He addressed twentieth-century issues of faith and reason. Having experienced Nazi attempts to get rid of the Old Testament, he interpreted the orthodox doctrine of scripture in such a way as to avoid misuse of the Bible either for fundamentalist purposes or to support forms of churchless individualism and eclecticism. His starting point and focus in this ongoing work remained firmly christocentric. This implied the application of Luther's insight expressed in classic terms by his 1525 challenge to Erasmus: 'Take Christ out of the Scriptures, and what will you find left in them?'[37] In Australia Sasse wrote a tract, 'Holy Church or Holy Writ?' (1967), and this, along with sufficient other essays for a collected volume, was published posthumously in 1981 under the title *Sacra Scriptura*. The relevance of Christian apologetics did not elude him in this new land. For, along with all the plurality and variety of churches (in every little country town, and suburb and city), the 'great South Land of the Holy Spirit' was also an adamantly secular country. With his background and experience he managed, at least in part, to reconnect theology with the university, and to give theology students a good conscience about being there.

Martin Luther, who was he really? Contrary to a virtual real presence of the Reformer as perceived by people of the seventeenth and eighteenth centuries, the nineteenth century hardly knew how to recognise him.[38] It took the talents of Karl Holl (1866–1926) and his school to restore an authentic reformatory profile to the Wittenbergian and to lift his teaching on faith and 'the righteousness of God' beyond the realm of pious phraseology. That it happened at all, and despite a second horrible war involving Germany, is something of a miracle. By the middle of the century students of Holl – Sasse was one of them – held most of the famous German chairs of church history. But it was Sasse who, along with outstanding British scholars such as Gordon Rupp and Philip Watson, and the American Roland Bainton, provided this 'Luther renaissance' with increasingly international forums. Here Sasse's most widely read and often translated book, *Here We Stand*, played an important role. In this work he debunks several significant and fashionable, but inadequate and misleading, interpretations of Luther in modern times; he goes on to mirror the real man, and to uncover his lasting significance for the Lutheran Church, as well as for the modern ecumenical world.

Thoroughly versed in the biblical and classical languages, Dr Sasse would at times walk into lectures reciting slabs of the Greek or Latin Fathers, or his favourite, Luther. He also required students to learn at least some texts by heart, one of the classics being the Reformer's early letter to the monk Spenlein:

> ... my dear Friar, learn Christ and him crucified. Learn to praise him and, despairing of yourself, say, 'Lord Jesus, you are my righteousness, just as I am your sin. You have taken upon yourself what is mine and have given to me what is yours. You have taken upon yourself what you were not and have given me what I was not' ...
>
> If you firmly believe this as you ought ... receive your untaught and hitherto erring brothers, patiently help them, make their sins yours, and, if you have any goodness, let it be theirs. Thus the Apostle teaches, 'Receive one another as Christ also received you to the glory of God.'[39]

Hermann Sasse was at heart ever a pastor, as Dr Henry Proeve said at his funeral. His love of people, the church and the sacrament of the altar were very closely connected. And his scholarship served these real and communal purposes. In Adelaide he authored a major study on the eucharist, *This is my Body*. His involvement in the Roman Catholic–Lutheran dialogue, which began in the 1970s, assisted closer relations and deeper mutual understanding on a local level. He remained ecumenical, soberly so, not expecting the reunion of the churches as a calculable result of countless interchurch discussions, but as a gift of God's love, touching people through the Gospel of Christ and in the holy sacraments, a gift to be thankfully received, in faith and hope.

Something of a sea change happened to arrive in Lutheran and other churches in this country in the middle of the century, related of course to ecumenical events that had touched Western and Eastern churches, 'a Copernican revolution in Christian thinking',[40] that would, with Vatican II, also deeply affect the Roman Communion. In hindsight it might well appear that, in this respect at least, the timing of Dr Sasse's arrival was more than fortuitous. He helped interpret the times in a new place. Moreover, his profile and presence in South Australia altered the fragile cultural and ecclesial self-perceptions of German groups here (whether descendants of earlier forebears or those beginning to arrive as New Australians). Here was a pastor and teacher who had stood his ground and was in meaningful contact both with Evangelicals and Reformed people, and with High Church Anglicans and Catholics, and with their leading or representative figures. His coming thus opened new doors (although he was often cautious about others actually going through them). In terms used by Sasse's younger friend from Confessing Church days, Professor Edmund Schlink: 'Whereas Christians previously viewed their own church as the centre of the body of Christ, now more and more of them see their church – with others – orbiting around Christ as the centre'.

This legacy is with us. However, while it remains true that, as Sasse wrote in his final essay, ecclesiology (the nature of the church) 'remains the great problem of theology in all churches',[41] the reception and transmission of that 'Copernican' legacy implies ongoing patient commitment both to the Centre and to what Kierkegaard called 'the works of love'.

Notes

1. See Sasse's 1936 essay, 'The Theologian of the Second Reich: Thoughts on the biography of Adolf von Harnack', in Hermann Sasse, *The Lonely Way: Selected essays and letters*, vol. 1 (1927–1939), Concordia, St Louis, Miss., 2002, pp. 311–20; also F.W. Graf, 'Adolf von Harnack, Friedrich Gundolf's "Goethe"', *Journal for the History of Modern Theology*, vol. 1, 1994, pp. 167ff.
2. Hermann Sasse, *In Statu Confessionis*, vol. 2, ed. Friedrich Hopf, Verlag die Spur, Hermannsburg, 1976, p. 274.
3. See the introduction in Sasse, *The Lonely Way*, vol. 1, p. 14.
4. Hans-Siegfried Huss, 'Was heisst lutherisch?", *Lutherische Kirche in der Welt*, vol. 42, 1995, p. 73.
5. Les Carlyon, *The Great War*, MacMillan, Sydney, 2006, pp. 509, 596.
6. Hermann Sasse, *The Lonely Way*, vol. 2 (1941–1976), Concordia, St Louis, Miss., 2005, p. 415.
7. Adrian Hastings, *A History of English Christianity 1920–1990*, SCM, London, 1991, p. 18.
8. In Kurt Ihlenfeld, *Stadtmitte: Kritische Gaenge in Berlin*, Eckart Verlag, Witten and Berlin, 1965, p. 311. Author's translation.
9. See Sasse, *The Lonely Way*, vol 1, pp. 15, 23–60.
10. Quoted by Tom Hardt, 'Hermann Sasse in his Letters', *Logia*, vol 4, 1995, p. 6.
11. Reinhard Frieling, as cited by Ronald Feuerhahn, 'Hermann Sasse as an Ecumenical Churchman', University of Cambridge dissertation, 1991, pp. 27ff.
12. For a discussion of this essay see Gordon Gerhardy, 'Hermann Sasse on Confession and Culture for a Younger Church', dissertation, St Paul, Minnesota, 1981, pp. 70–5.
13. See Deissmann's statement in *Die Religionswissenschaft der Gegenwart in Selbstdarstellungen*, ed. Erich Stange, Verlag Felix Meiner, Leipzig, 1925, pp. 73ff.
14. Sasse, *In Statu Confessionis*, vol 2, p. 364. That Sasse's views were at least in part shared by famed faculty colleagues can be seen in Karlmann Beyschlag's, *Die Erlanger Theologie* (Martin Luther Verlag, Erlangen, 1993), where the ethical writing of Paul Althaus is discussed, especially p. 202.
15. Alfred Rosenberg expounded the extreme Nazi doctrine in his book. For further information on the book and on the reception of Rosenberg's ideas, see Richard Steigmann-Gall, *The Holy Reich*, Cambridge Univ. Pr., Cambridge, 2003, pp. 91–101.
16. English text as in Peter Matheson (ed.), *The Third Reich and the Christian Churches*, T. & T. Clark, Edinburgh, 1981, pp. 1ff.

17 Sasse, *In Statu Confessionis*, vol. 1, pp. 297–99; cf. Stewart Hermann, *The Rebirth of the German Church*, Macmillan, Toronto, 1946, p. 62.
18 Dietrich Bonhoeffer, *Works*, vol. 6, ed. Wayne Floyd Jr., Fortress, Minneapolis, Minn., 2005, pp. 138–42.
19 Herbert Mees (ed.), *A German Church in the Garden of God*, BPA Print, Melbourne, 2004, pp. 409, 331.
20 Elert's remarks on how Nazi politics impinged on his faculty and its members and what he undertook by way of defending their rights etc. can be found in Beyschlag, pp. 266–86. Lowell Green's recent work, *Lutherans against Hitler* (Concordia, St Louis, Miss., 2007), contains a section, 'The Erlangen Faculty under Elert's Deanship (1935–1943)'. It provides insight into Elert's activity (p. 342), citing part of his report in translation as follows: 'Soon after Ulmer's dismissal, Specht and Molitoris informed me that also Prof. Sasse, who had been openly attacked by Rosenberg, would no longer be tolerable because he endangered the whole university. Also Strathmann stood for a while on the blacklist. I did everything I could to beat off these attacks, but I believe that the case of Sasse was mainly delayed because they first wanted to be sure they got someone who would listen to the [Nazi] Party as successor to Ulmer. At the beginning of the war, when the Old Testament scholar, Procksch, went into retirement, I also succeeded in winning Dr. [Friedrich] Baumgaertel, a non-[Nazi] Party man, as his successor. There was a rule that vacant assistantships should be posted on the bulletin boards of all other universities. As dean, I always evaded this requirement, in spite of numerous warnings from Molitoris, because it could be expected with certainty that, in this way, outside [Nazi] Party members would be placed in these positions. By managing to have the previous assistant renewed in his position for a longer time, the faculty could also at this point be protected against [Nazi] Party spies. *The Erlangen Theological Faculty is the only one in all Germany which remained without [Nazi] Party members*' (Elert's emphasis).
21 Hermann Sasse, *Zeugnisse: Erlanger Predigten und Vorträge vor Gemeinden, 1933–1944*, ed. Friedrich Hopf, Martin Luther Verlag, Erlangen, 1979, pp. 36, 51.
22 On Sasse's later urgent warning to his Munich bishop, Meiser, against circulating anti-judaistic theology in the church, see F.W. Graf in *Handbuch der Geschichte der evangelischen Kirche in Bayern*, vol. 2, EOS, St Ottilien, 2000, p. 323.
23 Klaus Scholder, *The Churches and the Third Reich*, vol 1, Fortress, Philadelphia, 1987, pp. 456ff.
24 Green 2006, pp. 63, 164, 177. See also *International Bonhoeffer Society Newsletter*, no. 94, 2008, p. 12.
25 See Armin Boyens, *Kirchenkampf und Oekumene 1933–39*, Kaiser Verlag, Munich, 1969, p. 48.

26 See Hardt 1995, p. 6.
27 Sasse, *Zeugnisse*, 1979, p. 91.
28 Sasse, *The Lonely Way*, vol 2, p. 142.
29 See Feuerhahn 1991, pp. 12, 249.
30 In Eugene Skibbe, *The Quiet Reformer: An introduction to Edmund Schlink's life and ecumenical theology*, Kirk House, Minneapolis, Minn., 1999, p. 131. Of course, a non-literal reading of Skibbe's statement is made necessary alone by virtue of Sasse's global view of the Church ('*oekumene*'). But on a more personal level, the Principal of Immanuel Seminary, whose faculty Sasse joined in 1949, was Dr S.P. Hebart, his outstandingly successful Australian doctoral student. Hebart had worked under his supervision at Erlangen shortly before the war. Furthermore, the educationist Carl Muetzelfeldt (also celebrated in this volume) had fortunately left Germany to join the same faculty in 1934. Muetzelfeldt too had recognised the Nazi danger (both directly affecting his family but also as being in sharp conflict with his philosophy and practice) at an early moment.
31 See Sasse's letter to Derek Van Abbe, 2 April 1956, Adelaide University Library, German settlers collection, C. D 22.
32 Faculty correspondence and documentation have been recently reviewed and assessed by former church historian at Erlangen, Bishop Emeritus Prof. Gerhard Müller: 'Hermann Sasse als Mitglied und als Kritiker der Theologischen Fakultät der Universität Erlangen 1933 bis 1949', *Zeitschrift fuer bayerische Kirchengeschichte*, vol. 75, 2006, pp. 176–217. See also Green 2006, pp. 335, 346–8.
33 J.J. Stolz to 'Dear Brother …', 1 Febuary 1949, Lutheran Archives, Adelaide.
34 Peter Noss, in *Biographisch-Bibliographisches Kirchenlexikon*, vol. 8, Verlag Bautz, Herzberg, 1994, p. 1383.
35 Thus his American biographer, Ronald Feuerhahn (1991, p. 11).
36 ibid., p. 240.
37 *Luther's Works*, American edition, vol. 33, Fortress Press, Philadelphia, 1972, p. 26.
38 Kurt Ihlenfeld, *Stadtmitte. Kritische Gaenge in Berlin*, Eckert Verlag, Witten & Berlin, 1964, p. 321.
39 *Luther's Works*, vol 48, pp. 11ff.
40 The term is used by Eugene Skibbe (1999, p. 107).
41 Sasse, *The Lonely Way*, vol 2, p. 419.

Nora Heysen
Art and war for a German-Australian family

Catherine Speck

Australian art is indebted to German artists. Some are visitors, like Nikolaus Lang (b. 1941), whose fascination with our environs led to his fabricating a landscape 'painting', *Dedicated to the vanished Adelaide tribe*, from the actual sands of a cliff face at Maslin Beach in 1987.[1] Others were immigrants whose iconic images have become an integral part of what we now call Australian art. The list is long and includes Louis Tannert (c.1833–c.1909), artist and teacher at Adelaide's School of Design in the 1880s; silversmith Julius Schomburgk (1819–1893); painter Alexander Schramm (1813–64); Bauhaus artist and teacher Ludwig Hirschfeld-Mack (1893–1965); furniture designer-maker Schulim Krimper (1893–1971) and printmaker and teacher Udo Sellbach (1927–2006). But few have won the accolades of German-born Hans Heysen (1877–1968) and his Australian-born daughter Nora Heysen (1911–2003).[2]

Hans Heysen was a much-celebrated artist; his work is held in all state and national collections and he was winner of the Wynne prize for landscape painting nine times. He was knighted for services to art in 1959.[3] His daughter Nora was also highly successful. She was the first woman to win the Archibald Prize in 1938 for her painting of Madame Elink Schurmann, the wife of the Dutch Consul General, and the first Australian woman to be appointed an official war artist in 1943. Later in life, in 1993, she was the recipient of an Australia Council Award for Achievement in the Arts and she received an Order of Australia in 1998. The focus for this chapter is her appointment as an official war artist, which was significant in itself; but, interestingly, it also unwittingly closes the period of anti-German behaviour her father Hans experienced during the First World War.

Nora grew up in a highly artistic and educated environment at The Cedars in Hahndorf. Her first art teacher was her father. Her mother Selma (Sallie) of the Bartels family was also of German heritage. Sallie was an educated woman, an avid reader, and a former student in Hans Heysen's art classes. Regular visitors to the household included Dame Nellie Melba, artists Lionel and Norman Lindsay, and art publisher Sydney Ure Smith. Their life was very much that of the artist and his family living the idyllic life in the country in order to be in touch with nature and to find inspiration in the bush – as artists have done for generations. Hans described this way of working to his friend Lionel Lindsay: 'I only try to paint as truthfully as I can, and that which my eyes see and perhaps what I unconsciously feel ... of course light interests me as much as ever, but I am seeking it more under the "everyday aspect of nature"'.[4] Hans also said, 'I believe isolation is good for an artist: he has a chance of finding himself and is not always too anxious to paint for exhibitions'.[5]

Adelaide had a high proportion of German settlers, almost 30,000, or one in ten, by the First World War,[6] and many established German settlements, such as Hahndorf, which were filled with German-speaking families, produce and ways of life.[7] Hans and Sallie Heysen's decision to move out of Adelaide to a German township in 1908 was dictated much more by romantic artistic ideals than those of their German heritage. They were cultured German-Australians and up-and-coming professionals, who, in choosing to live in a German rural environment where they had little in common culturally with the townsfolk, ran the risk of being isolated. But this was not case. They were well liked and respected.[8]

German was not spoken in the Heysen home, even though both parents were fluent speakers. This was not uncommon amongst German-Australians, although Hans spoke German to his neighbouring farmers.[9] However, from this traditional German setting Hans forged a vision of the Australian bush around the iconic gum tree and sunlight that moved the portrayal of the bush a step further than that rendered by the Heidelberg artists in the 1880s and 1890s. In place of Tom Roberts's and Arthur Streeton's youthful portrayals of settlers battling the bush, or dwelling in the bush and domesticating it, Hans Heysen focused on the beauty,

Hans Heysen, Australia 1877–1968, *Red Gold*, 1913, Hahndorf, South Australia, oil on canvas 129.5 x 174.5cm, gift of Rt Hon Sir Charles Booth 1913. (Art Gallery of South Australia, Adelaide)

integrity and maturity of the bush. For instance, in *Red Gold,* 1913 (above), the majestic gums stand timelessly and appear 'humanoid in their heroic posturing'[10] and epitomise a maturing, recently federated nation. The bright sunshine manifested the artist's belief that 'the essence of the Australian landscape … [is] sunshine … [it is] … the essence of life and atmosphere'.[11] Hans is credited with creating that maturing vision of Australia in the federation era.

Others of his paintings and drawings show the simplicity of rural life observed around him – farmers, farmyard animals, thatched rooves on traditional German sheds, and scenes reflecting centuries-old farming practices. This gave his work a timelessness, despite the impact of modernity. Nora also picked up on this German-ness of Hahndorf in her portrait of *Ruth*, 1933 (page 405), in which she portrays a local farm girl who worked nearby. Ruth, who is dressed simply, is semi-framed by a patchwork of paddocks, which stand more as a reference to her daily work than as landscape. Her arms cross her strong frame, while her hands are those of

Nora Heysen, Australia 1911–2003, *Ruth*, 1933, Hahndorf, South Australia,
oil on canvas 81.5 x 64.2 cm.
(Art Gallery of South Australia)

a manual worker who is an integral part of the rural life of the neighbourhood. She has a quiet but intriguing sense of belonging in that space.

During the First World War, when Nora was just four years of age, her father Hans was confronted with his German heritage, even though he had lived in Australia since 1884, was a naturalised Briton and held a British passport and considered himself an Australian. The British Empire, of which Australia was a member, was at war with Germany.

Animosity to German-Australians was not evident in the early days of the war. In this period Germans, who were well-respected citizens and the largest immigrant group outside Britons, could still join the Australian Imperial Forces (AIF).[12] Australia's quarrel was not with German people, but as the *Sydney Morning Herald* said, 'with the sword hand of Prussian militarism'.[13] However, anti-German feeling developed, and, by May 1915, the situation changed. Australians were informed that their patriotic duty was 'to hate the Hun',[14] and anti-German cartoons rapidly became the staple of Australia's daily press, magazines and recruiting posters.

Within this climate Hans was asked to resign from both the Australian Art Association, even though he was an invited founding member, and the South Australian Society of the Arts, because he refused to affirm his Australian patriotism. He thought it unnecessary since his entire painting style was devoted to portraying Australian light and bush. The insults continued. The National Gallery of Victoria had reserved a painting, *In sunset haze*, from his large and successful 1915 solo exhibition in Melbourne, but then decided against its purchase because the artist was German-born. Hans felt the insults acutely, especially as he had recently – without being asked – donated one of his paintings to the Melbourne Savage Club so it could be used to raise funds for the Lord Mayor's Patriotic Fund.[15] Fortunately, Hans was not interned at Torrens Island, as were many. His Sydney-based brother-in-law Rudolph Schneider was held at the Liverpool internment camp outside Sydney until 1920, despite his being an Australian citizen.

Rumours too were spreading in Adelaide that Hahndorf was the centre of clandestine spying and arms activities, and the All-British League even visited The Cedars to check allegations that Hans was circulating stories about the late King Edward VII. The artist was not, but he also had to assure his visitors he was not engaged in any such activities, and that he had no hidden wireless sets for transmitting signals.[16] During the war Hahndorf underwent a name change to Ambleside as a way of cleansing it of its German affiliation.[17]

The slurs didn't stop. In 1917 the Art Gallery of New South Wales refused to include Hans Heysen's paintings in their Loan Exhibition of Australian Art unless the artist 'definitely and satisfactorily declares whether his allegiances and sympathies are with the British Nation'.[18] Once again he felt this was not necessary, as is apparent in his letter to fellow German artist and pacifist Elioth

Gruner: 'I am sorry at not being represented, but as I disliked the approach of the Gallery Board on the question of nationality, I must take the consequences of what I thought right to stick up for – if a man's feeling for Australia cannot be judged by the work he has done – then no explanation on his part would dispel the mistrust ... I cannot give any explanation – it would not be understood in the present circumstances.'[19]

Hans may have been a pacifist. Certainly he abhorred the war, writing in the same letter to Gruner: 'My only hope is that this useless waste of human life with its millions of tragedies will soon be over – it's a constant prey on one's mind – no force will fade the colour of it from one's mind'.[20] As his biographer Colin Thiele observed: 'poor Hans, the gentlest and most peaceful of men, who barely knew which end of a rifle was which, and who hated all forms of killing so deeply that he wouldn't even suffer his own turkeys to be sacrificed for the Christmas dinner, was being envisaged in the role of spy'.[21]

This ill feeing towards the artist continued beyond the war years, and in 1921, Bernard Hall, Director of the National Gallery of Victoria, refused to speak to the artist at his solo exhibition in Melbourne, despite an attempt at an introduction by his dealer William Gill. As the *Argus* commented, 'the fact that Mr Heysen is of German parentage is said to have been the cause of the friction'.[22] Hans retaliated by withdrawing his painting, *Fruit*, which the Gallery had reserved for purchase, and instead sold it privately. It wasn't until the late 1920s that civility was restored between the two.

Remarkably, the artist bore no long-term animosity to those who ostracised him during the First World War because he was German-born. The irony, however, is that in the Second World War his daughter Nora was appointed an Australian official war artist and thus entrusted with the duty to represent Australians at war, and two of his sons, Michael and Stefan, joined the AIF. Nora actually sought the appointment. Inspired by the photographic work of Damien Parer and George Silk that was reproduced in the daily press, she decided: 'I might as well use what I can do in some capacity'. She spoke to her father's influential friends: Louis McCubbin, who was on the appointments committee of the Australian War Memorial, and James McGregor and Sydney Ure

Smith, both Trustees at the Art Gallery of New South Wales, about how to arrange it.[23]

In January 1943, McCubbin proposed that Nora be appointed an official war artist, along with Stella Bowen. The appointments broke new ground because no Australian women had ever held this post before. Pressure had been mounting from artists' groups to broaden appointments, and the women's services were now highly visible. In recommending Nora, McCubbin described her as 'not only one of the most accomplished women artists, but one of the leading artists in Australia ... She could be used in a variety of ways, painting portraits, and covering women's activities in South Australia.'[24] No mention was made of her German heritage, but then she was Australian-born, her father by now was extremely well connected and very senior in the art world, and the doubts people had about him during the First World War no longer applied to him or his family in the Second World War.[25] Both appointments were approved in February 1943; Nora's was not announced until August, and she finally took it up on 18 October 1943. The long delay was due to the fact that her appointment raised the issue of equal pay, which took months to solve.[26]

Hans was not wholly in favour of his daughter's decision to take on work as a war artist. He thought the position of official war artist would be too tough for her.[27] It is also probable he disliked the militaristic subject matter. However, she produced some remarkable paintings during this time. Her first experience, while still in Melbourne in her Flinders Street studios, gave her a taste for military culture and some of the hurdles she would face. She was asked, as a part of the Military History Unit's program of selecting important senior military personnel as appropriate subjects for the historical record, to paint portraits of the seven women who headed up the Women's Services. From their perspective, 'the interest of the portrait lies in the importance of the subject'.[28] These busy women had little time to sit to have their portrait painted and, instead of six two-hour sittings, they gave the artist only half an hour at a time.[29] Their khaki and blue uniforms were not inspiring and left little room for interpretation. When Annie Sage, matron-in-chief of the nursing services, arrived in her nurse's uniform Nora finally had something to work with.[30] She found the colour red a welcome relief

Nora Heysen, *Matron Annie Sage, Matron in Chief, AANS*, 1944, oil on canvas 76.6 x 56.4cm. (Australian War Memorial, ART 22218)

and commented: 'I was delighted to see Matron Sage's uniform, with its red cape. I find all this khaki a difficult colour to use.'[31] She drew on the style of the Flemish Old Masters and, in designing the portrait *Matron Annie Sage, Matron in Chief, AANS*, 1944, with its white nurse's veil, red cape and a fulsome figure beneath, she shows Sage as Madonna-like.[32]

Sage took a liking to Nora and wanted her transferred to New Guinea to portray nurses at work. Nora was sent there in April 1944 and was based at the recently recaptured Finschhafen, the area closest to the front where nurses were placed. Initially, she was lonely. The nurses were not welcoming, and her tent was not in their quarters, but some distance away. These women had served in North Africa and the Middle East, whereas Nora had not, and they resented her rank and her captain's pay. While working in

Melbourne on the portraits, she had been staying at the Menzies Hotel, and in the nurses' eyes, as Nora says, she 'had come right out of the Menzies Hotel with a captain's pips on her shoulders!'[33] As a consequence, she kept to herself and in a letter home said, 'Living amongst a crowd has the one advantage that one is left entirely alone so I spend a great deal of my time in my little tent'.[34] It is possible, that having observed her father working alone in his studio, she had a role model for working in isolation.

Apart from the ostracism and the loneliness, Nora had difficulty portraying the female nurses and medical aids, because the artist in her who had spent years developing a finely tuned sense of colour found their uniform colour problematic. As she commented, 'I was supposed to do the women's war effort, but that didn't please me because the women were dressed from head to knee in khaki with nets over their faces, and there wasn't any bit of female that you could see. Also I found the khaki colour very difficult to paint so I did the men in their jungle greens which was much more to my liking.'[35]

Her orders for her New Guinea posting were conveyed to her when she reached Port Moresby; namely, that 'for the most part [she would] be with the women's services, but will not necessarily be confined to those services'.[36] Given this, she decided, in addition to studies of nurses, to portray some of the men at Finschhafen. These included *Bluey (Sapper Bashforth)*, 1944, whom she described colourfully to her family as:

> A lumber man from Queensland, a hulking fellow of 6'4" with pale blue eyes with that distant horizon look, red headed, red moustached and red hairs all over his brawny chest. It was Bluey who blazed the trail up to Satelberg [sic] and who mowed down the jungle to make roads, all under fire ... He and 'dearest' (the bulldozer) ... were a law unto themselves and no one dared to give Bluey orders. He and dearest went their own dangerous way ... The war could not have advanced up here without them.[37]

She did manage to portray some women, including *Theatre Sister Margaret Sullivan*, 1945, whom she shows in mask and gown and holding her trademark surgical instruments. This particular nurse sometimes had to work on two operations simultaneously.[38]

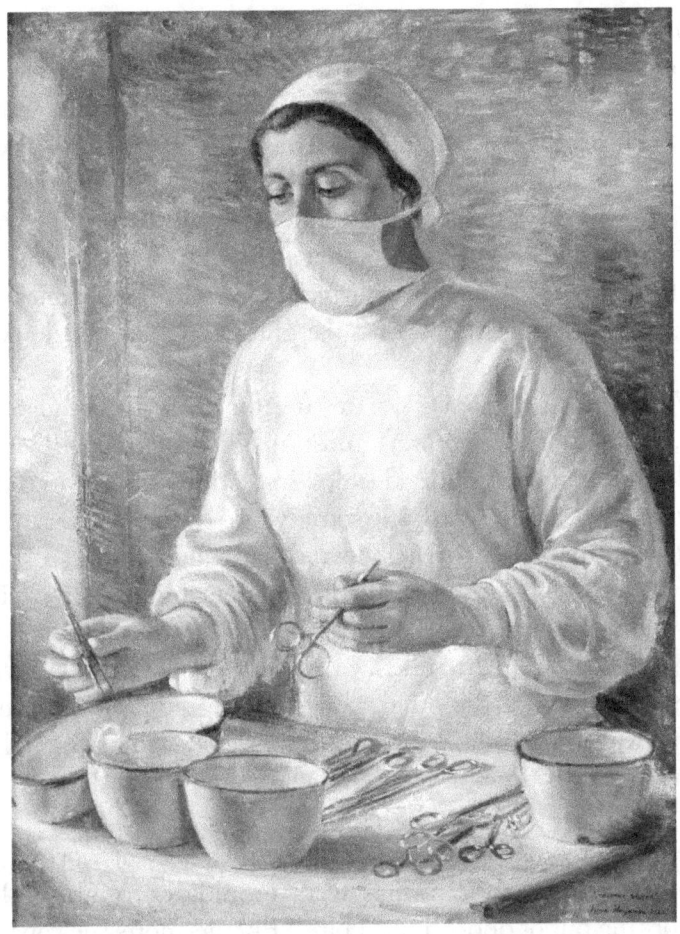

Nora Heysen, *Theatre Sister Margaret Sullivan*, 1945,
oil on canvas 91.8 x 66cm. (Australian War Memorial, ART 22234)

In order to paint this, Nora donned mask and gown and sketched in a makeshift operating theatre in a casualty clearing station as the surgery took place. She wrote home to her parents, describing the whole the experience as 'quite fantastic to find oneself in that atmosphere', adding, 'the war does strange and unpredictable things to us.'[39] In fact, she faced some initial resistance to her working in the operating theatre, but as she described in another letter home, she found a solution: 'I was frowned upon by the surgeon until I made a drawing of the theatre sister for him and now he's cooperative – I work in the sterile atmosphere of ether and whiteness.'[40]

One intriguing feature about this image is its clinical quality;

the focus is on the nurse and her instruments, with no appearance of the body she was assisting in repairing. This painting is not just of a nurse, however; it could be seen as a muted reference to what her daily work involved as she repaired damaged bodies and also how Nora observed this. Interestingly, when describing his daughter's work as a war artist to his friend Lionel Lindsay, Hans said she 'sees all sorts of operations and sights that she will find hard to obliterate from her mind with the years. I would *hate* it!' But beneath this comment was admiration for his daughter, as Colin Thiele pointed out.[41]

Working in the tropics was testing for an artist because it was damp, wet, and, furthermore, a most unsuitable climate in which to complete oil paintings. Nora decided instead to make drawings, but discovered when she sent back some work to the War Memorial's Military History Unit in Melbourne that Major John Treloar, the officer-in-charge of war artists, had no understanding of the climatic issues and wanted paintings, not drawings, or what he called 'head studies'. She was reprimanded, but defended herself ably, writing to Treloar, 'Many of the other artists will agree with me that it is not practical to attempt larger and more finished subjects up here – also that it takes time and experience to adapt oneself to working conditions'.[42]

Years later Nora commented on the difficulty of working with oils in New Guinea: 'Paintings went mouldy overnight and ... I was working out of doors quite a bit.'[43] Furthermore, she considered drawing a medium more appropriate to working in tropical conditions: 'You were working in the wet, and you had to be very quick working in the wards, working with patients or anything pertaining to war had to be done rather quickly and getting out oil paints and all this business ... and I don't work very much from memory. I work direct. The drawings can say as much as paintings, but paintings mean more to the War Memorial.'[44]

While Nora found working in the tropics, with its constant rain, difficult, she was captivated by the landscape around her. In one of her regular letters home to her parents, she commented, 'I wish I had more experience in landscape painting, it is rather a lovely spot around here with magnificent blue views of jungle-clad hills [but it is] difficult to know how to handle it in paint';[45] and one month later, 'The hills are beautiful even though the place is a shambles, [with its] dead trees and bomb craters, there is so much beauty'.[46] These are interesting observations, since there had been, so to speak, a division of labour in the Heysen household, once it became clear that Nora would also work as an artist. Her father had almost completely given up painting flowers to let Nora work on that genre, and he focused on landscape painting while Nora also focused on portraits. These family dynamics account for her wistful comments about landscape painting and explain why, working as a war artist, she focused almost exclusively on figurative work with landscape merely as a backdrop.

The climate was not the only problem. She also came into conflict with Major John Treloar on the grounds that she was portraying too few women and too many men. She was about to be recalled due to these perceived problems when dermatitis, a debilitating skin condition caused by living and working in the tropics, overtook her, and she was sent home to The Cedars to recover. While on leave, and at the request of Treloar, Louis McCubbin, Director of the National Gallery of South Australia and member of the War Memorial's Appointments Committee, visited her at Hahndorf to look over her work. McCubbin immediately realised she had many working drawings, covering all manner of subjects, she had not sent in because they were not yet finished. He notified Treloar of her method of working, the Military History Unit was satisfied, and once she was well enough her appointment was extended.

Nora's next posting was in far north Queensland, and in May 1945 she was based at the AIF Medical Air Evacuation Unit at the RAAF Station, Garbutt, Townsville. She spent several months going up and down the far north coast of Queensland, accompanying the Flying Sisters on medical evacuation trips from Lea and Morotai back to Cairns and Townsville. She called it her time of penance because, 'I'm not a very good flier and as for working in the air like that ... it was a bit of a trauma coming down with a wounded man without their legs and arms [sic] ... The amazing thing is they looked so happy to get out of it, no matter what they'd lost.'[47]

Later that same year, she was transferred to the RAAF base at Cairns, where she painted three memorable portraits: a transport driver, Aircraftswoman Florence Miles; a dispatch rider George Mayo; and a cook *Corporal Joan Whipp*, 1945, who for an army cook was unexpectedly proud of her cooking skills. She is a large woman, standing at her bench next to her bowls, basins and egg whisk. With conventional femininity cast aside, she is portrayed very much as an army cook – arms casually folded, strong upper torso framed by her army shirt with epaulettes on the shoulders, and a cook's apron – all of which give her an expansive air. She is in control of her kitchen, and as Nora said, 'she was such a jolly person, she got on very well with the men and she was such a good cook!'[48]

Nora also documented a little-acknowledged side of war in Cairns, at the Medical Research Unit, where research into the prevention and cure of malaria and the care of malaria patients was carried out. She painted entomologist Major Josephine Mackerras, whom she described as 'the only woman working in this capacity', an 'odd looking little person, ugly and interesting, bright intelligent eyes behind glasses, and a lined and pallid yellow face and grey wispy hair'.[49] She portrayed soldiers involved in the mosquito-breeding program, and as she reported in one of her weekly letters to Treloar, 'patients suffer as "guinea pigs" with malaria' for the progress of science; 'these volunteers do a good job, I think, and deserve recording.'[50]

Like everyone involved in the war, Nora was eager to go home once peace had been declared. She was also hungry for news about the art world, and in one letter to her parents asked, 'I hear there is a new book out on Australian painting by one Bernard Smith. Have you seen it?'[51] In October 1945 she commented, 'It won't be long now before I can close my paintbox on war work – a happy day'.[52] But she worked on as a war artist until February 1946, completing 155 paintings and drawings and three sketchbooks, all of which are in the collection of the Australian War Memorial.

After her discharge, she opted to finish off the remaining work in her own time. Her appointment was a high point in her career, and she produced some remarkable paintings of women, but it was also a difficult time for her – her tenacity was much needed, as had been the case for Hans during the First World War. Nora had sole responsibility for recording the women's services in the Pacific region, and as a consequence she was placed under more scrutiny than many of the other artists. But the prestigious appointment also meant the Heysen family had come full circle in relation to their national identity, of which their German heritage was an important part.

Notes

1. This painting is now in the collection of the Art Gallery of South Australia.
2. Hans Heysen's mother Elize and five children migrated to Australia in 1884, one year after his father Louis.
3. Hans Heysen became a Knight Bachelor in the Queen's Birthday Honours List of 12 June 1959 'in recognition of his unique contribution to Australian art' (cited in Colin Thiele, *Heysen of Hahndorf*, Rigby, Adelaide, 1968, p. 274).
4. Hans Heysen to Lionel Lindsay, 7 February 1919 (quoted in Thiele 1968, p. 289).
5. Hans Heysen to Lionel Lindsay, 1918, MS9104, La Trobe Collection, State Library of Victoria.
6. Ian Harmstorf, 'Germans', in Wilfrid Prest (ed.), *The Wakefield Companion to South Australian History,* Wakefield Press, Adelaide, 2001, pp. 224–5; Elizabeth Kwan, *Living in South Australia: A social history*, vol. 2, SA Government Printer, Netley, SA, 1987, p. 3.
7. Hahndorf was established in 1842 by Captain Hahn (Ian Harmstorf & Michael Cigler, *The Germans in Australia*, AE Press, Melbourne, 1985, p. 16).
8. The Heysen family moved into The Cedars in 1912.
9. This 'problem' of German-Australians not speaking German was commented on in the *Australische Zeitung* newspaper on 3 January 1900: 'English, the language of the country should and must be learnt, but that did not mean that German has to be thrown overboard as unnecessary ballast ... German should be kept alive not only in the Parish schools but in the family, because if the language died at home all other efforts would be in vain' (cited in Kwan 1987, p. 123).
10. Ian North, 'Gum-tree Imperial: Hans Heysen's *Red Gold* 1913', in Daniel Thomas, (ed) *Creating Australia: 200 Years of art 1788–1988*, International Cultural Corporation of Australia and Art Gallery Board of South Australia, Adelaide, 1988, pp. 140–1.
11. Hans Heysen letter quoted by Lionel Lindsay ('The art of Hans Heysen', *Art in Australia*, Sydney, special number, 1920, p. 8).
12. John Williams & Emily Kolb, 'Through media eyes: Australia and Germany 1913–1919, Comparative press perspectives', in *Journal of Australian Studies*, no. 60, 1999, pp. 40–1; Michele Langfield, 'Recruiting immigrants: The First World War and Australian immigration', in the *Journal of Australian Studies*, no. 60, 1999, p. 60.

13 *Sydney Morning Herald*, 10 October 1914; see also Williams & Kolb 1999, pp. 40–54.
14 ibid., p. 44.
15 Thiele 1968, p. 163.
16 ibid., p. 164.
17 This occurred in 1917 under the *Nomenclature Act* which was passed by the South Australian Government. It affected 69 German named towns and suburbs. Klemzig, Lobethal and Hahndorf were the earliest to revert to their former names in 1935 and 1936, some reclaimed their names in the 1970s and 1980s, but many lost their German names permanently (Prest [ed.] 2001, pp. 628–9).
18 Cited in John Tregenza, 'Hans Heysen: A biographical outline' in *Hans Heysen Centenary Retrospective 1877–1977*, Art Gallery Board of South Australia, 1977, p. 103.
19 Heysen to Gruner, 9 April 1918, Heysen Family papers, National Library of Australia (NLA), MS 5073.
20 ibid.
21 Thiele 1968, p. 164.
22 Probably 24 November 1921 (cited in Thiele 1968, p. 166).
23 Nora Heysen interviewed by the author, 15 September 1989.
24 Louis McCubbin to A.W. Bazley, Acting Director, Australian War Memorial, 28 January 1943, A.W.M. file 93, 50/4/1/1, part 1.
25 This happened more generally too (Harmstorf & Cigler 1985, p. 139).
26 A.W.M. file 50/4/2/131 and Heysen Family papers, NLA, MS 5073, folder 156, 1 October 1943. See also Catherine Speck, *Painting Ghosts: Australian Women Artists in Wartime*, Craftsman House/Thames and Hudson, 2004, Chapter 8, 'Nora Heysen's view from the Pacific Region'.
27 K. Nockles, 'Hidden from View: Nora Heysen', Master of Letters thesis, Australian National University, 1997, p. 59.
28 Treloar to the Acting Director, Australian War Memorial, 3 October 1941 (Cairo), A.W.M. file 93, 50/4/1/1, part 1.
29 Nora Heysen interviewed by the author, 15 September 1989.
30 Matron Annie Sage served in the Middle East, the Pacific area, New Guinea and Singapore during the Second World War. She was awarded a Royal Red Cross Medal in 1942, a Florence Nightingale Medal in 1947, and a Commander of the British Empire (C.B.E.) in 1951.
31 Nora Heysen, quoted in *Woman*, 14 February 1944.
32 Hans Heysen Papers, NLA, MS 5073, folder 158, nd.
33 Nora Heysen interviewed by the author, 15 September 1989, 23 February 1990.
34 Heysen Family papers, NLA, 14 July 1944, MS 5073, folder 163.

35 Heysen quoted in C. Craig, 'War and Art: Choice, impact and transformation: Australian artists recall their experiences 1939–45', *Oral History Association of Australia Journal*, no. 15, 1993, pp. 6–7. In actual fact, the nurses refused to wear khaki and wore their traditional grey uniforms; it was the AWAS (Australian Women's Army Service) who wore khaki uniforms (Jan Bassett, *Guns and Brooches: Australian Army nursing from the Boer War to the Gulf War*, Oxford University Press, Oxford, 1992, p. 3).
36 E.W. Woodward to headquarters, New Guinea force, 15 March 1944, AWM file 93, 206/2/17.
37 Heysen to her parents, May 1944, Heysen Family papers, NLA, MS 5073, folder 160.
38 Lola Wilkins & Joan Kerr, 'Nora Heysen: Theatre sister Margaret Sullivan', in Joan Kerr (ed.) *Heritage*, Craftsman House, Sydney, 1995, p. 262.
39 Heysen to her parents, 1 May 1944, Hans Heysen papers, NLA, MS 5073, folder 160.
40 Heysen to her parents, 19 August 1944, Hans Heysen papers, NLA, MS 5073, folder 160.
41 Thiele 1968, p. 252.
42 Heysen to Treloar, 24 July 1944, A.W.M. file 93, 206/2/17.
43 Nora Heysen interviewed by the author, 23 February 1990.
44 Nora Heysen interviewed by the author, 15 September 1989.
45 Nora Heysen to her parents, 31 July 1944, Hans Heysen papers, NLA, MS 5073, folder 163.
46 Nora Heysen to her parents, 31 August 1944, Hans Heysen papers, NLA, MS 5073, folder 163.
47 Nora Heysen interviewed by the author, 15 September 1989.
48 Ibid.
49 Nora Heysen to her parents, 1945, Cairns, Hans Heysen papers, NLA, MS 5073, folder 163.
50 Heysen to Treloar, 20 August 1945, A.W.M. file 206/2/17.
51 Heysen to her parents, 1945, Cairns, Hans Heysen papers, NLA, MS 5073, folder 164.
52 ibid.

Joining the club
German immigrants to South Australia after 1945

Ingrid Münstermann

Introduction

This chapter presents a sociological perspective of the settlement of German-born migrants who came to Australia after the Second World War. Most of them arrived in Australia in the 1950s, with South Australia having its largest intake in 1952.[1] Many Germans came with a chequered history, but they were admitted, despite strong criticisms by the Jewish Council to Combat Fascism and Anti-Semitism.[2] Most men were tradespersons (on entry officially classified as labourers), and most women were clerks (officially classified as domestics). The structure of Australian society was unfamiliar and their knowledge of English often minimal, so German ethnic clubs were created. These were meeting places where people could speak their mother tongue and maintain aspects of their culture without being ridiculed, and where emotional support was available to assist them to come to terms with a new life. It was important for the new settlers to create a buffer, a so-called comfort zone, to soften the settlement process. Measured by official statistics on workforce participation, education and training, income and home ownership, the majority of German-born newcomers succeeded in their efforts to take their place in an unfamiliar society.[3] There were also high rates of out-marriages, high rates of language shift from German to English as early as in the first generation, and high rates of naturalisation, all of which accelerated the transition into a new culture.

A very useful way of tracing this rapid process of acculturation is to examine the immigrants' membership of clubs. It is possible both quantitatively and qualitatively to draw insightful conclusions about these post-war immigrants from data extracted from such sources as the Australian Bureau of Statistics (ABS) (1945 to 2001), the Bureau of Immigration, Multicultural and Population Research (until 1996), and from publications such as *People and Place*.

In 1995, 1130 questionnaires were distributed within the German-born community of South Australia, and 164 responses were received. These questionnaires were semi-structured and left sufficient space for people to voice their opinions, representing the qualitative part of the research. Later on, 131 interviews were conducted with first-, second- and third-generation 'Germans'. The qualitative research included interviews on two occasions with the presidents and secretaries of nine different organisations which had been founded by German-born people. The presidents and secretaries of the Goethe Society and the Wagner Society were also interviewed; these institutions were founded by members of Adelaide University. These interviews were repeated in 2003.

In the early years of immigration, club membership was an important tool for the identification of migrants as they were looking for people of the same background for advice and support, and the most common place to meet compatriots were the ethnic organisations. It must be mentioned from the outset, however, that the 'ethnic' identification of members provided some difficulties. Determining ethnicity or even nationality (previous and current) of club members is almost impossible. It was difficult to establish exact figures of how many members were born in Germany, were ethnic Germans, were people of East European descent who spoke German fluently, or who were second-generation Germans. The registration forms for the largest German ethnic organisation, The Club, contain only the applicant's name, address, date of birth, telephone number and current occupational status. For my purposes here, self-identification and broad identification by the presidents and secretaries of the different organisations have been used to determine membership trends. Despite this shortcoming, it is argued that these trends are important signifiers of what is going on in the German immigrant community and whether ethnicity or group solidarity is increasing, is being maintained, or declining.

During the past 50 years several ways of thinking about settlement processes have been developed: assimilation, integration, accommodation, symbolic ethnicity, acculturation and multiculturalism. The ones which are thought most appropriate and convincing are Emory Bogardus's theory of acculturation, and Herbert Gans's theory of acculturation and of symbolic ethnicity.[4] Acculturation can be linked to Australia's concept of multiculturalism, since both rest on tolerance and the maintenance of old customs. Acculturation combines adaptation with learning, but does not necessarily create assimilation. Where assimilation requires changes in attitudes, which take a long time to achieve, acculturation requires changes in cultural patterns, which can more easily be achieved, as long as the following conditions exist: the tolerance level of the host society is high (the more tolerant the host society, the easier it is for the newcomer to abandon old customs and habits); and the immigrants want to fit into an overarching framework (law, language, and so on) and have a desire to succeed. To achieve acculturation, some characteristics and activities of the migrant group need to be modified to fit the requirements of the new environment, and the host society has to provide the conditions for this.

Clubs

In 1953 Jean Martin found that 38 ethnic associations existed in New South Wales, representing 19 different European nationalities or sociocultural groups.[5] She argued that these organisations functioned as centres of social life and provided a mechanism for the continuation of cultural traditions. Based on the limited information available at that time, she established the following characteristics of such associations. With very few exceptions, immigrant associations are not prototypes of groups that existed in the home country, but are formed to meet needs emerging from the immigrant situation. These associations represent an effort amongst immigrants to cope with unfamiliar situations, providing a structure within which the participants can win certain recognition, enabling them to recover self-respect and self-esteem, which are lost when arriving in unfamiliar territory. Further, most immigrant associations represent sectional interests within a nationality – geographical, cultural and linguistic. Martin concludes that the immigrants themselves are not a constant factor, and, as time progresses, they cannot be understood as a homogeneous group.

James Jupp, writing almost 50 years later, found that by the 1970s, and before multiculturalism was launched officially, there was a widespread network of ethnic organisations.[6] The Department of Social Security listed almost 2000 associations in all states and territories, suggesting a high degree of organisation. These ethnic structures were used by governments of different persuasions and by public agencies to discuss problems and to find avenues of communication. Jupp agrees with Martin that these organisations were used to cushion the effects of coming to terms with a new life in a foreign country.

As far as German immigrants are concerned, the following picture emerges. Joseph Vondra, researching in the 1970s, claimed that German-speaking immigrants arriving in the 1950s, 1960s and 1970s fashioned the dominant character of the post-war arrivals – the petty bourgeois nature of the group – hard-working, conservative, self-reliant and materialistic.[7] These people express their needs, tastes and lifestyles in the so-called club culture and have values fixed on increased affluence. Gisela Kaplan, writing approximately ten years later, expressed the view that most clubs were formed in the 1960s, but membership was already declining by the 1980s.[8] In her view the club culture was not representative of German residents in Australia, and it was not appealing to the younger generation. Sandra Kipp and others, writing a few years later than Vondra and Kaplan, found that there were approximately 30 German-speaking community organisations in Melbourne, but the majority of German speakers did not belong to any of them.[9]

In South Australia after 1945 the German-born population increased at first (from 1098 in 1947 to 16,393 in 1976), but then declined (to 12,660 in 2001, and to 11,971 in 2006) and, in 2006, constituted only 0.8% of the overall population.[10] In order to assess whether ethnicity, the feeling of identification with, and solidarity amongst, people of German background is persisting or declining, contact with 11 associations was established (1995 and 2003) and membership figures, scheduled events and attendances explored. In 2003 it was not possible to contact all organisations because two had folded. Two others still existed, but despite many attempts contact could not be established.

Table 1: German Ethnic Organisations and Organisations Communicating German Cultural Aspects

Association	Founded	Facilities	Membership						Estimat. Average Age 2003	Facilities and Activities
			Foun-dation	High-est	1995 Total	1995 German	2003 Total	2003 German		
Busy Bees – *Die Fleissigen Bienen*, Morphett Vale	1984	Hire	10	90	87	83	62	54	62	CommHall, bar; darts, cards, bingo, pool, bowling, coffee/cake, lunch, mystery tours, dances, talks.
Danube Swabians – *Donauschwaben*, Woodville	1972	Own	45	300	300	275	300	275	68	Bar; billiard, cards, darts, craftwork, library, Donauschwaben newspapers, BBQs, coffee/cake, dances.
Enzian Community Club, Hope Valley	1987	Hire	16	120	120	110		Estimate 100	Not known	CommHall, bar; folkdance, videos, BBQs, coffee/cake, dances.
German-Australian Association, Port Augusta	1956 1962	Own	50	130	56	45	32	16	70	Bar; cards, billiard, videos, coffee/cake, caberets, dances, German-language teaching.
German Club of Elizabeth	1979	Own	15	150	110	80	86	81	68	Bar; bowling, cards, eight ball, BBQ, garage sales, dances, Schützenfest.
German-Speaking Association, Whyalla	1968	Own	35	250	65	62	Has folded		N/A	Bar; needle work, cards, coffee/cake, videos, outings, BBQs

German immigrants after 1945

Organization	Founded	Premises								Activities
SA German Association, Flinders Street, Adelaide	1886 1911 1947	Own	N/K N/K 170	N/K 600 2000	1000	600	894	626	64	Bar, restaurant; Adelaider Liedertafel, choirs, accordion, Berliner, Bavarian, ladies' gymnastics, descendants, stamp collectors, social, carnival, pensioner, theatre, marksmen, gute Freunde, soccer, table tennis, tennis, bushwalkers, folk dance, cards, BBQs, Octoberfest, Schützenfest, library.
SA German Association of Mount Gambier	1960	Own	25	210	55	30		Estimate 10	Not known	Bar; marksmen, table tennis, eight ball, green ball, cards, darts, library, BBQs, dances.
Sociability Club Port Adelaide – *Gemütlichkeitsverein* Taperoo	1984	Hire	22	40	40	37		Has folded	N/A	Bar; dances and outings.
*Goethe Society	1952	Hire	4	90	75	68	120	108	60	Literature, music, travel reports.
*Wagner Society	1986	Hire	2	80	80	8	150	22	Not known	Music of Richard Wagner, lectures, videos, Wagner's wake, Richard and Cosima Wagner's birthdays.
Total membership			3460		1988	1398		1292		
Percentage of German-born Census population						10.5% of 13,241		10.2% of 12,660		

*not founded by German immigrants

Table 1 shows the emergence of 11 associations over a period of 40 years, 1947 to 1987. The table records the year the clubs were founded, whether facilities are owned or hired, the number of foundation members, the highest membership figures, figures for 1995 and for 2003, and the services offered. The table also shows figures of 'German' and of 'other' members. To address the issue of declining ethnicity, it was important to make this distinction. It is also assumed that without the so-called 'other' members, more associations would have disappeared by now.

South Australia's largest German organisation will serve as an example of the way these associations emerge, develop and sometimes perish. The South Australian General German Association in Adelaide (today officially named SA German Association, but affectionately called The Club) was founded in 1886. According to Ian Harmstorf, The Club was closed during the two wars.[11] It had 600 members in 1911, but only 200 members in 1936. During the 1930s strong internal divisions within The Club made it difficult to obtain patronage, because Nazi Party members used the organisation as a meeting place: 11 people were members of the German Nazi Party.[12] At the outbreak of the war in 1939, the Australian Government was suspicious of The Club's activities, but a report of the Commonwealth Investigation Branch in Canberra in 1946 stated: '... from an examination of the old Military Intelligence file it would appear that no action was taken by the Military authorities to close the Club under National Security (General) Regulations, the closing of the same would seem to have been voluntary'.[13]

In 1950 the membership was 170, and then there was a steady increase to 2000 in 1986, The Club's centenary. About 30 per cent of fee-paying members were 'other' members. But by 1995, membership had declined to 1000, and the participation rate of 'other' club members was 40 per cent. In 2003 the membership was 894, including 30 per cent of 'other' members. The Club had granted special privileges to everyone who spoke German fluently – only they could become full members with an entitlement to vote. This however was changed in 1993: non-German speakers could become full members and had the right to vote; meetings are now held in English and in German; and the bi-monthly newsletter is published in English and in German.

The most famous event staged by The Club is the annual *Schützenfest*, the King Shoot, which took place in the old German town of Hahndorf between 1964 and 1992. Since 1993, it has been staged in Bonython Park, Adelaide, and in 2003 it attracted 28,000 local, interstate and international visitors. Although The Club tends to date the *Schützenfest* from the post-Second World War era, according to Harmstorf,[14] the first *Schützenfest* had already been held in 1890 in the Adelaide suburb of Walkerville. The *Schützenfest* has played an important part in South Australia's cultural history, and, according to several interviews, The Club has promoted German culture within a multicultural Australian setting: there has never been any restriction to membership on ethnic grounds, and aspects of Australian culture are integrated into the club culture. The Club incorporates 20 different interest groups, which function well.

Between the 1950s and 1980s, eight other German associations were founded in South Australia and the following remark, made by an interviewee regarding the smaller associations, demonstrates the need for identification:

> Why did all these small German associations emerge? I am not quite sure but I think it is a matter of identification. We all get older and it is harder to get into the city and we need something to identify with, where we can relax and feel completely comfortable. Most of us are not working any more. The Club became at one stage quite impersonal, with a big membership of over two thousand. So, I think, when you have a small but well functioning group, people find it easier to identify. And all we elderly want is a dance every now and again, and a bit of a chat in our mother tongue once or twice per week. The small clubs certainly make this possible. This sort of identification is very important to me and my wife.

As Table 1 demonstrates, associations which were founded by members of the German immigrant community offer aspects of popular culture, such as dancing, folk dance, singing, films, card games, bingo, bowls, food, drinks, stamp collecting, tennis, table tennis, gymnastics, and walking. However, what is happening in societies which offer aspects of German high culture? The following two organisations deserve special mention, because firstly they were not established by German migrants but by academics of Adelaide University, and secondly because they deal with the so-called high culture, namely German literature, art and music.

In 1952 members of the German Department at the University of Adelaide set up the Goethe Society. At the foundation meeting it was determined that the main task would be to cultivate and maintain the literary and musical aspects of German culture. During the interviews one of the participants mentioned that 'Jewish people founded the Goethe Society and they kindly invited us to participate.' Many of the German-born migrants expressed appreciation for this opportunity. 'Culturally Australia lacked sophistication, but that was the price we had to pay in the beginning. The Goethe Society filled this void – up to a certain point.' The highest membership of the Goethe Society numbered around 120, and the figure remained more or less stable over the years. Approximately 90 per cent were native speakers, but the population was ageing. In 2002 it was decided to change the language during meetings, from German to English. This was to make it possible for the younger generation, who are not completely comfortable in the German language, to attend meetings and to contribute. Despite these changes, the Goethe Society was not able to continue, and it folded in 2007, after 55 years.

The other association is the Wagner Society. It deals with the music of Richard Wagner and was founded in 1986 by members of the Department of Music, Adelaide University. The patron is Wolfgang Wagner, a grandson of Richard Wagner. This organisation is very active: membership in 1995 was 80, but in 2003 it had increased to 150. It was thought that this considerable increase in membership may have been an effect of staging Wagner's *Ring* in the Adelaide Festival Theatre first in 2000 and then again in 2004; however, I was assured that there is a genuine interest in Wagner's music, apart from the *Ring,* and that the many activities which the society offers also contribute to the increase in membership: overseas trips to different Wagner festivals, sophisticated lecture and radio programs, get-togethers at stylish places, and a membership of mainly professional people. Only 15 per cent of members of the Wagner Society are German immigrants.

It seems that organisations providing high culture find it easier to maintain membership than those providing popular culture. Here it should be pointed out that the Goethe Society was and the Wagner Society is managed (voluntarily) by professional people, who are familiar with various government departments (the federal department of education; the *Goethe Gesellschaft* in Germany; the *International Wagner Verband* in Germany) and are able to access their assistance and to prepare grant applications. By comparison, highly motivated volunteers (mostly retirees) manage the German ethnic organisations; they are supporting the institutions by being financial members and donate time and effort to maintain them.

Table 1 shows a decrease in membership figures as well as in the number of associations promoting German popular culture. According to the presidents and secretaries of the different organisations, it is estimated that in the early 1980s membership was at its highest, with around 20 per cent of German-born people actively participating. This rate decreased to approximately 10 per cent in 2003. There could be several reasons for this. Generally the South Australian hospitality industry offers much more than 40 or 50 years ago, when ethnic clubs were the only places to get a meal and a drink after 6 pm or on weekends. There have also been changes to the laws relating to pub closing time (no longer 6 pm), and blood-alcohol limits for driving have been imposed. These issues will have had some influence on the declining membership. However, the most important reasons are related to the age of the German-born population and to the overall acculturation of German immigrants into Australian society. German-born people do not need ethnic clubs anymore. This theory is confirmed when analysing why club membership was or was not important.

The findings in Table 2 are based on answers given in questionnaires and during interviews. The answers were provided by 217 first-, and 34 second- and third-generation 'Germans'. The results show that 35 per cent of the first generation and 44 per cent of the second and third generation belong to a German ethnic organisation. The main reasons for membership are to maintain old customs, culture and language, and for the opportunity to meet people of the same background. For some first-generation German immigrants, club membership also meant the maintenance of status and self-respect, and this is further discussed later on.

Table 2: To belong or not to belong to an organisation promoting aspects of German culture

	First generation N = 217		Second/third Generation N = 34		Total N = 251	
Reasons for belonging	No.	%	No.	%	No.	%
Maintenance of customs /culture	59	27	6	18	65	26
Language maintenance	49	23	3	9	52	21
Opportunity to meet people of same background	49	23	2	6	51	20
Other (includes status, self-respect)	13	6	3	9	16	6
Total positive responses	170		14		184	
Reasons for not belonging						
Support is not needed No affinity with Germans anymore Germans in clubs live in the past	45	20	15	44	60	24
Club does not provide for young people	2	1	5	15	7	3
Total negative responses	47	100	20	100	67	100

An important finding relates to the second and third generation: only 18 per cent of the participants want to maintain old customs and culture, 9 per cent want to maintain the language, and only 6 per cent are interested in meeting people of the same ethnic background. The overall participation rate of second- and third-generation Germans in this research was small and conclusions should perhaps be drawn cautiously; however, claims such as support not being needed, that respondents have no affinity with Germans, that Germans in clubs live in the past, and that clubs do not provide for young people should raise the awareness of those in charge of these associations.

The other important findings are the negative responses of 20 per cent of first-generation Germans who also claim that support is not needed, and that they no longer feel any affinity towards

Germans. It may well be that these people arrived in Australia at a very young age and that they now are completely absorbed into Australian society.

Acculturation and identity

What do these trends in clubs and organisations tell us about the acculturation of post-war German immigrants to South Australia? Bogardus argues that 'one can more easily bear the loss of almost anything in life than the loss of social status'.[15] When a person immigrates to a foreign country and is not able to speak the language, or speaks with a strong accent and has mannerisms different from those of the host society, loss of status seems inevitable, especially within a working-class environment. Clubs acted as a buffer zone, offsetting the consequences of losing status, while ethnic organisations presented comfort zones where the old identities could be maintained.

Over time new, fragmented identities developed among German immigrants. People wanted to be accepted, and in trying to fit in they adapted to different situations. In other words, acculturation took place – people modified their behaviour to bring it into line with the norms of the new country without making too many changes to their private beliefs and feelings. They maintained old customs and values, but were well integrated and felt comfortable in the receiving society. Yet it was a process which fell short of assimilation, which, in the strictest sense, requires unconditional surrender to the new culture and total rejection of the interpersonal bonds among immigrants.[16]

Declining membership in clubs and organisations can be interpreted as a sign that the process of acculturation is drawing to a close. This conclusion is based on Gans's supposition that, after a certain period of time, ethnic groups no longer need ethnic cultures or organisations; instead, they resort to symbols such as foods and traditions and perhaps identify with national figures or church holidays. This can be observed among German immigrants in South Australia, who, apart from consuming traditional food and drinks on special occasions such as Christmas and Easter, continue to observe St Nikolaus Day and Advent Sundays, display Advent wreaths and Advent calendars in clubs, churches and homes, and celebrate Christmas on 24 December. Within their ethnic associations, participants foster customs as shown in Table 1, and they organise the *Schützenfest*. The ethnic organisations function still as a medium for ethnicity, but their role is diminishing, as the folding of the Goethe Society after 55 years demonstrates. The German-born population is well integrated into Australian society and resorts to symbolic ethnicity.

The process of acculturation is also evident when we look at patterns of out-marriage. Charles Price found that, even in the period 1947 to 1963, 61 per cent of Austrian and German men married women of Australian or other nationality, and 55 per cent of Austrian and German women married an Australian or a man of other than their own nationality.[17] These percentages increased over the years.[18] As for the second-generation Germans, Price found that in-group marriage varied from only 3 per cent to 4.5 per cent between 1981 and 1992.[19] Moreover, 80 per cent of Germans have taken up Australian citizenship.[20] Looking at the use of the English language provides another indicator of acculturation. In 1986 Michael Clyne found that almost 41 per cent of German-born immigrants used only English in everyday life.[21] Between 1986 and 1991 the number of German-born who reported speaking German at home decreased by around 3 per cent;[22] therefore, it can be assumed that 44 per cent of German-born immigrants speak English only. Looking at second-generation Germans, there is a much higher rate of English language use: within endogamous marriages it is 73 per cent, and within exogamous marriages it is more than 85 per cent.[23] Clyne and Kipp[24] also show that between 1991 and 1996 German as a community language decreased by 12.8 per cent (from 113,336 to 98,808). Some of the users may have died, but many will have switched to English only.

This sort of behaviour is not new. Peter Mühlhäusler established that during the nineteenth century Germans in German colonies in the Pacific would resort to English in everyday conversation, although they could have used their mother tongue.[25] Many people even resorted to pidgin English. Mühlhäusler recorded that the presence of only one speaker of the English language was sufficient to prompt a whole group of German men to communicate in more or less bad English. His general conclusion was that Germans had a well-developed sense of trying to fit in. But he also related the language shift in the Pacific to missing policies on language teaching and to the lack of teaching facilities.

Ian Harmstorf and Michael Cigler reveal similar circumstances.[26] Germans in South Australia in the nineteenth century willingly fitted into Australian society. Harmstorf demonstrates this by saying that, in 1913, when the German Consul General visited South Australia, he found that the Germans had readily given up their language and culture. The Consul General was only repeating the views of A. Heisig who had written as early as in 1853 in *Die Deutschen in Australien* (published in Berlin) that there was a strong tendency for Germans to be seduced by, and to adopt, the British language and way of life.[27]

Looking at German immigrants who arrived in South Australia from 1945, there can be no doubt that they, too, fitted into the overall structure of society, but that ethnic organisations fulfilled an important role in 'cushioning the effects of settlement and adjustment because they were important points of contact'.[28] Apart from socialising, experiences could be exchanged and advice obtained. But the number of people actively participating is, and always seems to have been, relatively small. My findings demonstrate that group solidarity and social networks are weak within the German immigrant population. One interviewee mentioned that it is 'a matter of outwitting rather than helping each other'. It is suggested that German immigrants 'cut across ties and pass the framework of bounded institutionalised groups'.[29] Official data confirm the theory of only minimal group solidarity: the proportion of immigrants from Germany having received help from relatives and friends to come to Australia, or after their arrival, was lower than that of any other place of birth group except Malaysia,[30] indicating a self-reliant and independent approach to an immigrant existence.

Conclusion

German immigrants who arrived in Australia from 1945 have not completely disappeared within Australian society, but they are highly acculturated. As my findings show, group identification is minimal – just over 10 per cent of South Australia's German-born population belongs to an ethnic organisation, and rates of out-marriage, naturalisation and language shift to English only are high. Gans argues that, when acculturation has taken place, ethnic populations no longer need ethnic cultures or organisations but resort to symbols such as foods, traditions and perhaps identification with national figures or church holidays. It can be argued that the customs of first-generation Germans in South Australia have indeed turned into what Gans calls 'symbolic ethnicity'. Sol Encel confirms Gans's argument by suggesting that ethnicity does not refer to a survival phenomenon by which groups cling to their past, but that, in a modern society, ethnicity is based on, and strengthened by, common occupational positions, residential stability and concentration, and dependence on universal institutions and services.[31] Social upward mobility (occupational, social and geographic) plays a more important role than the maintenance of ethnic heritage in the life of post-Second World War German immigrants to Australia.

Overall, the research shows an acculturated migrant population, but the results need to be treated with some caution. Further analysis should be undertaken to establish how long the study participants have been in Australia, at what age they arrived, and whether they are married to someone of German or other background. These are important points and influence behaviour. Looking at the Mühlhäusler and Harmstorf findings, which demonstrate the Germans having a well-developed sense of trying to fit into the host society, one could assume that German immigrants are more adaptable than other migrant groups; but one could also assume that the troubled past had something to do with the speedy acculturation of those who arrived after 1945. Whatever the reasons for the positive settlement outcome, the following passionate statement by Peter Heuzenroeder creates a sense of pride but also of responsibility in me, an immigrant of German background: 'The German heritage in all its forms – buildings, manners, relationships, beliefs, as well as festivals – is something unique and good in itself and therefore not only worthy of preservation, but something that should be fostered and kept for the benefit of all Australians whatever their ethnic background'.[32]

Notes

1. Australian Bureau of Statistics, *Immigration to SA, Australia and South Australia*, Census Data, AGPS, Canberra, 1986, p. 20.
2. Jewish Council to Combat Fascism and Anti-Semitism, 'German and Volks Migration will Flood Australia with Nazis', pamphlet printed by Moran Bros., St. Kilda, Vic., c.1952.
3. Bureau of Immigration and Population Research, *Community Profile, Germany Born, 1991 Census*, AGPS, Canberra, 1994, pp. 16–31; also Bureau of Immigration and Population Research, *Immigrant Families: A statistical profile*, AGPS, Canberra, 1994, p. 38.
4. Emory S. Bogardus, *The Development of Social Thought*, Longmans, Green & Co. New York, 1961, pp. 470–5; Herbert Gans, 'Symbolic Ethnicity: The future of ethnic groups and cultures in America', *Ethnic and Racial Studies*, vol. 2, no. 1, 1979, pp. 1–19; Herbert Gans, 'Second-Generation Decline: Scenarios for the economic and ethnic futures of post-1965 American immigrants', *Ethnic and Racial Studies*, vol. 15, no. 2, 1992, pp. 173–92.
5. Jean Martin, 'The social impact of New Australians', in J. Lack & J. Templeton (eds) *Bold Experiment*, Oxford UP, Melbourne, 1995, pp. 92–7.
6. James Jupp, *From White Australia to Woomera*, Cambridge UP, Melbourne, 2002, pp. 27–9.
7. Joseph Vondra, *German Speaking Settlers in Australia*, Cavalier Press, Melbourne, 1981, pp. 1–22.
8. Gisela Kaplan, 'Post-War German Immigrants', in J. Jupp (ed.) *The Australian People*, Angus and Robertson, Sydney, 1988, pp. 498–500.
9. Sandra Kipp, Michael Clyne & Anne Pauwels, *Immigration and Australia's Language Resources*, AGPS, Canberra, 1995, p. 137.
10. http://www.abs.gov.au.
11. Ian Harmstorf, *Insights into South Australian History, SA's German History and Heritage*, Gould Publishing Services, Adelaide, 1994, p. 28.
12. Australian National Archives SA D1915/0.
13. ibid.
14. Harmstorf 1994, p. 38.
15. Bogardus 1961, p. 471.
16. Martin Kovacs and Arthur Cropley, *Immigrants and Society*, McGraw-Hill, Sydney, 1975, p. 11.
17. Charles Price, 'Post-War Migration: Demographic background', in Allan Stoller (ed.), *New Faces*, Victorian Family Council by F.W. Cheshire, Melbourne, 1966, pp. 11–29.
18. Australian Bureau of Statistics, *Marriages: Relative birthplace of parties, South Australia*, cat. no. 3311.4, ABS, Canberra, 1991.

19 Charles Price, 'Ethnic Intermixture in Australia', *People and Place*, vol. 2, no. 4, 1994, pp 8–11.
20 Bureau of Immigration and Population Research 1994, p. 5.
21 Michael Clyne, *Community Languages: The Australian experience*, Cambridge UP, Melbourne, 1991, pp. 62–7.
22 Bureau of Immigration and Population Research 1994, p. 36.
23 Clyne 1991, pp. 62–7.
24 Michael Clyne & Sandra Kipp, 'Linguistic Diversity in Australia', *People and Place*, vol. 5, no. 3, 1997, p. 8.
25 Peter Muehlhaeusler, 'Die deutsche Sprache im Pazifik', in H. Hiery (ed.) *Die deutsche Suedsee 1884–1914: Ein Handbuch*, Ferdinand Schoeningh Verlag, Paderborn, 2000.
26 Ian Harmstorf, 'Guests or Fellow-Countrymen? A study in assimilation', Ph.D. thesis, Flinders University of SA, Adelaide, 1988, pp. 181–219; Ian Harmstorf, *The German Presence in South Australia*, Centre for Multicultural Studies, Flinders University of SA and University of SA, 1989, pp. 1–19; Harmstorf 1994, p. 28; Ian Harmstorf & Michael Cigler, *The Germans in Australia*, Australian ethnic heritage series, EA Press, Melbourne, 1989, pp. 93–165.
27 A. Hiesig, *Die Deutschen in Australien*, Berlin, 1853.
28 Joan Carr, 'Family Business in Australia and New Zealand', Ph.D. thesis, Flinders University of SA, Adelaide, 1988, p. 173.
29 B. Wellman & S.O. Berkowitz, *Social Structures: A network approach*, Cambridge UP, New York, 1991, p. 21.
30 Bureau of Immigration, Multiculturalism and Population Research, 'Immigration Update, September Quarter 1995', AGPS Canberra, 1996, p. 44.
31 Sol Encel, 'Ethnicity and Multiculturalism', national research conference paper, Australian Institute of Multicultural Affairs, University of Melbourne, 1986, p. 13.
32 Harmstorf & Cigler 1989, p. 161.

Notes on contributors

Michael Bollen is publisher at Wakefield Press, where during the last 24 years he has worked on an eclectic range of books, including many works of history. He is an occasional writer for magazines, and enjoys mining nineteenth-century Adelaide for untold stories. A fascination with the colony's medical squabbles led him to the city's putative German hospital, and thence to wider questions of early German immigration and integration.

W.H. (Bill) Edwards is a retired Minister of the Uniting Church in Australia. He served as Superintendent of Ernabella Mission in the Pitjantjatjara region in the north-west of South Australia (1958–72), Superintendent of Mowanjum Mission in the north-west of Western Australia (1972–73) and Minister of the Pitjantjatjara Parish (1976–80). He lectured in Indigenous Studies at the South Australian College of Advanced Education and the University of South Australia (1981–96). In retirement he is an Adjunct Senior Lecturer at the University of South Australia and has completed a thesis entitled 'Moravian Aboriginal Missions in Australia' for the award of the degree of Doctor of Philosophy at Flinders University. He interprets in Pitjantjatjara language in the health and legal sectors. His publications include *An Introduction to Aboriginal Societies* (2nd edn, Thomson, 2004) and, as editor, *Traditional Aboriginal Society* (2nd edn, Macmillan, 1998). In 2009 he was awarded membership of the Order of Australia for service to the Indigenous community.

Mary-Anne Gale has worked as a teacher and linguist in the field of Aboriginal education for nearly 30 years. She is currently working with the Ngarrindjeri community in the revival of their language, drawing from her experience working in bilingual schools in the

Northern Territory in strong languages such as Walrpiri and Yolngu Matha. She also has a keen interest in assisting Aboriginal people in writing their stories in their own voices, and collaborated with the late Auntie Veronica Brodie on her book *My Side of the Bridge*, and later with Uncle Lewis O'Brien on *And the Clock Struck Thirteen*. Mary-Anne's master's thesis was published in the book *Dhangum Djorra'wuy Dha:wu: a history of writing in Aboriginal languages*. Her PhD title was 'Poor Bugger Whitefella Got No Dreaming: the representation and appropriation of published Dreaming narratives with special reference to David Unaipon's writings'. She is now working on a book on David Unaipon's life and continues to work in the area of Aboriginal teacher training.

Angela Heuzenroeder has a PhD in history from the University of Adelaide. Her thesis, entitled 'A Food Culture Transplanted: Origins and development of the food of early German immigrants to the Barossa Region, South Australia (1839–1939)', examines the causes of change in the eating habits of migrating peoples. Angela is also the author of the book *Barossa Food*, a culinary history of the region, published by Wakefield Press and now in its third impression. A research fellow in the History Discipline at the University of Adelaide, Angela has delivered many papers and had several articles published about food history.

Philip Jones is a graduate of the University of Adelaide History Department and has worked as a curator in the South Australian Museum's Department of Anthropology since 1984. His doctoral thesis concerned the history of the Museum's anthropological collections. Fieldwork in the Simpson Desert region has resulted in several publications on the region's history and ethnography. He has curated more than 30 exhibitions at the South Australian Museum, ranging from Aboriginal art to the history of exploration and collecting. During 2007 he co-authored *Australia's Muslim Cameleers. Pioneers of the Inland 1860s–1930s* and published *Ochre and Rust*, a book of essays on museum objects and the Australian frontier which won the inaugural Prime Minister's literary award for non-fiction. He is currently writing on Aboriginal material culture, archival photography of Australia's inland, and the colonial artist George French Angas.

Janice Lally studied Fine Arts (Hons 1989) at the Australian National University and the University of Western Australia before completing a PhD in the history and philosophy of science, University of Melbourne (2002) with a thesis titled 'The Australian Aboriginal Collection in the Museum für Völkerkunde, Berlin, and the making of cultural identity'. As curator, gallery director and arts consultant she has managed numerous public art projects and exhibitions in Australia, Germany and Hong Kong. She recently left her position as Program Manager and Curator, Flinders University Art Museum, Adelaide, to become Curator for Public Art at the Adelaide City Council, South Australia. Exhibitions she has curated include *Identity: Portrait and Place–document or insight?* (2007); *Identity? echoes and voices – 40 years at the Flinders University Art Museum* (2006); *Light Black* (national tour and toured to Japan and Taiwan 2003–04); and *Ritual of Tea* (Adelaide Festival and national tour 2002). Published papers from recent conferences appear in *The Makers and Making of Indigenous Australian Museum Collections* (Melbourne University Publishing and Museum Victoria, 2008) and *Symposium Adolf Bastians Erbe im Ethnologischen Museum – ein universales Archiv der Menschheit? 25.2–27.2.2005* and *Baessler Archiv*, Berlin, 2005.

Christine Lockwood, formerly a high school teacher, lived and worked in various capacities in Papua New Guinea 1969–87 and USA 1991–2000. Through her time overseas, she has developed an interest in cross-cultural issues, cultural change and the relationship between theology and culture. Now living in the Adelaide area, she has resumed history studies, exploring the foundations of her adopted state of South Australia against the background of her overseas experience. She is currently a PhD candidate at the University of Adelaide.

Horst Lücke is a Professor Emeritus, University of Adelaide, and an Honorary Professor in the University of Queensland. He received his legal education at Cologne, New York and Adelaide universities and has been closely associated with the University of Adelaide since 1959, occupying *inter alia* the positions of Professor of Law (1967–84) and head of the Law School (1970–72, 1976–78). He has also taught at universities in New York, Oxford, Freiburg, Hamburg and at Bond University. He has published widely in Australian and international journals. One of his main interests is comparative law. His contribution continues work on the early German migrants to South Australia.

John Miles is the author of three volumes of poetry and *Lost Angry Penguins, D.B. Kerr & P.G. Pfeiffer: A path to the wind*. His poetry has received a number of Australian and international awards. For his research work on *Lost Angry Penguins*, he was granted an ArtsSA-funded Varuna residency. A former poetry editor for *Australian Writer*, he now acts in this capacity for Adelaide's *Independent Weekly*. Born in Kent, he grew up from age six in South Australia. After a number of years of living and working in the UK and South Africa, he now lives in Adelaide.

Peter Monteath is Associate Professor of History at Flinders University in Adelaide. He has a Masters Degree from the University of Siegen in Germany, a doctorate from Griffith University, and he is a Fellow of the Alexander von Humboldt Foundation. He has published widely in both European and Australian history. His previous book with Wakefield Press was *Encountering Terra Australis: The Australian Voyages of Nicolas Baudin and Matthew Flinders*.

Peter Mühlhäusler is the Foundation Professor of Linguistics at the University of Adelaide and Supernumerary Fellow of Linacre College, Oxford. He has taught at the Technical University of Berlin and the University of Oxford. He is an active researcher in several areas of linguistics, including ecolinguistics, language planning, language policy and language contact in the Australia-Pacific area. His current research focuses on the Pitkern-Norf'k language of Norfolk Island and the Aboriginal languages of the west coast of South Australia. His recent publications are (with Wurm and Tryon) *Atlas of Languages of Intercultural Communication in the Pacific, Asia and the Americas*; *Pidgin and Creole Linguistics*; *Language of Environment-Environment of Language*; (with Foster and Monaghan), *Early Forms of Aboriginal English in South Australia*; and (with Amery and Gara) *Hermann Koeler's Adelaide: Observations on the Language and Culture of South Australia by the First German Visitor*.

Ingrid Münstermann was born in Hamburg, Germany, and came to Australia in 1973. While working as a medical secretary at Flinders Medical Centre she began to study part-time in 1986, completed a BA Hons in 1992 and a PhD in Social Sciences at Flinders University in 1997. The title of her thesis was 'German immigrants in South Australia after 1945'. Since 2004 Ingrid has been teaching sociology at Charles Sturt University in Wagga Wagga, trying to convince students that multiculturalism and tolerance are still valid concepts. She is currently undertaking research on issues in mental health, and in matters relating to the Australian family farm and cross-boundary farming. Ingrid was awarded the 2008 Research Centre Fellowship in the Institute of Land, Water and Society of Charles Sturt University.

Pauline Payne is an Adelaide-based historical consultant. She comes from a rural background and is a graduate of the University of Adelaide and Oxford University. She is a Visiting Research Fellow in the School of History and Politics at the University of Adelaide, where she holds a doctorate. Currently she is President of the History of Science, Ideas and Technology Group (SA). Her publications include *Thebarton Old and New* (1996); *The Australian Barley Board: Making the right moves 1939–1999* (with Peter Donovan) (1999); *Helping Hand Aged Care 1953–2003: A history* (2003); and most recently *The Diplomatic Gardener: Richard Schomburgk: Explorer and Botanic Garden Director* (2007). Her previous career in public and social administration and research for heritage consultancies have combined with her own family history to give her a special interest in Australian settlement history, crop research and the contribution of German women pioneers.

Barbara Poniewierski, by profession a teacher of modern languages, graduated from the University of Western Australia in 1952 with Honours in German. One of the first post-war holders of a DAAD scholarship, she trained at the Interpreters Institute attached to the University of Heidelberg, 1954–55. She was awarded an MA from the University of Queensland for a thesis on the Australia-First Movement (1936–42), and a PhD for the 'Impact of Nazism on German Citizens in Australia, 1932–47'. Under the name 'Barbara Winter', she has had five books published in Australia and one in Germany.

Maurice Schild graduated in arts at Adelaide and studied theology at Immanuel Seminary. A DAAD scholarship allowed him to continue theology at Heidelberg, where he gained the doctorate in 1964. Ordained that year, he became pastor at Trinity Lutheran Church at Doncaster, Victoria. He subsequently joined the faculty at Luther Seminary and lectured in liturgical and church history. This job allowed further research and writing (in Reformation studies, Kierkegaard, Bonhoeffer). In 1996 he authored *The Lutherans in Australia* with Philip Hughes. Maurice was a foundation member of the Australian Roman Catholic–Lutheran Dialog and a participant in the Adelaide Theological Circle. He lives in retirement with his wife Beryl and supervises students, edits the *Journal* of Friends of Lutheran Archives and conducts services for Christian communities in English and German.

Wilfried Schröder has scholarly interests ranging from the history of science through ethnology and the geosciences; he is the author of some 45 books and over 400 scientific papers. Among his areas of expertise is the impact and influence of German scientific travellers in Australia, with a particular focus on Erhard Eylmann. Eylmann is not well known in Australia, although he travelled extensively here, made an important contribution to Australian anthropology and was well known to Baldwin Spencer and Francis Gillen. Wilfried Schröder's biography of Eylmann – the most significant of a number of publications by him on this topic – is published under the title *Ich reiste wie ein Buschmann. Zum Leben und Wirken des Australienforschers Erhard Eylmann* (Bremen, 2002).

Catherine Speck is an Associate Professor and Reader in Art History at the University of Adelaide, where she coordinates the postgraduate programs in Art History and Curatorial and Museum Studies delivered through the university and the Art Gallery of South Australia. She is the author of *Painting Ghosts: Australian Women Artists in Wartime* (Craftsman House House/Thames and Hudson 2004) and she is a member of the Adelaide Critics Circle. She is currently editing a book of letters between Hans Heysen and Nora Heysen (*Heysen to Heysen*), due for release by the National Library of Australia in 2011.

Volker Stolle was born in Stolp, Pomerania (now in Poland), and studied Protestant theology in Oberursel, Münster, Hamburg and Heidelberg. He took his first exam in theology in 1964, after which he became an assistant pastor in Bochum. After his second examination in 1966 he was ordained and worked as an assistant pastor and catechist in Berlin. In 1971–72 he was an academic assistant at the University of Münster's 'Instititum Judaicum Delitzschianum', before gaining his doctorate in theology. From 1972 to 1978 he was pastor in Bochum, and then from 1978 to 1984 he served as Director of the Lutheran Church Mission (Bleckmar Mission). From 1979 he also taught Mission Studies, serving from 1984 to his retirement in 2005 as Professor for the New Testament at the Lutheran Theological Seminary in Oberursel. His publications are in the areas of the New Testament, interpretation of Luther's writings, Christian–Jewish relations and the history of the Lutheran Mission. Since his retirement he has been living in Mannheim, where he continues to research and publish, including his book on Karl Mützelfeldt, *'Den christlichen Nichtariern nimmt man alles.' Der evangelische Pädagoge Karl Mützelfeldt angesichts der NS-Rassenpolitik* (Berlin, 2007).

Julie Holbrook Tolley recently completed her doctoral thesis, 'Stewed Cockatoo and a Glass of Grenache', an historical study of women in the South Australian wine industry. Dr Tolley has been published in several journals, including *History Australia*, which had sound bites of her interviews embedded in the article, a world first. She presented a paper at the first international conference on wine history in Avignon, published in *Wine, Society, and Globalization* in 2007. She is currently lecturing and tutoring at the University of South Australia and teaching at Christies Beach High School. She is also researching the Australian wartime artist, Sybil Craig.

Christine Winter (Postdoctoral Research Fellow, School of History, Philosophy, Religion and Classics, University of Queensland, and Visiting Fellow, Australian National University) is a historian whose work analyses transnational histories of European–Pacific relations and engagements. She has published on National Socialism in Oceania and on the politics of internment during the Second World War. She has been part of the team researching *The Official*

History of Australian Peacekeeping, Humanitarian and Post-Cold War Operations and has most recently been collaborating with Professor Tessa Morris-Suzuki and Dr Keiko Tamura on the ARC-funded project *Rethinking Impartial Humanitarianism*. The chapter is part of her wider research project *Legacies of the German Empire in Oceania: The transformation of German identity during the inter-war years*.

Lois Zweck completed a PhD in German at Adelaide University ('The Austrian Novel: Musil, Broch, Canetti') and undertook postdoctoral studies at Freiburg University before teaching German at all levels, from primary to tertiary, and in a range of contexts, from pioneering telephone-teaching at the Correspondence School, to adult evening classes. Working on German documents for the centenary history of her old school (Concordia College) led to an interest in the history of Australian Lutheranism, German migration to South Australia and her own ancestry. The challenge of learning to read the old German script has been amply rewarded by access to the rich early records of the local German and Lutheran communities, most of the members of which are unfortunately no longer able to read about their own heritage. Numerous visits to Europe have in recent years concentrated increasingly on research in archives and libraries in Germany and Poland. Besides her involvement with Lutheran Archives as a volunteer transcriber, translator and researcher, as Deputy Chairman of the Board and as Chairman of Friends of Lutheran Archives, she works as an occasional translator for the Ecumenical Council of the Roman Catholic Church.

Index

A

Abel, Wilhelm Friedrich 272
Adelaide Botanic Garden 126, 130–142, 148, 190, 208, 218, 220, 223, 243
Adelaide Children's Hospital 121
Adelaide Hospital 95, 98, 100, 107–109, 113, 115, 119, 121, 132
Alfred 88
Angas, George Fife 17, 19, 106, 174, 175–177, 180, 204, 238
Angas, George French 157, 163, 164
Angry Penguins xix, 334, 336–337, 342–343
Asmis, Dr Rudolf 271, 274, 276–278, 280, 283

B

Backhaus, Rev. Dr George Henry 100–102, 114, 116–117, 152
Barossa Valley 28, 41, 63, 121, 177, 208, 209, 215–218, 232, 237–240, 243–245, 247– 249, 251, 321, 329, 345, 376
Bartsch, Walter Ernst 272
Basedow, M.P.F. (Friedrich) 129, 139
Bauer, Ferdinand 144
Bayer, Dr Friedrich Carl/Frederick Charles xvi, 96–107, 109–114, 116, 119–123
Bayer, Emmeline 122

Beazley, George 223–224
Becker, Dr J. Heinrich 207, 270–276, 279–280, 284, 294
Beckler, Hermann 207
Behr, Hans Hermann 207, 214–216
Bejach, Curt 308–309, 319
Bethesda Mission 194, 198
Bieri, Otto 288, 292, 296
bis Winckel, Sophia 239, 243–244
Blandowski, Wilhelm/William 205, 207, 214, 218
Bodner, Johann M. 193, 198
Boehme, Dr C. 97, 99–101, 104
Bohlens, Oluf 272
Bohlmann, Ilma 278, 281–282, 284
Bonhoeffer, Dietrich 390–394
Bowen, Stella 408
Brougham 4
Büring, Hermann 148

C

Caleb Angas 65
Coppin, George 111, 112, 115–116, 119
Coromandel 2, 237
Crefeld 270

D

David, Christian 43, 44, 46
Deissmann, Adolf 384, 387–388

Destitute Board 109, 115, 123
Dietrich, Amalie 207, 211
Doehler, Pastor Ludwig 349, 362
Dresden Mission Aid Society 18–23, 25–31, 33, 37–39, 69, 174
Dutton, Francis 116, 120, 206
Dutton, Geoffrey 332, 334, 336, 343

E

Elsasser, Robert 308, 320
Evangelical Lutheran Mission Society, Dresden (*see also* Dresden Mission Aid Society) 17–18, 63–64, 174
Eylmann, Erhard 188–203 162, 188
Eyre, Edward John 34

F

Fiedler, Johanne 239, 243
Fienemann, Carl Christoph 272
Fisher, James Hurtle 116, 119, 166–167, 182
Foelsche, Paul Heinrich xiv, 138, 220–222, 229
Freund-Zinnbauer, Pastor Alfred 318–319, 321–323, 380
Fritzsche, Pastor Gotthard xii, 174, 176

G

Gawler, Governor George 17, 22–23, 34–35, 175
George Washington 89, 92
German Club xx, 271, 274–275, 277–278, 281, 298, 314, 422, 424–425
German Hospital xvi, 99, 108–110, 114, 116–117, 120–121, 123
Gerstäcker, Friedrich ix, xi
Gillen, Francis 191, 196, 202
Gilles, Osmond xvi, 106–107, 111, 113–114, 117–119, 177
Goethe Society 419, 423, 426–427, 430

Goyder line 219, 220, 326–327
Gramp, Johann 240
Grey, Governor George 23, 27–28, 34, 36, 39, 71, 177
Gruner, Elioth 407

H

Haacke, Dr Wilhelm 217–218, 223–225, 227
Haast, Julius 223
Hagenauer, Friedrich August 47, 49, 56
Hagen, Jacob 107, 109, 112–113
Hahn, Captain Dirk 175, 327, 340
Hahn, Harry 272
Hale, Archdeacon 29–30, 38
Hamburgh Hotel 96, 100, 103, 105–106, 115, 116
Hammond, William Edward 110
Harris, Max 332, 334–335
Hebart, Theodor 283–285, 291, 330, 333, 337
Helmke, Gottlieb 88, 90
Henschke, Prue 250
Hermannsburg Mission 41, 53, 191, 193, 197–198, 365
Hermann von Beckerath 214–215
Heuzenroeder, Moritz 214–215
Heysen, Hans xx, 402–404, 406, 408, 414
Heysen, Nora 402–417 402, 405, 409, 411
Hill, Charles 158
Hillebrand, William 214, 216
Hindmarsh, Governor Sir John 21, 167
Hirschfeld-Mack, Ludwig 402
Hitler, Adolf xvii, xviii, 259, 274, 276, 278, 280–282, 284–286, 289–293, 314–316, 323, 345–346, 348, 368, 375, 382, 390, 393

Holtze, Maurice (Waldeman) Wilhelm/William 141, 222–223, 226
Homburg, Friedrich/Fritz 258–259, 276, 279, 290, 293
Homburg, Hermann 275, 278–281
Hübbe, Ulrich xvi, 121, 166–168, 170–185
Hus, Jan 42

I

Immanuel College 315, 327, 329–333, 336–337, 342, 378
Immanuel Seminary 372, 401
Investigator 144

J

Jansen, Frederick William 103
Janzow, Dr William 284, 292, 301, 305, 307–309, 314–315, 319–320, 323, 378
Jung, Joanna 275
Jury, Charles Rischbieth 332, 334–336, 343
Jüttner, F. 253, 255–256

K

Kappler, Pastor Andreas 92, 102–103
Kaurna people xiv, 1, 8–11, 13, 23–25, 28, 38, 65, 156
Kavel, August xii, 21, 23, 31, 89, 103, 106, 174, 176, 204, 237–238, 327
Kent, Dr Benjamin 98, 113, 117
Kerr, Donald Beviss (D.B.) 331–336, 341, 343
Killalpaninna Mission (*see also* Hermannsburg Mission) 50, 52, 54–57, 60, 194, 196–198
Klose, Samuel 17, 23, 28, 33, 37, 65
Koeler, Hermann xiii, xiv, 1–14, 162
Köln 348–349
Kopperamanna Mission 52–58

Kramer, Carl 48–49, 51, 52, 55–56, 58
Krawinkel, Heinrich 271, 278–280
Kreusler, Marianne xv, 207, 208, 210–213, 215–216
Krichauff, F.E.H.W. 139, 214
Krimper, Schulim 402
Kristallnacht 305, 311
Kronk, Nicolaus 103, 113, 119
Kuehn, Wilhelm 48–52, 58–59

L

Lady Wellington 3–4
Lange, Leonie 250
Lindsay, Lionel 403, 412
Lindsay, Norman 403
Linger, Carl xv, 148, 210, 277
Listemann, G. 12, 129, 148
Loehe, Johannes Paul 283, 331
Löwy, Nelly 307–308, 319
Luck, August 90–92
Luck, Christian 82–85, 88–89
Luck, Friedrich 88, 90, 92
Luck, Johann 86–87
Lutheran Immigration Aid Society 316–317, 321, 378–379
Luther, Martin 42, 44, 170, 314, 318, 337, 384, 389, 391, 393, 396–397

M

Main 270
McCubbin, Louis 407–408, 413
McGregor, James 407
Meier, Pastor Julius 276, 283–285, 288, 299
Meissel, Gottlieb 48–49, 51–52, 55, 58
Menge, Johannes 176, 207–209, 231, 237–238
Merchant Shipping Act 1854 167, 183
Methsieder, Pastor Lorenz 275, 283

Meyer, Heinrich August Eduard 17,
    26, 28–31, 37–39, 63–66, 68, 69,
    70–78, 103, 112, 162
Moeller, Fritz 92
Montefiore, Jacob 304
Moorhouse, Matthew 23, 25, 34, 36,
    39, 71
Moravian Church 41–42, 44–45, 59,
    371
Mücke/Muecke, Dr Carl xv, 124, 126,
    129, 139, 148, 208, 210
Mützelfeldt, Karl xix, 316–317, 321,
    364–382

N

Native Training Institute 23, 30, 36
Niemöller, Pastor Martin 391–392
Noltenius, Henry 97, 99, 103, 110–
    113, 119

O

Odewahn, Johannes 207–208,
    212–213
Offe, Victor Rudolph 289–290
Osswald, Ferdinand 214

P

Pestonjee Bomanjee 175
Pfeiffer, Paul Gotthilf 326-344 xviii,
    xix, 326–343
Phoenix 331–336
Pohlmann, Wilhelm/William 96
Point McLeay Mission 38, 48–49, 51,
    58, 60, 64, 70, 77, 194, 197
Point Pearce Mission 50, 59–60
Princess Louise xv, 126, 129–130, 148–
    149, 210

R

Rau, Otto 224–225
Real Property Act 1858 (SA) 168, 180,
    182

Renner, Erich 327, 332
Reuther, Pastor R.B. 355–356, 361
Riedel, Johannes 283, 287
Riedel, Werner 283
Robe, Governor Frederick Holt 29,
    34, 37, 98
Rodemann, Louis 103–104
Rohde, Karl Johann 272
Royal Exchange Hotel 110–111
Runge, Gustav 137

S

Sage, Annie 408–409, 416
Salomon, Horst 317, 321, 379
Sasse, Hermann xix, 377, 384–386,
    388, 392, 397
Schirmer, Johann Wilhelm/John 116,
    160
Schomburgk, Julius 402
Schomburgk, Otto xv, 124, 126–130,
    141, 210
Schomburgk, Richard xiv, xv, 126–
    128, 130–131, 134, 140–142, 148, 208,
    215, 218, 220, 223, 225, 243
Schondorf, Cristoph 58–59
Schramm, Alexander xiv, xv, 144,
    146–162, 210, 402
Schrapel, Tania 250
Schultze, Friedrich 215, 218–220
Schulz, J.F.W. 256–257, 259
Schürmann, Clamor Wilhelm 8–9,
    13, 17–18, 22–32, 34, 36–39, 65–66,
    76, 162, 175, 207, 215
Schützenfest xx, 425, 430
Sellbach, Udo 402
Seppelt, Johanna Charlotte 239, 244
Seppelt, Joseph 244
Short, Bishop Augustus 37
Skipper, John Michael 158
Solway 2, 240
Southall, Ivan 339–343

South Australia Act 1834 33–34
South Australian Aboriginal Missionary Society 31, 37
South Australian Company 2, 17, 19, 23, 106, 176, 204, 238
South Australian 2
Spencer, Baldwin 196, 202–203
Starke, Ernst Emil 271–272, 274–275
Stilling, Joseph 110–111, 113–114
Stirling, Edward 227–229
St John's Anglican Church 106
Stolz, Johannes Julius 282–283, 315–316, 318–319, 321–324, 348, 353–355, 361, 364, 369, 377–378, 381, 394–395
Strehlow, Carl 162, 193, 198

T

Taglione 166
Tannert, Louis 128, 402
Taplin, George 38, 48–49, 64, 77, 196–197
Teichelmann, Christian Gottlob 8–9, 13, 17–19, 23, 25, 28, 32, 38, 162, 175, 207
Tepper, Johann Gottlieb (Otto) 207, 216–219, 224, 289–292, 295, 296
Teusner, Berthold 287, 295
Theile, Friedrich Otto 353–354, 361
Thiele, Colin 331–333, 336, 339, 343, 407, 412
Tivoli Hotel 116
Torrens, Robert R. 167–168, 177, 179–181, 183–185
Torrens System 166–167, 179–180, 183, 185

U

United Evangelical Lutheran Church in Australia (UELCA) 282–286, 292, 315, 321, 323, 333, 345–351, 353–354, 364, 369, 372, 374–378, 394
Ure Smith, Sydney 403, 407

V

Verco, Joseph 227
Vogelsang, Hermann 41, 54
von Guérard, Eugène 160–162, 165
von Humboldt, Alexander 127, 129, 206, 210
von Humboldt, Wilhelm 206–207
von Mueller, Dr Ferdinand xv, 133, 138, 205–208, 212, 214–217, 220, 223–225, 227

W

Wagner Society 419, 423, 426–427
Walder, Heinrich 48–53, 55–58
Wallenstein, Heinrich 272
Wandrahm 92
Waste Lands Act 1841 34
Waterhouse, Frederick 213, 218, 220–221, 223
Wehl, Eduard 208, 214–215
Wehrstedt, Otto 208
Wesley, John 46, 393
Westall, William 144–146
White Australia Policy 309
Wichmann, Adolph 103
Wilhelmi, Charles/Carl xiv, 29, 215
Willows Hospital 121

Y

Young, Govnernor Sir Henry Fox 29, 30, 34, 37, 108

Z

von Zinzendorf, Count Nicholas 41, 43–46, 60
Zebra 175, 327
Zietz, Amandus 190, 207, 225–227, 229

Wakefield Press is an independent publishing and
distribution company based in Adelaide, South Australia.
We love good stories and publish beautiful books.
To see our full range of titles, please visit our website at
www.wakefieldpress.com.au.

www.ingramcontent.com/pod-product-compliance
Lightning Source LLC
Chambersburg PA
CBHW071433300426
44114CB00013B/1413